T0210566

Lecture Notes in Computer Science 9613

Commenced Publication in 1973
Founding and Former Series Editors:
Gerhard Goos, Juris Hartmanis, and Jan van Leeuwen

More information about this series at http://www.springer.com/series/7407

Oleg Kiselyov · Andy King (Eds.)

Functional and Logic Programming

13th International Symposium, FLOPS 2016
Kochi, Japan, March 4–6, 2016
Proceedings

 Springer

Editors
Oleg Kiselyov
Tohoku University
Sendai
Japan

Andy King
School of Computing
University of Kent
Canterbury
UK

ISSN 0302-9743   ISSN 1611-3349   (electronic)
Lecture Notes in Computer Science
ISBN 978-3-319-29603-6   ISBN 978-3-319-29604-3   (eBook)
DOI 10.1007/978-3-319-29604-3

Library of Congress Control Number: 2015960824

LNCS Sublibrary: SL1 – Theoretical Computer Science and General Issues

Printed on acid-free paper

This Springer imprint is published by SpringerNature
The registered company is Springer International Publishing AG Switzerland

Preface

This volume contains the proceedings of the 13th International Symposium on Functional and Logic Programming – FLOPS 2016 – held in Kochi, Japan, March 4–6, 2016.

FLOPS brings together practitioners, researchers, and implementers of declarative programming, to discuss mutually interesting results and common problems: theoretical advances, their implementations in language systems and tools, and applications of these systems in practice. The scope includes all aspects of the design, semantics, theory, applications, implementations, and teaching of declarative programming. FLOPS specifically aims to promote cross-fertilization between theory and practice and among different styles of declarative programming.

FLOPS 2016 put a particular stress on the connections between theory and practice. This stress was reflected in the composition of the Program Committee, in the call for submissions and, ultimately, in the program of the symposium.

The call for papers attracted 36 submissions, of which the Program Committee, after careful and thorough discussions, accepted 14. The accepted papers cover not just functional and logic programming but also program transformation and re-writing, and extracting programs from proofs of their correctness. The invited speakers, Kazunori Ueda and Atze Dijkstra, reflected on the lessons of two projects (one of which was a national, Japanese project), with declarative programming at their center. In addition to the invited talks and contributed papers, the symposium program included, for the first time, tutorials and a poster session. The tutorials on "Attribute Grammars", "Agda", and "Programming in Picat" were presented, respectively, by Atze Dijkstra, Andreas Abel, and Neng-Fa Zhou. These tutorials were designed to complement the invited talk with in-depth expositions.

This year we initiated an award for the best paper submitted to the symposium. We were delighted to announce that the award for FLOPS 2016 went to Arthur Blot, Pierre-Evariste Dagand, and Julia Lawall for their article entitled "From Sets to Bits in Coq."

Putting together FLOPS 2016 has been a team effort. First of all, we would like to thank the authors of the submitted papers and the presenters of the invited talks and the tutorials. Without the Program Committee (PC) we would have had no program either, and we are very grateful to the PC members for their hard work. Supporting the PC were a number of additional reviewers, and we and the PC would like to acknowledge their contribution. The reviews were unusually detailed and helpful. An author of one rejected paper wrote to us, not to complain but to praise the reviews of his submission. We are greatly indebted to the general chair, Yukiyoshi Kameyama for his advice, encouragement, and support throughout the process and taking on many administrative chores. The local chair, Kiminori Matsuzaki, and the local Organizing Committee were invaluable in setting up the conference and making sure everything ran smoothly.

Finally, we would like to thank our sponsor, the Japan Society for Software Science and Technology (JSSST) SIGPPL, for their continuing support. We acknowledge the cooperation of ACM SIGPLAN, the Asian Association for Foundation of Software (AAFS), and the Association for Logic Programming (ALP).

January 2016   Oleg Kiselyov
                                                               Andy King

Organization

Program Chairs

Andy King   University of Kent, UK
Oleg Kiselyov   Tohoku University, Japan

General Chair

Yukiyoshi Kameyama   University of Tsukuba, Japan

Local Chair

Kiminori Matsuzaki   Kochi University of Technology, Japan

Program Committee

Andreas Abel	Gothenburg University, Sweden
Lindsay Errington	USA
Makoto Hamana	Gunma University, Japan
Michael Hanus	CAU Kiel, Germany
Jacob Howe	City University London, UK
Makoto Kanazawa	National Institute of Informatics, Japan
Hsiang-Shang Ko	National Institute of Informatics, Japan
Julia Lawall	Inria-Whisper, France
Andres Löh	Well-Typed LLP, UK
Anil Madhavapeddy	Cambridge University, UK
Jeff Polakow	USA
Marc Pouzet	École normale supérieure, France
Vítor Santos Costa	Universidade do Porto, Portugal
Tom Schrijvers	KU Leuven, Belgium
Zoltan Somogyi	Australia
Alwen Tiu	Nanyang Technological University, Singapore
Sam Tobin-Hochstadt	Indiana University, USA
Hongwei Xi	Boston University, USA
Neng-Fa Zhou	CUNY Brooklyn College and Graduate Center, USA

External Reviewers

Guillaume Baudart

Timothy Bourke

Benoit Desouter

Sandra Dylus

Adrien Guatto

Geoff Hulette

Kazuhiro Inaba

Georgios Karachalias

Anthony Widjaja Lin

Lunjin Lu

Kazutaka Matsuda

Shin-Cheng Mu

Björn Peemöller

Lutz Strassburger

Jan Rasmus Tikovsky

Paolo Torrini

UHC: Coping with Compiler Complexity (Keynote Abstract)

Atze Dijkstra

Utrecht University, Department of Information and Computing Sciences
atze@uu.nl

Abstract. Programming language design may be difficult, but by now doing an actual design of a language feature is an often repeated and relatively well understood process involving known ingredients: construct a minimal language incorporating the desired feature, define (operational) semantics, a declarative type system, an algorithmic type system, and a prototype implementation. Obviously, this is a gross simplification ignoring the mathematic craftsmanship involved, and not always all of the above ingredients are being dealt with. Still, this is the raw material and mechanics of design found in many conference proceedings on programming languages and their design.

In contrast however, how to implement a designed programming language feature and incorporating it into an existing programming language seems to be less well exposed. A sketch of an implementation and its related issues often is given but of the actual code and its details often at best is summarized by a footnote referring to the (repository of the) implementation. Of course publications exist which specifically address an implementation itself [8] but the size limited nature of a publication forces such descriptions of implementations to narrow down to a limited set of language features and often simplification of the implementation itself is required to obtain clarity and compactness. With the risk of oversimplification we conjecture that design and implementation of individual programming language features is well understood but it is less clear how the implementation of the combination of such individual features can be done in a systematical and predictable way, or, in other words: how do we deal with the complexity arising out of programming language feature implementation both in isolation and combination (as it occurs in a compiler)?

Here we will deal with this issue of compiler complexity by looking at the approaches taken for UHC (Utrecht Haskell Compiler) [4, 3, 2]. UHC is a Haskell compiler intended to be experimented with, both in terms of the use of tools for construction and in terms of being a platform for (relatively) easy experimentation with language features and their implementation. In particular, within UHC two more general sources of complexity are being dealt with:

1. Specification of semantics specifically for implementation. The complexity lies in how to algorithmically specify computations over an AST (Abstract Syntax Tree).
2. Combination of implementation of individual programming language features into a full compiler. The complexity lies in the interaction between language features.

Over the lifespan of the UHC project the following approaches and solutions have been explored:

- (*addressing complexity source 1*) The use of attribute grammars for the specification of programming language feature implementations. The UUAG [9] is mostly used for the implementation of UHC. The AG formalism is further explored into various directions, for example Ruler (*also addressing complexity source 2*) [5] specifically targets type system specification, Viera [10] embeds the tools for description of programming language implementation (i.e. parser, attribute grammar) as a DSL into Haskell (GHC [7]).
- (*addressing complexity source 2*) Partitioning the full implementation description into smaller fragments as belonging to a particular language feature; these are then combined together when constructing a compiler using Shuffle [1].
- (*addressing complexity source 1*) The use of CHR (Constraint Handling Rules) [6] for type related computations involving backtracking.

The above approaches vary in their success. We will discuss our experience with these approaches, in particular what more formal counterparts can be implemented with our tools, small examples of this looks, and what (in retrospect) did or did not work.

References

1. Dijkstra, A.: Shuffle. http://foswiki.cs.uu.nl/foswiki/Ehc/Shuffle
2. Dijkstra, A.: Stepping through Haskell. Ph.D. thesis, Utrecht University, Department of Information and Computing Sciences (2005)
3. Dijkstra, A., Fokker, J., Swierstra, S.D.: The architecture of the Utrecht Haskell compiler. In: Haskell Symposium 2009. ACM Request Permissions, September 2009
4. Dijkstra, A., Fokker, J., Swierstra, S.D.: UHC Utrecht Haskell Compiler. Technical report (2009)
5. Dijkstra, A., Swierstra, S.D.: Ruler: programming type rules. In: FLOPS 2006. Proceedings of the 8th International Conference on Functional and Logic Programming, pp. 30–46. Springer-Verlag, April 2006
6. Frühwirth, T.: Constraint Handling Rules. Cambridge University Press (2009)
7. GHC Team: The Glasgow Haskell Compiler. https://www.haskell.org/ghc/
8. Jones, M.P.: Typing Haskell in Haskell. In: Haskell Workshop. http://www.cse.ogi.edu/~mpj/thih/thih-sep1-1999/ (1999)
9. Swierstra, S.D., Middelkoop, A., Bransen, J.: UUAG (Utrecht University Attribute Grammar) system. http://foswiki.cs.uu.nl/foswiki/HUT/AttributeGrammarSystem
10. Viera, M.: First class syntax, semantics, and their composition. Ph.D. thesis, Universiteit Utrecht, Department of Information and Computing Sciences, March 2013

Contents

Logic/Constraint Programming and Concurrency: The Hard-Won Lessons
of the Fifth Generation Computer Project.   1
   Kazunori Ueda

From Sets to Bits in Coq.   12
   Arthur Blot, Pierre-Évariste Dagand, and Julia Lawall

From Proposition to Program: Embedding the Refinement Calculus in Coq. . .   29
   Wouter Swierstra and Joao Alpuim

The Boolean Constraint Solver of SWI-Prolog (System Description).   45
   Markus Triska

Probabilistic Inference by Program Transformation in Hakaru
(System Description).   62
   Praveen Narayanan, Jacques Carette, Wren Romano,
   Chung-chieh Shan, and Robert Zinkov

An Interaction Net Encoding of Gödel's System T: Declarative Pearl.   80
   Ian Mackie and Shinya Sato

Space-Efficient Planar Acyclicity Constraints: A Declarative Pearl   94
   Taus Brock-Nannestad

Executable Relational Specifications of Polymorphic Type Systems Using
Prolog. 109
   Ki Yung Ahn and Andrea Vezzosi

Proof Relevant Corecursive Resolution 126
   Peng Fu, Ekaterina Komendantskaya, Tom Schrijvers,
   and Andrew Pond

A Coq Library for Internal Verification of Running-Times. 144
   Jay McCarthy, Burke Fetscher, Max New, Daniel Feltey,
   and Robert Bruce Findler

A Transformational Approach to Parametric Accumulated-Cost Static
Profiling 163
   R. Haemmerlé, P. López-García, U. Liqat, M. Klemen, J.P. Gallagher,
   and M.V. Hermenegildo

Polymorphic Types in Erlang Function Specifications   181
   Francisco J. López-Fraguas, Manuel Montenegro,
   and Juan Rodríguez-Hortalá

Declarative Foreign Function Binding Through Generic Programming   198
   Jeremy Yallop, David Sheets, and Anil Madhavapeddy

Incremental Computing with Abstract Data Structures   215
   Akimasa Morihata

Declarative Programming with Algebra   232
   Andre van Delft and Anatoliy Kmetyuk

Author Index   253

Logic/Constraint Programming and Concurrency: The Hard-Won Lessons of the Fifth Generation Computer Project

Kazunori Ueda[✉]

Department of Computer Science and Engineering, Waseda University,
3-4-1, Okubo, Shinjuku-ku, Tokyo 169-8555, Japan
ueda@ueda.info.waseda.ac.jp

1 Introduction

The technical goal of the Fifth Generation Computer Systems (FGCS) project (1982–1993) was to develop *Parallel Inference* technologies, namely systematized technologies for realizing knowledge information processing on top of parallel computer architecture [8].

The design space of methodologies for bridging parallel computers and knowledge information processing is immense. For this reason, it was considered necessary to set up a *working hypothesis* to conduct research in a coherent manner, and the Logic Programming paradigm was adopted as the working hypothesis. The FGCS project decided to develop a *Kernel Language*[1] based on Logic Programming as the core of systematized technologies for bridging the architecture layer and the application layer.

When the FGCS project started, the language specification and the implementation techniques of Prolog was reasonably well established already, and the Warren Abstract Machine (WAM), which became the de-facto standard of the implementation technique of Prolog, was under design. However, the understanding of the leading people of the FGCS project was that realizing a system of technologies for Parallel Inference necessarily meant to develop a new form of *general-purpose* computing technologies that encompass (but are not limited to) knowledge information processing. In particular, being able to describe a *full operating system* for the Parallel Inference Machine (PIM) to be developed in the project and to express and execute various *parallel algorithms* was considered to be a fundamental requirement on the Kernel Language.

Consequently, the research goal of the Kernel Language was set to designing a concurrent and parallel programming language under the working hypothesis of Logic Programming, and soon after I joined the project in 1983, the Kernel Language Task Group started the overall language design with international collaboration. After many discussions on the requirement specification

---

[1] The FGCS project designed and implemented two Kernel Languages, KL0 and KL1, of which this article focuses on KL1 for the Parallel Inference Machine. KL0 was a Kernel Language for the Sequential Inference Machine developed for quick startup of the project.

© Springer International Publishing Switzerland 2016
O. Kiselyov and A. King (Eds.): FLOPS 2016, LNCS 9613, pp. 1–11, 2016.
DOI: 10.1007/978-3-319-29604-3_1

of the language, we became convinced by the end of 1983 that Concurrent Logic Programming—more specifically, Concurrent Prolog introduced to us by Ehud Shapiro [15]—was basically the right choice as the basis of the Kernel (as opposed to user-level) Language of the project for its simplicity and expressive power I will describe later.

Both Logic Programming (and Constraint Programming as its relative) and concurrent programming (and concurrency theory as its foundation) build upon basic concepts quite different from mainstream programming models such as imperative and functional programming, which requests researchers and technicians to switch their mindset to work on them. Furthermore, Concurrent Logic Programming (and Concurrent Constraint Programming as its generalization) that emerged from the interaction of these two paradigms requests the switching of mindset not only to users and researchers of mainstream programming languages but also to researchers of Logic Programming and concurrency. Appreciating its essence and significance was not straightforward in spite of its technical simplicity. This is still true thirty years later, and makes it rather difficult for researchers of neighboring fields to be aware of the paradigm.

Nevertheless, Concurrent Logic Programming yielded various spin-off technologies in its thirty years of history. In particular, Concurrent Constraint Programming (CCP) formulated from Concurrent Logic Programming and Constraint Logic Programming attracted great attention as a theoretical model of concurrency rather than a tool for programming (hence we refer to CCP as *Constraint-Based Concurrency*).

The aim of this article is to convey the essence of Concurrent Logic Programming and Constraint-Based Concurrency and to describe how their research and development evolved after their conception.

I published several articles related to the present topic in the past [8, 19–21]. The exciting design process of the Kernel Language is detailed in [8], while the development of the paradigm until mid 1990's and my own view and vision of the paradigm are detailed in [19] and summarized in [20]. This article is a revised version of [21]. The references are not exhaustive; more extensive bibliography can be found in [8, 19] and other technical papers.

2   Emergence and Contribution of Concurrent Logic Programming

In the early 1980's, concurrent execution of logic programs was becoming an area of active research. It started with the introduction of coroutines into Prolog, but Relational Language (1981) was the first to feature *don't-care* nondeterminism (a.k.a. choice nondeterminism, as found in concurrent programming and concurrency theory) in place of *don't-know* nondeterminism, i.e., nondeterminism in the sense of solution search (as found in Prolog and nondeterministic automata). The time was the eve of the FGCS project. Started with Relational Language, researchers vied for Concurrent Logic Programming languages with clear semantics and high expressive power.

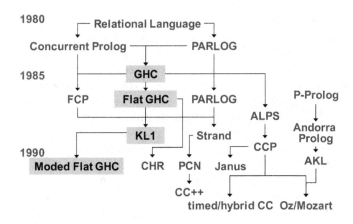

Fig. 1. Genealogy of concurrent logic programming and constraint-based concurrency

Figure 1 shows a genealogy of Concurrent Logic Programming and Constraint-Based Concurrency. An arrow indicates direct technical influence from one to another. I was involved in the design of the four shaded languages. Guarded Horn Clauses (GHC) [17], which became the model of the Fifth Generation Kernel Language (KL1), was born from close investigation and reconstruction of the language constructs of Concurrent Prolog and PARLOG. GHC in turn motivated the refinement of those two languages, and its key concept was further inherited to many other computational models and languages.

The over twenty languages and models shown in Fig. 1 differ in their goals and functionalities but shares one concept: *dataflow synchronization*. A major reason why imperative concurrent programming is difficult lies in the separation of control dependency and data dependency. The idea of dataflow synchronization, namely *to wait until a necessary piece of data become available*, resolves this dissociation and plays an important role in describing the cooperative behavior of concurrent processes correctly and clearly.

While message passing in other computational models also can be seen as dataflow synchronization, message passing in Concurrent Logic Programming enabled the passing of *incomplete messages*, namely messages containing uninstantiated variables to be used as reply boxes. Incomplete messages make intriguing use of *partial information* (data structure with not yet determined parts), a key feature of logic and constraint programming. The contribution of Concurrent Prolog was that it demonstrated the effective use of partial information in concurrent programming for the first time.

Incomplete messages contain logical variables (a.k.a. single-assignment variables). Those logical variables can be used not only for a single reply to a message but also as channels or streams for subsequent communication (a.k.a. *sessions*) between concurrent processes. Thus incomplete messages realized what the process calculi community later called *channel mobility*. Just like records and pointers form dynamic data structures, processes and channels form *dynamic process structures.* Programming of dynamically evolving process structures is an essential feature of flexible concurrent programming languages. The fact that the FGCS project adopted a Kernel Language featuring channel mobility and started its parallel implementation in the mid 1980's seems to indicate the project's fore-sight, considering that concurrency theory for evolving process structures—the π-calculus and its asynchronous variants—was developed after the late 1980's.

Concurrent Logic Programming was unfortunately often regarded as "a version of Logic Programming without search capabilities," but its technical contribution is better appraised in the light of concurrency and communication.

Models and languages that emerged in the same period (early to mid 1980's) include the theoretical model of Communicating Sequential Processes (CSP), MultiLisp, the functional language Id, and the concurrent object-oriented language ABCL. The *future* construct of MultiLisp, the I-structure of Id, and future-type messages of ABCL are all closely related to logical variables in (Concurrent) Logic Programming.

3   From Guarded Horn Clauses to Constraint-Based Concurrency

When the basics of Concurrent Logic Programming was established in the early 1980's, CCS (Calculus of Communicating Systems) and Structural Operational Semantics were still quite new formalisms. To my knowledge, there was almost no technical interaction between those formalisms and Concurrent Logic Programming in the early 1980's, which is to say that the development of Concurrent Logic Programming was not driven by the methodology of theoretical computer science such as formal semantics but by close investigation of language constructs through prototype implementation and by the study of properties and consequences deduced from language specifications. Guarded Horn Clauses was actually born by the study of the (informal) semantics of Concurrent Prolog, in particular the study of its atomic (indivisible) operations in fine-grained parallel execution. The study went in parallel with a (sequential) implementation project of Concurrent Prolog, based on our principle that the best way to understand a programming language was to implement it.

The design of Guarded Horn Clauses was also influenced by discussion with the architecture group of the FGCS project led by Shunichi Uchida. When the design of the Kernel Language started, an alternative approach was to introduce coarse-grained parallel processing while retaining the functionalities of Prolog. However, the architecture group maintained that the Kernel Language should embrace as fine-grained concurrency as possible in order to promote the research and development of novel parallel architectures. This guideline acted as one of the key design principles of the Kernel Language, leading to the study of its atomic actions, and contributed to the stability of the resulting language.

Another design principle the project members agreed upon after big discussions on the research direction was Occam's Razor; that is, we asked ourselves the following research question: *What was the minimum set of language constructs to turn Logic Programming into an expressive concurrent programming language?* This was influenced by the design philosophy of Concurrent Prolog which came with only two constructs, *read-only unification* and *guard*, and was chosen as a concrete working hypothesis towards KL1. However, through our intensive study including three implementations of Concurrent Prolog, the apparently simple language specification turned out to have some semantical difficulties. This made me seek an alternative language specification, and Guard Horn Clauses was devised in the end of 1984 as an alternative with just one additional syntactic construct, *guard*, which bore the semantics of dataflow synchronization. It did not take too long until GHC was accepted by the project as a new working hypothesis towards KL1. It did not take too long until GHC was then subsetted to Flat GHC (GHC without nested guards), the language that finally became the basis of KL1. Thus the design process of the Kernel Language could be phrased as "evolution by devolution" [16,19].

When we design programming languages and computational models, formal semantics is not an ultimate goal but a step towards further study. The most important thing for languages and models to be of value is to give deep insight into them and find out useful properties.

Let us give one example of such study in the design process of GHC. In sequential computing, the value of a variable at a given time point is a well-defined notion. On the other hand, I had thought in studying the properties of GHC that the value of a variable observed at some time point and place would not necessarily a well-defined notion. I thought that the model of concurrency we wanted to establish should allow the observation of the value of a variable to take time and the value of a variable to be transmitted asynchronously to each occurrence of the variable. At a workshop on Functional and Logic Programming held in Trento, Italy in December 1986, I asked if there was a theory that made clear distinction between variables and occurrences of variables. Per Martin-Löf responded that Jean-Yves Girard of the University of Paris 7 was considering Linear Logic.

Linear Logic, published immediately after that, did have no direct connection to asynchrony I was thinking about, but it turned out to have close relationship to Concurrent Logic Programming in a different sense. Around that time, choice nondeterminism of Concurrent Logic Programming was often criticized for the lack of logical interpretation. For instance, consider a scheduling program and a goal which returns either `precedes(a,b)` or `precedes(b,a)` depending on what nondeterministic choice is made. Here, both `precedes(a,b)` and `precedes(b,a)` can be deduced from the original program and the initial goal, but their conjunction "`precedes(a,b)` and `precedes(b,a)`" should not be derivable. This problem of classical logic was not addressed until the mid 1980's, but Linear Logic enabled us to interpret it appropriately by introducing additive conjunction. It was around 1990 that a number of programming languages based on Linear Logic were proposed, starting with the language LO (Linear Objects).

In the late 1980's, another connection between Concurrent Logic Programming and Logic emerged, which was unexpected when the former was designed.

Slightly after the advent of Concurrent Logic Programming, *Constraint Logic Programming* was proposed by generalizing the data domain of Logic Programming (finite terms), and inspired by that, the synchronization and transmission mechanisms of Concurrent Logic Programming—and GHC in particular—were formulated as the implication relation between constraint store (containing partial information about the values of variables) and the information that are expected to be received [12]. Logical implication thus received a new light as an account of the synchronization mechanism of Concurrent Logic Programs.

This attempt to integrate Concurrent Logic Programming and Constraint Logic Programming lead to *Concurrent Constraint Programming*, namely the theory of Constraint-Based Concurrency formulated using structural operational semantics. I pointed out in the mid 1980's that the essence of the computation of GHC was interprocess communication based on the observation and generation of substitutions, namely bindings between variables and values [19], and Constraint-Based Concurrency reformulated it in a general form termed *ask* and *tell* without assuming particular data domains. The initial proposal of Constraint-Based Concurrency considered both *atomic tell* (in which publication of constraints is done atomically upon nondeterministic choice of a clause) and *eventual tell* (in which publication of constraints is done after nondeterministic choice of a clause), but through heated discussions with Vijay Saraswat and Ken Kahn, the framework converged to its eventual tell version ([8], article by Ken Kahn) that reflects the semantics of GHC and admits my view of the (eventual) value of a variable described above.

Despite its concise operational semantics, the significance and the essence of Constraint-Based Concurrency is not yet sufficiently disseminated and understood properly. The basic concepts of process calculi such as CCS, CSP and the π-calculus are not difficult to understand since they handle communication channels explicitly. On the other hand, Constraint-Based Concurrency is often described as "concurrent processes sharing a constraint store and communicating by *ask*ing and *tell*ing constraints to the store." This tends one to remind imperative concurrent programming using shared memory which may hinder proper understanding of the framework. The reality is that a constraint store does not only allow one to express (i.e., encode) communication channels using lists but allows one to express *private* channel communication and channel mobility because variables in a constraint store can be accessed only from processes to which those variables are explicitly distributed. However, this important secrecy property of Constraint-Based Concurrency is not necessarily recognized even by experts of the paradigm, suggesting the difficulty of balancing abstraction and concretion in the research and dissemination of computing paradigms.

Both Constraint-Based Concurrency and the π-calculus were born in the end of the 1980's. The International Conference on Fifth Generation Computer Systems 1988 (FGCS'88), held slightly before that, had a big panel discussion on the Theory and Practice of Concurrent Systems, attended by Ehud Shapiro, William Dally, Geoffrey Fox, Carl Hewitt, Robin Milner, David H. D. Warren, and the myself. Personal and technical collaboration originated by this conference lead to the advance of research on the models of concurrency in Japan. The asynchronous π-calculus by Kohei Honda (1990) was born in this background.

4 Development After the 1990's and Diversification

Concurrent Logic Programming and Constraint-Based Concurrency yielded various new frameworks of computation that opened up new application domains.

One such framework is *Hybrid Concurrent Constraint Programming* [7] focusing on hybrid systems in which the states of systems may cause both continuous and discrete changes.

Variables in Concurrent Logic Programming are single-assignment; the partial information of their values may be accumulated incrementally in the course of program execution but will not change destructively. Still, it allow us to represent a history of state changes as streams of states. The use of streams is however limited to systems with discrete time. A natural way of modeling systems with continuous time in Constraint Programming is to let state variables be functions over time which may cause discrete and/or continuous changes.

With this view, two paradigms were born as extensions of Constraint-Based Concurrency: Timed Concurrent Constraint Programming (Timed CC) for handling discrete changes, and Hybrid Concurrent Programming (Hybrid CC) for handling both discrete and continuous changes. Once one regards the value of a variable as a function over time, its evolution over time can be fully formulated in the framework of Constraint Programming with the aid of differential equations. The mainstream approach to the modeling and analysis of hybrid systems uses automata as a central tool, and developing high-level language constructs including those for abstraction and modularization is still an important challenge. Hybrid Concurrent Constraint Programming was a step towards this direction.

Another important framework originated from Concurrent Logic Programming is Constraint Handling Rules (CHR) [6]. CHR has syntax similar to Concurrent Logic Programming languages but allows multisets of atomic formulae on both the left-hand side the right-hand side of rules, making it a multiset rewriting language. CHR was designed for programming constraint solvers rather than concurrency. It did not aim at a stand-alone programming language but at providing host languages including functional, logic, and object-oriented languages with constraint programming capabilities. It is interesting to see that a closely related computational model finds its place in an area very different from concurrent programming and is accumulating various applications.

One of the initial goals of Concurrent Logic Programming was to make the development of parallel software significantly easier. Its scope is not limited to knowledge information processing, and it was actually applied to high-performance computing. Languages born in the 1990's in this line of research include PCN (Program Composition Notation) [5], CC++ (Compositional C++) [3], and HPC++ [11]. PCN allows one to parallelize sequential code in C and Fortran using the idea of Concurrent Logic Programming, and its overall design deeply reflects that of Concurrent Logic Languages. The subsequent languages, CC++ and HPC++, aimed at exploiting the nice properties of logical variables in program parallelization while minimizing the change of the base languages. This thread of research was driven by researchers including Ian Foster who lead Grid Computing later on.

After the mid 1990's, research on language constructs in the practice of concurrent and parallel computing became less popular. Java, which smartly appeared in this period, took an extremely conservative approach to concurrency. However, next trends are visiting mainstream programming languages in the 21st century. IBM's X10 [4] aims at wholesale redesign of Java's concurrent and parallel programming constructs, in which Vijay Saraswat, the founder of Constraint-Based Concurrency, is deeply involved and inherits its basic principles. Another example is Cω [2], an extension of C$\sharp$, one of whose goals is to improve the description of asynchronous concurrency. Although Cω was born in the research thread of the Join calculus, it shares the basic idea of dataflow synchronization with Constraint-Based Concurrency.

Another language we need to mention is Erlang [1] that was developed as a industrial-strength concurrent language. Erlang shares its design principles with Concurrent Logic Programming in that both adopt single-assignment variables and fine-grained concurrency based on message passing, and strong similarity is found in programs written in those languages. Erlang did not employ flexible interprocess communication as found in Concurrent Logic languages; instead it featured error recovery and real-time processing which are essential in some practical applications.

Finally, we should mention MGTP, a Model-Generation Theorem Prover implemented on top of the Kernel Language KL1 [9,10]. The adoption of Concurrent Logic Programming for the Fifth Generation Kernel Language was simply a result of separation of concerns, and how to implement higher-level Parallel Inference on top of KL1 was always an important subject of the FGCS project. MGTP has shown that a reasonably large class of full first-order logic can be encoded into Concurrent Logic programs and runs scalably on parallel computers.

5   Challenges in Computational Models for the 21st Century

The biggest challenge in the theory and practice of concurrent programming is to establish "the λ-calculus in the world of concurrency" [19]. The fact that numerous models of concurrency have been proposed after the π-calculus implies that we have not yet agreed upon a model which is as stable and unifying as the λ-calculus. We do not know if this endeavor will end with a success, but I believe it is a rewarding challenge.

In the 21st century, Robin Milner proposed Bigraphical Reactive Systems (BRS) [13] as the next step of the π-calculus. Its main motivation was to formulate systems in which hierarchical structures (such as administrative domains) and connection structures (for communication) co-exist. Indeed, while the majority of concurrency models were concerned with connection structures, some models that appeared since the 1990's, such as the Chemical Abstract Machine and the Ambient calculus, featured hierarchical structures and its evolution.

Guarded Horn Clauses did not support hierarchical structuring, but the key requirement of the Fifth Generation Kernel Language KL1, designed based on GHC, was to be capable of describing operating systems for parallel computers. The major difference between GHC and KL1 was that KL1 featured a *Shoen*[2] construct for the hierarchization and management of computation. Shoen was designed from practical requirements, but the hierarchical graph rewriting language LMNtal [22], designed and implemented in an attempt to reunify Constraint-Based Concurrency and CHR, happened to be our second challenge towards the unification of hierarchy and connectivity. LMNtal also happened to share its design motivation with BRS in that both addressed the integration of the two structuring mechanisms. Although initially designed as a unifying model of concurrency, our LMNtal implementation features state-space search and LTL model checking of hierarchical graph rewriting systems [23]—don't-know nondeterminism is now back and programs with more than 10^9 states can be handled.

Another important challenge in concurrency will be to develop powerful type systems for non-sequential computing. Those type systems are expected to play even more important roles than the roles played by traditional type systems, because it is important in non-sequential computing to analyze physical as well as logical aspects such as the cost of communication and the resource needed for computation. In the FGCS project, I designed and implemented Moded Flat GHC [18], a Concurrent Logic Programming language with a static type system for reasoning about interprocess communication using mobile channels represented by logical variables. Similar type systems were designed in process calculi. However, many things remain to be done towards type systems for concurrency and type systems covering both logical and physical properties of computation.

Computing environments around us are changing towards wide-area, nanoscale, many-core, and low-power computation. The main theoretical models that supported 20th-century computing were Turing machines for computability, RAM model for complexity, and the λ-calculus for programming. However, it is hard to believe that they are sufficient to support 21st-century computing. Since concurrency is now ubiquitous, it seems important to upgrade our foundational theories and software technologies. University curricula also need to reflect the trends of computing environments.

Concurrent Logic Programming and related technologies born in the 1980's found rather limited places for use in the 20th-century mainstream computing, but 21st-century computing environments may give us opportunities of reassessment and new development of this technology.

---

[2] A Japanese word meaning a manor.

References

1. Armstrong, J.: Erlang. Commun. ACM **53**(9), 68–75 (2010)
2. Benton, N., Cardelli, L., Fournet, C.: Modern concurrency abstractions for C$^\sharp$. In: Magnusson, B. (ed.) ECOOP 2002. LNCS, vol. 2374, pp. 415–440. Springer, Heidelberg (2002)
3. Chandy, K.M., Kesselman, C.: CC++: A Declarative Concurrent Object-Oriented Programming Notation. In: Research Directions in Concurrent Object-Oriented Programming, The MIT Press, 281–313 (1993)
4. Charles, P., et al.: X10: An object-oriented approach to non-uniform cluster computing. In: OOPSLA 2005, pp. 519–538. ACM (2005)
5. Foster, I., Olson, R., Tuecke, S.: Productive parallel programming: The PCN approach. Sci. Program. **1**(1), 51–66 (1992)
6. Frühwirth, T.: Theory and practice of Constraint Handling Rules. J. Log. Program. **37**(1–3), 95–138 (1998)
7. Gupta, V., Jagadeesan, R., Saraswat, V., Bobrow, D.G.: Programming in hybrid constraint languages. In: Antsaklis, P.J., Kohn, W., Nerode, A., Sastry, S.S. (eds.) HS 1994. LNCS, vol. 999. Springer, Heidelberg (1995)
8. Fuchi, K., Kowalski, R., Furukawa, K., Ueda, K., Kahn, K., Chikayama, T., Tick, E.: Launching the new era. Commun. ACM **36**(3), 49–100 (1993)
9. Fujita, H., Hasegawa, R.: A model-generation theorem prover in KL1 using a ramified stack algorithm. In: 8th International Conference on Logic Programming (ICLP'91), pp. 535–548. The MIT Press (1991)
10. Hasegawa, R., Fujita, H., Koshimura, M., Shirai, Y.: A model generation based theorem prover MGTP for first-order logic. In: Kakas, A.C., Sadri, F. (eds.) Computational Logic: Logic Programming and Beyond. LNCS (LNAI), vol. 2408, pp. 178–213. Springer, Heidelberg (2002)
11. Johnson, E., Gannon, D.: HPC++: Experiments with the parallel standard template library. In: 11th International Conference on Supercomputing, pp. 124–131. ACM (1997)
12. Maher, M.J.: Logic semantics for a class of committed-choice programs. In: Fourth International Conferenceon Logic Programming (ICLP'87), pp. 858–876. The MIT Press (1987)
13. Milner, R.: The Space and Motion of Communicating Agents. The Cambridge University Press, Cambridge (2009)
14. Saraswat, V.A., Rinard, M.: Concurrent constraint programming (Extended Abstract). In: POPL 1990, pp. 232–245. ACM (1990)
15. Shapiro, E.Y.: A Subset of Concurrent Prolog and Its Interpreter. ICOT Tech. Report TR-003, Institute for New Generation Computer Technology (ICOT), Tokyo (1983)
16. Tick, E.: The deevolution of concurrent logic programming languages. J. Log. Program. **23**(2), 89–123 (1995)
17. Ueda, K.: Guarded Horn Clauses. ICOT Technical Report TR-103, Institute for New Generation Computer Technology (ICOT), Tokyo (1985). In: Wada, E. (ed.) Logic Programming. LNCS, vol. 221, pp. 168–179. Springer, Heidelberg (1986)
18. Ueda, K., Morita, M.: Moded Flat GHC and its message-oriented implementation technique. New Gener. Comput. **13**(1), 3–43 (1994)
19. Ueda, K.: Concurrent logic/constraint programming: The next 10 years. In: Apt, K.R., Marek, V.W., Truszczynski, M., Warren, D.S. (eds.) The Logic Programming Paradigm: A 25-Year Perspective, pp. 53–71. Springer, Heidelberg (1999)

20. Ueda, K.: Logic programming and concurrency: A personal perspective. ALP News Lett. **19**(2), 37–52 (2006)
21. Ueda, K.: Logic and constraint programming versus concurrency. Comput. Softw. **25**(3), 49–54 (2008). http://doi.org/10.11309/jssst.25.3_49
22. Ueda, K.: LMNtal as a hierarchical logic programming language. Theor. Comput. Sci. **410**(46), 4784–4800 (2009)
23. Ueda, K., Ayano, T., Hori, T., Iwasawa, H., Ogawa, S.: Hierarchical graph rewriting as a unifying tool for analyzing and understanding nondeterministic systems. In: Leucker, M., Morgan, C. (eds.) ICTAC 2009. LNCS, vol. 5684, pp. 349–355. Springer, Heidelberg (2009)

From Sets to Bits in Coq

Arthur Blot[(⊠)], Pierre-Évariste Dagand, and Julia Lawall

Sorbonne Universités, UPMC Univ Paris 06, CNRS, Inria, LIP6 UMR 7606,
Paris, France
arthur.blot@ens-lyon.org

Abstract. Computer Science abounds in folktales about how — in the
early days of computer programming — bit vectors were ingeniously used
to encode and manipulate finite sets. Algorithms have thus been developed to minimize memory footprint and maximize efficiency by taking
advantage of microarchitectural features. With the development of automated and interactive theorem provers, finite sets have also made their
way into the libraries of formalized mathematics. Tailored to ease proving, these representations are designed for symbolic manipulation rather
than computational efficiency. This paper aims to bridge this gap. In the
CoQ proof assistant, we implement a bitset library and prove its correctness with respect to a formalization of finite sets. Our library enables
a seamless interaction of sets for computing — bitsets — and sets for
proving — finite sets.

1 Introduction

Sets form the building block of mathematics, while finite sets are a fundamental
data structure of computer science. In the world of mathematics, finite sets
enjoy appealing mathematical properties, such as a proof-irrelevant equality [17]
and the extensionality principle for functions defined over finite sets. Computer
scientists, on the other hand, have devised efficient algorithms for set operations
based on the representation of finite sets as bit vectors and on bit twiddling
[3,27], exploiting the hardware's ability to efficiently process machine words.

With interactive theorem provers, sets are reinstituted as mathematical
objects. While there are several finite set libraries in CoQ, these implementations
are far removed from those used in efficient code. Recent work on modeling low-
level architectures, such as the ARM [14] or x86 [18] processors, however, have
brought the magical world of bit twiddling within reach of our proof assistants.
We are now able to specify and reason about low-level programs. In this paper,
we shall tackle the implementation of bitsets and their associated operations.

Beyond the goal of certifying low-level programs, our work can contribute
to mechanized reasoning itself. Indeed, our work is deeply rooted in the Curry-
Howard correspondence, which blurs the line between proofs and computations.
As shown by SSREFLECT, proof-by-reflection [2] is a powerful technique to scale
proofs up. At the heart of this technique lies the fact that computation happens
within the type theory. Last but not least, it is revealing that the finite set library

O. Kiselyov and A. King (Eds.): FLOPS 2016, LNCS 9613, pp. 12–28, 2016.
DOI: 10.1007/978-3-319-29604-3_2

provided by the COQ standard library originates from the CompCert [19] project, whose certified compiler crucially relies on such efficient datastructures.

This paper recounts an investigation from the concrete world of bit vectors to the abstract world of finite sets. It grew from a puzzled look at the first page of Warren's *Hacker's Delight* [27], where lies the cryptic formula $x \& (x-1)$. How do we translate the English specification given in the book into a formal definition? How do we prove that this formula meets its specification? Could COQ generate efficient and trustworthy code from it? And how efficiently could we simulate it within COQ itself? We aim to answer those questions in the following.

This paper makes the following contributions:

- in Sect. 3, we establish a bijection between bitsets and sets over finite types. Following a refinement approach, we show that a significant part of SSRE-FLECT finset library can be refined to operations manipulating bitsets;
- in Sect. 4, we develop a trustworthy extraction of bitsets down to OCaml's machine integers. While we are bound to axiomatize machine integers, we adopt a methodology based on exhaustive testing to gain greater confidence in our model;
- in Sect. 5, we demonstrate our library through two applications. We have implemented a Bloom filter datastructure, proving the absence of false negatives. We have also implemented and verified the n-queens algorithm [13].

The source code of our development is available at

https://github.com/artart78/coq-bitset

2 Finite Sets and Bit Vectors in Coq

Let us first recall a COQ formalization of finite sets and a formalization of bit vectors. The former provides basic algebraic operations, such as union, intersection, complement, *etc.*, and more advanced ones, such as cardinality and minimum. The latter offer extended support for describing bit-level computations, such as logical and arithmetic operation on memory words.

2.1 A Finite Set Library: finset

To manipulate finite sets in COQ, we rely on the finset library [20], provided by the Mathematical Components platform [15]. The finset library provides set-theoretic operators for dealing with sets of elements of a finite type, *i.e.* sets of finite cardinality. A finite set being a finite type itself, we also make extensive use of SSREFLECT's fintype library [25]. We recall their key definitions in Table 1.

Remark 1. It is crucial to constrain the underlying type to be finite: a bitset represents collections thanks to their finite enumeration. Indeed, the bitset encodes the fact that, for any given set, every element of this enumeration is either present or absent. □

Table 1. Key operations on finite sets [20, 25]

CoQ judgment	Informal semantics
T : finType	card(T) is finite
T : finType ⊢ {set T} : Type	type of finite sets of T-elements
A : {set T} ⊢ #| A | : nat	cardinality of the set A
x : A ⊢ x \in A : bool	membership test
k : T ⊢ k |: A : {set T}	insertion of the element k in A
A :\ k : {set T}	removal of the element k from A
P : T → bool ⊢ [set x : T | P] : {set T}	subset of T satisfying P
A, B : {set T} ⊢ A :|: B : {set T}	union of A and B
A, B : {set T} ⊢ A :&: B : {set T}	intersection of A and B
A, B : {set T} ⊢ A :\: B : {set T}	difference of A and B
i0 : T ⊢ [arg min_(i < i0 in A) M] : T	an i \in A minimizing M

Table 2. coq-bits API (fragment)

CoQjudgment	Informal semantics
n : nat ⊢ BITS n : Type	vector of n bits
bs : BITS n, k : nat ⊢ getBit bs k : bool	test the kth bit
xs, ys : BITS n ⊢ andB xs ys : BITS n	bitwise and
xs, ys : BITS n ⊢ orB xs ys : BITS n	bitwise or
xs, ys : BITS n ⊢ xorB xs ys : BITS n	bitwise xor
xs : BITS n ⊢ invB xs : BITS n	bitwise negation
xs : BITS n, k: nat ⊢ shrBn xs k : BITS n	right shift by k bits
xs : BITS n, k: nat ⊢ shlBn xs k : BITS n	left shift by k bits

The canonical example of a finite set is the type 'I_n : Type (where n : nat is an index) of the finite ordinals below n. Intuitively, 'I_n represents the set $\{0, \cdots, n-1\}$. Every finite set of cardinality n is isomorphic to 'I_n.

Remark 2. We are confident that our development could carry over to different formalizations of finite sets and finite ordinals such as, *e.g.*, the MSets library [10] and the Finite_sets library [9] provided by the CoQ standard library.

2.2   A Bit Vector Library: coqBits

To model operations on bitsets, we rely on coq-bits [18], a formalization of logical and arithmetic operations on bits. A bit vector is defined as an SSREFLECT tuple [26] of bits, *i.e.* a list of booleans of fixed (word) size. The key abstractions offered by this library are listed in Table 2. The library characterizes the interactions between these elementary operations and provides embeddings to and from $\mathbb{Z}/2^n\mathbb{Z}$.

3   Sets as Bit Vectors, Bit Vectors as Sets

There is an obvious bijection between a finite set of cardinality n and a bit vector of size n. Since we can sequentially enumerate each inhabitant of a finite type, we can uniquely characterize an inhabitant by its *rank* in this enumeration. Thus, a finite set can be concisely represented by setting the kth bit to true if and only if the element of rank k belongs to the set.

In Coq, this bijection is captured by the (extensional) definition

```
Definition repr {n}(bs: BITS n) E := E = [ set x : 'I_n | getBit bs x ].
```

where the right-hand side reads a standard set comprehension. We shall therefore say that a bit vector `bs` *represents* a set `E` if `repr bs E` holds.

The crux of this definition is to establish a relation between the abstract notion of finite sets — convenient for mathematical proofs — and the concrete artefact of bit vectors — enabling efficient computations. This relational presentation establishes a *data refinement* of finite sets by bitsets [8,12].

In the following sections, we show that logical operations on finite sets are reflected by concrete manipulations on bitsets. In each case, we also prove that the refinement relation is preserved. As a result, an algorithm defined parametrically over the representation of a finite set will be instantiable to finite sets — for proofs — *and* bit sets — for computations. We shall illustrate this technique in Sect. 5.1.

3.1   Set Membership

Over finite sets, set membership merely requires checking whether an element belongs to an enumeration of the set's elements. It is therefore a decidable property, provided by the finset operator `x : T, A : set T ⊢ x \in A : bool`

In terms of bitsets, this can be implemented by shifting the kth bit to the least significant position and masking the resulting bit vector with 1:

```
Definition get {n}(bs: BITS n)(k: 'I_n): bool
  := (andB (shrBn bs k) #1) == #1.
```

We then prove that our refinement of finite sets is respected by `get`. To do so, we show that, given a finite set `E` represented by a bitset `bs`, testing the membership of an element `k` in `E` is equivalent to getting the kth bit in `bs`:

Lemma 1 (Representation of Membership). *For a non-empty finite set E of cardinality n.+1 represented by a bitset bs, get agrees with the set membership operation for every element of E, i.e.*

```
Lemma get_repr: forall n (k: 'I_n.+1)(bs: BITS n.+1) E, repr bs E →
    get bs k = (k \in E).
```

3.2   Inserting and Removing Elements

Inserting an element `k` into a bitset `bs` amounts to setting the kth bit to 1. For instance, to set a specific bit, we apply an or-bitmask

```
Definition insert {n}(bs: BITS n) k: BITS n := orB bs (shlBn #1 k).
```

Once again, the formal specification and the computational realizer are related through a representation lemma, *e.g.*:

Lemma 2 (Representation of Insertion). *For a finite set* E *represented by a bitset* bs, *set insertion is refined by* insert:

```
Lemma insert_repr: forall n (bs: BITS n) (k: 'I_n) E, repr bs E →
    repr (insert bs k) (k |: E).
```

3.3   Algebra of Sets

The refinement relation holds for the standard algebra of sets. For two finite sets `A, B : set T`, we have that

- the complement ~: `A` is realized by `invB` (bitwise negation),
- the intersection `A :&: B` is realized by `andB` (bitwise and),
- the union `A :|: B` is realized by `orB` (bitwise or), and
- the symmetrical difference `(A :\: B) :|: (B :\: A)` is realized by `xorB` (bit-wise xor).

For each of these definitions, we prove the corresponding representation lemmas.

3.4   Cardinality

Computing the cardinality of a bitset requires counting the number of bits set to 1. To the delighted hacker, this merely amounts to implementing a *population count* algorithm [27, Sect. 5–1]. Several efficient implementations of this algorithm exist: we refer our reader to the above reference for a tour of each of them.

We chose to implement the population count *via* a lookup table. The gist of the algorithm is as follows. Let us consider a bitvector `bs` of size n (*e.g.*, $n = 64$) and let k be a divisor of n (*e.g.*, $k = 8$). We tabulate the number of 1s in all the bit vectors of size k. The idea is that for a sufficiently small value of k, this table fits within a single cache line. Therefore, to compute the number of 1s in `bs`, we can add the number obtained by looking up the key corresponding to the segment $[k \times i, k \times (i+1) - 1]$ in the table, for $i \in [0, n/k - 1]$.

For example, on a 64-bit architecture, one would typically split the bit vector into segments of 8 bits, pre-computing a lookup table of 256 elements. Because the table fits in a single cache line, the individual lookups are fast. We have thus traded space (an impossibly large lookup table covering all 64-bit numbers) for time (by iterating the lookup 8 times instead of performing it once).

The first step, which happens off-line, thus involves computing a lookup table mapping any number between 0 and 2^k to its number of bits set:

```
Definition pop_table {n}(k: nat): seq (BITS n).
```

Looking up the number of bits set in the segment $[i \times k, i \times (k+1) - 1]$ is a matter of right shifts followed by a suitable and-mask to extract the segment. We obtain the segment's population count by a lookup in the pre-computed map:

```
Definition pop_elem {n}(k: nat)(bs: BITS n)(i: nat): BITS n
  := let x := andB (shrBn bs (i * k)) (decB (shlBn #1 k)) in
     nth (zero n) (pop_table k) (toNat x).
```

Finally, we obtain the total population count by iterating over the i segments of bit vectors of size k, adding their individual population counts:

```
Fixpoint popAux {n}(k: nat)(bs: BITS n)(i: nat): BITS n :=
  match i with
  | 0 => zero n
  | i'.+1 => addB (pop_elem k bs i') (popAux k bs i')
  end.
```

```
Definition cardinal {n}(k: nat)(bs: BITS n): BITS n
  := popAux k bs (n %/ k).
```

As before, the implementation has been shown to refine its specification.

3.5   Minimal Element

Finding the minimal element of a bitset amounts to identifying the least significant bit that is set to one. To put it another way, the rank of the minimal element is the *number of trailing zeros* [27, Sect. 5–4]. The classical formula for computing the number of trailing zeros for a bit vector of size n is given by

```
Definition ntz {n}(k: nat)(bs: BITS n): BITS n
  := subB #n (cardinal k (orB bs (negB bs))).
```

The intuition is that `orB bs (negB bs)` has the same number of trailing zeros as `bs` while all the bits beyond the minimal element are set. Therefore, the cardinality of this bit vector is its length minus the number of trailing zeros. We prove the usual representation lemma.

4   Trustworthy Extraction to OCaml

While bit vectors provide a faithful *model* of machine words, their actual representation in COQ — as lists of booleans — is far removed from reality. To extract our programs to efficient OCaml code, we must bridge this last gap and develop an axiomatic presentation of OCaml's machine integers.

We shall specify the semantics of this axiomatization by means of the coq-bits primitives. Once again, we rely on a refinement relation, stating that OCaml's integers refine coq-bits's integers (in fact, they are in bijection) and asserting that each axiomatized operation on OCaml's integers is a valid refinement of the corresponding operation in the coq-bits library. In effect, each abstract operation can be seen as a *specification*.

However, introducing new logical axioms cannot be taken lightly: one invalid assumption and the actual behavior of an OCaml operation could significantly diverge from its COQ specification. Built on such a quicksand, a formal proof is close to useless. For example, when extracting a COQ model of 8-bits integers onto OCaml 63-bit integers, it is all too easy to forget to clear the 55 most significant bits[1]. An operation overflowing a byte followed by a left shift — such as shrB (shlB #0 9) 1 — would incorrectly expose the overflow, thus betraying the encoding. We can however take advantage of the fact that there is only a finite number of OCaml integers and that our specifications are decidable properties: we gain a higher level of trust in our model by exhaustively testing each specification against its OCaml counterpart.

4.1 Axiomatization and Extraction of Int8

Our axiomatization of machine integers merely involves importing the functions relative to integers defined in the OCaml standard library [23]. The list of axiomatized operations is summarized in Table 3. Concretely, the axioms and their realizers are defined as follows:

```
Axiom Int8: Type.
Extract Inlined Constant Int8 => "int".

Axiom lt: Int8 → Int8 → bool.
Extract Inlined Constant lt => "(<)".
```

To mediate between machine integers and bit vectors, we define two conversion functions

```
Definition bitsToInt8  : BITS 8 → Int8 := (..).
Definition bitsFromInt8 : Int8 → BITS 8 := (..).
```

which ought to establish a bijection between Int8 and BITS 8. This fact cannot be established within COQ: bitsFromInt8 and bitsToInt8 perform various shifts and tests on machine integers, operations of which COQ has no knowledge of since they were axiomatized. To COQ, an axiomatized operation is nothing but a constant, *i.e.* a computationally inert token.

4.2 Gaining Trust in Extraction

Although our axiomatisation of machine integers is computationally inert, it can be extracted to OCaml, where it computes. In OCaml, we can therefore easily *run* the tests bitsFromInt8 (bitsToInt8 bs) = bs for all 8-bit vector bs. If this equality is experimentally verified, this provides a strong (meta-level) indication that bitsToInt8 is cancelled by bitsFromInt8. We thus propose to

---

[1] Needless to say, this example is drawn from the authors' harsh experience.

gain trust in our model by (exhaustively) testing it [14]. We adopt a systematic infrastructure, inspired by translation validation [22]. Let us illustrate with the cancelativity property.

First of all, bit vectors of size 8 being finitely enumerable, we can write a test — in Coq — checking the cancelativity property for all possible bit vectors:

```
Definition bitsToInt8K_test: bool :=
 [forall bs , bitsFromInt8 (bitsToInt8 bs) == bs ].
```

After extraction to OCaml, we can inspect the value bitsToInt8K_test: if it is false, then our specification is definitely incorrect. If it is true, then we may confidently accept the validation axiom

```
Axiom bitsToInt8K_valid: bitsToInt8K_test.
```

that reflects in SSReflect/Coq[2] the fact that we observed true in OCaml. Using this axiom and by the very definition of our test, we can *prove* the cancelativity property:

```
Lemma bitsToInt8K: cancel bitsToInt8 bitsFromInt8.
Proof.
  move=> bs; apply/eqP; move: bs.
  by apply/forallP: bitsToInt8K_valid.
Qed.
```

We follow the same methodology for the remaining specifications. For a desired specification Spec, we

1. implement an exhaustive test spec_test checking this property;
2. check that the extracted code returns true;
3. reflect its validity through an axiom spec_valid;
4. prove the desired property Spec from the test and its axiomatized validity.

To establish a bijection between BITS 8 and Int8, we chose to test for injectivity of bitsFromInt8. From injectivity, we easily deduce cancelativity and bijectivity follows naturally. The injectivity lemma is stated as follows:

```
Lemma bitsFromInt8_inj: injective bitsFromInt8.
```

We can reflect the concluding equality in terms of the decidable equality == of bit vectors. However, the premise refers to the propositional equality of two Int8 values. As such, we have no way to turn this statement into a checkable assertion. Morally, however, we know that the propositional equality over Int8 should be consistent with OCaml's equality, which we have axiomatized as eq. This leads us to introduce the following — uncheckable — axiom:

```
Axiom eqInt8P : Equality.axiom eq.
```

where eq is an axiom that extracts to OCaml's structural equality test.

---

[2] Boolean values are transparently lifted to types through the is_true: bool → Prop predicate that assigns the empty set to false and the unit set otherwise.

```
exception TestFailure of int ;;

let forall_int wordsize k =
  try
    for i = 0 to (1 lsl wordsize) - 1 do
      if (not (k i)) then
        raise (TestFailure i)
    done;
    true
  with (TestFailure i) →
Printf.printf "failed %d\n" i; false

let forall_int8 = forall_int 8
let forall_int16 = forall_int 16
let forall_int32 = forall_int 32
```

Fig. 1. Realizer for the `forallInt8` quantifier

Similarly, we need a device for verifying universal quantifications over bit vectors. This decision procedure is realized by a simple enumeration routine (Fig. 1) postulated as an axiom in COQ:

```
Axiom forallInt8 : (Int8 → bool) → bool.
Extract Inlined Constant forallInt8 => "Forall.forall_int8".
```

The reflection property is once again uncheckable and therefore postulated

```
Axiom forallInt8P : forall P PP,
  viewP P PP →
    reflect (forall x, PP x) (forallInt8 (fun x => P x)).
```

Remark 3 (Trusted Proving Base). The axioms `eqInt8P` and `forallInt8P` are the only axioms whose validity is not safeguarded by experimental validation. `eqInt8P` seems rather innocuous since it merely asserts that equality over OCaml's integers is defined precisely by OCaml's implementation of equality. An error in `forallInt8P` would be more consequential: if, for instance, the bounds `min_int` and `max_int` are both mistakenly set to 0, then many false properties of machine integers would be presented as "experimentally true." As usual with a mathematical definition, it is only by confronting this definition against expected properties (such as, for example, the cyclic properties of `Int8`) that confidence can be gained in its validity.   □

Using these two devices, we can test injectivity of `bitsFromInt8` with

```
Definition bitsFromInt8_inj_test: bool :=
  forallInt8 (fun x =>
    forallInt8 (fun y =>
      (bitsFromInt8 x == bitsFromInt8 y) ==> (eq x y))).
```

Running this test confirms its validity, which we can then postulate in our model. Injectivity follows, by a small proof involving the reflection of integer equality and of quantification over integers. From which we conclude by establishing the existence of a bijection between `Int8` and `BITS 8`:

```
Lemma bitsFromInt8_bij: bijective bitsFromInt8.
```

Remark 4. The execution of the OCaml-extracted test takes 4 s for to cover all 8-bits integers. The equivalent test for 16-bit integers did not complete after several hours. Using manually optimized (and, therefore, less trustworthy) OCaml code, we were able to run the tests in 0.23 s for 8-bit integers and in 7 h 27 for 16-bit integers. Our hand-tuned test routine includes the following optimizations:

– factorizing the conversion from integers to bitsets across multiple tests;
– avoiding Peano integers by directly manipulating native OCaml integers.

The last point is essential for keeping a quadratic algorithm. Running the test for 32-bit integers is feasible, but is likely to take years of CPU time. Obviously, 64-bit integers cannot be exhaustively tested.

   Despite our best efforts, our extraction remains *unverified* in a formal sense: it is trustworthy in as much as it gives consistent results with a particular version of the OCaml compiler (or interpreter), running on a particular operating system and a specific machine. To all intents and purposes, we have not provided a proof of correctness of our extraction: we have merely developed an experimental process by which to test its validity.

4.3   Refining Bit Vectors to Integers

The bijection naturally leads us to a refinement relation from Coq's bit vectors down to OCaml's machine integers. We thus define

```
Definition native_repr (i: Int8)(bs: BITS wordsize): bool
  := eq i (bitsToInt8 bs).
```

that is to say: an integer refines a bit vector if they are in bijection.

   Following the refinement methodology, we then show that each operation on bit vectors is refined by a corresponding operation on machine integers. Let us consider the case of bitwise negation. We would like to prove that `lnot`, which extracts to OCaml's `lnot`, is a valid refinement of `invB`:

```
Lemma lnot_repr: forall i bs,
    native_repr i bs → native_repr (lnot i) (invB bs).
```

This statement reads as follows: if `i` is a native integer corresponding to the bitset `bs`, then the `lnot` operator acts exactly the same way as `invB` on it. The operator `invB` — bitwise negation — thus provides a specification for the operation `lnot` axiomatized in Coq. To prove this property, we craft a exhaustive test

```
Definition lnot_test: bool
  := forallInt8 (fun i =>
       native_repr (lnot i) (invB (bitsFromInt8 i))).
```

that we extract and run in OCaml. The result being `true`, we feel confident in asserting its validity to CoQ:

```
Axiom lnot_valid: lnot_test.
```

The lemma `lnot_repr` follows from the definition of `lnot_test` and `lnot_valid`. We similarly specified, tested and proved the validity of all remaining operations (Table 3).

Table 3. Specifications, axioms and the realizers of `Int8`

Informal semantics	CoQ axiom	OCaml extraction
Zero	zero	0
Successor	suc	fun x → (x + 1) land 0xff
Arithmetic negation	neg	fun x → (-x) land 0xff
Addition	add	fun x y → (x + y) land 0xff
Bitwise negation	lnot	fun x → (lnot x) land 0xff
Bitwise and	land	(land)
Bitwise or	lor	(lor)
Bitwise xor	lxor	(lxor)
Shift left	lsl	fun x y → (x lsl y) land 0xff
Shift right	lsr	(lsr)
Equality	eq	(=)
Comparison	lt	(<)

4.4   Refining Sets to Machine Integers

In Sect. 3, we have established a refinement relation between `BITS n` and finite sets. In Sect. 4.1, we have established another refinement relation between `Int8` and `BITS 8`. By transitivity, we obtain a refinement of finite sets to `Int8`:

```
Definition machine_repr (n: Int32)(E: {set 'I_wordsize}): Prop :=
  exists bv, native_repr n bv ∧ repr bv E.
```

The desired representation lemmas then carry over from finite sets to integers, trickling through bit vectors. For example, one defines the complement and easily proves its associated representation lemma

```
Definition compl (bs: Int32): Int32 := lnot bs.
Lemma compl_repr: forall i E,
    machine_repr i E → machine_repr (compl i) (~: E).
```

5   Applications

To illustrate our approach, we now tackle two examples of algorithms that rely on finite sets for their proof and bitsets for their efficient execution. In Sect. 5.1, we present a certified Bloom filter [4] implementation. In Sect. 5.2, we implement an algorithm solving the n-queens problem.

5.1 Bloom Filters

A Bloom filter is an efficient — but approximate — abstraction for monotone sets. It offers an operation for inserting an element into the set and another for testing membership. It is approximate in the sense that it is subject to *false positives*: an element might be signaled as belonging to a set into which it has never been inserted. However, it is free of *false negatives*: if the membership test fails, then it is indeed the case that the element has never been inserted. Combined with its small memory footprint, this last property makes this data structure very useful in practice.

Under the hood, a Bloom filter relies on a collection (H_i) of hashing functions onto 'I_n, for some integer n (usually, the architecture's word size). Upon inserting an element p, we compute the i hashes of p and collect them in a single *signature set* of cardinality n:

```
Fixpoint bloomSig_aux (curFilter: T)(H: seq (P → 'I_wordsize))(e: P): T
 := match H with
  | [::] => curFilter
  | h :: H => bloomSig_aux ((singleton (h e)) \cup curFilter) H e
  end.
```

```
Definition bloomSig (H: seq (P → 'I_wordsize))(e: P): T
 := bloomSig_aux \emptyset H e.
```

The kth element of the signature set is thus set if and only if there is hashing function reducing to this value. To update the Bloom filter, we simply take the union of this signature set and the previously-computed ones:

```
Definition bloomAdd (S: T)(H: seq (P → 'I_wordsize))(add_elt: P): T
 := S \cup (bloomSig H add_elt).
```

To check whether an element belongs to the filter, we once again compute its signature. If all the signature is a subset of the Bloom filter, then the corresponding element *may* have been inserted into the set. Otherwise, it definitely was not:

```
Definition bloomCheck (S: T)(H: seq (P → 'I_wordsize))(e: P) : bool
 := let sig := bloomSig H e in (sig \cap S) = sig.
```

The correctness of our implementation is established by

Theorem 1 (Absence of False Negatives). *Let (H_i) be a collection of hashing functions. If an element belongs to the Bloom filter, then this element belongs to any subsequent extension of the Bloom filter. Or, contrapositively:*

```
Lemma bloom_correct: forall T T' H add check, machine_repr T T' →
  (~ bloomCheck (bloomAdd T H add) H check) →
   (~ bloomCheck T H check) ∧ (add <> check).
```

This ensures that the element is still detected in all subsequent Bloom filters generated by adding more elements, i.e. it will never be a false negative.

Remark 5. Although insertion (`bloomAdd`) and membership test (`bloomCheck`) are implemented over native integers for efficiency, the correctness argument is more easily established by reasoning over abstract sets. To bridge this gap, we merely instantiate our parametric definition to use finite sets (Sect. 4.4), thus obtaining an abstract specification `bloomAdd_finset`. Parametricity tells us that the specification and its implementation verify the refinement relation.

5.2   The n-queens Problem

Our second application is a freshman's classic. The n-queens problem involves finding the number of ways to place n queens on a $n \times n$ board so that no queen threatens another, *i.e.* belongs to the same row, column or diagonal. To do so, the algorithm recursively fill the board row-by-row, making sure at each step to put the queen on a safe column. To enforce this invariant, Richards [24] has shown that it is sufficient to maintain a (finite) set of occupied columns and of the left and right diagonals at the given position. Upon moving to the next row, we update the occupied column and the diagonal sets: the new queen occupies a new column, while the diagonals are merely shifted by one element.

A particularly eager freshman (or one of Filliâtre's students [13]) would use a bitset `ld` to store the occupied left diagonals (relative to the current line), a bitset `rd` to store the occupied right diagonals (relative to the current line), and a bitset `col` to store the occupied columns. The set of possible positions is then concisely described by the set `~: (ld :|: rd :|: col)`. To decide on the next position to explore, we may take the minimal element of this set, using `ntz` (Sect. 3.5). The algorithm terminates when the set of columns `col` is full.

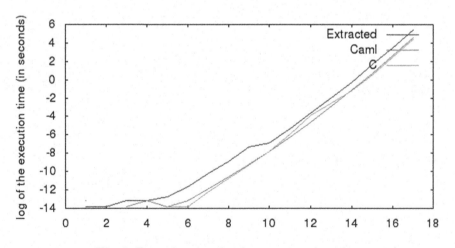

Fig. 2. Execution time for the n-queens algorithm

The correctness proof covers about 1300 lines of code, including about 50 lines of intermediairy definitions. Once again, we crucially rely on the equivalence between machine integers and finite sets (Sect. 4.4) to streamline the proof. We provide the performance of the extracted code in Fig. 2, comparing it against a hand-written OCaml implementation and a C implementation. The hand-coded OCaml executes within 30 % of the execution time of a reference C implementation, as is common for OCaml code. The extracted CoQ code is twice as slow as the OCaml one. We attributes this slow-down to the naivety of our CoQ implementation that encodes mutual recursion through an indexed type. The resulting extracted code thus repeatedly performs a (needless) boolean test in a tight loop.

6   Related Work

Our treatment of bitsets is rooted in the *data refinement* approach [1]. This approach involves relating a formal specification to a concrete implementation, refining the model at each step. Refinements have made their way into interactive theorem provers, such as Isabelle [7,16] and CoQ [11]. Our presentation builds upon the work of Denes *et al.* [12] in the CoQ proof assistant. In particular, we follow the authors in using parametricity to abstract over representations and obtain the representation lemmas for (almost) free [8].

We demonstrated our library by implementing and verifying two algorithms in CoQ. By doing so, we use CoQ as a software verification platform. This approach is reminiscent — although at a much smaller scale — of the CFML [6] tool. Indeed, CFML provides a verification platform for OCaml programs by embedding an axiomatic model — the characteristic formula — in CoQ and providing a program logic suitable to higher-order, effectful programs in CoQ. We took the more lightweight (but also more restrictive) approach of writing programs directly in CoQ, relying on extraction to obtain executable OCaml programs.

Why3 [5] is another platform for deductive program verification. It uses a collection of SMT solvers and interactive theorem provers to prove that programs meet their specifications. It supports manipulation of and reasoning about bitsets. To this end, the SMT solvers are extended with an axiomatic theory of bitsets. This theory has been shown consistent through a CoQ model. Whenever an SMT solver fails to discharge a proof obligation, the CoQ formalization can be used to, manually and interactively, prove the corresponding statement. Why3 is thus able to reason about algorithms manipulating bitsets automatically. For example, the n-queens algorithm was proved correct by Filliâtre [13]. Amazingly, most proof obligations (35 out of 41) are discharged automatically by the SMT solvers, freeing the programmer from the burden of writing formal proofs. The remaining proof obligations were proved in CoQ, in as little as 142 lines of tactics in total. Our proof was meant to exercise our library and was thus developed without automated assistance. As a consequence, it is much longer (1200 lines of tactics) and admittedly more pedestrian.

Table 4. Refined operations over finite sets

Informal semantics	finset definition	bitset definition
Membership:	`\in : T → {set T} → bool`	`get: Int8 →` `'I_wordsize → bool`
Insertion:	`|: : T →` `{set T} → {set T}`	`insert: Int8 → Int8 → Int8`
Removal:	`:\ : T →` `{set T} → {set T}`	`remove: Int8 → Int8 → Int8`
Empty set:	`set0 : {set T}`	`zero: Int8`
Full set:	`setT : {set T}`	`one: Int8`
Complement:	`~: : {set T} → {set T}`	`compl: Int8 → Int8`
Intersection:	`:&: : {set T} →` `{set T} → {set T}`	`inter: Int8 → Int8 → Int8`
Union:	`:|: : {set T} →` `{set T} → {set T}`	`union: Int8 → Int8 → Int8`
Sym. difference:	`:\: : {set T} →` `{set T} → {set T}`	`symdiff: Int8 → Int8 → Int8`
Cardinality:	`#|_| : {set T} → nat`	`cardinal: Int8 → Int8`
Minimal element:	`[arg min_(i < _ in _) i]` `: T → {set T} → T`	`ntz: Int8 → Int8`

7 Conclusion

In this paper, we have developed an effective formalization of bitsets, covering a significant fragment of SSREFLECT's finset library. We summarize the equivalences we have established in Table 4. Through this work, we hope to rejoice both Hackers and Mathematicians with delights [27]. To account for both — often divergent — point of views, we have adopted the data refinement approach advocated by Denes *et al.* [8]. We leveraged parametricity — a deep metamathematical property — to relate the proof-oriented and the computation-oriented specializations of our generic programs.

We would like to extend our work beyond a single machine word so as to support arbitrarily large bitsets. To this end, we would need native support for persistent (or non-persistent) arrays in COQ. Finally, our bitset library is but a first step toward building certified domain-specific compilers for programming low-level systems. In particular, device drivers are typically configured through intricate combinations of bitsets, *e.g.* for setting flags or checking the configuration status. We wish for our library to provide a verified connecting rod between the low-level interaction with the device and its high-level specification [21].

Acknowledgements. We are grateful to Arthur Charguéraud and Maxime Dénès for several discussions on these questions. We also thank Jean-Christophe Filliâtre for suggesting the *n*-queens example, and Clément Fumex and Claude Marché for pointers to the literature. We finally thank the anonymous FLOPS reviewers, whose remarks helped us to streamline our presentation.

References

1. Abrial, J.R.: The B-book: Assigning Programs to Meanings. Cambridge University Press, New York (1996)
2. Allen, S.F., Constable, R.L., Howe, D.J., Aitken, W.E.: The semantics of reflected proof. In: Symposium on Logic in Computer Science (LICS 1990), pp. 95–105 (1990)
3. Beeler, M., Gosper, R.W., Schroeppel, R.: Hakmem. Tech. report Massachusetts Institute of Technology (1972). http://hdl.handle.net/1721.1/6086
4. Bloom, B.H.: Space/time trade-offs in hash coding with allowable errors. Commun. ACM **13**(7), 422–426 (1970)
5. Bobot, F., Filliâtre, J.C., Marché, C., Melquiond, G., Paskevich, A.: The Why3 platform. LRI, CNRS & Univ. Paris-Sud & INRIA Saclay (2015)
6. Charguéraud, A.: Characteristic formulae for the verification of imperative programs. In: International Conference on Functional programming (ICFP 2011), pp. 418–430 (2011)
7. Klein, G., Cock, D., Sewell, T.: Secure microkernels, state monads and scalable refinement. In: Mohamed, O.A., Muñoz, C., Tahar, S. (eds.) TPHOLs 2008. LNCS, vol. 5170, pp. 167–182. Springer, Heidelberg (2008)
8. Cohen, C., Dénès, M., Mörtberg, A.: Refinements for free!. In: Gonthier, G., Norrish, M. (eds.) CPP 2013. LNCS, vol. 8307, pp. 147–162. Springer, Heidelberg (2013)
9. Coq Standard Library: Finite sets. https://coq.inria.fr/library/Coq.Sets.Finite_sets.html
10. Coq Standard Library: Modular implementation of finite sets. https://coq.inria.fr/library/Coq.MSets.MSets.html
11. Delaware, B., Pit-Claudel, C., Gross, J., Chlipala, A.: Fiat: deductive synthesis of abstract data types in a proof assistant. In: Principles of Programming Languages (POPL 2015), pp. 689–700 (2015)
12. Dénès, M., Mörtberg, A., Siles, V.: A refinement-based approach to computational algebra in Coq. In: Beringer, L., Felty, A. (eds.) ITP 2012. LNCS, vol. 7406, pp. 83–98. Springer, Heidelberg (2012)
13. Filliâtre, J.-C.: Verifying two lines of C with Why3: an exercise in program verification. In: Joshi, R., Müller, P., Podelski, A. (eds.) VSTTE 2012. LNCS, vol. 7152, pp. 83–97. Springer, Heidelberg (2012)
14. Fox, A., Myreen, M.O.: A trustworthy monadic formalization of the ARMv7 instruction set architecture. In: Kaufmann, M., Paulson, L.C. (eds.) ITP 2010. LNCS, vol. 6172, pp. 243–258. Springer, Heidelberg (2010)
15. Gonthier, G., Mahboubi, A.: A small scale reflection extension for the Coq system. Technical report RR-6455, INRIA (2008)
16. Haftmann, F., Krauss, A., Kunčar, O., Nipkow, T.: Data refinement in Isabelle/HOL. In: Blazy, S., Paulin-Mohring, C., Pichardie, D. (eds.) ITP 2013. LNCS, vol. 7998, pp. 100–115. Springer, Heidelberg (2013)
17. Hedberg, M.: A coherence theorem for Martin-Löf's type theory. J. Funct. Program. **8**(4), 413–436 (1998)
18. Kennedy, A., Benton, N., Jensen, J.B., Dagand, P.E.: Coq: The world's best macro assembler? In: Symposium on Principles and Practice of Declarative Programming (PPDP 2013), pp. 13–24 (2013)
19. Leroy, X.: Formal verification of a realistic compiler. Commun. ACM **52**(7), 107–115 (2009)

20. Mathematical Components: Finite sets. http://ssr2.msr-inria.inria.fr/doc/math comp-1.5/MathComp.finset.html

21. Mérillon, F., Réveillère, L., Consel, C., Marlet, R., Muller, G.: Devil: an IDL for hardware programming. In: Symposium on Operating Systems Design and Implementation (OSDI 2000) (2000)

22. Necula, G.C.: Translation validation for an optimizing compiler. In: Conference on Programming Language Design and Implementation (PLDI 2000), pp. 83–94 (2000)

23. OCaml Standard Library: Pervasives. http://caml.inria.fr/pub/docs/manual-oc aml/libref/Pervasives.html

24. Richards, M.: Backtracking algorithms in MCPL using bit patterns and recursion (1997)

25. Ssreflect library: Finite type. http://ssr.msr-inria.inria.fr/doc/ssreflect-1.5/Ssreflect. fintype.html

26. Ssreflect library: Tuple. http://ssr.msr-inria.inria.fr/doc/mathcomp-1.5/MathCo mp.tuple.html

27. Warren, H.S.: Hacker's Delight. Addison-Wesley Professional, Boston (2012)

From Proposition to Program
Embedding the Refinement Calculus in Coq

Wouter Swierstra[1]($\boxtimes$) and Joao Alpuim[2]

[1] Universiteit Utrecht, Utrecht, The Netherlands
w.s.swierstra@uu.nl
[2] RiskCo, Utrecht, The Netherlands
joao.alpuim@riskco.nl

Abstract. The *refinement calculus* and *type theory* are both frameworks that support the specification and verification of programs. This paper presents an embedding of the refinement calculus in the interactive theorem prover Coq, clarifying the relation between the two. As a result, refinement calculations can be performed in Coq, enabling the semi-automatic calculation of formally verified programs from their specification.

1 Introduction

The idea of *deriving* a program from its specification can be traced back to Dijkstra (1976); Floyd (1967) and Hoare (1969). The *refinement calculus* (Back 1978; Morgan 1990; Back and Wright 1998) defines a formal methodology that can be used to construct a derivation of a program from its specification step by step. Crucially, the refinement calculus presents single language for describing both programs and specifications.

Deriving complex programs using the refinement calculus is no easy task. The proofs and obligations can quickly become too complex to manage by hand. Once you have completed a derivation, the derived program must still be transcribed to a programming language in order to execute it – a process which can be rather error-prone (Morgan 1990, Chap. 19).

To address both these issues, we show how the refinement calculus can be embedded in Coq, an interactive proof assistant based on dependent types. Although others have proposed similar formalizations of the refinement calculus (Back and von Wright 1990; Hancock and Hyvernat 2006), this paper presents the following novel contributions:

– After giving a brief overview of the refinement calculus (Sect. 2), we begin by developing a library of predicate transformers in Coq, based on indexed containers (Altenkirch and Morris 2009; Hancock and Hyvernat 2006), making extensive use of dependent types (Sect. 3). We will define a *refinement relation*, corresponding to a morphism between indexed containers, enabling us to prove several simple refinement laws in Coq.

© Springer International Publishing Switzerland 2016
O. Kiselyov and A. King (Eds.): FLOPS 2016, LNCS 9613, pp. 29–44, 2016.
DOI: 10.1007/978-3-319-29604-3_3

- This library of predicate transformers can be customized to cope with different programming languages and programming constructs. We show how to define a refinement relation between programs in the WHILE language (Nielson et al. 1999) (Sect. 4).
- These definitions give us the basic building blocks for formalizing derivations in the refinement calculus. They do, however, require that the derived program is known *a priori*. We address this and other usability issues (Sect. 5).
- Finally, we validate our results by proving a soundness result and performing a small case study (Sect. 6). This soundness result relates our definitions to the usual weakest precondition semantics for imperative languages. The case study, taken from Morgan's textbook on the refinement calculus (Morgan 1990), derives a binary search algorithm for the square root of a positive integer. Such a program has many properties that make it difficult to formalize directly in Gallina, the fragment of Coq that is used for programming, such as non-structural recursion and mutable references.

2   Refinement Calculus

The refinement calculus, as presented by Morgan (1990), extends Dijkstra's Guarded Command language with a new language construct for specifications. The specification $[pre, post]$ is satisfied by a program that, when supplied an initial state satisfying the precondition *pre*, can be executed to produce a final state satisfying the postcondition *post*. Crucially, this language construct may be mixed freely with (executable) code constructs.

Besides these specifications, the refinement calculus defines a *refinement relation* between programs, denoted by $p_1 \sqsubseteq p_2$. This relation holds when **forall** $P, \mathsf{wp}(p_1, P) \Rightarrow \mathsf{wp}(p_2, P)$, where wp denotes the usual weakest precondition semantics of a program and its desired postcondition. Intuitively, you may want to read $p_1 \sqsubseteq p_2$ as stating that p_2 is a 'more precise specification' than p_1.

A program is said to be *executable* when it is free of specifications and only consists of executable statements. Morgan (1990) refers to such executable programs as *code*. To calculate an executable program C from its specification S, you must find a series of refinement steps, $S \sqsubseteq M_0 \sqsubseteq M_1 \sqsubseteq ... \sqsubseteq C$. Typically, the intermediate programs, such as M_0 and M_1, mix executable code fragments and specifications.

To find such derivations, Morgan (1990) presents a catalogue of lemmas that can be used to refine a specification to an executable program. Some of these lemmas define when it is possible to refine a specification to code constructs. These lemmas effectively describe the semantics of such constructs. For example, the following law may be associated with the **skip** command:

Lemma 1 (skip). *If pre $\Rightarrow$ post, then* $[pre, post] \sqsubseteq$ **skip**.

Besides such primitive laws, there are many recurring patterns that pop up during refinement calculations. For example, combining the rules for sequential composition and assignment, the *following assignment* lemma holds:

$$[x = X \land y = Y, x = Y \land y = X]$$
$\sqsubseteq$ { by the following assignment law }
$$[x = X \land y = Y, t = Y \land y = X]; x ::= t$$
$\sqsubseteq$ { by the following assignment law }
$$[x = X \land y = Y, t = Y \land x = X]; y ::= x; x ::= t$$
$\sqsubseteq$ { by the following assignment law }
$$[x = X \land y = Y, y = Y \land x = X]; t ::= y; y ::= x; x ::= t$$
$\sqsubseteq$ { by the law for skip }
skip$; t ::= y; y ::= x; x ::= t$

Fig. 1. Derivation of the swap program

Lemma 2 (Following Assignment). *For any term E,*

$$[pre, post] \sqsubseteq [pre, post\,[w \backslash E]]; w ::= E$$

We will illustrate how these rules may be used to calculate the definition of a program from its specification. Suppose we would like to swap the values of two variables, x and y. We may begin by formulating the specification of our problem as:

$$[x = X \land y = Y, x = Y \land y = X]$$

Using the two lemmas we saw above, we can refine this specification to an executable program. The corresponding calculation is given in Fig. 1. Note that we have chosen to give a simple derivation that contains some redundancy, such as the final **skip** statement, but uses a modest number of auxiliary lemmas and definitions.

For such small programs, these derivations are manageable by hand. For larger or more complex derivations, it can be useful to employ a computer to verify the correctness of the derivation and even assist in its construction. In the coming sections we will develop a Coq library for precisely that.

3   Predicate Transformers

In this section, we will assume there is some type S, representing the state that our programs manipulate. In Sect. 4 we will show how this can be instantiated with a (model of a) heap. For now, however, the definitions of specifications, refinement, and predicate transformers will be made independently of the choice of state.

We begin by defining a few basic constructions in Coq:

Definition *Pred* $(A : Type) : Type := A \to Prop.$

This defines the type *Pred A* of predicates over some type A. Using this definition we can define a subset relation between predicates as follows:

Definition *subset* $(A : Type)$ $(P_1\ P_2 : Pred\ A) : Prop :=$ **forall** $x, P_1\ x \rightarrow P_2\ x$.

A predicate P_1 is a subset of the predicate P_2, if any state satisfying P_1 also satisfies P_2. In the remainder of this paper, we will write $P_1 \subseteq P_2$ when the property *subset* $P_1\ P_2$ holds.

Next we can define the *PT* data type, consisting of a precondition and postcondition:

Record *PT* : *Type* :=
  MkPT { *pre* : *Pred S*;
           post : **forall** $s : S$, *pre s* $\rightarrow$ *Pred S* }.

The postcondition is a ternary relation between the input state, a proof that this input state satisfies the precondition, and the output state. Such a ternary relation is typical when modeling post-conditions in type theory to avoid the need for 'ghost variables', relating the input and output states (Nanevski et al. 2008; Swierstra 2009a; Swierstra 2009b). We will sometimes use the notation $[P, Q]$ rather than the more verbose *MkPT P Q*.

As its name suggests, the *PT* type has an obvious interpretation as a *predicate transformer*, i.e., a function from *Pred S* to *Pred S*:

Definition *semantics* $(pt : PT) : Pred\ S \rightarrow Pred\ S :=$
  fun $P\ s \Rightarrow \{ p : pre\ pt\ s\ \&\ post\ pt\ s\ p \subseteq P \}$.

The *semantics* function computes the condition necessary to guarantee that the desired postcondition P holds after executing a program satisfying the given specification *pt*. Intuitively, the precondition of the specification must hold and the postcondition must imply P. We will sometimes write $[\![pt]\!]$ rather than *semantics pt* for the sake of brevity.

Next, we characterize the refinement relation between two values of type *PT* as follows:

Inductive *Refines* $(pt_1\ pt_2 : PT) : Type :=$
  Refinement : **forall** $(d : pre\ pt_1 \subseteq pre\ pt_2)$,
    (**forall** $(s : S)\ (x : pre\ pt_1\ s)$, *post* $pt_2\ s\ (d\ s\ x) \subseteq post\ pt_1\ s\ x) \rightarrow$
    Refines $pt_1\ pt_2$.

We consider pt_2 to be a refinement of pt_1 when the precondition of pt_1 implies the precondition of pt_2 and the postcondition of pt_2 implies the postcondition of pt_1. As our postconditions are ternary relations, we need to do some work to describe the latter condition. In particular, we need to transform the assumption that the initial state holds for the precondition of pt_1 to produce a proof that the precondition of pt_2 also holds for the same initial state. To do so, we use the first condition, d, that the precondition of pt_1 implies the precondition of pt_2. We will use the notation, $pt_1 \sqsubseteq pt_2$, for the proposition *Refines pt_1 pt_2*.

To validate the correctness of this definition, we will show that it satisfies the characterization of refinement in terms of weakest precondition semantics given in Sect. 2. To do so, we have proven the following soundness result:

> **Theorem** *soundness* : **forall** pt_1 pt_2,
> $pt_1 \sqsubseteq pt_2 \leftrightarrow$ **forall** $P, [\![pt_1]\!] \ P \subseteq [\![pt_2]\!] \ P$.

In other words, the *Refines* relation adheres to the characterization of the refinement relation in terms of predicate transformer semantics. The proof is almost after unfolding the various definitions involved.

Even if we have not yet fixed the state space S, we can already prove that the structural laws of the refinement calculus, such as strengthening of postconditions, hold:

> **Lemma** *strengthenPost* $(P : Pred \ S) \ (Q_1 \ Q_2 : \textbf{forall} \ s, P \ s \rightarrow Pred \ S)$:
> (**forall** $(s : S) \ (p : P \ s), Q_1 \ s \ p \subseteq Q_2 \ s \ p) \rightarrow$
> $[P, Q_2] \sqsubseteq [P, Q_1]$.

To prove this lemma, we need to show that $P \subseteq P$ and that the postcondition Q_1 implies Q_2. The first proof is trivial; the second follows immediately from our hypothesis. Similarly, we can show that the refinement relation is both transitive and reflexive.

These definitions by themselves are not very useful. Before we can perform any *program* derivation, we first need to fix our *programming language*.

4 The While Language

In this paper, we will focus on deriving programs in the WHILE programming language (Nielson et al. 1999). The syntax of the WHILE language may be defined as follows:

$$S ::= \textbf{skip} \mid S_1; S_2 \mid x ::= a \mid \textbf{if } e \textbf{ then } S_1 \textbf{ else } S_2 \mid \textbf{while } e \textbf{ do } S$$

Like Dijkstra's Guarded Command Language (1976), the WHILE language has the most common constructs from any imperative language: assignment, branching, and iteration. Although it lacks many features, such as memory management, methods, classes, or user-defined types, the WHILE language is a suitable minimal language for the purpose of our study.

Before defining our syntax any further, we emphasize that this development is parametrized over some fixed type of identifiers, *Identifier*. Next, we fix our choice state S to be a finite map from identifiers to natural numbers, representing the values of variables stored on the heap, using the finite map modules from Coq's standard library. This choice is somewhat limited, but there are numerous alternative definitions using a universe construction and indexed data types to store heterogeneous data on the heap (Nanevski et al. 2008; Swierstra 2009b).

It is straightforward to model the syntax of the WHILE language as an inductive data type in Coq:

Inductive *Statement* : *Type* :=
| *Skip* : *Statement*
| *Seq* : *Statement* → *Statement* → *Statement*
| *Assign* : *Identifier* → *Expr* → *Statement*
| *If* : *BoolExpr* → *Statement* → *Statement* → *Statement*
| *While* : *Pred heap* → *BoolExpr* → *Statement* → *Statement*
| *Spec* : *PT* → *Statement*.

In what follows we will use the shorthand notation $c_1; c_2$ for *Seq* c_1 c_2 and $x ::= e$ for *Assign* x e.

Our development is parametrized over some (ordered) type representing identifiers. We have omitted the definition of expressions, consisting of integer and boolean constants, variables, and several numeric and boolean operators. Note that every *While* statement must also include a loop invariant of type *Pred heap*.

In addition to the constructs given by the EBNF grammar above, this data type includes a constructor *Spec*, containing the specification of an unfinished program fragment. The refinement laws we will define shortly determine how such specifications may be refined to executable code.

Semantics

Before discussing the refinement calculation further, we need to fix the semantics of our language. We shall do so by associating a predicate transformer, i.e., a value of type PT, with every constructor of the *Statement* data type.

Each rule in Fig. 2 associates pre- and postconditions, i.e., a value of type PT, with a syntactic constructs of the WHILE language. We use the somewhat suggestive notation, $\{P\}$ c $\{Q\}$ to associate with the statement c the conditions $[P, Q]$. These rules are not added as axioms to Coq; nor are they the constructors of an inductive data type. Rather, we can assign semantics to our *Statement* data type directly, as a recursive function:

Fixpoint *semantics* (c : *Statement*) : *PT*

In addition to the rules from Fig. 2, this function simply maps specifications, represented by the *Spec* constructor, to their associated predicate transformer.

Let us examine the rules in Fig. 2 a bit more closely. Each precondition may refer to an initial state s; each postcondition is formulated as a binary relation between an initial state s and a final state s', ignoring the (proof of the) precondition on s for the moment. For example, the postcondition of the SKIP rule states that the initial state s is equal to the final state s'. Similarly, the rule assignment states that the postcondition is equal to the precondition, where the value associated with the identifier x has been updated to the result of evaluating the right-hand side of the assignment statement, $[\![e]\!]$. Note that the semantics of expressions requires an additional environment argument, recording the state of all variables, that we have omitted for the sake of brevity.

$$\frac{}{\{\,True\,\}\ \textbf{skip}\ \{\,s = s'\,\}}\ \text{S{\small KIP}}$$

$$\frac{}{\{\,True\,\}\ x ::= e\ \{\,s' = s\,[x \mapsto [\![e]\!]]\,\}}\ \text{A{\small SSIGN}}$$

$$\frac{\{P_1\}\ c_1\ \{Q_1\} \qquad \{P_2\}\ c_2\ \{Q_2\}}{\{P_1\ s \wedge \textbf{forall}\ t, Q_1\ s\ t \to P_2\ t\}\ c_1; c_2\ \{\textbf{exists}\ (t : S), Q_1\ s\ t \wedge Q_2\ t\ s'\}}\ \text{S{\small EQ}}$$

$$\frac{\{P_1\}\ t\ \{Q_1\} \qquad \{P_2\}\ e\ \{Q_2\}}{\left\{ \begin{array}{l} [\![b]\!] \to P_1\ s\ \wedge \\ \neg\,[\![b]\!] \to P_2\ s \end{array} \right\}\ \textbf{if}\ b\ \textbf{then}\ t\ \textbf{else}\ e\ \left\{ \begin{array}{l} [\![b]\!] \to Q_1\ s\ s'\ \wedge \\ \neg\,[\![b]\!] \to Q_2\ s\ s' \end{array} \right\}}\ \text{I{\small F}}$$

$$\frac{\{P\}\ c\ \{Q\}}{\left\{ \begin{array}{l} I\ s\ \wedge\ (\textbf{forall}\ t, [\![b]\!] \wedge I\ t \to P\ t)\ \wedge \\ \textbf{forall}\ t\ t', [\![b]\!] \wedge I\ t \wedge Q\ t\ t' \to I\ t' \end{array} \right\}\ \textbf{while}\ b\ \textbf{do}\ c\ \left\{ \neg\,[\![b]\!] \wedge I\ s' \right\}}\ \text{W{\small HILE}}$$

Fig. 2. Semantics of W{\small HILE}

The rules for compound statements are slightly more complicated. To sequence two commands c_1 and c_2, the rule S{\small EQ} requires the precondition of c_1 should hold and its postcondition should imply the postcondition of c_2. The postcondition of the composition states that there is an intermediate state t, that relates the postconditions of both statements.

The rule for conditionals, I{\small F}, is reasonably straightforward: when the boolean condition b holds, the precondition of the **then**-branch must be satisfied and its postcondition is the postcondition of the entire statement. When the boolean condition is not satisfied, a similar statement holds for the **else**-branch.

Finally, the W{\small HILE} rule is the most complex. Besides the precondition, P, and postcondition, Q, associated with the body of the loop, the W{\small HILE} rule requires the programmer to specify the loop invariant, I. The precondition of the W{\small HILE} rule consists of three conjuncts:

- the invariant I must hold initially;
- the boolean guard b holds and the invariant must together imply the precondition of the loop body;
- the loop body must preserve the invariant.

The postcondition merely states that the boolean guard no longer holds, but the invariant has been maintained. Note that this formulation captures *partial correctness*; there is no variant ensuring that the loop must terminate eventually.

Using these semantics, we now define a refinement relation between statements in the W{\small HILE} language:

Definition *RefinedBy* $c_1\ c_2 := Refines\ (semantics\ c_1)\ (semantics\ c_2)$.

Once again, we will use the notation $c_1 \sqsubseteq c_2$ when *RefinedBy* $c_1\ c_2$ holds.

Example: Swap

With these definitions in place, we can now formalize the proof in Fig. 1. To do so, we need to find a proof of the *swapCorrect* lemma, formulated as follows:

Definition *swapSpec* :=
[*In X s* ∧ *In Y s, find s' X = find s Y* ∧ *find s' Y = find s X*].

Definition *swap* : *Statement* := *Skip*;
$$T ::= Ref\ Y;$$
$$Y ::= Ref\ X;$$
$$X ::= Ref\ T.$$

Lemma *swapCorrect* : *swapSpec* ⊑ *swap*.

Here we use the *Ref* constructor to include variables in our expression language. The proof is reasonably straightforward: we repeatedly apply the transitivity of the refinement relation, explicitly passing the mediating *Statement* that we read off from Fig. 1. The only non-trivial proof obligations that arise concern reading from and writing to our heap.

Unfortunately, this form of post-hoc verification is very different from the program calculation that we would like to perform. The proof requires repeatedly stating the 'next step' in the refinement proof explicitly, every time we apply transitivity of the refinement relation. As a result, the straightforward proof script is lengthy and error-prone. In the next section we will develop machinery to enable the interactive discovery of programs, rather than the mere transcription of an existing proof.

5   Interactive Refinement

Although we can now take any pen-and-paper proof of refinement and verify this in Coq, we are not yet playing to the strengths of the *interactive* theorem prover that we have at hand. In this section, we will show how to develop lemmas and definitions on top of those we have seen so far that facilitate the interactive calculation of a program from its specification. Carefully choosing the formulation of our lemmas and the order of their assumptions will help guide the refinement process.

We start by defining a function that determines when a statement is executable, i.e., when there are no occurrences of the *Spec* constructor:

Fixpoint *isExecutable* (*c* : *Statement*) : *Prop*

Rather than fixing the exact program upfront, we can now reformulate the correctness lemma of swap as follows:

Lemma *swapCalc* : { *c* : *Statement* | *SwapSpec* ⊑ *c*
∧ *isExecutable c*}.

The notation { *x* : *A* | *P x*} in Coq is used to denote a dependent pair consisting of a witness *x* : *A* and a proof that *x* satisfies the property *P*.

To prove this lemma we need to provide an executable $c : Statement$ and a proof that $SwapSpec \sqsubseteq c$. This is a superficial change – we could now complete the proof by providing our *swap* program as the witness c and reuse our previous correctness lemma. Instead of doing this, however, we wish to explore how to reformulate typical refinement calculus laws to enable the interactive construction of a suitable program.

Consider the *following assignment rule*, given in Lemma 2. We can formulate and prove the lemma in Coq as follows:

Lemma $followAssign_1$
$(x : Identifier) (e : Expr)$
$(P : Pred\ S) (Q : \textbf{forall } (s : S), P\ s \rightarrow Pred\ S) :$
let $Q' := \textbf{fun } s\ pres\ s' \Rightarrow Q\ s\ pres\ (s'[x \mapsto [\![e]\!]])$ **in**
$[P, Q] \sqsubseteq [P, Q']; x ::= e.$

Here we use the notation $s'[x \mapsto [\![e]\!]]$ to indicate that the value associated with the identifier x in s' has been updated to $[\![e]\!]$. The proof of this lemma is reasonably straightforward. After applying the *Refinement* constructor, the remaining proof obligations are trivial to discharge. Having proven this lemma, however, we cannot immediately use it to prove a goal of the shape $\{c : Statement \mid spec \sqsubseteq c \wedge isExecutable\ c\}$. To do so, we need to define an additional wrapper.

Lemma $followAssign_2 \{P : Pred\ S\} \{Q\}$
$(x : Identifier) (e : Expr) :$
let $spec_1 := Spec\ ([P, Q])$ **in**
let $spec_2 := Spec\ ([P, \textbf{fun } s\ pres\ s' \Rightarrow Q\ s\ pres\ (s'[x \mapsto [\![e]\!]])])$ **in**
$\{c : Statement \mid (spec_2 \sqsubseteq c) \wedge isExecutable\ c\} \rightarrow$
$\{c : Statement \mid (spec_1 \sqsubseteq c) \wedge isExecutable\ c\}.$

We can now use this lemma to finish our derivation, *swapCalc*. Every application of the *followAssign_2* lemma changes the postcondition; once we have completed our three assignments, we will need to show that our postcondition is a direct consequence of our precondition. This last step is the most important and is the only step that requires any verification effort.

Looking at the formulation of the *followAssign_2* lemma more closely, however, we see that we can *always* apply this rule, regardless of the pre- and postconditions of our specification. By heedlessly applying this lemma, we can paint ourselves into a corner, leaving an unprovable goal *later on in the refinement derivation*. Put differently, applying this rule defers all the verification work, whereas we would like to derive the overall correctness of a program from the correctness of a sequence of refinement steps.

To address this, we have defined the following final version of the *following assignment rule*:

Lemma *followAssign* $\{P : Pred\ S\}\ \{Q\}$
$(x : Identifier)\ (e : Expr)\ (Q' : \textbf{forall}\ (s : S),\ P\ s \to Pred\ S)$:
let $spec_1 := Spec\ ([P, Q])$ **in**
let $spec_2 := Spec\ ([P, Q'])$ **in**
$(\textbf{forall}\ s\ pres\ s',\ Q'\ s\ pres\ s' \to Q\ s\ pres\ (s'[x \mapsto [\![e]\!]])) \to$
$\{c : Statement \mid (spec_2 \sqsubseteq c) \wedge isExecutable\ c\} \to$
$\{c : Statement \mid (spec_1 \sqsubseteq c) \wedge isExecutable\ c\}.$

Applying this rule yields *two* subgoals: the explicit proof relating the two postconditions and the remainder of the refinement calculation. Furthermore, when applying this rule the user must explicitly pass the 'new' postcondition Q'. This formulation of the following assignment rule, however, has one significant advantage: it encourages users to perform a small amount of verification, corresponding to the proof of first subgoal, every time it is applied. Where the previous formulations made it possible to rack up arbitrary 'verification debt', this last version enables the incremental development of the correctness proof.

This section has focused on a single lemma, *followAssign*. This lemma is representative for the design choices that we have made in the implementation of several related refinement laws. We have tried to capture our methodology in a handful of following design principles, that we applied when formulating further refinement laws:

- Any refinement law should prove a statement of the form $\{c : Statement \mid spec \sqsubseteq c \wedge isExecutable\ c\}$. Users are expected to formulate their specifications in this fashion. Fixing this form enables us to assume the open (sub)goals have a certain shape, which we can exploit during the program calculation and proof automation.
- There is at least one lemma implementing each of the refinement rules shown in Fig. 2. Often we provide several composite definitions, that refine specific parts of a composite command, such as the body of a loop or one component of a sequential composition.
- The order of hypotheses in lemmas matters. Coq presents the user with the remaining subgoals in the same order in which they occur as arguments to the lemma being invoked. Therefore subgoals that are most likely to be problematic should come first. For example, a poor choice of postcondition Q' in the final version of the *followAssign* lemma could yield unprovable subgoals. Requiring that problematic subgoals are completed first, minimizes the chance of a complete refinement calculation getting stuck on an unproven subgoal arising from an earlier step.
- We never assume anything about the shape of the pre- or postcondition of the specifications involved. For example, consider the usual rule for sequential composition from Hoare logic:

$$\frac{\{P\}\ c_1\ \{Q\} \qquad \{Q\}\ c_2\ \{R\}}{\{P\}\ c_1;c_2\ \{R\}}\ \text{SEQUENCE}$$

To apply this rule, we require the precondition of c_1 and postcondition of c_2 to be *identical*. This is not necessarily the case in the middle of a refinement calculation. Instead of requiring users to weaken postconditions and strengthen preconditions explicitly, it can be useful to provide an equivalent, yet more readily applicable, alternative definition:

$$\frac{\{P\}\, c_1\, \{Q_2\} \qquad \{Q_1\}\, c_2\, \{R\} \qquad Q_2 \to Q_1}{\{P\}\, c_1; c_2\, \{R\}} \text{ SEQUENCE}$$

Here we have turned the explicit relation between the postcondition of c_1 and the precondition of c_2 into an additional subgoal. As a result, the rule can always be applied, but it now carries an additional proof obligation.

6 Validation

This section presents two separate results, validating our work. We will show how our choice of pre- and postconditions associated with the WHILE are sound and complete with respect to the usual weakest precondition semantics. Later, we will use our definitions to formalize a derivation by Morgan (1990).

Soundness

In Fig. 2, we are free to associate any choice of pre- and postconditions with the syntax of the WHILE language – how can we validate that our choice of pre- and postconditions are correct? Or what does 'correctness' even mean in this context? In this section, we will show how our definitions relate to those found in the literature.

Typically, weakest precondition semantics are specified by associating *predicate transformers* with the constructs from a programming language. For example, the rules typically associated with the WHILE language are give in Fig. 3.

On the surface, the pre- and postconditions we have chosen in Fig. 2 are not at all similar. Yet we can relate these two semantics precisely. The semantics given in Fig. 3 define a function wp with the following type:

Fixpoint $\mathsf{wp}\,(c : Statement)\,(R : Pred\,S) : Pred\,S$

$$\mathsf{wp}\,(\mathbf{skip}, R) = R$$
$$\mathsf{wp}\,(x ::= e, R) = R\,[x\,/\,[\![e]\!]]$$
$$\mathsf{wp}\,(c_1; c_2, R) \qquad = \mathsf{wp}\,(c_1, \mathsf{wp}\,(c_2, R))$$
$$\mathsf{wp}\,(\mathbf{if}\ c\ \mathbf{then}\ t\ \mathbf{else}\ e, R) = [\![c]\!] \to \mathsf{wp}\,(t, R)$$
$$\wedge \neg\,[\![c]\!] \to \mathsf{wp}\,(e, R)$$
$$\mathsf{wp}\,(\mathbf{while}\ c\ \mathbf{do}\ b, R) \qquad = I \wedge [\![c]\!] \to \mathsf{wp}\,(b, I)$$
$$\wedge \neg\,[\![c]\!] \to R$$

Fig. 3. Weakest precondition semantics of WHILE

Recall from Sect. 3 that we can assign semantics to any value of PT, interpreting it as a predicate transformer of type $Pred\ S \rightarrow Pred\ S$. Using this semantics, we can now relate our definitions with the traditional semantics in terms of weakest preconditions:

Theorem $soundness\ (c : Statement)\ (P : Pred\ S):$
forall $s, \text{wp}\ c\ P\ s \leftrightarrow [\![c]\!]\ P\ s.$

This result is important: our choice of semantics in Fig. 2 is sound and complete with respect to the usual axiomatic semantics in terms of predicate transformers.

Case Study: Square Root

Now that we have covered the basic design principles and semantics of our embedding of the refinement calculus, we aim to validate our results through a case study. In this section, we will repeat the calculation of a program to performs a binary search to find the integer square root of its input integer. This example is taken from Morgan's textbook on refinement calculus (Morgan 1990, Chap. 9). The complete calculation can be found in Fig. 4. Note that we have numbered every refinement step explicitly.

Given the desired postcondition, $r = \lfloor \sqrt{s} \rfloor$, we apply several refinement laws until we are left with an executable program. To avoid repetition, we use the notation $P \trianglelefteq Q$ when the term P contains a single specification that can

$$[true, r^2 \leqslant s < (r+1)^2]$$
$\sqsubseteq$ { choosing I to be $r^2 \leqslant s < q^2$ (*Step 1*) }
$$[true, I \wedge r+1 \equiv q]$$
$\sqsubseteq$ { sequence (*Step 2*) }
$$[true, I]; [I, I \wedge r+1 = q]$$
$\sqsubseteq$ { assignment and sequential composition (*Step 3*) }
$$q ::= s+1; r ::= 0; [I, I \wedge r+1 = q]$$
$\trianglelefteq$ { while (*Step 4*) }
while $r+1 \not\equiv q$ **do** $[r+1 \not\equiv q \wedge I, I]$
$\trianglelefteq$ { sequence (*Step 5*) }
$$[r+1 < q \wedge I, r < p < q \wedge I]; [r < p < q \wedge I, I]$$
$\sqsubseteq$ { assignment (*Step 6*) }
$$p ::= (q+r) \div 2; [r < p < q \wedge I, I]$$
$\trianglelefteq$ { conditional introduction (*Step 7*) }
if $s < p^2$ **then** $[s < p^2 \wedge p < q \wedge I, I]$ **else** $[s \geqslant p^2 \wedge r < p \wedge I, I]$
$\sqsubseteq$ { assignment (*Step 8*) }
if $s < p^2$ **then** $q ::= p$ **else** $r ::= p$

Fig. 4. Calculating the integer square root program

be refined by Q. In particular, any executable code fragments in P will not be repeated in Q (or the remainder of the derivation). This is a slight variation on the notation that Morgan uses, that more closely follows the intuition of 'open subgoal' with which users of interactive theorem provers will already be familiar.

The first step strengthens the postcondition, requiring that the additional condition I must also be satisfied. In later steps, this will become our loop invariant, stating that our current approximation lies between the upper bound q and lower bound r. The proof continues by splitting off a series of assignments that ensure I holds initially (*Step* 2).

Once we have established that the loop invariant holds initially (*Step* 3), we introduce a **while** statement (*Step* 4). The loop will continue until the lower bound, r, can no longer be increased without overlapping with the upper bound q. Although we could refine the body of the **while** with the **skip** command, this would cause our program to diverge. Instead, we begin by assigning to the variable p the 'halfway point' between our bounds q and r (*Step* 6). Finally, we check whether p is too large or too small to be the integer square root (*Step* 7). Both branches of the conditional update our bounds accordingly, after which the loop body is finished (*Step* 8).

How difficult is it to perform such a refinement proof in Coq? Most individual refinement steps correspond to a single call to an appropriate lemma. Discharging the subgoals arising from the application of each lemma typically requires a handful of tactics, many of which we believe could be automated further. The only non-obvious steps arise from having to apply several custom lemmas about division by two. The entire proof script weighs in at just under 200 lines, excluding general purpose lemmas defined elsewhere; as some of our lemmas require explicit pre- and postconditions, the proof scripts can become rather verbose. This is unfortunate, as adapting the specification may require updating the conditions mentioned explicitly in the proof script. We believe that it should be able to halve the length of the proof by tidying up the proof and investing in better automation.

Interactive verification in this style has several important advantages. Firstly, it is impossible to fudge your 'proofs.' On paper, it can be easy to gloss over certain verification conditions that you believe to hold. The proof assistant keeps you honest. Furthermore, the interactive derivation in this style produces an abstract syntax tree of the executable code. This can be easily traversed to generate imperative (pseudo)code. Some of the errors that Morgan describes arise from the fact that, even after the pen and paper proof has been completed, the resulting code still needs to be transcribed to a programming language. This need not be a concern in this setting.

7   Discussion

The choice of our PT types and definition of refinement relation are not novel. Similar definitions of *indexed containers* (Altenkirch and Morris 2009) and *interaction structures* (Hancock and Setzer 2000a,b) can already be found in the literature. Indeed, part of this work was triggered by Peter Hancock's remark that these structures are closely related to *predicate transformers* and the refinement relation between them, as we have made explicit in this paper.

We are certainly not the first to explore the possibility of embedding a refinement calculus in a proof assistant. One of the first attempts to do so, to the best of our knowledge, was by Back and Von Wright (Back and von Wright 1989). They describe a formalization of several notions, such as weakest precondition semantics and the refinement relation, in the interactive theorem prover HOL. This was later extended to the *Refinement Calculator* (Butler et al. 1997), that built a new GUI on top of HOL using Tcl/Tk. More recently, Dongol et al. have extended these ideas even further in HOL, adding a separation logic and its associated algebraic structure (Dongol et al. 2015). There are far fewer such implementations in Coq, Boulmé (2007) being one of the few exceptions. In contrast to the approach taken here, Boulmé explores the possibility of a monadic, shallow embedding, by defining the *Dijkstra Specification Monad*.

There is a great deal of work marrying effects and dependent types. Swierstra's thesis explores one potential avenue: defining a functional semantics for effects (Swierstra 2009b; Swierstra and Altenkirch 2007). For some effects, such as non-termination, defining such a functional semantics in a total language is highly non-trivial. Therefore, systems such as Ynot take a different approach (Nanevski et al. 2008)s. Ynot extends Coq with several axioms, corresponding to the different operations various effects support, such as reading from and writing to mutable state. The type of these axioms captures all the information that a programmer may use to reason about such effects. These types are similar to those presented here in Fig. 2. Contrary to the approach taken here, however, Ynot lets users write their programs without considering their specification. Users only need to write proofs after specifying the pre- and postconditions for a certain function. The refinement calculus, on the other hand, starts from a specification, which is gradually refined to an executable program.

In the future, we hope to investigate how these various approaches to verification may be combined. One obvious next step would be to re-use the separation logic and associated proof automation defined by later installments of Ynot (Chlipala et al. 2009) as the model of the heap in our refinement calculus. Furthermore, we have (for now) chosen to ignore the variants associated with loops. As a result, the programs calculated may diverge. Embellishing our definitions with loop variants is straightforward, but will make our definitions even more cumbersome to use.

Type theory and the refinement calculus are both frameworks that combine specification and calculation. By embedding the refinement calculus in type theory, we study their relation further. The interactive structure of many proof assistants seems to fit well with the idea of *calculating* a program from its specification step-by-step. How well this approach scales, however, remains to be seen. For now, the embedding presented in this paper identifies an alternative point in the spectrum of available proof techniques for the construction of verified programs.

Acknowledgments. The first author would like to thank Peter Hancock for his patience in explaining the relation between interaction structures and the refinement calculus. The first author's visit to Scotland was funded by the *London Mathematical Society's* Scheme 7 grant.

References

Altenkirch, T., Morris, P.: Indexed containers. In: 24th Annual IEEE Symposium on Logic in Computer Science, LICS 2009, pp. 227–285 (2009)

Back, R.J.R., von Wright, J.: Refinement concepts formalized in higher order logic. Formal Aspects Comput. **2**, 247–272 (1989)

Von Wright, J.: Refinement Calculus: Refinement Calculus. Texts in Computer Science. Springer, New York (1998)

Back, R.J.R., von Wright, J.: Refinement concepts formalised in higher order logic. Formal Aspects Comput. **2**(1), 247–272 (1990)

Back, R.J.R.: On the Correctness of Refinement in Program Development. PhD thesis, University of Helsinki (1978)

Boulmé, S.: Intuitionistic refinement calculus. In: Della Rocca, S.R. (ed.) TLCA 2007. LNCS, vol. 4583, pp. 54–69. Springer, Heidelberg (2007)

Butler, M.J., Grundy, J., Långbacka, T., Ruksenas, R., Wright, J.V.: The refinement calculator. In: Formal Methods Pacific (1997)

Chlipala, A., Malecha, G., Morrisett, G., Shinnar, A., Wisnesky, R.: Effective interactive proofs for higher-order imperative programs. In: International Conference on Functional Programming, ICFP 2009, pp. 79–90 (2009)

Dijkstra, E.W.: A Discipline of Programming. Prentice-Hall, Englewood Cliffs (1976)

Dongol, B., Gomes, V.B.F., Struth, G.: A program construction and verification tool for separation logic. In: Hinze, R., Voigtländer, J. (eds.) MPC 2015. LNCS, vol. 9129, pp. 137–158. Springer, Heidelberg (2015)

Floyd, R.W.: Assigning meanings to programs. Math. Aspects Comput. Sci **19**(19–32), 1 (1967)

Hancock, P., Hyvernat, P.: Programming interfaces and basic topology. Ann. Pure Appl. Logic **137**(1), 189–239 (2006)

Setzer, A., Hancock, P.: Interactive programs in dependent type theory. In: Clote, P.G., Schwichtenberg, H. (eds.) CSL 2000. lncs, vol. 1862, pp. 317–339. Springer, Heidelberg (2000)

Hancock, P., Setzer, A.: Specifying interactions with dependent types. In: Workshop on subtyping and dependent types in programming (2000b)

Hoare, C.A.R.: An axiomatic basis for computer programming. Commun. ACM **12**(10), 576–580 (1969)

Morgan, C.: Programming from specifications. Prentice-Hall Inc, Upper Saddle River (1990)

Nanevski, A., Morrisett, G., Shinnar, A., Govereau, P., Birkedal, L.: Ynot: Dependent types for imperative programs. In: International Conference on Functional Programming, ICFP 2008, pp. 229–240 (2008)

Flemming, N., Nielson, H.R., Hankin, C.: Principles of Program Analysis. Springer, Heidelberg (1999)

Swierstra, W.: A hoare logic for the state monad. In: Berghofer, S., Nipkow, T., Urban, C., Wenzel, M. (eds.) TPHOLs 2009. LNCS, vol. 5674, pp. 440–451. Springer, Heidelberg (2009)

Swierstra, W.: A functional specification of effects. PhD thesis, University of Nottingham (2009)

Swierstra, W., Altenkirch, T.: Beauty in the beast: In: Proceedings of the ACM SIGPLAN Workshop on Haskell Workshop, pp. 25-36. ACM (2007)

The Boolean Constraint Solver of SWI-Prolog (System Description)

Markus Triska$^{(\boxtimes)}$

Database and Artificial Intelligence Group, Vienna University of Technology,
Vienna, Austria
triska@dbai.tuwien.ac.at
http://www.metalevel.at

Abstract. We present a new constraint solver over Boolean variables, available as library(clpb) (documentation: http://eu.swi-prolog.org/man/clpb.html) in SWI-Prolog. Our solver distinguishes itself from other available CLP($\mathcal{B}$) solvers by several unique features: First, it is written entirely in Prolog and is hence portable to different Prolog implementations. Second, it is the first freely available BDD-based CLP($\mathcal{B}$) solver. Third, we show that new interface predicates allow us to solve new types of problems with CLP($\mathcal{B}$) constraints. We also use our implementation experience to contrast features and state necessary requirements of attributed variable interfaces to optimally support CLP($\mathcal{B}$) constraints in different Prolog systems. Finally, we also present some performance results and comparisons with SICStus Prolog.

Keywords: CLP(B) · Boolean unification · Decision diagrams · BDD

1 Introduction

CLP($\mathcal{B}$), Constraint Logic Programming over Boolean variables, is a declarative formalism for reasoning about propositional formulas. It is an important instance of the general CLP($\cdot$) scheme introduced by Jaffar and Lassez [11] that extends logic programming with reasoning over specialized domains. Well-known applications of CLP($\mathcal{B}$) arise in circuit verification and model checking tasks.

There is a vast literature on SAT solving, and there are many systems and techniques for detecting (un)satisfiability of Boolean clauses (see [14,18,22] and many others).

However, a CLP($\mathcal{B}$) system is different from common SAT solvers in at least one critical aspect: It must support and take into account *aliasing* and unification of logical variables, even *after* SAT constraints have already been posted. Generally, CLP($\mathcal{B}$) systems are more algebraically oriented than common SAT solvers: In addition to unification of logical variables, they also support variable quantification, conditional answers and easy symbolic manipulation of formulas. In this paper, we discuss several use cases and consequences of these features.

This paper is organized as follows: In Sect. 2, we briefly outline the current state of available CLP($\mathcal{B}$) systems, followed by a brief discussion of Binary

© Springer International Publishing Switzerland 2016
O. Kiselyov and A. King (Eds.): FLOPS 2016, LNCS 9613, pp. 45–61, 2016.
DOI: 10.1007/978-3-319-29604-3_4

Decision Diagrams. In Sect. 4, we present the interface and implementation of a new CLP($\mathcal{B}$) system, its distinguishing new features, a comparison of attributed variable interfaces and necessary requirements for optimally supporting CLP($\mathcal{B}$) solvers on top of Prolog. Section 5 describes new applications made possible by the new features of our library, followed by performance results and a brief discussion of implementation variants and planned features.

2   CLP($\mathcal{B}$) Systems and Implementation Methods

Support of CLP($\mathcal{B}$) constraints has been somewhat inconsistent between and even within different Prolog systems over the last few decades. CHIP [9] was one of the first widely used systems to support CLP($\mathcal{B}$) constraints, and shortly after, SICStus Prolog supported them too [4], up until version 3. However, more recent versions of SICStus Prolog, while shipping with a port of the clpb library, do not officially support the solver in any way.[1] In contrast, Prolog IV [1] and GNU Prolog [8] do support Boolean constraints.

Implementation methods of CLP($\mathcal{B}$) systems are likewise diverse. We find two main implementation variants used in major Prolog systems: (1) implementations based on Binary Decision Diagrams (BDDs) and (2) approximation of CLP($\mathcal{B}$) constraints by other constraints, using for example indexicals. SICStus Prolog is an instance of the former variant, and GNU Prolog one of the latter.

Each of these variants has strengths and weaknesses: Among the major advantages of BDD-based implementations we find *completeness* and some algebraic virtues which we will explain in later sections of this paper. In comparison, approximation-based implementations are generally simpler, more scalable and much more efficient on selected benchmarks [5]. However, they are *incomplete* in general and require an explicit search to ensure the existence of solutions after posting constraints.

3   Binary Decision Diagrams (BDDs)

A Binary Decision Diagram (BDD) is a rooted, directed and acyclic graph and represents a Boolean function [2,12]. In this paper, we assume all BDDs to be *ordered* and *reduced*. This means, respectively, that all variables appear in the same order on all paths from the root, and that the representation is minimal in the sense that all isomorphic subgraphs are merged and no redundant nodes occur.

In the Prolog community, BDDs have already appeared several times: Apart from the CLP($\mathcal{B}$) library used in SICStus Prolog, we also find BDDs in the form of small Prolog code snippets. For example, Richard O'Keefe has generously made a small library available for his COSC410 course in the year 2011.[2]

---

[1] The documentation of SICStus Prolog 4.3.2 contains the exact wording of current support terms of the clpb module that ships with the system: "The library module is a direct port from SICStus Prolog 3. It is not supported by SICS in any way.".

[2] Source: http://www.cs.otago.ac.nz/staffpriv/ok/COSC410/robdd.pl.

BDDs also occur in publications that introduce or use closely related data structures [19,20]. Within the logic programming community, important applications of BDDs arise in the context of *probabilistic* logic programming [13] and termination analysis of Prolog programs [3,6].

4   A New CLP($\mathcal{B}$) System: `library(clpb)` in SWI-Prolog

We have implemented a new CLP($\mathcal{B}$) system, freely available in SWI-Prolog [21] as `library(clpb)`. In this section, we present the design choices, interface predicates and implementation. Subsections 4.5, 4.6 and 4.7 are targeted at implementors and contributors of Prolog systems and constraint libraries, and assume familiarity with BDDs and Prolog interfaces for attributed variables.

4.1   Implementation Choices: BDDs, SAT Solvers, Libraries

Before presenting the actual features and implementation of our new system, we present a brief high-level overview of the various implementation options and their consequences, and give several reasons that justify the choices we have made in our implementation.

When implementing a new CLP($\mathcal{B}$) system, we typically have a clear idea of what we need from it. Also in our case, the intended use was very clear from the start: Since 2004, the author has been working on facilitating a port of Ulrich Neumerkel's GUPU system [16,17] to SWI-Prolog so that more users can freely benefit from it. GUPU is an excellent Prolog teaching environment, and one of its integrated termination analyzers, cTI [3], heavily depends on the CLP($\mathcal{B}$) implementation of SICStus Prolog. Already a cursory glance at the source code of cTI makes clear that it depends on features that only a BDD-based solver can provide, since cTI goes as far as inspecting the concrete structure of BDDs in its implementation.

Still, we initially hoped for a shortcut: Our hope was that we could simulate the behaviour of a BDD-based CLP($\mathcal{B}$) system by using a simpler (external or internal) SAT solver. For example, we envisioned that checking for tautologies could be easily handled by looking for counterexamples of the accumulated constraints, and checking consistency of accumulated constraints could be handled by trying to generate concrete solutions after posting each constraint.

Alas, such a simplistic approach falls short for several reasons. One of those reasons is efficiency: For example, detecting tautologies (a prominent operation in cTI) is hard in general, but easy after BDDs have been built. Another, more fundamental reason is that many use cases of CLP($\mathcal{B}$) depend on *symbolic* results instead of "only" detecting satisfiability, and such results are much more readily obtained with BDD-based approaches.

As a simple example, consider the integrated circuit shown in Fig. 1 (a). A Prolog program that describes the circuit with CLP($\mathcal{B}$) constraints (see Sect. 4.2) is shown in Fig. 1 (b). No concrete solutions are asked for by that program: To verify the circuit, we care more about the *symbolic expressions* that are obtained as residuals goals of this program, and *less* about concrete solutions. For example, with the given program, the query ?- xor(x, y, Z). yields the residual goal sat(Z=:=x#y), expressing Z as a function of the intended input variables, which are universally quantified. From this, we see at one glance that the circuit indeed describes the intended Boolean XOR operation. When producing residual goals, existential quantification is implicitly used by the Prolog toplevel to project away variables that do not occur in the query.

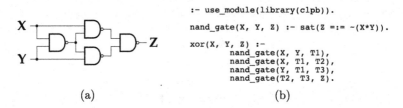

```
:- use_module(library(clpb)).

nand_gate(X, Y, Z) :- sat(Z =:= -(X*Y)).

xor(X, Y, Z) :-
        nand_gate(X, Y, T1),
        nand_gate(X, T1, T2),
        nand_gate(Y, T1, T3),
        nand_gate(T2, T3, Z).
```

(a)   (b)

Fig. 1. (a) Expressing XOR ($X \oplus Y = Z$) with four NAND gates and (b) describing the circuit with CLP($\mathcal{B}$) constraints. ?- xor(x, y, Z). yields sat(Z=:=x#y).

To efficiently provide such features and others (see also Sect. 4.4), we decided to base our implementation on BDDs instead of only emulating them.

Having made the decision to implement a BDD-based CLP($\mathcal{B}$) system, the next arising question was how to actually use BDDs so that they work in the context of CLP($\mathcal{B}$). Even though the excellent implementation description of an existing BDD-based CLP($\mathcal{B}$) system [4] was of course available to us, many unsettled questions still remained, such as: How is an existing BDD changed after unification of two variables? How do we handle unification of two variables that reside in different BDDs? How exactly does the notion of *universally* quantified variables affect all operations on BDDs? How are residual goals produced? Finally, are there not some subtly misguiding mistakes in the implementation description, e.g., is a BDD really represented by a *ground* Prolog term in SICStus Prolog, or are there not variables also involved?

In the face of so many initially unsettled questions, we anticipated a lot of prototyping and rewriting in the initial phase of our implementation, which also turned out to be necessary. To facilitate prototyping, enhance portability, and to study and answer high-level semantic questions separated from lower-level issues, we are consciously *not* hard-wiring our solver with an external BDD package until semantic aspects (see Sect. 4.7) are settled to provide a more stable basis for low-level changes. Therefore, we have created a new high-level Prolog implementation of BDDs that forms the basis of our new CLP($\mathcal{B}$) system.

We consider the availability of a completely free CLP($\mathcal{B}$) system where the above questions are answered in the form of an executable specification an integral part of our contribution, since it also shows the places where, if at all, external BDD libraries can be most meaningfully plugged in.

4.2   Syntax of Boolean Expressions

We have strived for compatibility with SICStus Prolog and provide the same syntax of Boolean *expressions*. Table 1 shows the syntax of all Boolean expressions that are available in both SICStus and SWI-Prolog. Universally quantified variables are denoted by Prolog *atoms* in both systems, and universal quantifiers appear implicitly in front of the entire expression. Atoms are useful for denoting *input* variables: In residual goals, intended output variables are expressed as functions of input variables. The expression `card(Is,Exprs)` is true iff the number of true expressions in the list `Exprs` is a member of the list `Is` of integers and integer ranges of the form `From-To`.

In addition to the Boolean expressions shown in Table 1, we have also chosen to support two new Boolean expressions. These new expressions are shown in Table 2. They denote, respectively, the disjunction and conjunction of all Boolean expressions in a list. We have found this syntax extension to be very useful in many practical applications, and encourage their support in other CLP($\mathcal{B}$) systems. This syntax was kindly suggested to us by Gernot Salzer.

Table 1. Syntax of Boolean expressions available in both SICStus and SWI

Expression	Meaning
0, 1	**false, true**
variable	unknown truth value
atom	universally quantified variable
~ *Expr*	logical NOT
Expr + *Expr*	logical OR
Expr * *Expr*	logical AND
Expr # *Expr*	exclusive OR
Var ^ *Expr*	existential quantification
Expr =:= *Expr*	equality
Expr =\= *Expr*	disequality (same as #)
Expr =< *Expr*	less or equal (implication)
Expr >= *Expr*	greater or equal
Expr < *Expr*	less than
Expr > *Expr*	greater than
`card(Is,Exprs)`	*see description in text*

Table 2. New and useful Boolean expressions in SWI-Prolog

Expression	Meaning
+(Exprs)	disjunction of list **Exprs** of expressions
*(Exprs)	conjunction of list **Exprs** of expressions

4.3   Interface Predicates of `library(clpb)`

Regarding interface predicates of our system, we have again strived primarily for compatibility with SICStus Prolog, and all CLP($\mathcal{B}$) predicates provided by SICStus Prolog are also available in SWI-Prolog with the same semantics. In particular, the interface predicates available in both systems are:

sat(+Expr): True iff the Boolean expression Expr is satisfiable.

taut(+Expr, -T): Succeeds with T=0 if Expr cannot be satisfied, and with T=1 if T is a tautology with respect to the stated constraints. Otherwise, it fails.

labeling(+Vs): Assigns a Boolean value to each variable in the list Vs in such a way that all stated constraints are satisfied.

4.4   New Interface Predicates

BDDs have many important virtues that can be easily made available in a BDD-based CLP($\mathcal{B}$) system. The core idea of efficient algorithms on BDDs is often to combine the solutions for the two children of every BDD node in order to obtain a solution for the parent node.

In addition to the interface predicates presented in the previous section, we have implemented three new predicates that are not yet available in SICStus Prolog:

sat_count(+Expr, -N): N is the number of different assignments of truth values to the variables in the Boolean expression Expr, such that Expr is true and all posted constraints are satisfiable.

random_labeling(+Seed, +Vs): Assigns a Boolean value to each variable in the list Vs in such a way that all stated constraints are satisfied, and each solution is *equally likely*, using random seed Seed and committing to the first solution.

weighted_maximum(+Weights, +Vs, -Maximum): Assigns 0 and 1 to the variables in Vs such that all stated constraints are satisfied, and Maximum is the maximum of $\sum w_i v_i$ over all admissible assignments. On backtracking, all admissible assignments that attain the optimum are generated.

As we show in the following section, these predicates are of great value in many applications, and we encourage their support in other CLP($\mathcal{B}$) systems based on BDDs. This is because these predicates are very easy to implement with BDD-based approaches, and omitting them deprives users of these benefits, unnecessarily.

Using the new +/1 syntax to express the disjunction of Boolean expressions in a list, we also suggest the new idiom sat_count(+[1|Vs], N) to count the number of assignments of truth values to variables in Vs that satisfy all constraints that are posted so far, without further constraining the set of solutions.

4.5   Implementation

We briefly outline the underlying ideas of our implementation. Perhaps most strikingly, our library is written *entirely* in Prolog. This is a deliberate design decision, facilitating rapid prototyping and portability. To the best of our knowledge, ours is the first BDD-based CLP($\mathcal{B}$) system that is freely available. Our library comprises about $1,700$ LOC, including documentation and comments.

Internally, we are using the following representation, using *attributed variables* as in hProlog [7]: Each CLP($\mathcal{B}$) variable belongs to exactly one BDD. Each CLP($\mathcal{B}$) variable gets an attribute of the form index_root(Index,Root), where Index is the variable's unique integer index, and Root is the root of the BDD that the variable belongs to.

Each CLP($\mathcal{B}$) variable is also equipped with an association table that helps us keep the BDD reduced. The association table of each variable must be rebuilt on occasion to remove nodes that are no longer reachable. We rebuild the association tables of involved variables after BDDs are merged to build a new root. This only serves to reclaim memory: Keeping a node in a local table even when it no longer occurs in any BDD does not affect the solver's correctness.

A *root* is a logical variable with a single attribute, a pair of the form Sat-BDD, where Sat is the Boolean expression (in original form) that corresponds to BDD. Sat is necessary to rebuild the BDD after variable aliasing, and to project all remaining constraints to a list of sat/1 goals.

Finally, a *BDD* is either: (1) The integers **0** or **1**, denoting **false** and **true**, respectively, or (2) a node of the form node(ID,Var,Low,High,Aux), where:

- ID is the node's unique integer ID
- Var is the node's branching variable
- Low and High are the node's low (Var = 0) and high (Var = 1) children
- Aux is a free variable, one for each node, that can be used to attach attributes and store intermediate results.

This representation means that we are using (assuming SWI-Prolog and machine-sized integers) 48 bytes per node on 64-bit systems, and we need to store this roughly *twice* because each node is also represented in the association table of its branching variable.

In addition to this considerable memory overhead, our choice to use association tables incurs a logarithmic runtime overhead compared to hashing. On the plus side, association tables scale very predictably and do not require any *ad hoc* considerations and complex treatment of edge-cases.

Figure 2 shows an essential predicate of our library: It is called make_node/4, and given a branching variable and its two children, it builds (low_high_key/3) a unique Key and, depending on whether such a node already exists, either yields that node, or builds a new node. A unique ID is generated for each new node by incrementing a global backtrackable variable called $clpb_next_node. The predicates lookup_node/3 and register_node/3 (implementation omitted) access the branching variable's association table to fetch or store a node. In

```
1    make_node(Var, Low, High, Node) :-
2             (    Low == High -> Node = Low
3             ;    low_high_key(Low, High, Key),
4                  (   lookup_node(Var, Key, Node) -> true
5                  ;   clpb_next_id('$clpb_next_node', ID),
6                      Node = node(ID,Var,Low,High,_Aux),
7                      register_node(Var, Key, Node)
8                  )
9             ).
```

Fig. 2. make_node/4, the essential predicate for creating a BDD node

addition, if the two children are identical, then the resulting node is simply that child itself. Thus, make_node/4 automatically keeps the BDD reduced.

Many of the implemented algorithms use *memoization* to store intermediate results for later use. We are using DCGs and semicontext[3] notation in several internal predicates to implicitly thread through stored results. We refer interested readers to the source code of our library for the fully detailed picture of the implementation.

4.6   Consistency Notions in the Context of CLP($\mathcal{B}$)

Completeness of our CLP($\mathcal{B}$) system follows from the well-known fact that, for fixed variable order and function, the corresponding BDD is *canonical*. Hence, as long as all BDDs that represent the posted constraints are different from **0**, there is at least one admissible solution.

In addition, the well-known CLP(FD) notion of *domain consistency* is of course equally applicable to CLP($\mathcal{B}$): For example, when posting the constraint sat(X*Y + ~X*Y), then a domain consistent CLP($\mathcal{B}$) solver must yield the unification Y = 1. We implement domain consistency in our CLP($\mathcal{B}$) system, and, although this is not documented and does not directly follow from its implementation description, library(clpb) in SICStus Prolog seems to implement this as well.

In fact, SICStus Prolog goes even beyond domain consistency, and seems to implement an undocumented additional property that, for lack of an established terminology (see also [10]), we shall call *aliasing* consistency. By this, we mean that if taut(X =:= Y, 1) holds for any two variables X and Y, then X = Y is posted. For example, when posting sat((A#B)*(A#C)), then an aliasing consistent CLP($\mathcal{B}$) solver must yield the unification B = C.

We implement both consistency notions as follows: First, in a single global sweep of the BDD, we collect all variables that are not skipped in any branch of the BDD that leads to **1**. It is easy to see that if a variable is skipped in a branch that leads to **1**, then it can assume both possible truth values, and cannot be involved in any aliasing. The collected variables are further classified into (1) variables that allow only a single truth value, (2) *further-branching* variables

---

[3] A Prolog DCG primer is available at http://www.metalevel.at/dcg.html.

(i.e., variables that do not have **1** as any child in any node) and (3) *negative-decisive* variables (i.e., variables that have **0** as one child in all nodes). It is easy to see that any potential aliasing must involve one further-branching and one negative-decisive variable, and in additional partial sweeps of the BDD, we determine all unifications that hold among the collected variables.

We have tested the impact of enabling domain and aliasing consistency on a range of benchmarks, and generally found the impact to be very acceptable and sometimes even improving the running time. For this reason, we have opted to enable both consistency notions and benefit from their algebraic properties.

4.7 Unification of Attributed Variables

At the time of this writing, there is no consensus across different Prolog systems regarding the interface predicates for attributed variables. Two different interfaces used by major implementations are, respectively, the one used by SICStus Prolog, and the one used by hProlog and SWI-Prolog. The most striking difference between these two interfaces (see [7]) is that in SICStus Prolog, unifications are *undone* before verify_attributes/3 is called, whereas for example in SWI-Prolog, attr_unify_hook/2 is called with the unification already in place.

Using our implementation experience, we strongly endorse the SICStus interface and its greater generality. We justify this with three different arguments:

(1) The interface used in SWI-Prolog is not general enough to express what we need. For example, according to the documentation of SICStus Prolog, the unification P = Q of two CLP($\mathcal{B}$) expressions P and Q is equivalent to posting sat(P =:= Q). In SWI-Prolog, we cannot fully implement this semantics, because at the time the unification hook is called, the unification has already taken place and may have created a *cyclic* term instead of retaining variables.

(2) The interface used in SWI-Prolog makes it extremely hard to reason about simultaneous unifications. Critically, two variables may be instantiated simultaneously, using for example [X,Y] = [0,1]. This may not pose any problem when admissible unifications can be determined from ground values alone, but it is a severe limitation when additional structures such as decision diagrams, typically stored in attributes, are required. This is because when the unification hook is called for X, then Y is *no longer a variable* and its previous attributes cannot be directly accessed.

(3) The interface used in SWI-Prolog makes reasoning about unifications extremely error-prone. For example, when unifying two CLP($\mathcal{B}$) variables, the unification hook is called with the two variables already *aliased* and in fact identical. In our experience, failure to take possible aliasings into account is a common mistake when working with the SWI interface, and it would improve ease of use considerably if, as in the SICStus interface, unifications were *undone* before the unification hook is invoked by SWI-Prolog.

It is clear that the SICStus interface has some performance impact, because unifications have to be *undone*. In our view, this small disadvantage is completely negligible when taking into account the increased generality and ease of use of the SICStus interface.

5   New Applications of `library(clpb)`

In this section, we present new applications of our $\mathrm{CLP}(\mathcal{B})$ system to illustrate the value of the new interface predicates that we provide. Importantly, these applications all rely *exclusively* on the $\mathrm{CLP}(\mathcal{B})$ interface predicates that are explained in the previous section. In other words, they do not use any low-level primitives that directly manipulate a BDD. Instead, everything is expressed as sat/1 constraints, and the new interface predicates are used to count solutions and select solutions etc. Similar functionality is also available in many BDD packages. However, a $\mathrm{CLP}(\mathcal{B})$ system is much more convenient to use than a low-level library, and different formulations of the same problem can be tried more easily.

5.1   Counting Solutions

We now apply the new interface predicates of our $\mathrm{CLP}(\mathcal{B})$ solver to solve a problem that asks for the number of solutions. It is one of the problems posed in the well known set of challenging mathematical tasks called *Project Euler*.[4] Specifically, it is:

Project Euler Problem 172: How many 18-digit numbers n (without leading zeros) are there such that no digit occurs more than three times in n?

One way to solve this problem is to find a recursive formula that breaks the problems into smaller parts, and to use memoization to make computed intermediate results quickly available for later reference.

However, in our experience, such a way to solve this problem is comparatively tedious and error-prone: It is easy to overlook a case, or to accidentally count some combinations multiple times. Thus, it is hard to be absolutely certain about the correctness of a recursive formula in such cases.

In contrast, the problem has a completely straight-forward and short formulation using $\mathrm{CLP}(\mathcal{B})$ constraints: We can use Boolean variables v_i ($0 \le i \le 9$) to represent a single digit d, where $v_i = 1$ indicates that $d = i$. This method naturally scales to multiple digits by using further sets of variables for subsequent digits. Figure 3 shows how to indicate the number 2016 in this way, where each row corresponds to one digit.

$$\begin{pmatrix} 0\,0\,1\,0\,0\,0\,0\,0\,0\,0 \\ 1\,0\,0\,0\,0\,0\,0\,0\,0\,0 \\ 0\,1\,0\,0\,0\,0\,0\,0\,0\,0 \\ 0\,0\,0\,0\,0\,0\,1\,0\,0\,0 \end{pmatrix}$$

Fig. 3. Representing 2016 with a Boolean 4×10 matrix, using one row per digit

---

[4] See http://projecteuler.net for more information.

Obviously, exactly one of v_i must be 1 to specify the unique value of a single digit. Thus, if v_i are represented as a Prolog list Ls of 10 Boolean variables, we state sat(card([1],Ls)) in terms of CLP($\mathcal{B}$).

The main constraint of the puzzle is readily expressed over each *column* of the resulting matrix, using sat(card([0,1,2,3],Ls)) to constrain each digit to occur at most 3 times.

Figure 4 shows the complete Prolog code to solve the problem with CLP($\mathcal{B}$). The query euler_172(N) yields N = 227485267000992000 after about 7 hours of computation time, using an Intel Core i7 CPU (2.67 GHz) and about 20 GB RAM with SWI 7.3.7.

```
1    :- use_module(library(clpb)).
2    :- use_module(library(clpfd)).
3
4    euler_172(N) :-
5            findall(Ds, (between(1,18,_),length(Ds,10)), Digits),
6            Digits = [[0|_]|_],   % no leading zero
7            transpose(Digits, DigitsT),
8            maplist(card([0,1,2,3]), DigitsT),
9            maplist(card([1]), Digits),
10           append(Digits, Vs),
11           sat_count(+[1|Vs], N).
12
13   card(C, Ls) :- sat(card(C, Ls)).
```

Fig. 4. Using CLP($\mathcal{B}$) constraints to solve Project Euler Problem 172

In contrast to the recursive version and complex combinatorial considerations, there is hardly any room for errors with such a simple CLP($\mathcal{B}$) model.

5.2   Random Solutions

In our second example, we apply CLP($\mathcal{B}$) constraints to model an *exact cover* problem. The task is to cover an $N \times N$ chessboard with *triominoes*, which are rookwise connected pieces with three cells.

We use the following CLP($\mathcal{B}$) encoding: Each cell of the chessboard corresponds to a column of a matrix (b_{ij}), and each possible placement of a single triomino corresponds to one row. $b_{ij} = 1$ means that placing a triomino according to row i covers cell j. For each row, we introduce a Boolean variable x_k, where $x_k = 1$ means that we choose to place a triomino according to row i. An *exact cover* of the chessboard means that for each set S_l of Boolean variables, $S_l = \{x_k \mid b_{kl} = 1\}$, exactly *one* of the variables in S_l is equal to 1, i.e., sat(card([1],$list(S_l)$)) holds, with $list(S_l)$ denoting a Prolog list corresponding to S_l.

In Fig. 5, subfigures (a) and (b) illustrate a common phenomenon when using CLP(FD) constraints to solve such tasks: Successive solutions are often very much alike. Simply adding randomization to labeling/2 is in general *not* sufficient to guarantee random solutions due to potential clustering of solutions. Subfigures (c) and (d) illustrate that solutions can be selected with uniform probability with CLP($\mathcal{B}$) constraints, using the new interface predicate random_labeling/2.

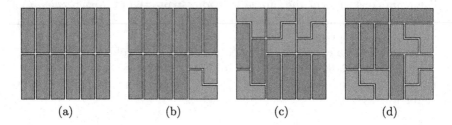

Fig. 5. Exact covers of a 6 × 6 chessboard. (a) and (b) are successive solutions found with CLP(FD) constraints. (c) and (d) are found with CLP($\mathcal{B}$), using random seeds 0 and 1, respectively.

5.3   Weighted Solutions

In the third example, we use the new interface predicate weighted_maximum/3 to *maximize* the number of Boolean variables that are **true**.

The example we use to illustrate this concept is a simple matchsticks puzzle. The initial configuration is shown in Fig. 6 (a), and the task is to keep as many matchsticks as possible in place while at the same time letting no subsquares remain. For example, in Fig. 6 (b), exactly 7 subsquares remain, including the 4 × 4 outer square. Figure 6 (c) shows an admissible solution of this task.

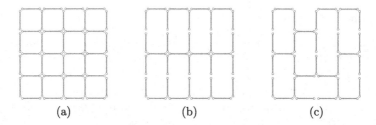

Fig. 6. (a) A grid of matchsticks, (b) Exactly 7 subsquares remaining and (c) Removing the minimum number of matchsticks so that no subsquares remain

Such puzzles are readily formulated with CLP($\mathcal{B}$) constraints, using one Boolean variable to indicate whether or not a matchstick is placed at a particular position. Our new interface predicates make it easy to find and count solutions, and also to maximize or minimize the number of used matchsticks.

CLP($\mathcal{B}$) constraints are not limited to very small puzzles and toy examples though: For tasks of suitable structure, CLP($\mathcal{B}$) constraints scale quite well and let us solve tasks that are hard to solve by other means.

In the next example (taken from [12]), we use CLP($\mathcal{B}$) constraints to express maximal independent sets of graphs: Boolean variables b_i denote whether node i is in the set. In addition, each node i is assigned a weight w_i. The task is to find a maximal independent set that maximizes the total weight $\sum b_i w_i$. For concreteness, let us consider the cycle graph C_{100}, and assign each node i the weight $w_i = (-1)^{\nu(i)}$, where $\nu(i)$ is the number of ones in the binary representation of i. The grey nodes in Fig. 7 show a maximal independent set of C_{100} with maximum total weight. In the figure, nodes with negative weight are drawn as squares, and nodes with positive weight are drawn as circles.

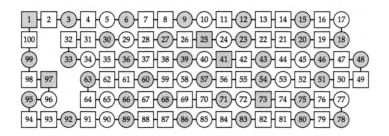

Fig. 7. Maximal independent set of C_{100} with maximum weight ($= 28$)

CLP($\mathcal{B}$) constraints yield the optimum (28) within a few seconds in this example. Moreover, we can use our new interface predicates to compute other interesting facts. For example, C_{100} has exactly 792,070,839,848,372,253,127 independent sets, and exactly 1,630,580,875,002 *maximal* independent sets.

6 Benchmark Results

We now use several benchmarks to compare the performance of our system with the CLP($\mathcal{B}$) library that ships with SICStus Prolog. We are using SWI-Prolog version 7.3.7, and SICStus Prolog version 4.3.2. All programs are run on an Intel Core i7 CPU (2.67 GHz) with 48 GB RAM, using Debian 8.1.

The benchmarks comprise examples[5] from the literature that are also used in [4] and other publications:

pigeon8x9: The task of attempting to place 9 pigeons into 8 holes in such a way that each hole contains at most one pigeon. Clearly, this problem is unsatisfiable.

queens N: Placing N queens on an $N \times N$ chessboard in such a way that no queen is under attack.

schur N: Distribute the numbers $1, \ldots, N$ into 3 *sum-free* sets. A set S is sum-free iff $i, j \in S$ implies $i + j \notin S$. This is satisfiable for all N up to and including the *Schur number* $S(3) = 13$, and unsatisfiable for $N > 13$.

---

[5] The code of all benchmarks is available at http://www.metalevel.at/clpb-bench.

triominoes N: Triomino cover (see Sect. 5.2) of an $N \times N$ chessboard.

We benchmark each example in three different ways, and the results are summarized in Table 3: First, we build a single conjunction C of all clauses and post sat(C). The columns titled sat show the timing results (in seconds) of this call for SWI and SICStus, respectively. Then, we build a list Cs of clauses and post maplist(sat, Cs). The timing result of this is shown in the sats columns. Finally, we invoke taut(C, _), and the timing results of this call are shown in the taut columns.

Table 3. Running times (in seconds) of different benchmarks

name	vars	clauses	SWI 7.3.7			SICStus 4.3.2		
			sat	sats	taut	sat	sats	taut
pigeon8x9	72	17	1.2	1.2	1.2	0.07	0.01	0.05
queens6	36	302	12.7	12.8	12.9	0.01	2.7	0.01
queens7	49	490	65.7	65.9	67.3	3.62	22166	0.03
schur13	39	139	10.6	10.7	10.7	0.31	2.8	0.19
schur14	42	161	13.1	13.2	13.3	0.57	7.63	0.41
triominoes5	94	25	3.6	3.7	3.7	0.01	–	0.02
triominoes6	148	36	22.6	22.7	23.3	–	–	0.08

There are several things worth pointing out about these results: First, it is evident that the CLP($\mathcal{B}$) solver of SICStus Prolog often vastly outperforms our library. We can safely expect the SICStus library to be at least two orders of magnitude faster than ours on many benchmarks. In part, this huge difference in performance may certainly be attributed to the fact that SWI-Prolog itself is already more than three times slower than SICStus Prolog on benchmarks that are in some sense deemed to be representative of many applications. Neng-Fa Zhou, the author of B-Prolog, kindly maintains a collection of these results at http://www.picat-lang.org/bprolog/performance.htm. Since our library is written entirely in Prolog, it strongly depends on the performance of the underlying Prolog system.

Second, there is a large relative difference between the sat and sats columns within SICStus Prolog. In the queens7 case, it is particularly pronounced. In SWI-Prolog, there is virtually no difference between these variants, because we *always* implicitly post individual sat/1 constraints if the given formula is a compound term with principal functor */2, i.e., a conjunction.

Third, some of the benchmarks cannot be solved at all with SICStus Prolog on this machine: We use "–" to denote an *insufficient memory* exception.

7   CLP($\mathcal{B}$) with Other Types of Decision Diagrams

BDDs are not the only kind of decision diagrams that are practically useful, and the question arises whether other types of decision diagrams are not at least equally suitable as the basis of CLP($\mathcal{B}$) systems.

To collect preliminary experiences with different implementation variants, we have created a variant[6] of library(clpb) that is based on Zero-suppressed Binary Decision Diagrams (ZDDs). The key idea of ZDDs [15] is to assign a slightly different meaning to the diagram: In ZDDs, a branch leading to 1 only means **true** if all variables that are *skipped* in that branch are *zero*. ZDDs are therefore especially useful when many variables are zero in solutions.

The ZDD-based variant of library(clpb) does not feature all the functionality that the BDD-based version provides. This is due to two main reasons: The first reason is that, due to the different semantics of the diagrams, a ZDD-based approach necessitates that all variables be known *in advance*, at least if we want to avoid rebuilding all ZDDs every time a new variable occurs. Therefore, a special library predicate must be called before using the ZDD-based version in order to "declare" all Boolean variables that appear in the formulation. The ZDD-based variant is thus not a drop-in replacement of the BDD-based version that ships with SWI-Prolog.

The second reason is that the shortcomings (see Sect. 4.7) of SWI-Prolog's interface predicates for attributed variables are especially severe when ZDDs are involved. This is because simultaneous unifications, such as [A,B] = [0,1], significantly complicate the reasoning when deciding whether a variable (still) occurs in a ZDD. With BDDs, these limitations are a bit less severe, because a variable that does not occur in a BDD can assume either truth value.

So far, we have collected only very limited experience with ZDDs, in part also due to the mentioned limitations of SWI-Prolog's interface predicates. Nevertheless, we would like to point out two interesting tasks for which the ZDD-based variant is very well suited, and hint at planned future developments.

First, we extend the triomono tiling task to a 9×12 grid. One solution is shown in Fig. 8 (a). Project Euler Problem 161 asks for the *number* of such tilings. Using the ZDD-based variant, it takes about 13 GB RAM and 2 days of computation time to construct a ZDD that represents all solutions and compute the number (which is 20,574,308,184,277,971). Using the BDD-based version of library(clpb) requires more than 4 times as much memory.

Second, we allow, in addition to triominoes, also monominoes and dominoes, and cover an 8×8 chessboard. Figure 8 (b) shows one solution. With the ZDD-based variant, 1 GB RAM suffices to compute the number of possible coverings (there are exactly 92,109,458,286,284,989,468,604 of them). Using BDDs takes about 10 times as much memory.

Many other interesting applications of ZDDs are described in [12], and we plan to make many of them accessible in future versions of this library variant. This may require suitable additional interface predicates.

---

[6] The variant is freely available at http://www.metalevel.at/clpb-zdd.

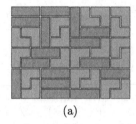
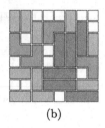

(a)   (b)

Fig. 8. (a) Project Euler Problem 161: Covering a 9 × 12 grid with triominoes; (b) Covering a chessboard with monominoes, dominoes and triominoes

8   Conclusion and Future Work

We have presented the first BDD-based CLP($\mathcal{B}$) system that is freely available. It features new interface predicates that allow us to solve new applications with CLP($\mathcal{B}$) constraints.

Implementing the system in Prolog has allowed us to prototype many ideas quickly. The implementation provides a high-level description of all relevant ideas, and is portable to other Prolog systems that support attributed variables.

We hope that the availability of a free BDD-based CLP($\mathcal{B}$) system leads to increased interest in CLP($\mathcal{B}$) constraints within the Prolog community, and encourages other vendors to likewise support such libraries.

Ongoing and future work is focused on additional test cases to ensure the system's correctness, porting the system to other Prolog systems such as YAP and SICStus Prolog, and improving performance. Stefan Israelsson Tampe is currently porting the solver to Guile-log, a Prolog system based on Guile.

Additional interface predicates may be needed to cover further applications of BDDs and ZDDs. Careful design of these predicates is necessary to provide sufficient generality without exposing users to low-level details of the library.

Acknowledgments. First and foremost, I thank Ulrich Neumerkel for introducing me to constraint logic programming and to testing constraint solvers. For their encouragement about CLP($\mathcal{B}$), I thank Nysret Musliu and Fred Mesnard. My gratitude also goes to Jan Wielemaker for providing a robust and free Prolog system, for his fast reaction times and much appreciated support when discussing and implementing new features. I thank Mats Carlsson for the visionary CLP($\mathcal{B}$) solver of SICStus Prolog and sending me a complimentary version of his system. For their supremely well-written documents about BDDs, I thank Donald Knuth and Henrik Reif Andersen. These books and papers further increased my interest in the subject and were very useful during development. I also thank the anonymous reviewers for their helpful comments.

With all my heart, I thank my partner Barbara for her love.

References

1. Benhamou, F., Touraïvane, T.: Prolog IV: langage et algorithmes. In: JFPLC, pp. 51–64 (1995)

2. Bryant, R.E.: Graph-based algorithms for boolean function manipulation. IEEE Trans. Comput. **35**(8), 677–691 (1986)
3. Burckel, S., Hoarau, S., Mesnard, F., Neumerkel, U.: cTI: Bottom-up termination inference for logic programs. In: 15. WLP, pp. 123–134 (2000)
4. Carlsson, M.: Boolean Constraints in SICStus Prolog. SICS TR, T91, 09 (1991)
5. Codognet, P., Diaz, D.: A simple and efficient boolean solver for constraint logic programming. J. Autom. Reason. **17**(1), 97–129 (1996)
6. Colin, S., Mesnard, F., Rauzy, A.: Un module Prolog de mu-calcul booléen: une réalisation par BDD. In: JFPLC 1999, Huitièmes Journées Francophones de Programmation Logique et Programmation par Contraintes, pp. 23–38 (1999)
7. Demoen, B.: Dynamic attributes, their hProlog implementation, and a first evaluation. Report CW 350, Department of Computer Science, K.U. Leuven, October 2002
8. Diaz, D., Abreu, S., Codognet, P.: On the implementation of GNU Prolog. TPLP **12**(1–2), 253–282 (2012)
9. Dincbas, M., Hentenryck, P.V., Simonis, H., Aggoun, A., Graf, T., Berthier, F.: The constraint logic programming language CHIP. In: FGCS, pp. 693–702 (1988)
10. Hooker, J.N.: Projection, consistency, and George Boole. Constraints **21**(1), 59–76 (2016). http://dx.doi.org/10.1007/s10601-015-9201-2
11. Jaffar, J., Lassez, J.L.: Constraint logic programming. In: POPL, pp.111–119 (1987)
12. Knuth, D.E.: The Art of Computer Programming, Volume 4, Fascicle 1: Bitwise Tricks & Techniques; Binary Decision Diagrams, 12th edn. Addison-Wesley Professional, Reading, Massachusetts (2009)
13. Mantadelis, T., Rocha, R., Kimmig, A., Janssens, G.: Preprocessing boolean formulae for BDDs in a probabilistic context. In: Janhunen, T., Niemelä, I. (eds.) JELIA 2010. LNCS, vol. 6341, pp. 260–272. Springer, Heidelberg (2010)
14. Marques-Silva, J.: Algebraic Simplification Techniques for Propositional Satisfiability. In: Dechter, R. (ed.) CP 2000. LNCS, vol. 1894, p. 537. Springer, Heidelberg (2000)
15. Minato, S.: Zero-suppressed BDDs for set manipulation in combinatorial problems. In: Design Automation Conference (DAC), pp. 272–277 (1993)
16. Neumerkel, U.: Teaching Prolog and CLP (tutorial). In: ICLP (1997)
17. Neumerkel, U., Kral, S.: Declarative program development in Prolog with GUPU. In: Proceedings of the 12th International Workshop on Logic Programming Environments, WLPE, pp. 77–86 (2002)
18. Selman, B., Kautz, H., Cohen, B.: Local search strategies for satisfiability testing. In: Second DIMACS Implementation Challenge (1993)
19. Tarau, P.: Pairing functions, boolean evaluation and binary decision diagrams. CoRR abs/0808.0555 (2008). arxiv.org/abs/0808.0555
20. Tarau, P., Luderman, B.: Boolean evaluation with a pairing and unpairing function. In: SYNASC 2012, pp. 384–390 (2012)
21. Wielemaker, J., Schrijvers, T., Triska, M., Lager, T.: SWI-Prolog. TPLP **12**(1–2), 67–96 (2012)
22. Zhang, H.: SATO: an efficient propositional prover. In: McCune, W. (ed.) CADE 1997. LNCS, vol. 1249. Springer, Heidelberg (1997)

Probabilistic Inference by Program Transformation in Hakaru (System Description)

Praveen Narayanan[1(⊠)], Jacques Carette[2], Wren Romano[1],
Chung-chieh Shan[1], and Robert Zinkov[1]

[1] Indiana University, Bloomington, USA
{pravnar,wrengr,ccshan,zinkov}@indiana.edu
[2] McMaster University, Hamilton, Canada
carette@mcmaster.ca

Abstract. We present Hakaru, a new probabilistic programming system that allows composable reuse of distributions, queries, and inference algorithms, all expressed in a single language of measures. The system implements two automatic and semantics-preserving program transformations—*disintegration*, which calculates conditional distributions, and *simplification*, which subsumes exact inference by computer algebra. We show how these features work together by describing the ideal workflow of a Hakaru user on two small problems. We highlight our composition of transformations and types in design and implementation.

1 Introduction

To perform probabilistic inference is to answer a query about a probability distribution. The longstanding enterprise of probabilistic programming aims to perform probabilistic inference in a modular way, so that the distribution, query, and inference algorithm can be separately reused, composed, and modified.

The modularity we envision is motivated by the typical machine-learning paper published today. Often the first section presents a problem, the second section presents a distribution and query, and the third section presents an inference algorithm that answers the particular query for the particular distribution. Just as the second section composes its content using words such as "mixture" and "condition", the third section composes its content using words such as "proposal" and "integrate out". From this description using English and math, a person skilled in the art of probabilistic inference can write the specialized code that reproduces the results of the paper.

We aim to automate this code-generation task, so that changes to programs that perform probabilistic inference become easier to try out and carry out.

Thanks to Mike Kucera and Natalie Perna for helping to develop Hakaru.

This research was supported by DARPA grant FA8750-14-2-0007, NSF grant CNS-0723054, Lilly Endowment, Inc. (through its support for the Indiana University Pervasive Technology Institute), and the Indiana METACyt Initiative. The Indiana METACyt Initiative at IU is also supported in part by Lilly Endowment, Inc.

O. Kiselyov and A. King (Eds.): FLOPS 2016, LNCS 9613, pp. 62–79, 2016.
DOI: 10.1007/978-3-319-29604-3_5

We focus on making inference compositional—that is, on making the third section of the typical machine-learning paper executable—because less is known about it.

Contributions. Hakaru is a new, proof-of-concept probabilistic programming system that achieves unprecedented modularity by two means:

1. a language of measures that represents distributions and queries as well as inference algorithms;
2. semantics-preserving program transformations based on computer algebra.

The two main transformations are

1. *disintegration*, which calculates conditional distributions and probability densities, and
2. *simplification*, which subsumes exact inference and supports approximate inference, by making use of Maple.

All our transformations take input and produce output in the same language, so we can compose them to express inference algorithms.

This paper shows how these features work together by describing the ideal workflow of a Hakaru user on two small problems.

2   Inference Example on a Discrete Model

In Pearl's classic textbook on probabilistic reasoning [9], Example 1 (page 35) begins as follows:

> Imagine being awakened one night by the shrill sound of your burglar alarm. What is your degree of belief that a burglary attempt has taken place?

The workflow of a Hakaru user is that of Bayesian inference:

1. Model the world as a *prior* probability distribution on what is observed (alarm or not) and what is to be inferred (burglary or not). Hakaru defines a language of distributions that formalizes this modeling.
2. Turn the prior into a *conditional* distribution, which is a function that maps what is observed to a distribution on what is to be inferred. Hakaru provides transformations that automate this conditioning.
3. Apply the function to what is actually observed (true, the alarm did sound) to get the *posterior* distribution on what is to be inferred (burglary or not, given that the alarm did sound). Hakaru can show the distribution not only by generating a stream of samples, but also as a term in the language.

2.1   Modeling

We start with an example of step 1. The prior distribution given by Pearl can be expressed as the following Hakaru term:

```
model :: (Mochastic repr) => repr (HMeasure (HPair HBool HBool))
model = bern 0.0001 `bind` \burglary ->
        bern (if_ burglary 0.95 0.01) `bind` \alarm ->
        dirac (pair alarm burglary)
```

Hakaru is a language embedded in Haskell in "finally tagless" form [1], so the code above is actually parsed and type-checked by the Haskell compiler GHC. In the type signature, (Mochastic repr) => repr is due to the finally-tagless embedding, HBool is Hakaru's boolean type, HPair is Hakaru's product type constructor, and HMeasure turns a type of values into a type of distributions. The type constructor HMeasure is a monad [3,10], whose unit and bind operations are spelled dirac and bind. In this embedding style the types of dirac and bind do not unify with Haskell's return and >>=. Although we could use -XRebindableSyntax to obtain do notation, we avoid doing so in this work.

As usual, the monad HMeasure is made interesting by the primitive operations Hakaru provides for it. In the model above, bern 0.0001 is the distribution on booleans that is true 0.01% of the time and false the other 99.99% of the time. Its type is (Mochastic repr) => repr (HMeasure HBool). The boolean randomly produced by this distribution is fed to Hakaru's if_, which models how burglary influences alarm.

Besides reading it, another way to understand this model is to run it as a sampler. Each run produces a pair of booleans: runSample model usually prints Just (False,False). The sampler chooses burglary, the second component of the pair, followed by alarm, the first component.

2.2   Conditioning

To answer Pearl's question, we should focus on the portion of the distribution where alarm is true. We could run model over and over as a sampler and collect only the samples where alarm is true, but the vast majority of samples would have alarm be false, so it would take a long time to gather enough samples to answer Pearl's question with any accuracy. Instead, we move to step 2 of our workflow. We apply Hakaru's disintegrate transformation to obtain the conditional distribution of burglary *given* alarm:

```
conditional :: (Mochastic repr, Lambda repr)
            => repr (HBool :-> HMeasure HBool)
conditional = disintegrate model
```

In general, Hakaru's disintegrate transformation turns a Hakaru program of type HMeasure (HPair a b) into a Hakaru function (:->) from a to HMeasure b.

The particular function produced in this case is shown in Fig. 1. This is produced by Hakaru's pretty-printer.

The generated code is large and full of reducible expressions, such as

```
superpose [(1, weight (19/20) $
                weight (1/10000) $
                dirac true),
            (1, weight (1/100) $
                superpose [])]
```

To explain what this expression means and how it can be reduced, we need to describe the semantics of Hakaru.

```
lam $ \x1 ->
superpose [(1,
            superpose [(1,
                        superpose [(1,
                                    superpose [(1,
                                                if_ x1
                                                  (superpose [(1,
                                                               weight (19/20) $
                                                               weight (1/10000) $
                                                               dirac true),
                                                              (1,
                                                               weight (1/100) $ superpose [])])
                                                  (superpose [])),
                                               (1,
                                                superpose [(1, superpose []),
                                                           (1,
                                                            if_ x1 (superpose []) (superpose []))])]),
                                   (1,
                                    superpose [(1, if_ x1 (superpose []) (superpose [])),
                                               (1,
                                                superpose [(1, superpose []),
                                                           (1,
                                                            if_ x1
                                                              (superpose [])
                                                              (superpose [(1,
                                                                           weight (1/20) $
                                                                           weight (1/10000) $
                                                                           dirac true),
                                                                          (1,
                                                                           weight (99/100) $
                                                                           superpose [])]))])])]),
                       (1,
                        superpose [(1,
                                    superpose [(1,
                                                if_ x1
                                                  (superpose [(1, weight (19/20) $ superpose []),
                                                              (1,
                                                               weight (1/100) $
                                                               weight (9999/10000) $
                                                               dirac false)])
                                                  (superpose [])),
                                               (1,
                                                superpose [(1, superpose []),
                                                           (1,
                                                            if_ x1 (superpose []) (superpose []))])]),
                                   (1,
                                    superpose [(1, if_ x1 (superpose []) (superpose [])),
                                               (1,
                                                superpose [(1, superpose []),
                                                           (1,
                                                            if_ x1
                                                              (superpose [])
                                                              (superpose [(1,
                                                                           weight (1/20) $
                                                                           superpose []),
                                                                          (1,
                                                                           weight (99/100) $
                                                                           weight (9999/10000) $
                                                                           dirac false)]))])])])]),
           (1, superpose [])]
```

Fig. 1. The output of disintegrating the burglary model

A Hakaru program of HMeasure type can be understood in two ways: as an *importance sampler* and as a *measure*. An importance sampler is a random procedure that produces an outcome along with a weight (or fails, which is like producing the weight 0). A weight is a non-negative real number. For example, dirac true produces the outcome true with the weight 1. In general, dirac always produces the weight 1, whereas the weight produced by m `bind` \x -> k x is the product of the weights produced by m and k x. The weight produced by weight (1/10000) $ m is 1/10000 times the weight produced by m. A typical use of an importance sampler is to run it repeatedly while maintaining a running weighted average of some function of the outcome.

The syntax of superpose in Hakaru is that it takes a list of weight-measure pairs $[(w_1, m_1), \ldots, (w_n, m_n)]$ and produces a measure. What a sampler built with superpose does is to choose one of the measures m_i, with probability proportional to the weights w_i, and sample from it. The weight produced by superpose is $\sum_{i=1}^{n} w_i$ times the weight produced by m_i. If the list is empty (that is, $n = 0$) then superpose simply fails. Hence, the fragment displayed above produces the outcome true with weight $(1 + 1) \cdot (19/20) \cdot (1/10000)$ half of the time, and fails the other half of the time.

This sampler is *not* preserved when we simplify a Hakaru expression. What is preserved is the measure. A measure is like a probability distribution, but it doesn't necessarily sum to 1, thanks to weight and superpose in the language. The measure denoted by weight (1/10000) $ m is the measure denoted by m scaled by 1/10000. And superpose represents a linear combination of measures, so superpose [] denotes the zero measure.

The following equations on measures are valid, like in linear algebra:

```
weight w $ superpose []                 = superpose []
weight w $ weight w' $ m                = weight (w * w') $ m
superpose [(w, m), (w', m)]             = weight (w + w') $ m
superpose [(w, m), (w', superpose [])]  = weight w $ m
```

Consequently, the fragment displayed above denotes the same measure as the simpler expression: weight ((19/20) * (1/10000)) $ dirac true.

This latter program as a sampler always produces the outcome true with weight $(19/20) \cdot (1/10000)$. This behavior is not the same but *better*, because a running weighted average would converge to the same result more quickly when we don't throw away half of our samples.

Instead of simplifying Fig. 1 by hand, we can apply Hakaru's simplify transformation:

```
simplified = simplify conditional
```

The result produced by Hakaru's pretty-printer is:

```
lam $ \x1 ->
if_ x1
    (superpose [(19/200000, dirac true), (9999/1000000, dirac false)])
    (superpose [(1/200000, dirac true), (989901/1000000, dirac false)])
```

This result both runs more efficiently (because again, it fails less often) and reads more easily (because again, it is shorter). It is a Hakaru function (constructed using `lam`) that takes the observed `alarm` as input and returns a measure on `burglary`. In this instance, Hakaru performed linear-algebra-like reductions with the help of the computer algebra system Maple, and produced a compact representation of the conditional distribution. In this sense, simplification subsumes exact inference. We can easily read off that, if we `apply` this function to `true` in step 3 of our workflow, then we would get a posterior distribution that is 19/200000 parts burglary and 9999/1000000 parts no burglary. (These numbers do not sum to 1, nor do we expect them to.)

2.3   Sampling

The simplified posterior is a Hakaru program and it can be run as a sampler: `runSample (app simplified true)` usually prints `Just False`.

3   Inference Example on a Continuous Model

We now turn to an example that involves random real numbers. Imagine the task of building thermometers to measure room temperatures. To build a reliable thermometer we would like to calibrate two attributes of the device. The first attribute is the amount of temperature noise—how much the room temperature fluctuates over time. The second attribute is the amount of measurement noise—how much the thermometer measures the same actual temperature as a different value each time it is used because of its imperfections. Calibrating a thermometer would mean approximating these attributes as best as possible. We can then build a thermometer that corrects its measurements with accurate knowledge of the temperature noise and measurement noise.

3.1   Modeling

To perform our calibration task, we would like to make several experimental measurements and then infer the noises from these measurements. We need step 2 of our workflow to produce a conditional distribution on noises given measurements. So we begin in step 1 by defining a distribution on pairs of measurements and noises:

```
thermometer :: (Mochastic repr)
            => repr (HMeasure (HPair (HPair HReal HReal)
                                     (HPair HProb HProb)))
thermometer =
    liftM unsafeProb (uniform 3 8) `bind` \noiseT ->
    liftM unsafeProb (uniform 1 4) `bind` \noiseM ->
    normal 21 noiseT `bind` \t1 ->
    normal t1 noiseM `bind` \m1 ->
```

```
normal t1 noiseT `bind` \t2 ->
normal t2 noiseM `bind` \m2 ->
dirac (pair (pair m1 m2) (pair noiseT noiseM))
```

The type of `thermometer` shows it is a measure on pairs. The first component of the pair has type `HPair HReal HReal`. That is, we take only two measurements in this simplistic model. To determine the noises accurately, we should use thousands of measurements, not just two. That is why we need to add arrays to Hakaru. In order to handle arrays, the simplification and disintegration program transformations would have to be modified, which is the focus of ongoing work. Here we describe a system without container data-types and show its use on examples having a low number of dimensions.

The second component is a pair of non-negative reals, which are denoted by the `HProb` type in Hakaru. The `HProb` type is like `HReal` but records the knowledge that the number is non-negative. This knowledge is useful in at least two ways. First, knowing that `noiseT` is positive helps the simplification transformation produce `noiseT` instead of `sqrt(noiseT^2)`. Second, during sampling an `HProb` number is typically a probability and represented by its log in floating point. This alleviates the common probabilistic computation problem of underflow errors in extremely small probabilities.

In `thermometer` we express prior beliefs about how noises are distributed, which are seen in the calls to `uniform`. Often such beliefs about distributions (and their parameters such as $3, 8$ and $1, 4$ above) come from domain knowledge. Furthermore, we model temperatures and measurements as being Gaussian distributed with some noisy perturbations. This is expressed in Hakaru by `normal`:

```
normal :: (Mochastic repr) => repr HReal -> repr HProb -> repr (HMeasure HReal)
normal mu sd = lebesgue `bind` \x ->
                superpose [( exp_ (- (x - mu)^2
                                   / fromProb (2 * pow_ sd 2))
                           / sd / sqrt_ (2 * pi_)
                          , dirac x )]
```

The first argument to `normal` is the mean of the Gaussian distribution. The second argument is the standard deviation, which must be non-negative, as the type `HProb` above shows. Actually, it has to be positive. The term `lebesgue` denotes the Lebesgue measure on the reals.

Besides expressing these distributions, we model the network of influences among the random variables. First we draw the candidate noise values `noiseT` and `noiseM` from their respective distributions. We want to use these noises as standard deviations for the `normal` distributions. However, the `uniform` distribution is over `HReal` values since uniform distributions can, in general, produce negative real numbers. But, because the parameters to the `uniform` distributions are positive, we know that values drawn from them must in fact be positive. Thus, we use the `unsafeProb` construct (which is safe in this case) to produce the `HProb`-typed `noiseT` and `noiseM`.

The initial room temperature `t1` is centered around $21°C$, and the later temperature `t2` is centered around `t1`. Both are drawn with standard deviation noiseT. We can think of this as a random walk starting at 21°C. Finally, measurements m1 and m2 are taken of each temperature, with standard deviation noiseM. These dependencies amount to a hidden Markov model, more specifically a linear dynamic model in one dimension.

3.2 Conditioning

For our inference goal we need to obtain a conditional distribution on the noises given the measurements. We can get it by applying the disintegration transformation, as in Sect. 2. A conditional distribution on noises given measurements is a function from measurements to a distribution on noises. This is precisely what the function type of thermConditional says.

```
thermConditional :: (Mochastic repr, Lambda repr)
                  => repr (HPair HReal HReal
                             :-> HMeasure (HPair HProb HProb))
thermConditional = disintegrate thermometer
```

Hakaru's pretty-printer, used on thermConditional, produces Fig. 2. Of course, this expression is different from thermometer. The measurements m1 and m2, which used to be drawn from normals, are now the input variables x2 and x3 (bound by deconstructing the argument x1 using unpair). In place of the two measurement calls to normal, the distribution is now weighted by the *density* of each Gaussian at the corresponding measurement. Unlike a distribution, a density is a function from HReal to HProb.

```
lam $ \x1 ->
x1 `unpair` \x2 x3 ->
uniform 3 8 `bind` \x4 ->
normal 21 (unsafeProb x4) `bind` \x5 ->
uniform 1 4 `bind` \x6 ->
normal x5 (unsafeProb x4) `bind` \x7 ->
weight (exp_ (-(x3 - x7) * (x3 - x7)
                / fromProb (2 * pow_ (unsafeProb x6) 2))
           / unsafeProb x6
           / sqrt_ (2 * pi_)) $
weight (exp_ (-(x2 - x5) * (x2 - x5)
                / fromProb (2 * pow_ (unsafeProb x6) 2))
           / unsafeProb x6
           / sqrt_ (2 * pi_)) $
dirac (pair (unsafeProb x4) (unsafeProb x6))
```

Fig. 2. The thermometer model after disintegration

The reader might wonder why Fig. 1 is rather large, given the simple model it came from, while Fig. 2 is modest though the model it comes from seems more complex. This is because the burglar model contains discrete choices (calls to bern), which tend to inflate the output of disintegration, while the thermometer model is a straight-line program.

While `thermConditional` represents the correct posterior distribution, it is not yet efficient for inference. This is because of the two calls to `normal` that still exist. Our prior distribution `thermometer` does not return the variables drawn from these `normals`, which are the temperatures `t1` and `t2`. The measure is a *marginal* distribution on only `m1`, `m2`, `noiseT`, and `noiseM`. Similarly, `thermConditional`, when given measurements, returns a distribution only on the noises, not on the variables `x5` and `x7`. Because the distribution uses the random variables `x5` and `x7` only internally, running it as a sampler amounts to naive numerical integration over them, which is inaccurate and slow.

It would be better to integrate over `x5` and `x7` exactly. We can use the simplification transformation to do it:

`thermSimplified = simplify thermConditional`

The pretty-printed output of simplifying the conditional distribution is shown in Fig. 3. The remaining calls to `normal` have disappeared and all the weight factors are combined into a single formula. By removing `x5` and `x7` and storing the intermediate factors that are the results of integrating these variables, Hakaru has performed what is known as marginalization or variable elimination.

```
lam $ \x1 ->
weight (recip pi_ * (1/6)) $
uniform 3 8 `bind` \x2 ->
uniform 1 4 `bind` \x3 ->
weight (exp_ ((x2 * x2
              * ((x1 `unpair` \x4 x5 -> x4) * (x1 `unpair` \x4 x5 -> x4))
              * 2
              + x2 * x2 * (x1 `unpair` \x4 x5 -> x4) * (x1 `unpair` \x4 x5 -> x5)
              * (-2)
              + x2 * x2
              * ((x1 `unpair` \x4 x5 -> x5) * (x1 `unpair` \x4 x5 -> x5))
              + x3 * x3
              * ((x1 `unpair` \x4 x5 -> x4) * (x1 `unpair` \x4 x5 -> x4))
              + x3 * x3
              * ((x1 `unpair` \x4 x5 -> x5) * (x1 `unpair` \x4 x5 -> x5))
              + x2 * x2 * (x1 `unpair` \x4 x5 -> x4) * (-42)
              + x3 * x3 * (x1 `unpair` \x4 x5 -> x4) * (-42)
              + x3 * x3 * (x1 `unpair` \x4 x5 -> x5) * (-42)
              + x2 * x2 * 441
              + x3 * x3 * 882)
             * recip (x2 * x2 * (x2 * x2) + x2 * x2 * (x3 * x3) * 3
                      + x3 * x3 * (x3 * x3))
             * (-1/2))
         * recip (sqrt_ (unsafeProb (x2 ** 4 + x2 ** 2 * x3 ** 2 * 3
                                     + x3 ** 4)))
         * 3) $
dirac (pair (unsafeProb x2) (unsafeProb x3))
```

Fig. 3. The result of simplifying `thermConditional`

Once again, simplification subsumes exact inference with help from computer algebra. While this code could be made yet more concise by let-binding, it already makes for an efficient sampler.

3.3   Sampling

The next step in the workflow of a Hakaru user is to sample from the posterior. In this example, the posterior distribution is only 2-dimensional, so it is easy to tune the noise parameters by importance sampling or by searching a grid exhaustively. In higher dimensions, most parameter combinations are very bad, and exhaustive search is intractable, so we often want to use a *Markov chain Monte Carlo* (MCMC) technique in order to get an answer in a reasonable amount of time. That is what we demonstrate here.

MCMC means that the sampler generates not a single random sample but a chain of them, each dependent on the previous one. Most MCMC algorithms require specifying an easy-to-sample *proposal distribution* that depends on the current element of the chain [7]. This distribution is sampled to propose a candidate for the next element in the chain. We show here the Metropolis–Hastings method (MH), a popular MCMC algorithm that compares the posterior and proposal densities at the current and proposed elements in order to decide whether the next element of the chain should be the proposed element or a repetition of the current element. This decision mathematically ensures that the chain is composed of samples that represent the posterior accurately.

A good proposal distribution will propose samples that are representative of the posterior. In this sense, the proposal embodies a strategy for searching and approximating the posterior space. Hakaru lets us specify our own proposal distribution based on our understanding of the model. MH practitioners know that custom proposal distributions are an important way to improve MH performance. Here we show a proposal distribution that a Hakaru user could write for the current example.

```
proposal :: (Mochastic repr)
        => repr (HPair HReal HReal)
        -> repr (HPair HProb HProb)
        -> repr (HMeasure (HPair HProb HProb))
proposal _m1m2 ntne =
  unpair ntne $ \noiseTOld noiseEOld ->
  superpose [(1/2, uniform 3 8 `bind` \noiseT' ->
                dirac (pair (unsafeProb noiseT') noiseEOld)),
             (1/2, uniform 1 4 `bind` \noiseE' ->
                dirac (pair noiseTOld (unsafeProb noiseE')))]
```

This particular proposal distribution leaves one noise parameter unchanged and draws an update to the other noise parameter from a **uniform** distribution. Thus, once the Metropolis–Hastings sampler finds a good setting for one parameter, it can remember it and more or less leave it alone for a while as it fiddles with the other parameter. In contrast, importance sampling tries to hit upon good settings for both parameters at once, which is less likely to happen. On the other hand, the chain dependency of Metropolis–Hastings sampling means it can stay stuck in a globally sub-optimal part of the search space for a long time.

A generic MH algorithm can be defined as a reusable transformation on Hakaru terms. It has this type:

```
mh  :: (Mochastic repr, Integrate repr, Lambda repr,
         env ~ Expect' env, a ~ Expect' a, Backward a a)
     => (forall r'. (Mochastic r') => r' env -> r' a
                                            -> r' (HMeasure a))
     -> (forall r'. (Mochastic r') => r' env -> r' (HMeasure a))
     -> repr (env :-> (a :-> HMeasure (HPair a HProb)))
```

The various constraints in the type are a consequence of the finally tagless embedding. The Expect, Integrate and Lambda constraints require the interpretation (repr) to define operations for expectation, integration, and the lambda calculus. The Backward constraint is required for the density calculation step that forms a part of the MH procedure. The sampling interpretation satisfies these constraints.

We cam apply the generic mh to our custom proposal and the desired posterior thermSimplified:

```
mhKernel = mh proposal thermSimplified
```

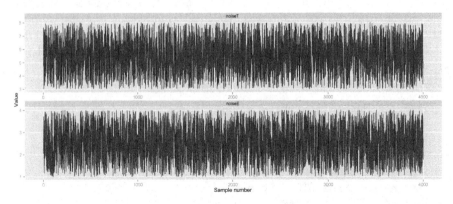

(a) Traceplot of sampled parameter values given observed temperatures (29°C,26°C)

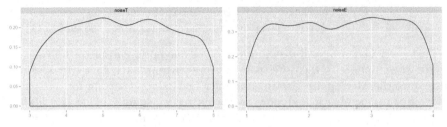

(b) Density plots for the noise parameters

Fig. 4. Sampling from the conditioned posterior using Metropolis–Hastings

This invocation generates a Metropolis–Hastings transition kernel that can be used to produce samples from the posterior. We first condition the kernel on observed temperature measurements – `pair 29 26`. We then run this sampler for 20000 iterations and use every 5th sample (a process known as *thinning*) to produce the plot in Fig. 4.

Knowing that the MH kernel likely contains large mathematical expressions from density calculation, and knowing that the `simplify` transformation is modular and reusable, we can attempt to speed up the computation at each iteration of the MH kernel by invoking `simplify mhKernel`. The performance gained from this reuse of algebraic simplification is shown in the middle row of Table 1.

Table 1. Time needed to draw 20,000 MH samples averaged over 10 runs.

Source of Hakaru code	Average run time
Generated by disintegrator	2,015± 4ms
Generated, then automatically simplified	569 ± 4
Written by hand	529 ± 10

Simplification here introduces efficiency with respect to wall clock time and not in the number of samples needed for convergence. The third program in Table 1 is a hand-coded Hakaru sampler written non-compositionally. For comparison, we also wrote a model of `thermometer` in the probabilistic language WebPPL [5]; it generates a Metropolis-Hastings sampler that takes 948±8ms. All measurements were produced on a quad-core Intel i5-2540M processor running 64-bit Ubuntu 14.04. Hakaru's samplers use GHC 7.8.3 `-O2`, and WebPPL's sampler is compiled to JavaScript and run on Node.js version 0.10.28.

4   Inference by Composable Program Transformations

As the examples above show, Hakaru transforms a probabilistic program to other programs in the same language that generate samples or otherwise perform inference. This major design decision contrasts with most other probabilistic programming systems, which handle a probabilistic program either by producing code in a different language, or by generating samples or otherwise performing inference directly—without staging.

Because Hakaru transformations stay in the same language, we can compose them. For example, we use disintegration and simplification together to generate efficient densities, which are at the heart of Metropolis–Hastings sampling, as well as conditional distributions, which are at the heart of Gibbs sampling. Even after we apply an approximate inference technique such as Metropolis–Hastings to a problem, we can still inspect and optimize the generated solution before running it. We can also compose inference techniques (such as particle filtering and Metropolis–Hastings) as well as analyses (perhaps to estimate the running time or accuracy of a sampler).

4.1   Semantic Specifications of Transformations

Although all our transformations operate on Hakaru syntax, we specify what they do by referring to Hakaru semantics based on *integrators*. For example, for the models in Sects. 2 and 3, the specification of disintegration guarantees that the denotations of the model and the posterior are related as below.

```
model = superpose [(1, dirac true),          thermometer = lebesgue `bind` \m1 ->
                   (1, dirac false)]                        lebesgue `bind` \m2 ->
        `bind` \alarm ->                                    app (disintegrate thermometer)
        app (disintegrate model) alarm                         (pair m1 m2)
        `bind` \burglary ->                                 `bind` \noise ->
        dirac (pair alarm burglary)                         dirac (pair (pair m1 m2) noise)
```

We describe elsewhere the implementation of this specification, which involves reordering integrals and computing a change of variables [12].

The specification of simplification is just that its output has the same measure semantics as the input. Implementing the specification involves translating to and from an integrator representation of measures, and improving the integral using computer algebra. We describe this process in detail elsewhere [2].

4.2   Comparison with Other Embeddings

Like us, Kiselyov and Shan [6] and Ścibior et al. [11] both embed a probabilistic language in a general-purpose functional language, respectively OCaml and Haskell. Like us, they both express and compose inference techniques as transformations that produce programs in the same language. But unlike our embedding, their embeddings are "shallower": the language defines a handful of constructs for manipulating distributions, and reuses the host languages' primitives for all other expressions.

On one hand, their transformations consequently cannot inspect most of the input source code, notably deterministic computations and the right-hand side of >>=. Thus, Hakaru can compute densities and conditional distributions in the face of deterministic dependencies, and Hakaru can generate Metropolis–Hastings samplers using a variety of proposal distributions. On the other hand, a shallow embedding ensures that any deterministic part of a probabilistic program runs at the full speed of the host language.

WebPPL is a probabilistic language embedded in Javascript, providing inference methods to transform input programs into a different language [5]. Venture [8] and Anglican [13] are probabilistic programming systems that build upon Lisp and Clojure respectively to define strict, impure languages for composing inference procedures. In all these works, the code – derived via transformations or building blocks – can perform direct inference but not stage any computation.

5   Expressing Semantic Distinctions by Types

We make crucial use of types to capture semantic distinctions in Hakaru. These distinctions show up both in the implementation and in the language itself.

Figure 5 illustrates the types of each construct or macro described in this paper, grouped by the interface (such as `Mochastic`) that an interpretation (such as `Sample`) would need to implement.

```
class (...) => Base (repr :: Hakaru * -> *) where
  pair   :: repr a -> repr b -> repr (HPair a b)
  unpair :: repr (HPair a b) -> (repr a -> repr b -> repr c) -> repr c
  true, false :: repr HBool
  if_          :: repr HBool -> repr c -> repr c -> repr c
  unsafeProb :: repr HReal -> repr HProb
  fromProb   :: repr HProb -> repr HReal
  exp_   :: repr HReal -> repr HProb
  pow_   :: repr HProb -> repr HReal -> repr HProb
  sqrt_  :: repr HProb -> repr HProb

class (Base repr) => Mochastic (repr :: Hakaru * -> *) where
  dirac :: repr a -> repr (HMeasure a)
  bind  :: repr (HMeasure a) ->
             (repr a -> repr (HMeasure b)) -> repr (HMeasure b)
  superpose :: [(repr HProb, repr (HMeasure a))] -> repr (HMeasure a)
  uniform   :: repr HReal -> repr HReal -> repr (HMeasure HReal)
  normal    :: repr HReal -> repr HProb -> repr (HMeasure HReal)

class Lambda (repr :: Hakaru * -> *) where
  lam :: (repr a -> repr b) -> repr (a :-> b)
  app :: repr (a :-> b) -> repr a -> repr b

bern   :: (Mochastic repr) => repr HProb -> repr (HMeasure HBool)
weight :: (Mochastic repr) => repr HProb -> repr (HMeasure w) -> repr (HMeasure w)
liftM  :: (Mochastic repr)
          => (repr a -> repr b) -> repr (HMeasure a) -> repr (HMeasure b)
```

Fig. 5. The types of language constructs and macros used in the examples

5.1 Distinguishing Hakaru from Haskell

The foremost distinction is between Hakaru's type system and Haskell's type system. That is, we distinguish between the universe[1] of Hakaru types, `Hakaru`, and the universe of Haskell types, `*`.

At first this distinction may seem unnecessary, since we can identify Hakaru types as those which are the argument to some `repr`. However, making the distinction eliminates two broad classes of bugs.

First, there are many types in `*` which we do not want to allow within `Hakaru`. For example, Hakaru has support for arbitrary user-defined regular recursive polynomial data types. However, Haskell's data types are far richer, including: non-regular recursive types, non-strictly-positive recursive types, exponential types, higher-rank polymorphism, GADTs, and so on. Consequently, we must not allow users to embed arbitrary Haskell data types into `Hakaru`. The kind `*` is much too large for Hakaru, so by introducing the `Hakaru` kind we can statically prohibit all these non-Hakaru types.

---

[1] We implement this universe of types by defining our own Haskell kind using GHC's `-XDataKinds` extension. Thus, we call `Hakaru` and `*` both "universes" and "kinds".

Second, distinguishing between `Hakaru` and `*` guarantees a form of hygiene in the implementation. Without the kind distinction it is easy to accidentally equivocate between Haskell's types and Hakaru's types. This equivocation introduces confusion about what exists within the Hakaru language itself, versus what exists within the interpretation of Hakaru programs. One example of this confusion is the `lub` operator used by disintegration to make a nondeterministic choice between two Hakaru programs that mean the same measure. When introducing the `Hakaru` kind we noticed that it was not entirely clear whether the `lub` operator is in the language or a mere implementation detail.

5.2 Distinguishing Values and Distributions

Hakaru's type system draws a hard distinction between individual values (of type `a`) and distributions on values (of type `HMeasure a`). To see why this is necessary, consider the pseudo-program "`x = uniform 0 1; x + x`". As written it is unclear what this pseudo-program should actually mean. On one hand, it could mean that the value `x` is drawn from the distribution `uniform 0 1`, and then this fixed value is added to itself. On the other hand, it could mean that `x` is defined to be the distribution `uniform 0 1`, and then we draw two samples from this distribution and add them together.

To distinguish these two meanings, stochastic languages like Church [4] must introduce a memoization operator; however, it is often difficult to intuitively determine where to use the memoization operator to obtain the desired behavior. In contrast, Hakaru distinguishes these meanings by distinguishing between let-binding and monadic-binding:

```
sampleOnce  = uniform 0 1 `bind` \x -> dirac (x + x)
sampleTwice = uniform 0 1 `let_` \x -> liftM2 (+) x x
```

Importantly, there is no way to mix up the second lines of these programs. If `x` is monadically bound, and hence has type `HReal`, then the expression `liftM2 (+) x x` does not type check, because `HReal` is not a monad so it cannot be the type of arguments to `liftM2 (+)`. Whereas, if `x` is let-bound, and hence has type `HMeasure HReal`, then the expression `dirac (x + x)` does not type check, because we do not define `(+)` on measures; but even if we did define `(+)` on measures, then the expression would have type `HMeasure (HMeasure HReal)` which doesn't match the signature.

5.3 Distinguishing Values in Different Domains

It is often helpful to distinguish between various numeric domains. Although the integers can be thought of as real numbers, it is often helpful to specify when we really mean integers. Similarly, although the natural numbers can be thought of as integers and the positive reals can be thought of as reals, it is often helpful to explicitly capture the restriction to non-negative numbers. Thus, Hakaru provides four primitive numeric types: `HNat`, `HInt`, `HProb`, and `HReal`.

There are at least four reasons for making these distinctions. First, it helps with human understanding to say what we mean. Second, many of the built-in distributions are only defined for non-negative parameters, thus the non-negative types HNat and HProb are necessary to avoid undefinedness. Third, capturing the integral and non-negative constraints helps with algebraic simplification since we do not have to worry about the non-occurring cases. Fourth, for the situations where we must actually compute values (e.g., the sampling interpretation), knowing that HProb is non-negative means that we can represent these values in the log-domain in order to avoid problems with underflowing.

5.4 Distinguishing Different Interpretations of Hakaru

We use a "finally tagless" embedding of Hakaru in Haskell [1]. Thus an *interpretation* of Mochastic is implemented as an instance. We have several such interpretations—a sampler, a pretty-printer, and two variants of embedding our language into Maple. *Transformations* are also instances, but where repr appears as a free variable. For example, we have an expectation transformation Expect, which takes a measure expression and returns its expectation functional. Another transformation implements disintegration, which is performed by lazy partial evaluation of measure terms.

As our use of bind indicates, we use Higher Order Abstract Syntax (HOAS) to encode Hakaru binding. In exchange for preventing scope extrusion, HOAS makes some manipulations of bindings difficult to express. Basically, one significant advantage of finally tagless is that if we can write your transformation compositionally, then it will compose beautifully with other such transformations. But some transformations are hard to write compositionally. For example, it is easy to write "macros" such as liftM2, as well as the Expect transformation, but it is hard to implement lazy partial evaluation.

Even for a compositional transformation, finally-tagless style makes our code hard to debug, because for example Expect repr is implemented in terms of an abstract repr that is not required to be an instance of Show. This rules out using Debug.Trace.traceShow in the middle of the implementation of Expect.

We love how the Haskell type of a Hakaru term tracks how the term will be interpreted, such as Expect PrettyPrint. The flip side is that to apply multiple interpretations to the same term (like to scale a distribution so it sums to 1), we must either create the "product" of two interpretations (and using it to interpret a term takes time exponential in the number of nested binders in the term), or the Haskell type of a term must be universally quantified over repr. The latter is very natural for experienced Haskell programmers, but is hard to explain to others, thus limiting the potential of Hakaru as a general-purpose probabilistic programming language. Another issue is that the very hygiene which is a strength of finally-tagless makes it awkward to have "free variables" (parameters) in a term; these must all be lam bound before a term can be disintegrated or simplified. This contrasts sharply with how easily a computer algebra system handles free variables in equivalent terms [2].

6   Conclusion

A major challenge faced by every probabilistic programming system is that probabilistic models and inference algorithms do not compose in tandem: just because a model we're interested in can be built naturally from two submodels does not mean a good inference algorithm for the model can be built naturally from good inference algorithms for the two submodels. Due to this challenge, many systems with good support for model composition resort to a fixed or monolithic inference algorithm and do their best to optimize it.

Hakaru demonstrates a new way to address this challenge. On one hand, Hakaru supports model composition like any other embedded monadic DSL does: on top of primitive combinators such as dirac, bind, and superpose, users can define Haskell functions to express common patterns of samplers and measures. On the other hand, because each inference building block is a transformation on this DSL, Hakaru supports inference composition like a compiler construction kit or computer algebra system does: users can define Haskell functions to express custom pathways from models to inference.

We are working to extend the Hakaru language, to express high-dimensional models involving arrays and trees, and to express more inference algorithms, including parallel and streaming ones. We are also working to make Hakaru more usable: by representing the abstract syntax as a data type, by customizing the concrete syntax, and by inviting user interaction for transforming subexpressions.

References

1. Carette, J., Kiselyov, O., Shan, C.-c.: Finally tagless, partially evaluated: Tagless staged interpreters for simpler typed languages. J. Funct. Program. **19**(5), 509–543 (2009)
2. Carette, J., Shan, C.-c.: Simplifying probabilistic programs using computer algebra (2015). http://www.cs.indiana.edu/ftp/techreports/TR719.pdf
3. Giry, M.: A categorical approach to probability theory. In: Banaschewski, B. (ed.) Categorical Aspects of Topology and Analysis. Lecture Notes in Mathematics, vol. 915, pp. 68–85. Springer, Heidelberg (1982)
4. Goodman, N.D., Mansinghka, V.K., Roy, D., Bonawitz, K., Tenenbaum, J.B.: Church: A language for generative models. In: Proceedings of the 24th Conference on Uncertainty in Artificial Intelligence, pp. 220–229. AUAI Press (2008)
5. Goodman, N.D., Stuhlmüller, A.: The design and implementation of probabilistic programming languages. http://dippl.org (2014). Accessed 20 November 2015
6. Kiselyov, O., Shan, C.-c.: Embedded probabilistic programming. In: Taha, W.M. (ed.) DSL 2009. LNCS, vol. 5658, pp. 360–384. Springer, Heidelberg (2009)
7. MacKay, D.J.C.: Introduction to Monte Carlo methods. In: Jordan, M.I. (ed.): Learning and Inference in Graphical Models. Kluwer (1998)
8. Mansinghka, V.K., Selsam, D., Perov, Y.N.: Venture: a higher-order probabilistic programming platform with programmable inference. CoRR abs/1404.0099 (2014). http://arxiv.org/abs/org/abs/1404.0099

9. Pearl, J.: Probabilistic Reasoning in Intelligent Systems: Networks of Plausible Inference. Morgan Kaufmann, San Francisco (1988). revised 2nd printing (1998)
10. Ramsey, N., Pfeffer, A.: Stochastic lambda calculus and monads of probability distributions. In: Conference Record of the Annual ACM Symposium on Principles of Programming Languages POPL 2002, pp. 154–165. ACM Press (2002)
11. Ścibior, A., Ghahramani, Z., Gordon, A.D.: Practical probabilistic programming with monads. In: Proceedings of the 8th ACM SIGPLAN Symposium on Haskell, pp. 165–176. ACM (2015)
12. Shan, C.-c., Ramsey, N.: Symbolic Bayesian inference by lazy partial evaluation (2015). http://www.cs.tufts.edu/~nr/pubs/disintegrator-abstract.html
13. Wood, F., van de Meent, J.W., Mansinghka, V.: A new approach to probabilistic programming inference. In: Proceedings of the 17th International conference on Artificial Intelligence and Statistics, pp. 1024–1032 (2014)

An Interaction Net Encoding of Gödel's System $\mathcal{T}$

Declarative Pearl

Ian Mackie[1]([⊠]) and Shinya Sato[2]

[1] LIX, CNRS UMR 7161, École Polytechnique, 91128 Palaiseau Cedex, France
mackie@lix.polytechnque.fr
[2] University Education Center, Ibaraki University,
2-1-1 Bunkyo, Mito-shi, Ibaraki 310-8512, Japan

Abstract. The graph rewriting system of interaction nets has been very successful for the implementation of the lambda calculus. In this paper we show how the ideas can be extended and simplified to encode Gödel's System $\mathcal{T}$—the simply typed λ-calculus extended with numbers. Surprisingly, using some results about System $\mathcal{T}$, we obtain a very simple system of interaction nets that is significantly more efficient than a direct encoding for the evaluation of programs.

1 Introduction

Gödel's System $\mathcal{T}$ [7] is the simply typed λ-calculus, with functions and product types, extended with natural numbers. It is a very simple system, yet has enormous expressive power—well beyond that of primitive recursive functions.

Interaction nets [9] are a model of computation, based on graph rewriting. They are user defined rewrite systems and because we can write systems which correspond to term rewriting systems we can see them as specification languages. But, because we must also explain all the low-level details (such as copying and erasing) then we can see them as a low-level operational semantics or more specifically, as an implementation language. Supporting this latter point, we remark that in general graph rewriting, locating (by graph matching) a reduction step is considered an expensive operation, but in interaction nets there is a very simple mechanism to locate a redex (called an active pair in interaction net terminology), and there is no need to use expensive matching algorithms. There are interesting aspects of interaction nets for parallel evaluation—we will hint at some of these aspects later in the paper.

Over the last years there have been several implementations of the λ-calculus using interaction nets. These include optimal reduction [8], encodings of existing strategies [12,15], and new strategies [13,14]. One of the first algorithms to implement Lévy's [11] notion of optimal reduction for the λ-calculus was presented by Lamping [10]. Asperti et al. [3] devised BOHM (Bologna Optimal Higher-Order Machine) building on the ideas of Lamping.

© Springer International Publishing Switzerland 2016
O. Kiselyov and A. King (Eds.): FLOPS 2016, LNCS 9613, pp. 80–93, 2016.
DOI: 10.1007/978-3-319-29604-3_6

The purpose of this paper is to add to this list of interaction net implementations and to bring together on one hand the successful study of encoding λ-calculus and related systems into interaction nets mentioned above, together with the result that Gödel's System $\mathcal{T}$ can be encoded with the linear λ-calculus and an iterator [2]. Specifically, there are redundancies in System $\mathcal{T}$—copying and erasing can be done either by the iterator or by the λ-calculus. We can remove the copy and erasing power of the λ-calculus, and still keep the expressive power. Taking this further, we can also get primitive recursive functions as a subset of this system. The key motivation for bringing these works together is that the linear λ-calculus can be very easily encoded into interaction nets, and therefore there is a hope for a very efficient implementation of this language.

The rest of this paper is structured as follows. In the next section we recall the basic notations of interaction nets, to fix notation, and also give the definition of linear System $\mathcal{T}$. In Sect. 3 we give a compilation of the calculus into interaction nets and give the dynamics of the system together with some examples. In Sect. 4 we discuss some aspects of this work, and finally we conclude in Sect. 5.

2   Background

2.1   Interaction Nets

In the graphical rewriting system of interaction nets [9], we have a set Σ of *symbols*, which are names of the nodes in our diagrams. Each symbol has an arity ar that determines the number of *auxiliary ports* that the node has. If $ar(\alpha) = n$ for $\alpha \in \Sigma$, then α has $n + 1$ *ports*: n auxiliary ports and a distinguished one called the *principal port*.

Nodes are drawn as circles. A *net* built on Σ is an undirected graph with nodes at the vertices. The edges of the net connect nodes together at the ports such that there is only one edge at every port. A port which is not connected is called a *free port*.

Two nodes $(\alpha, \beta) \in \Sigma \times \Sigma$ connected via their principal ports form an *active pair*, which is the interaction nets analogue of a redex. A rule $((\alpha, \beta) \implies N)$ replaces the pair (α, β) by the net N. All the free ports are preserved during reduction, and there is at most one rule for each pair of nodes. The following diagram illustrates the idea, where N is any net built from Σ.

The most powerful property of this graph rewriting system is that it is one-step confluent: the order of rewriting is not important, and all sequences of rewrites are of the same length (in fact they are permutations). This has practical consequences: the diagrammatic transformations can be applied in any order, or even in parallel, to give the correct answer. We write $\Longrightarrow$ for a single interaction, and $\Longrightarrow^*$ for the transitive reflexive closure. An interaction net is in normal form when there are no active pairs. The notation $N \Downarrow N'$ indicates that there exists a finite sequence of interactions $N \Longrightarrow^* N'$ such that N' is a net in normal form. Thus N is (strongly) normalising if $N \Downarrow N'$.

2.2   System $\mathcal{T}$

In this section we recall the main notions of Gödel's System $\mathcal{T}$. This is an applied λ-calculus with, in addition to function types, products and natural numbers. Intuitively, we can think of it as a minimal higher-order language that is an extension to the simply typed λ-calculus. From an alternative perspective, it is a language that has greater computational power than primitive recursive functions—we can define Ackermann's function for instance.

We refer the reader to [7] for a detailed description of System $\mathcal{T}$. In [2] it was shown that there are redundancies in this calculus: copying and erasing can be done either in the λ-calculus or using the iterator. This leads to a simplified presentation using the linear λ-calculus. In this paper we refine the calculus further by introducing pattern matching. There is nothing deep in this step, but it allows us to present the same computational power as System $\mathcal{T}$ in a very precise syntax. In the following we assume familiarity with the λ-calculus [4], and also some basic recursion theory.

Table 1 summarises the syntax of this linear System $\mathcal{T}$. The first four lines give the linear λ-calculus with pairs. The construct $\lambda p.t$ is the usual abstraction, extended to allow patterns of variables or pairs of patterns (as defined at the bottom of the table). The remaining three rules define the syntax for constructing numbers and the iteration. We work with terms modulo α-conversion as usual.

The pattern notation requires a little explanation. In the term $\lambda p.t$, if the pattern p is a variable, say x, then we have the usual abstraction. However, we allow richer patterns built from pairs. It is through these patterns that we are able to access the components of the pairs constructed in the syntax (so we do not need explicit projection functions). Thus we can write terms such as $\lambda \langle x, y \rangle.t$, $\lambda \langle x, \langle y, z \rangle \rangle.t$, etc. Because the language is typed, we will always have arguments of the correct shape for the pattern matching.

In Fig. 1 we give the (linear) typing rules for this calculus. We write judgements as $p_1 : A_1, \ldots, p_n : A_n \vdash t : B$. The typing rules also capture the linear variable constraints in an alternative way.

Our version of linear System $\mathcal{T}$ has a number of useful properties: it is confluent, strongly normalising and reduction preserves types. Reduction also preserves the variable constraints, and is adequate to give normal forms for programs of type nat. We first define reduction, then give explanations below.

Context

$$\frac{}{x : A \vdash x : A} \text{ (Var)} \qquad \frac{\Gamma, p : A, q : B \vdash t : C}{\Gamma, \langle p, q \rangle : A \otimes B \vdash t : C} \text{ (Pattern Pair)}$$

$$\frac{\Gamma, p : A, q : B, \Delta \vdash t : C}{\Gamma, q : B, p : A, \Delta \vdash t : C} \text{ (Exchange)}$$

Logical Rules:

$$\frac{\Gamma, p : A \vdash t : B}{\Gamma \vdash \lambda p.t : A \multimap B} \text{ ($\multimap$Intro)} \qquad \frac{\Gamma \vdash t : A \multimap B \qquad \Gamma \vdash u : A}{\Gamma \vdash tu : B} \text{ ($\multimap$Elim)}$$

$$\frac{\Gamma \vdash t : A \qquad \Delta \vdash u : B}{\Gamma, \Delta \vdash \langle t, u \rangle : A \otimes B} \text{ (Pair)}$$

Numbers:

$$\frac{}{\Gamma \vdash 0 : \text{nat}} \text{ (Zero)} \qquad \frac{\Gamma \vdash t : \text{nat}}{\Gamma \vdash \mathsf{S}\, t : \text{nat}} \text{ (Succ)}$$

$$\frac{\Gamma \vdash t : \text{nat} \qquad \Delta \vdash u : A \qquad \Theta \vdash v : A \multimap A}{\Gamma, \Delta, \Theta \vdash \text{iter } t\, u\, v : A} \text{ (Iter)}$$

Fig. 1. Linear system $\mathcal{T}$

Table 1. Terms

Terms	Variable constraint	Free variables (fv)
x	–	$\{x\}$
tu	$\mathsf{fv}(t) \cap \mathsf{fv}(u) = \varnothing$	$\mathsf{fv}(t) \cup \mathsf{fv}(u)$
$\lambda p.t$	$\mathsf{bv}(p) \subseteq \mathsf{fv}(t)$	$\mathsf{fv}(t) \smallsetminus \mathsf{bv}(p)$
$\langle p, q \rangle$	$\mathsf{fv}(p) \cap \mathsf{fv}(q) = \varnothing$	$\mathsf{fv}(p) \cup \mathsf{fv}(q)$
0	–	$\varnothing$
$\mathsf{S}\, t$	–	$\mathsf{fv}(t)$
iter $t\, u\, v$	$\mathsf{fv}(t) \cap \mathsf{fv}(u) = \mathsf{fv}(u) \cap \mathsf{fv}(v) = \varnothing$ $\mathsf{fv}(t) \cap \mathsf{fv}(v) = \varnothing$	$\mathsf{fv}(t) \cup \mathsf{fv}(u) \cup \mathsf{fv}(v)$
Pattern	Variable constraint	Bound variables (bv)
x	–	$\{x\}$
$\langle p, q \rangle$	$\mathsf{bv}(p) \cap \mathsf{bv}(q) = \varnothing$	$\mathsf{bv}(p) \cup \mathsf{bv}(q)$

Definition 1 (Reduction). *The main reduction rules for this calculus are given in the following table:*

Reduction		Condition
$(\lambda p.t)v$ $\longrightarrow$ $[p \ll v].t$		$\mathsf{fv}(\lambda p.t) = \varnothing$
iter $(\mathsf{S}\ t)\ u\ v \longrightarrow$ iter $t\ (vu)\ v$		$\mathsf{fv}(v) = \varnothing$
iter $0\ u\ v$ $\longrightarrow u$		$\mathsf{fv}(v) = \varnothing$

The conditions on the rules are used to constrain the possible reductions and preserve the linearity of the terms. The matching operation $[p \ll u].t$ is inspired by that of the ρ-calculus [5]. $\lambda p.t$ is a generalised abstraction—it can be seen as a λ-abstraction on a pattern p instead of a single variable. $[p \ll u].t$ is a matching constraint denoting a matching problem $p \ll u$ whose solutions will be applied to t. The reduction rules for the matching construct are:

$$[x \ll v].t \longrightarrow t[v/x]$$
$$[\langle p, q \rangle \ll \langle t, u \rangle].t \longrightarrow [p \ll t].[q \ll u].t$$

Thus matching creates substitutions. Substitution is a meta-operation defined as usual, and reductions can take place in any context. Matching forces evaluation of terms, and will always succeed.

This calculus has a number of properties: it is terminating and confluent, and reduction preserves types. We will not give an extensive study of those properties here however, as we are interested in implementing this calculus in interaction nets. We will simply give an important property of reduction that will be essential to prove any results about the encoding later. Define $t \Downarrow n$ if $t \longrightarrow^* u$ and u is a normal form (*i.e.*, no further reduction is possible).

Lemma 1. *Let t be a closed linear System $\mathcal{T}$ term. If $t \Downarrow u$ then exactly one of the following occurs:*

1. *if $t : \mathsf{nat}$, then $u = S^n(0)$.*
2. *if $t : A \otimes B$, then $u = \langle v, w \rangle$, for some terms v and w.*
3. *if $t : A \multimap B$, then $u = \lambda x.v$, for some term v.*

Proof. We show the case for nat. Since t is closed and reduction preserves types, u can only be a number, an application or an iter construct. If u is an application, say $(\lambda x.a)b$, then since u is closed, $(\lambda x.a)$ must also be closed, and therefore it is not a normal form as a reduction can take place (contradiction). If u is an iter, say iter $n\ a\ b$, then since u is closed, n must also be closed, and therefore it is not a normal form as a reduction can take place (contradiction). Therefore, u must be a number. The other two cases follow similar reasoning.

2.3   Examples

Here we give a several examples to illustrate how to use the syntax and what terms look like.

– Pairs and pattern matching:

$$\lambda\langle x, y\rangle.\langle y, x\rangle : A \otimes B \multimap B \otimes A$$
$$\lambda\langle x, \langle y, z\rangle\rangle.\langle\langle x, y\rangle, z\rangle : A \otimes (B \otimes C) \multimap (A \otimes B) \otimes C$$

– Addition, multiplication and exponentiation can be defined as:

$$\text{add} = \lambda mn.\text{iter } m \ n \ (\lambda x.Sx) : \text{nat} \multimap \text{nat} \multimap \text{nat}$$
$$\text{mult} = \lambda mn.\text{iter } m \ 0 \ (\text{add } n) : \text{nat} \multimap \text{nat} \multimap \text{nat}$$
$$\text{exp} = \lambda mn.\text{iter } n \ (S \ 0) \ (\text{mult } m) : \text{nat} \multimap \text{nat} \multimap \text{nat}$$

Note in particular that each function satisfies the linearity constraints.
– When we need to copy or erase, we can do that as shown in the following examples for numbers:

$$C = \lambda x.\text{iter } x \ \langle 0, 0\rangle \ (\lambda\langle a, b\rangle.\langle Sa, Sb\rangle) : \text{nat} \multimap \text{nat} \otimes \text{nat}$$
$$\text{fst} = \lambda\langle n, m\rangle.\text{iter } m \ n \ (\lambda x.x) : \text{nat} \otimes \text{nat} \multimap \text{nat}$$
$$\text{snd} = \lambda\langle n, m\rangle.\text{iter } n \ m \ (\lambda x.x) : \text{nat} \otimes \text{nat} \multimap \text{nat}$$

– Ackermann's function is a standard example of a non primitive recursive function:

$$ack(0, n) = S \ n$$
$$ack(S \ n, 0) = ack(n, S \ 0)$$
$$ack(S \ n, S \ m) = ack(n, ack(S \ n, m))$$

In a higher-order functional language, there is an alternative definition that we can write in our syntax:

$$\text{ack} = \lambda m.\lambda n.(\text{iter } m \ (\lambda x.S \ x) \ (\lambda xy.\text{iter } (S \ y) \ (S \ 0) \ x))n$$

We can simplify this definition slightly by using the usual η-rule: $\lambda x.tx = t$, (we remark that $x \notin \text{fv}(t)$ because of the linearity constraint).

$$\text{ack} = \lambda m.\text{iter } m \ (\lambda x.S \ x) \ (\lambda xy.\text{iter } (S \ y) \ (S \ 0) \ x)$$

3   Interaction Net Encoding

In this section we give a translation $\mathcal{T}(\cdot)$ of linear System $\mathcal{T}$ into interaction nets. A term t with $\text{fv}(t) = \{x_1, \ldots, x_n\}$ will be translated as a net $\mathcal{T}(t)$ with the root edge at the top, and n free edges corresponding to the free variables:

The labelling of free edges is just for the translation (and convenience), and is not part of the system. The nodes needed for this compilation will be introduced on demand, and we give the interaction rules later in the section. We will occasionally make some assumptions about the order of the free edges to make the diagrams simpler below.

Variable. When t is a variable, say x, then $\mathcal{T}(t)$ is translated into an edge:

Abstraction. If t is an abstraction, say $\lambda p.t'$, then there are two alternative translations of the abstraction, which are given as follows:

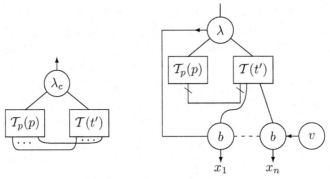

In these diagrams, we use an auxiliary function for the translation of patterns $\mathcal{T}_p(p)$ which is given by the following two rules.

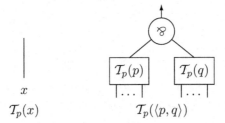

$$\mathcal{T}_p(x) \qquad\qquad \mathcal{T}_p(\langle p, q \rangle)$$

If p is a variable, then it is translated into an edge. Otherwise, if it is a pair pattern, then it is translated as shown in the right hand diagram above.

Returning to the compilation of abstraction, in the first case, shown on the left in the above diagram, is when $\mathsf{fv}(\lambda p.t') = \varnothing$. Here we use a node λ_c to represent a *closed abstraction* and we explicitly connect the occurrence of the variable of the body of the abstraction to the λ_c node.

The second case, shown on the right, is when $\mathsf{fv}(\lambda p.t') = \{x_1, \ldots, x_n\}$. Here we introduce three different kinds of node: λ of arity 3, for abstraction, and two kinds of node representing a list of free variables. A node b is used for each free variable, and we end the list with a node v. The idea is that there is a pointer to the free variables of an abstraction; the body of the abstraction is encapsulated in a box structure. We assume, without loss of generality, that the (unique) occurrence of the variable x is in the leftmost position of $\mathcal{T}(t')$.

It is worth noting that a closed term will never become open during reduction, but crucially for this system to work, terms may become closed during reduction. The distinction between open and closed terms is important in the dynamics of the interaction system that is given later.

Application. If t is an application, say uv, then $\mathcal{T}(uv)$ is given by the following net, where we have introduced a node @ of arity 2 corresponding to an application.

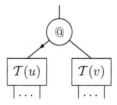

Pair. If t is a pair, say $\langle u, v \rangle$, then $\mathcal{T}(\langle u, v \rangle)$ is given by the following net, where we have introduced a node $\otimes$ of arity 2 corresponding to a pair.

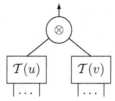

Numbers. A number will be represented by a chain of successor nodes (S), terminating with a zero (0) node. S has one auxiliary port, and 0 has none. Therefore, if t is a number, it is either 0 or $S(u)$, for some term u. These two cases are translated as follows:

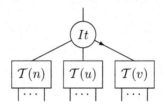

Iterator. If t is iter n u v, then we introduce one new node. The principal port of this node points to the function v, because we must wait for this to become a closed term before starting the interaction process.

This completes the compilation function. A closed term will be translated as a net with one edge at the root of the term. We give some examples before defining the reduction rules for the interaction nodes that we introduced in the above compilation. The first example is the net $\mathcal{T}(\lambda\langle x, y\rangle.\langle y, x\rangle)$, which illustrates the pattern and pairing construct:

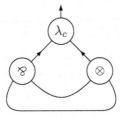

The second example shows the function snd defined previously. The compilation $\mathcal{T}(\lambda\langle m, n\rangle.\text{iter } m \ n \ (\lambda x.x))$ gives the following net:

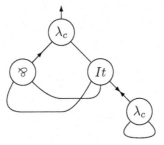

The final example, given in Fig. 2 is the net corresponding to the Ackermann function: $\mathcal{T}(\lambda m.\text{iter } m \ (\lambda x.\text{S } x) \ (\lambda xy.\text{iter } (\text{S } y) \ (\text{S } 0) \ x))$.

3.1   Reduction

We next give the rules to complete the interaction net system. In Fig. 3 we give the first seven interaction rules that encode β-reduction, pattern matching and substitution. The first rule starts the implementation of β-reduction, connecting the body of the abstraction to the result, and the argument becomes a substitution. The second rule implements the matching. The remaining rules propagate a substitution through a net, and an important rule is v interacting with λ, where a closed abstraction is created.

The rules so far are similar to some other interaction net systems for the λ-calculus, so could be considered standard. The next three rules implement the iterator operation that we explain in more detail. When the iterator node interacts with a closed abstraction we have the following rule:

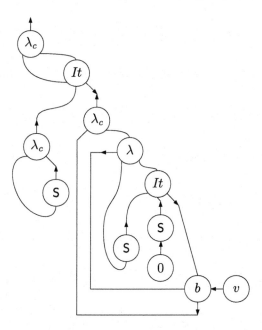

Fig. 2. Ackermann function

This rule creates a new node It_c that will interact with numbers. The node also holds on to the body and the variable edge of the abstraction. The two rules for the It_c node are as follows. The first rule is when we erase the function, and connect the result to the base value.

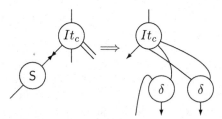

The final rule is when we unfold one level of iteration. Here the function is duplicated with δ nodes, and one copy is applied to the base value as required. Because the function being duplicated is closed, the duplication process is easily proved to be correct.

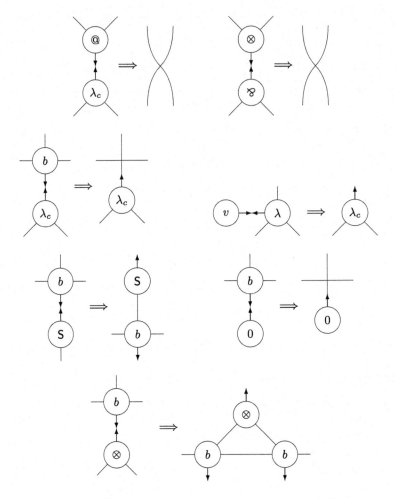

Fig. 3. Interaction rules

In Fig. 4 we give the final rules for duplication and erasing, where we use α to range over all other nodes in the system.

These rules are all that we need to implement our linear System $\mathcal{T}$. By showing that we simulate the reduction rules we get the following result.

Theorem 1. *Let t : nat be a closed linear System $\mathcal{T}$ term with normal form u, then $\mathcal{T}(t) \Downarrow \mathcal{T}(u)$.*

It is possible to give an encoding of Gödel's System $\mathcal{T}$ directly to interaction nets, however this comes at a cost as we must incorporate the non-linear aspects of the λ-calculus: copying and erasing. With our encoding, we have isolated the copying and erasing to closed functions, which is a much simpler operation (and we do not need many of the so-called bookkeeping operations of the general systems).

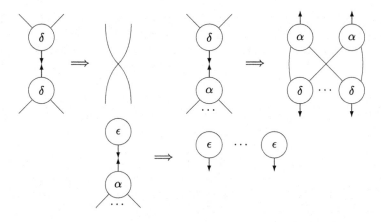

Fig. 4. Duplication and erasing interaction rules

Thus, using a result from [1], stating that the linear version is as powerful as the non-linear version, gives a greatly simplified interaction system.

Moreover, we can go further. Using a result of Dal Lago [6]: if we take the linear λ-calculus where iterated functions must be *closed by construction* (*i.e.*, $\mathsf{fv}(v) = \varnothing$ in iter $t\ u\ v$) then this system captures exactly the primitive recursive functions. If we are building functions to iterate that must be closed by construction, then we no longer need the box structure to identify when a term becomes closed. The consequence of this result here is that we can eliminate b, v and λ nodes (and the associated interaction rules), so that λ_c and @ are sufficient to encode the linear λ-calculus.

Theorem 2. *An interaction system built from the nodes* 0, S, It, It_c, δ, ϵ, λ_c, *and* @ *is complete for primitive recursive functions.*

The encoding of the linear λ-calculus as a system of interaction nets is particularly simple, since substitution is implemented for free: β-reduction is a constant time operation. This is a consequence of the fact that substitution is essentially implemented as an assignment. What we have achieved therefore is a very simple, with no overheads, implementation of Gödel's System $\mathcal{T}$ and primitive recursive functions in interaction nets.

4 Discussion

Very few people write programs with unary arithmetic (zero and successor). Nevertheless, the same techniques are used to represent lists and other data-structures that are ubiquitous. All our results can be adapted to work for a version of System $\mathcal{T}$ with built-in numbers (and also richer data-types), together with operations that work directly with these numbers. Our belief is that to understand complex languages and make them efficient, it is fruitful to start with simple subsets and build up. This is the approach we have taken in this paper.

Implementations of the λ-calculus are made complicated by the non-linear aspects of the calculus. Using the linear λ-calculus with iterators gives a simpler formulation of many algorithms, and even simpler when the iterated function is closed. It is possible to use compilation techniques to transform a non-linear algorithm in System T to our linear version, and in addition find ways to close functions. This approach uses some standard ideas from compilation such as continuations, but applied to a linear setting. We hope to report on some of these details in a future work, and also the impact on implementation efficiency.

Finally, we mention that there are a number of parallel implementations of interaction nets, and consequently the system presented in this paper can directly take advantage of this. However, some choices in the encoding can give different results: the most efficient sequential system is not necessarily the best system to try to run on parallel hardware. Again, we hope to be able to understand this aspect better through extensive benchmark testing.

5   Conclusion

We have given a very simple and efficient implementation of Gödel's System T using the graph rewriting formalism of interaction nets. The aim of this paper was initially to apply some of the ideas used for the representation of the λ-calculus in interaction nets to the the linear version of System T to investigate if the resulting system provides a useful implementation technique.

This work is a building block in a larger programme of research to investigate when interaction nets are useful for the evaluation of programs (either because they are more efficient than standard techniques, of if they offer some other advantage such as parallelism, small run-time system, etc.). A first step in this direction is the extension of the language with data-types, in particular lists, and investigate if other algorithms can also benefit from the techniques used here.

References

1. Alves, S., Florido, M., Fernández, M., Mackie, I.: The power of linear functions. In: Ésik, Z. (ed.) CSL 2006. LNCS, vol. 4207, pp. 119–134. Springer, Heidelberg (2006)
2. Alves, S., Fernández, M., Florido, M., Mackie, I.: Gödel's system T revisited. Theor. Comput. Sci. **411**(11–13), 1484–1500 (2010)
3. Asperti, A., Giovannetti, C., Naletto, A.: The Bologna optimal higher-order machine. J. Funct. Program. **6**(6), 763–810 (1996)
4. Barendregt, H.P.: The Lambda calculus: its syntax and semantics. Studies in Logic and the Foundations of Mathematics, vol. 103. North-Holland Publishing Company, Amsterdam (1984)
5. Cirstea, H., Kirchner, C.: The rewriting calculus - Part I and II. Logic J. Interest Group Pure Appl. Logics **9**(3), 427–498 (2001)
6. Lago, U.D.: The geometry of linear higher-order recursion. In: Panangaden, P., (ed.) Proceedings of the 20th Annual IEEE Symposium on Logic in Computer Science, LICS 2005, pp. 366–375. IEEE Computer Society Press, June 2005

7. Girard, J.-Y., Lafont, Y., Taylor, P.: Proofs and Types. Cambridge Tracts in Theoretical Computer Science, vol. 7. Cambridge University Press, Cambridge (1989)

8. Gonthier, G., Abadi, M., Lévy, J.-J.: The geometry of optimal lambda reduction. In: Proceedings of the 19th ACM Symposium on Principles of Programming Languages (POPL 1992), pp. 15–26. ACM Press, January 1992

9. Lafont, Y.: Interaction nets. In: Proceedings of the 17th ACM Symposium on Principles of Programming Languages (POPL 1990), pp. 95–108. ACM Press (1990)

10. Lamping, J.: An algorithm for optimal lambda calculus reduction. In: Proceedings of the 17th ACM Symposium on Principles of Programming Languages (POPL 1990), pp. 16–30. ACM Press, January 1990

11. Lévy, J.-J.: Optimal reductions in the lambda calculus. In: Hindley, J.P., Seldin, J.R., (eds.) To H.B. Curry: Essays on Combinatory Logic, Lambda Calculus and Formalism, pp. 159–191. Academic Press (1980)

12. Lippi, S.: λ-calculus left reduction with interaction nets. Math. Struct. Comput. Sci. **12**(6) (2002)

13. Mackie, I.: YALE: yet another lambda evaluator based on interaction nets. In: Proceedings of the 3rd ACM SIGPLAN International Conference on Functional Programming (ICFP 1998), pp. 117–128. ACM Press, September 1998

14. Mackie, I.: An interaction net implementation of closed reduction. In: Scholz, S.-B., Chitil, O. (eds.) IFL 2008. LNCS, vol. 5836, pp. 43–59. Springer, Heidelberg (2011)

15. Sinot, F.-R.: Call-by-name and call-by-value as token-passing interaction nets. In: Urzyczyn, P. (ed.) TLCA 2005. LNCS, vol. 3461, pp. 386–400. Springer, Heidelberg (2005)

Space-Efficient Planar Acyclicity Constraints
A Declarative Pearl

Taus Brock-Nannestad[✉]

Inria & LIX/École Polytechnique, Palaiseau, France
`taus.brock-nannestad@inria.fr`

Abstract. Many constraints on graphs, e.g. the existence of a simple path between two vertices, or the connectedness of the subgraph induced by some selection of vertices, can be straightforwardly represented by means of a suitable *acyclicity* constraint. One method for encoding such a constraint in terms of simple, local constraints uses a 3-valued variable for each edge, and an $(N + 1)$-valued variable for each vertex, where N is the number of vertices in the entire graph. For graphs with many vertices, this can be somewhat inefficient in terms of space usage.

In this paper, we show how to refine this encoding into one that uses only a single bit of information, i.e. a 2-valued variable, per vertex, assuming the graph in question is planar. We furthermore show how this same constraint can be used to encode *connectedness* constraints, and a variety of other graph-related constraints.

1 Introduction

In this paper, we aim to present an "encoding pearl" that shows how to encode various graph constraints in terms of an acyclicity constraint, and also how to decompose such an acyclicity constraint into a space-efficient (in terms of the combined sizes of the variable domains) collection of low-level constraints.

Our acyclicity constraint can be seen as a refinement of an intuitive, obviously correct, but space-inefficient constraint, which, to the best of our knowledge, is due to Tamura [5], although it is an obvious enough encoding that it may simply be *folklore*. To the best of our knowledge, the space-optimised constraint we present here is novel.

We will present our constraints both using a high-level, prose description, but also in terms of the more explicit language of *finite linear integer constraints*. We choose this as the target for our encoding because of its flexibility — we will freely make use of the fact it straightforwardly permits the encoding of e.g. conditionals and reified constraints.

In many cases, using a specialised acyclicity constraint, such as the one presented by Gebser *et al.* [1], will be more efficient for finding solutions to constraint satisfaction problems, as it can use domain-specific knowledge to propagate constraints in a way that a naïve encoding may not be able to.

On the other hand, there are often large gains to be had from encoding a problem using high-level constraints into e.g. a boolean satisfiability (SAT) problem, as seen in the *Sugar* CSP solver [6].

© Springer International Publishing Switzerland 2016
O. Kiselyov and A. King (Eds.): FLOPS 2016, LNCS 9613, pp. 94–108, 2016.
DOI: 10.1007/978-3-319-29604-3_7

Given the above considerations, we make no claims about the *real-world* efficiency of the solution we present in this paper, and rather present it as a neat theoretical *curiosity*.

The remainder of the paper is structured as follows. In Sect. 2, we show how acyclicity plays a crucial rôle in encoding path constraints. In Sect. 3, we present a straightforward but space-inefficient encoding of such a constraint, in a subset of planar graphs which we call *grid graphs*, followed by a few improvements in Sect. 4. In Sect. 5, we present our optimised encoding, and we prove its correctness in Sect. 6. In Sect. 7, we show how to extend the results concerning grid graphs to general planar graphs without a loss in efficiency. Section 8, we consider other kinds of graph constraints, and show how these can also be encoded using our acyclicity constraint. Finally, in Sect. 9, we conclude and discuss future work.

2 Making Use of Acyclicity

In this section, we will show exactly how an acyclicity constraint can be used to correctly enforce certain constraints on graphs. First, let us assume we are given some fixed graph G with two distinguished vertices s and t, and that we wish to select some subset of the edges so that they make up a single simple path from s and t. We will associate a variable to each edge of the graph, and say this variable has the value 1 if the edge is selected, and 0 otherwise. To ensure that the path is simple, we can add constraints that restrict the number of selected edges meeting a vertex as follows:

- Around s and t, we require that there is exactly one selected edge.
- For any other vertex v, we require that the number of selected edges around v is either 0 or 2.

These constraints already eliminate many incorrect selections, but unfortunately not all of them. The problem is that the above constraints ensure that the solution must be path-like around each vertex, but this is not enough:

Any part of a cycle is *also* path-like around each vertex in the cycle, hence we may get spurious cycles with just the above constraints. At this point it should hopefully be clear that if we find some way of preventing cycles from appearing in our assignment of edges, we may ensure that the solution consists of only a single, simple path.

Before we present a way of encoding such an acyclicity constraint, we will briefly remark on two simplifying assumptions we can make in this setting. First of all, we may assume that the graph in question is simple, i.e. there is at most one edge between any two vertices, and no edges from a vertex to itself. This can be justified by noting that if we have selected two edges that have the same start and end vertices, then we have already created a cycle. Similarly, any edge that is not part of any cycle of the graph can also be disregarded for the purposes of enforcing acyclicity. Thus, in the remainder of this paper, we will assume that the underlying graph is simple and bridgeless.

3   A Basic Encoding of the Acyclicity Constraint

First, we'll describe an inefficient, but hopefully intuitive encoding of an acyclicity constraint. To simplify the presentation, we'll only present the results in this section for a very simple and well-behaved graph. The graph we will consider has a vertex for each point $(i, j) \in \mathbb{Z} \times \mathbb{Z}$, and edges between any two vertices that are a unit distance apart. For the variables representing these paths, we will use $h_{i,j}$ for the horizontal edge extending rightwards from the vertex at (i, j), and $v_{i,j}$ for the edge extending vertically at this vertex. Furthermore, we will in certain situations rely on these edges having values that indicate not just whether they are selected, but also marking them with a specific direction. In this case, we will assume that the variables $h_{i,j}$ and $v_{i,j}$ may take on values from the set $\{-1, 0, 1\}$. A negative value indicates that the direction of the edge is to the left or down, and a positive value indicates that the direction of the edge is to the right or up. Thus,

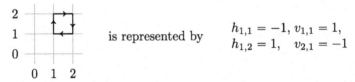

is represented by
$$h_{1,1} = -1, \; v_{1,1} = 1,$$
$$h_{1,2} = 1, \quad v_{2,1} = -1$$

To avoid having to consider truly infinite graphs, we will assume that all variables that are indexed by positions (i, j) take on the default value 0 on all but finitely many points. This essentially restricts us to working within a finite subgraph of the grid graph. The benefit of doing this, as opposed to working with finite graphs to begin with, is that this presentation allows for a uniform presentation of the constraints, and in particular avoids nasty boundary conditions that might otherwise arise.

Essentially, the constraints we will add have the following effect:

– First, all paths are forced to be *simple* — paths may not touch or cross each other:
$$\forall i, j. \quad |h_{i,j}| + |v_{i,j}| + |h_{i-1,j}| + |v_{i,j-1}| \in \{0, 1, 2\}.$$

– Secondly, all paths are forced to be *directed*. If a vertex has two edges connected (which is the maximum as per the previous constraint), then one edge must be pointing *towards* the vertex, and the other must point *away* from the vertex. This can be encoded as follows:
$$\forall i, j. \quad |h_{i,j} - h_{i-1,j} + v_{i,j} - v_{i,j-1}| \leq 1$$

This constraint may seem a bit unintuitive, but it is a straightforward matter to check that this (along with the preceding constraint) forces paths to be directed.

Next, we associate a variable $u_{i,j}$ to each vertex (i,j). This variable will take on values from the set $\{0, \ldots, N\}$ where N is the number of vertices of the subgraph we are considering. These variables are constrained as follows:

- Along any directed edge, the value of the source vertex must be strictly greater than the value of the target vertex:

$$\forall i, j. \quad (h_{i,j} > 0) \supset (u_{i,j} > u_{i+1,j})$$
$$\forall i, j. \quad (h_{i,j} < 0) \supset (u_{i,j} < u_{i+1,j})$$
$$\forall i, j. \quad (v_{i,j} > 0) \supset (u_{i,j} > u_{i,j+1})$$
$$\forall i, j. \quad (v_{i,j} < 0) \supset (u_{i,j} < u_{i,j+1})$$

The effect of these constraints is the following: first, all cycles must become *directed* cycles, as enforced by the first constraint. Second, the vertices appearing in a directed path must have values that are strictly decreasing along this path. Having both of these constraints thus precludes any cycles from appearing in the graph. Of course, this constraint might be too strict, for instance by excluding paths that should be allowed, but it's easy to see that any directed path can have strictly decreasing values assigned to it, since the domain of these values is larger than the number of vertices in the graph.

The main problem with this encoding is the size of the domain of the values. We require that each vertex (i,j) has a unique variable $u_{i,j}$ associated to it, and that these variables may take on values from the domain $\{0, \ldots, N\}$ where N is the total number of vertices in the graph. Thus, the more vertices our graph has, the greater this domain must be, leading to a quadratic growth in terms of space.

4   Potential Refinements

In this section, we will explore a few possible refinements that unfortunately do not quite improve matters. Although it is not customary to present approaches that do not work, we believe that in this case it gives a useful glimpse into the genesis of the encoding that will be presented in the next section.

The first and most obvious way of reducing the domains of the vertex variables would be to just reduce the domain. Unfortunately, this will in general also exclude some paths, which is not always desirable. The main problem with this approach is that the values along a path must still be strictly decreasing, hence whatever bounds we put on the values will also be a bound on the lengths of the paths it is possible to represent in the graph.

Of course, it is not necessary to strictly decrease the value along *every* edge in the graph. We could instead require that the values are non-increasing everywhere, as long as we have some guarantee that it will be strictly decreasing along at least one edge of any given cycle.

One way of enforcing this would be to pick a subset of the edges in advance, and tailor the constraints to be enforce a strict decrease along these edges, and allow any kind of decrease everywhere else.

How should one choose such a subset? An easy way to do so is to find a spanning tree of the graph, and then select all the edges that are *not* in this spanning tree to be the strictly decreasing ones. This works because any cycle must contain at least one of these edges, since the tree by definition cannot contain any cycles.

How much of an improvement is this? In a graph with N vertices, the spanning tree will contain $N-1$ edges, and hence the number of strictly decreasing edges will be $E-(N-1)$ where E is the number of edges in the graph. In the worst case, there exists a path that traverses all of these edges, and hence the domain of values associated to the vertices must have at least as many elements as the length of this path. In the case of the grid graph, we can define a spanning tree by taking all of the vertical edges, and a single horizontal line of edges. This leaves roughly half the edges of the graph as strictly decreasing.

Instead of choosing the strictly decreasing edges in advance, we might also select them in a more dynamic fashion. The basic idea is the following: if we can identify some feature (or set of features) that is guaranteed to be part of every cycle, we can use this to add strictly decreasing edges only at the points where these features occur. For instance, every cycle must contain at least one top-left corner, hence we could choose to make the vertical edge of each such corner strictly decreasing.

This is again an improvement on the previous situation, as the number of such corners in any path can be bounded in advance. Note that any top-left corner cannot have a similar corner immediately below or to the right, hence in a grid with N vertices, $N/3$ is certainly an upper bound on the number of top-left corners. Unfortunately, we can still construct paths that contain many top-left corners, hence this is not an asymptotic improvement on the efficiency of the encoding.

Here are two examples of paths that have many top-left corners, which we have marked using circles:

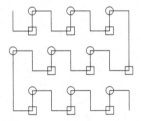 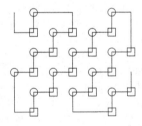

If we consider these and other examples, it quickly becomes apparent that any path that contains many top-left corners must also contain many bottom-right corners, which are marked with squares above. Moreover, if we follow the paths given by these examples, we find that we *alternate* between top-left and bottom-right corners.

5   An Optimised Encoding

As the refinements in the previous section hinted, there seems to be a relationship between the number of top-left corners and bottom-right corners.

First, we will change our encoding slightly. Instead of requiring a set of values to be (strictly) decreasing along the edges, we will instead keep just a single bit of information at each vertex. Our goal will be to give conditions that impose either equality or disequality constraints between vertices that are connected by an edge, in such a way that any cycle must contain an *odd* number of disequality constraints. If we can ensure this behaviour, then we will have succeeded in disallowing all cycles. Intuitively, we can imagine walking along the cycles with a single bit, following the directed edges, and flipping the value of our bit whenever we encounter a certain configuration of edges. As long as we make an odd number of flips, we are guaranteed to end up with the opposite parity when we return to the starting position. Naturally, paths with be unaffected by these constraints.

To encode these constraints, we first assign a binary-valued variable $p_{i,j}$ to each vertex (i, j). We next add the following constraints:

- For all edges directed downwards or to the left, we simply enforce equality between the values at each end:

$$\forall i, j. \quad (h_{i,j} < 0) \supset (p_{i+1,j} = p_{i,j})$$
$$\forall i, j. \quad (v_{i,j} < 0) \supset (p_{i,j+1} = p_{i,j})$$

- For edges directed upwards or to the right, we similarly constrain the values at each end, but choose whether to enforce equality or disequality depending on whether the edges in question form an "up-then-right" or "right-then-up" corner:

$$\forall i, j. \quad (h_{i-1,j} > 0) \supset (p_{i-1,j} = p_{i,j} \oplus (v_{i,j} > 0))$$
$$\forall i, j. \quad (v_{i,j-1} > 0) \supset (p_{i,j-1} = p_{i,j} \oplus (h_{i,j} > 0))$$

Here, $\oplus$ is the "exclusive or" operation.

Note that these four constraints cover all the possibilities for which the value of $h_{i,j}$ and $v_{i,j}$ is non-zero. Moreover, the four constraints are also *disjoint*, i.e. for any given edge, at most one of the above constraints apply. Here is an example that shows how the above constraints force the assignment of the $p_{i,j}$ values for a particular directed path (where we have arbitrarily set the value of p at the beginning of the path to 0):

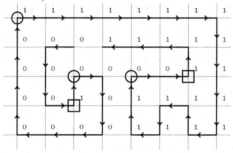

The circles and squares indicate the vertices at which the flips take place. Observe that if we were to close the cycle by adding an extra edge going left, there would be no way of reconciling the values of p.

All that remains now is to show that closed simple cycles must always contain an odd number of corners at which the parity flips. This will be the subject of the next section.

6   Turning Number Parity

In this section we will prove that the turning number of a simple closed cycle is always equal to either 1 or -1.

This result is known already for suitably well-behaved curves in the plane [7] and also for polygons [2], but to keep this paper somewhat self-contained, we will present a proof from first principles.

First, we must define precisely what kinds of directed paths we allow.

Definition 1. *A directed path consists of a sequence of steps of unit length going either up, right, left or down. We furthermore require that whenever a path changes direction, it does so by $\pm 90°$. We say a path is* closed *if the last step of the path ends at the beginning of the path. We say a path is* simple *if it does not cross or touch itself, that is, every point is the source or target of at most two segments of the path.*

Definition 2. *A* corner *of a given path is any point at which the path makes a turn. We use the notation $\ulcorner$ for a corner at which the path moves up and then right, and define $\urcorner$, $\lrcorner$, $\llcorner$, $\urcorner$, $\ulcorner$, $\llcorner$, and $\lrcorner$ similarly . In arithmetic expressions, we use the same notation to represent the* number *of such corners in the path in question. Thus, $\ulcorner + \ulcorner$ represents the total number of $\ulcorner$ and $\ulcorner$ corners in the given path.*

We will first present a way of calculating the *turning number* of a path, i.e. the number clockwise rotations a person following the path would make. Note that this need not be a whole number.

Intuitively, whenever the path turns to the right locally ($\ulcorner$, $\urcorner$, $\lrcorner$ or $\llcorner$), the turning number increases by $1/4$, and conversely whenever it turns to the left locally ($\urcorner$, $\ulcorner$, $\llcorner$ or $\lrcorner$), the turning number decreases by $1/4$. Based on this, we define the turning number of a path as follows:

Definition 3. *The* turning number *of a path is defined as*

$$1/4(\ulcorner + \urcorner + \lrcorner + \llcorner) - 1/4(\urcorner + \ulcorner + \llcorner + \lrcorner).$$

Of course, this definition is a bit cumbersome to work with, but luckily there is an easier way to calculate the turning number in the case of *closed* paths. To see this, we first need the following lemma:

Lemma 1. *For any closed path, the following equalities hold:*

$$\ulcorner - \lrcorner = \llcorner - \urcorner = \lrcorner - \ulcorner = \urcorner - \llcorner$$

Proof. Consider any ┌ or └ corner. Following the path in the direction of the arrow, we must eventually end up at a ┘ or ┐ corner, since the path is closed. A similar argument shows that any ┘ or ┐ corner is preceded by a ┌ or └ corner. Thus, we have the following equality relating the number of such corners in the path:

$$ ┌ \; + \; └ \; = \; ┘ + ┐. $$

By rearranging this equality, we get

$$ ┌ \; - ┘ = ┐ - └ \, , $$

which gives us one part of the desired equality. The remaining equalities follow in the same way. □

Corollary 1. *The turning number of a closed path is given by* ┌ − ┘.

Proof. Rearranging the definition of the turning number, we find that it is equal to

$$ {}^1\!/_4 ((┌ \; - ┘) + (└ - ┐) + (┘ − ┌) + (┐ − └)). $$

By the preceding lemma, each of the four differences is equal to ┌ − ┘, and hence the entire expression reduces to simply ┌ − ┘. □

In addition to this, we also have the nice result that the turning number of a closed path is well-behaved with regard to various transformations of this path:

Corollary 2. *Rotating a closed path does not change the turning number. Mirroring or reversing the direction of a closed path inverts the turning number.*

Proof. We show here one of the cases. Consider a given closed path. By the previous corollary, it has turning number equal to ┌ − ┘. If the direction of the path is reversed, every ┌ corner becomes a ┌ corner, and every ┘ corner becomes a ┘ corner. Thus, the value of ┌ − ┘ is equal to ┌ − ┘ after reversing the direction of the path. We now have

$$ ┌ − ┘ = -(┘ − ┌), $$

and from the previous lemma, it follows that ┘ − ┌ is the turning number of the reversed path. We thus conclude that reversing the direction of the path inverts the turning number. The remaining cases are similar. □

Next, we need to show that any closed, *simple* path has a turning number of either +1 or −1. We prove this in two steps. First, we show that any closed, simple path can be reduced to a path with only four edges (i.e. a square) by a sequence of local reductions. By observing that the local reductions preserve the turning number, we get the desired result.

Theorem 1. *Any closed, simple path with length greater than 4 can be reduced using local reductions to a closed, simple path with a strictly smaller length and with the same turning number.*

Proof. Formally, we prove this by induction on the length of the path. We will leave these appeals to the induction hypothesis implicit, however, and simply present the reductions. Additionally, we will present the reductions in terms of *undirected* paths, and only consider the turning number once we've established exactly what the reductions are.

First, we want to find an appropriate place to reduce the path. This will be a horizontal segment of some length where each end of the segment points downwards:

First, however, we must establish that there must exist such a segment. We do this with a sequence of observations:

Observation 1: There is at least one horizontal segment. As the path has length greater than 4, it must contain *some* segment, either horizontal or vertical. If the segment is horizontal, we are done. If the segment is vertical, we can follow it upwards until it turns (which it must, as the path is closed), and there we will find a horizontal segment.

Observation 2: The topmost horizontal segment must turn downwards at each end. If at either end it turns upwards, we may follow the path upwards until it turns again. At this point, we will have found a horizontal segment which is higher up than the topmost horizontal segment, and this is a contradiction.

Having now established the existence of the desired segment, we will pick a segment of this form for which the length is *minimal*, i.e. no segment of this form with strictly smaller length exists. It is this segment we will reduce locally.

We first consider the case where the left end of the segment turns *under* the segment. We ignore the right end of the segment for now:

The dotted lines at the bottom indicate the directions in which the path may proceed. Note that the path cannot turn up, as this would make it either non-simple or of length exactly 4.

In this case, we reduce the path as follows:

In a similar fashion, we can reduce the right end of the segment in the cases where it too turns underneath the segment. This leaves the following remaining case:

We would like to reduce it as follows:

To do so, however, we need to argue that this does not make the path intersect itself, otherwise we would be unable to apply the induction hypothesis. We will therefore establish that there cannot be any horizontal segments immediately below the given horizontal segment. Assume for the purposes of contradiction that there exists such a segment. Following the segment to the left, it must eventually turn downwards. Turning upwards would make the path intersect itself. Similarly, the right end of the segment must also turn downwards. At this point, however, we would have a horizontal segment, turning down at both ends, and with a length that is strictly smaller than the length of the segment we started with, and this is a contradiction. As we have now established that there are no horizontal segments directly beneath our chosen segment, we may now reduce it as previously shown.

This takes care of all possible cases. All that remains now is to note that the above reductions preserve the turning number. This can either be done the *hard* way, by checking every single case separately, or it can be done the *clever* way, by using Corollary 2. Note that rotating the path does not change the turning number, and reversing and mirroring it only changes the sign of the turning number, hence it is sufficient to observe that all the configurations seen in the reductions above can be rotated, mirrored or reversed in such a way that there are no ⌐ or ⌟ corners either before or after the reduction. It is then immediate that all the reductions preserve the turning number.   □

Armed with the above theorem, we may now prove that the desired property of closed, simple paths indeed holds.

Corollary 3. *The turning number of a closed, simple path is either* 1 *or* −1.

Proof. Using the previous theorem, any closed, simple path of length greater than 4 may be reduced to one with a strictly smaller length, without changing the turning number. All that remains, then, is to check that all closed paths of length at most 4 have turning number ±1. There are exactly two of these paths, and the result thus follows from a simple inspection of these.   □

Now that we have established that

$$\ulcorner \; - \lrcorner = \pm 1, \qquad \text{and thus} \qquad \ulcorner \; + \lrcorner \equiv 1 \mod 2$$

we have shown that the constraint presented in the previous section indeed has the property that any closed simple cycle induces an odd number of disequalities, and thus leads to a contradiction.

7   From Grid Graphs to General Planar Graphs

In this section, we will show how to extend the results of the previous section to general planar graphs.

One obvious way of doing this would be to use the fact that any planar graph can obviously be approximated by a suitable subgraph of the grid graph, by suitably "rasterising" an embedding of the planar graph. This would not be particular efficient, however, as the approximation might use many more vertices than the original graph.

Instead, we will show how a certain kind of planar graph embedding gives rise to a straightforward way of assigning appropriate turning number parity constraints to a general planar graph.

Our main tool for this purpose will be the so-called *visibility representation* [3,4] of a planar graph. Put briefly, any planar graph can be represented in a form where every edge is a vertical line, and every vertex is a horizontal line:

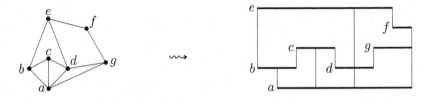

Now, this is already a much better representation than simply approximating an arbitrary planar embedding. First, note that the turning number parity does not change along any vertical edge, hence we can simply think of these as very *tall* single edges. Thus, we can easily represent any planar graph as one that is locally grid-like, by putting d vertices for each vertex of degree d in the original graph. However, we can in fact do better still. To see this, consider the ways in which a path can traverse a vertex in the visibility representation. If the path crosses the vertex without changing direction from up to down or vice versa, it is clear that the turning number parity does not change. This takes care of four of the possibilities. If, on the other hand, the path changes direction at the vertex, we must consider whether it moves leftwards or rightwards across said vertex. In the former case, the parity is unchanged, and in the latter case, it is flipped. This fully sums up the local behaviour of paths going through a vertex.

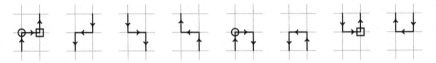

The key observation now is that we can enforce exactly this behaviour on any straight-line embedding of the planar graph. To do this, we will mark each vertex in the original graph embedding with information from the visibility representation that will enable us make the former act exactly as the latter. We will mark this as a small dotted arrow traversing each vertex. Every edge to the left of the arrow (when looking in the direction the arrow is pointing) will be among the edges above this vertex in the visibility representation, and dually the edges on the right of the arrow will be the edges below the vertex. Similarly, the edges will be ordered according to which order they occur around the vertex, using the direction of the arrow to distinguish between the possibilities. Essentially, one can think of this representation as one in which all the vertices in the visibility representation have been contracted into a single vertex again.

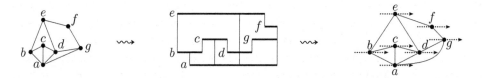

The question of whether the parity should flip when traversing a vertex in this graph can now be easily explained in terms of this additional arrow: if the path "bounces off" the arrow, and is travelling in the direction the arrow is pointing, the parity should flip. In all other cases, the parity should remain the same.

8   Further Graph Constraints

In this section, we will consider a variety of further graph constraints that may be achieved by adapting our acyclicity constraint.

First, let us consider the problem of connectedness. Given a subset of the vertices, we would like to enforce that the subgraph containing exactly these vertices (and the edges that connect them with each other) is in fact connected. For the sake of simplicity, we will assume that we have selected one vertex r that is guaranteed to be in the subset. We now enforce the constraint as follows:

- we associate a 2-valued variable $s_{i,j}$ to each vertex, representing whether said vertex is part of the selected subset.
- For each vertex in this subset, except for the vertex r, we require that at exactly one of its edges is selected, and that it points *away* from the vertex:

$$\forall (i,j) \in \mathbb{Z} \times \mathbb{Z} \setminus \{r\}. \quad (h_{i,j} > 0) + (v_{i,j} > 0) + (h_{i-1,j} < 0) + (v_{i,j-1} < 0) = 1$$

This constraint subsumes the constraints from Sect. 3 that forced the solution to contain only simple, directed paths, hence we discard these constraints.

The effect of these requirements is that our selected edges now induce a *tree* structure on the subgraph induced by the selected vertices. The vertex r then acts as the root of this induced tree. As there is only one root vertex, and as the tree will contain only edges from the subgraph, it is immediate that the subgraph in question must be connected.

Again, the acyclicity constraint becomes crucial — without it, a tree may end in a cycle, and thus might fail to be eventually connected to the root. All that remains, then, is to ensure that the possibility of having multiple edges entering a vertex does not break the acyclicity constraint we have already defined. The only way this could happen is if there were some way to constrain a given edge to take on two unequal values at the same time. As we only constrain the value of an edge entering a vertex based on the local configuration of it and the edge (if any) leaving the vertex, and as there is at most one edge leaving a vertex, it is impossible for the acyclicity constraint to overconstrain the variables. Note that this is not the case if we allow more than one edge to exit a given vertex.

8.1   Single-Cycle Constraints

Previously, we have seen how to constrain the solution to consist of a single path. We will now consider how to constrain the solution to consist of a single cycle instead. Off-hand, this may seem a bit strange, as we would then simultaneously constrain the solution to contain *no* cycles, and yet also a single cycle, which would be a contradiction.

To get the desired behaviour, we will first adapt the acyclicity constraint to allow this constraint to be broken at exactly one vertex in the graph. We first associate a 2-valued variable $b_{i,j}$ to each vertex. This variable will be constrained as follows:

- Among all the vertices, at most one of them can have $b_{i,j} = 1$. This is easily enforced by the following constraint:

$$\sum_{i,j} b_{i,j} = 1$$

- At any vertex, the acyclicity constraint is only enforced if the value of $b_{i,j}$ is equal to zero. For each constraint $C(i,j)$ concerning the vertex (i,j) this amounts to adding a precondition as follows:

$$\forall i, j. \quad (b_{i,j} = 0) \supset C(i,j)$$

At this point we have enough to encode the single-cycle constraint, but in fact we can do even better in this particular situation. One drawback of the acyclicity constraint we presented previously is that it requires a domain of size 3 for the variables associated to edges. If, on the other hand, our solution is known to consist of only cycles, we do not need this extra information to be encoded in the edges. The crucial observation is the following: if the solution consists of only cycles, we can keep track of the number of cycles (modulo 2) that any given face of the graph is inside. This allows us to associate a direction to each edge by stating that the face to the left of a given edge (as seen in the implicit direction of the edge) is always the outside face.

The benefit of this optimisation is clear: instead of constraining the 3-valued edges to ensure that they give rise to directed cycles, we may assume they are 2-valued, and simply add a single 2-valued variable $f_{i,j}$ for each face of the graph. As there are generally more edges than faces in a given planar graph, this is an improvement. If we define that $f_{i,j}$ is the face that is immediately above $h_{i,j}$

and immediately to the right of $v_{i,j}$, it is a straightforward matter to propagate the inside/outside information by the following constraints (recall that the edges now have domain $\{0,1\}$):

$$\forall i,j. \quad f_{i,j-1} = f_{i,j} \oplus h_{i,j}$$
$$\forall i,j. \quad f_{i-1,j} = f_{i,j} \oplus v_{i,j}$$

where we previously used, say, $h_{i,j} < 0$, we may now instead put $(f_{i,j-1} = 0) \wedge (f_{i,j} = 1)$, and thus restate the constraints from Sect. 5 in terms of the $f_{i,j}$ variables.

In fact, by doing this, we can eliminate the $h_{i,j}$ and $v_{i,j}$ variables *entirely*, and rewrite any expression referring to these variables into one using the $f_{i,j}$ variables instead.

9   Conclusion and Future Work

In this paper, we presented a novel way of encoding acyclicity constraints for planar graphs by means of a notion of *turning number parity*.

Although this encoding is efficient in terms of space, it is less clear whether it is actually practical to use. One benefit of the basic encoding is that cycles may be detected by simple interval constraint propagation where

$$x \in \{k,\ldots,\ell\}, \quad y \in \{m,\ldots,n\}, \quad x < y$$

immediately induces the constraints $k < y$ and $x < n$, and thus constrains the domain of x and y to be $\{k,\ldots,\min(\ell,n-1)\}$ and $\{\max(k+1,m),\ldots,n\}$ respectively. If moreover we know that $y < x$, propagating the above constraint will eventually exclude all possibilities in the domain of either x or y, and thus create a contradiction.

For the refined constraint, the picture is less clear. Essentially, we induce a sequence of equalities and disequalities between the parity variables in our directed cycle. If we decide on the parity of some variable in a path, the consequences of this choice will immediately propagate to every other vertex in the path, and if the path is in fact a cycle, this propagation will ultimately fail. If, on the other hand, no such choice has been made, the constraint propagation engine may fail to detect the contradiction. Consider for instance the following (dis)equalities:

$$a \neq b, \quad b = c, \quad c = d, \quad d = a, \quad a,b,c,d \in \{0,1\}$$

With these constraints, there is no local way to make progress by pruning the domains of the variables.

On the other hand, only a small bit of propagation is required to obtain a contradiction. If we add the following propagation rules

$$x \neq y, y = z \Longrightarrow x \neq z \qquad x \neq y, y \neq z \Longrightarrow x = z,$$

and apply it to the above example, it will eventually derive $a \neq a$, and get a contradiction. In fact, for path and cycle constraints, we can use the above as *simplification* rules, and allow them to consume both of the input constraints (for the connectedness constraint, this is no longer valid).

As we have shown, there exists an efficient encoding for *planar* graphs. It would be interesting to see how one might adapt the present constraints to handle *non-planar* graphs as well. One thing that should be noted is that the present approach does not immediately extend to more general graphs. Consider for instance the following graph embedded on the following planar representation of the torus (where the top and bottom edges are identified, and likewise for the left and right edges).

Here, it is easy to construct cycles that e.g. have no corners at all — in which case the turning number parity certainly doesn't change — or an even number of corners:

Thus, it is necessary to add further constraints to ensure that these cycles are also excluded.

Acknowledgements. This work is funded by the ERC Advanced Grant *ProofCert*.

References

1. Rintanen, J., Janhunen, T., Gebser, M.: SAT modulo graphs: acyclicity. In: Fermé, E., Leite, J. (eds.) JELIA 2014. LNCS, vol. 8761, pp. 137–151. Springer, Heidelberg (2014)
2. Grünbaum, B., Shephard, G.C.: Rotation and winding numbers for planar polygons and curves. Trans. Am. Math. Soc. **322**(1), 169–187 (1990)
3. Otten, R., Van Wijk, J.: Graph representations in interactive layout design. In: Proceedings of the IEEE International Symposium on Circuits and Systems, pp. 914–918 (1978)
4. Rosenstiehl, P., Tarjan, R.E.: Rectilinear planar layouts and bipolar orientations of planar graphs. Discrete Comput. Geom. **1**(1), 343–353 (1986)
5. Tamura, N.: Solving puzzles with Sugar constraint solver. Slides, August 2008. http://bach.istc.kobe-u.ac.jp/sugar/puzzles/sugar-puzzles.pdf
6. Tamura, N., Taga, A., Kitagawa, S., Banbara, M.: Compiling finite linear CSP into SAT. Constraints **14**(2), 254–272 (2009)
7. Whitney, H.: On regular closed curves in the plane. Compositio Mathematica **4**, 276–284 (1937)

Executable Relational Specifications of Polymorphic Type Systems Using Prolog

Ki Yung Ahn[1]([⊠]) and Andrea Vezzosi[2]

[1] Portland State University, Portland, OR, USA
kya@pdx.edu
[2] Chalmers University of Technology, Gothenburg, Sweden
vezzosi@chalmers.se

Abstract. A concise, declarative, and machine executable specification of the Hindley–Milner type system (HM) can be formulated using logic programming languages such as Prolog. Modern functional language implementations such as the Glasgow Haskell Compiler support more extensive flavors of polymorphism beyond Milner's theory of type polymorphism in the late 70's. We progressively extend the HM specification to include more advanced type system features. An interesting development is that extending dimensions of polymorphism beyond HM resulted in a multi-staged solution: resolve the typing relations first, while delaying to resolve kinding relations, and then resolve the delayed kinding relations. Our work demonstrates that logic programing is effective for prototyping polymorphic type systems with rich features of polymorphism, and that logic programming could have been even more effective for specifying type inference if it were equipped with better theories and tools for staged resolution of different relations at different levels.

Keywords: Hindley–Milner · Functional language · Type system · Type inference · Unification · Parametric polymorphism · Higher-kinded polymorphism · Type constructor polymorphism · Kind polymorphism · Algebraic datatype · Nested datatype · Logic programming · Prolog · Delayed goals

1 Introduction

When implementing the type system of a programming language, we often face a gap between the design described on paper and the actual implementation. Sometimes there is only an ambiguous description in English (or in other natural languages). Even when there is a mathematical description of the type system on paper, there can be a gap between the description and the implementation. Language designers and implementers can suffer from this gap because it is difficult to determine whether a problem originated from a flaw in the design or a bug in the implementation. Having a declarative (i.e., structurally similar to the design) and flexible (i.e., easily extensible) machine executable specification is extremely helpful, especially for prototyping or testing experimental extensions

© Springer International Publishing Switzerland 2016
O. Kiselyov and A. King (Eds.): FLOPS 2016, LNCS 9613, pp. 109–125, 2016.
DOI: 10.1007/978-3-319-29604-3_8

to the language's type system. Jones' attempt of *Typing Haskell in Haskell* [20] is an exemplary work that demonstrates the value of such a concise, declarative, and machine executable specification: the authors report that 90+ pages of Hugs type checker implementation in C could be specified in only 400+ lines of readable Haskell script.

Logic programming languages like Prolog are natural candidates for the purpose of specifying type systems that support type inference: the syntax and semantics are designed to represent logical inference rules (which is how type systems are typically formalized) and they offer native support for unification (which is the basic building block of type inference algorithms). As a result, type system specifications become even more succinct in Prolog than in functional languages. More importantly, the specifications are *relational*, capturing both type checking and type inference without duplication.

Our contributions are demonstrating

- A relational specification for a polymorphic type system that can be executed for both purposes of type checking and type inference (Sect. 2.1).
- A succinct and declarative specification for several dimensions of polymorphism (type, type constructor, kind) in less than 35 lines of Prolog (Sect. 2.2).
- A specification that is easily extend from the prior specifications with several pragmatic features such as pattern matching, recursion schemes, and polymorphic recursion (with the help of a few type annotation) (Sect. 3).
- A two-staged inference scheme for types and kinds using delayed goals (Sect. 2.2): We discovered that kind inference can be delayed after type inference (it is in some sense quite natural).
- A motivating example for a dualized view on variables in logic programming: Type variables are viewed as unifiable logic variables in type inference but they are viewed as concrete/atomic variables (or identifiers) in kind inference in our specification. Better way of organizing this concept is desirable to produce better relational specifications for polymorphic type systems.

We give a step-by-step tutorial style explanation of our specification in Sect. 2, gradually extending from the Prolog specification of the simply-typed lambda calculus. In Sect. 3, we demonstrate that our method of specification is flexible for extensions with other language features. All our Prolog specification in Sects. 2 and 3 are tested on SWI Prolog 7.2 and its source code are available online.[1] We contemplate on more challenging language features such as GADTs and term indices in Sect. 4, discuss related work in Sect. 5, and summarize our discussion in Sect. 6.

2   Polymorphic Type Inference Specifications in Prolog

We start from a Prolog specification for the Hindley–Milner type system (HM) in Sect. 2.1 and then extend the specification to support type constructor polymorphism and kind polymorphism in Sect. 2.2.

---

[1] http://kyagrd.github.io/tiper/.

The following two lines should be loaded into the Prolog system before loading the specifications in this paper.

```
:- set_prolog_flag(occurs_check,true).
:- op(500,yfx,$).
```

The first line sets Prolog's unification operator = to perform an occurs check, which is needed for the correct behavior of type inference. The second line declares $ as a left-associative infix operator, which is used to represent the application operator in the object language syntax. For instance, E1$E2 is an application of E1 to E2. Note that $ is left associative because we want E1$E2$E3 to mean ((E1$E2)$E3).[2]

2.1 HM

The four rules defining the type predicate in the specification of HM (Fig. 1) are almost literal transcriptions of the typing rules of HM. The query type(C,E,T) represents a typing judgment usually denoted by C ⊢ E : T on paper, meaning that the expression E can be assigned a type T under the typing context C. A typing context is a list of bindings. There are two kinds of bindings in HM: monomorphic bindings (X:mono(A)) and polymorphic bindings (X:poly(C,A)). Expressions in HM are either variables (X), lambda expressions (lam(X,E)), applications (E1$E2), or let-expressions (let(X=E0,E1)).

The first rule for finding a type (T1) of a variable (var(X)) amounts to instantiating (instantiate(T,T1)) the type (T) from the first binding (X:T) that matches the variable (X) bound in the typing context (C). The two rules for lambda expressions and applications are self-explanatory. The last rule for let-expressions introduces polymorphic bindings. HM supports rank-1 polymorphic types (a.k.a. type schemes), which are introduced by this polymorphic

```
type(C,var(X),      T1) :- first(X:T,C), instantiate(T,T1).
type(C,lam(X,E), A -> B) :- type([X:mono(A)|C],E,B).
type(C,X $ Y,      B ) :- type(C,X,A -> B), type(C,Y,A).
type(C,let(X=E0,E1), T ) :- type(C,E0,A), type([X:poly(C,A)|C],E1,T).

first(K:V,[K1:V1|Xs]) :- K = K1, V=V1.
first(K:V,[K1:V1|Xs]) :- K\==K1, first(K:V, Xs).

instantiate(poly(C,T),T1) :- copy_term(t(C,T),t(C,T1)).
instantiate(mono(T),T).
```

Fig. 1. Executable relational specification of HM in Prolog

---

[2] We intentionallay adopted the same symbol as the application operator $ in the Haskell standard library. In contrast to the right-associative operator in Haskell, our operator represents the default function application most often denoted by empty spaces and left-associative by convention.

let-bindings.[3] The typing context C inside the polymorphic binding poly(C,A) is the typing context of the let-expression where A is being generalized.

The instantiate predicate cleverly implements the idea of the polymorphic instantiation in HM. The built-in predicate copy_term makes a copy of the first argument and unifies it with the second argument. The copied version is identical to the original term except that all the Prolog variables have been substituted with freshly generated variables. The instantiation of a polymorphic type poly(C,T) is implemented as copy_term(t(C,T),t(C,T1)). Firstly, a copied version of t(C,T) is made. Say t(C2,T2) is the copied version with all variables in both C and T are freshly renamed in C2 and T2. Secondly, t(C2,T2) is unified with t(C,T1), which amounts to C2=C and T2=T1. Because C2 is being unified with the original context C, all freshly generated variables in C2 are unified with the original variables in C. Therefore, only the variables in T that do not occur in its binding context C will effectively be freshly instantiated in T1. For example, the result of copy_term(t([X:T],Y->X),t([X:T],T1)) is T1 = Y1->X, where only Y is instantiated to a fresh variable Y1 but X stays the same because it appears in the typing context [X:T]. This exactly captures generalization and instantiation of polymorphic types in HM.

One great merit of this relational specification is that it also serves as a machine executable reference implementation. We can run it for type checking:

```
?- type([], lam(x,var(x)), A -> A).
true .
```

as well as for type inference:

```
?- type([], lam(f,lam(x,var(f)$var(x))), T).
T = ((_G1571->_G1572)->_G1571->_G1572) .
```

and, although it is not the focus of this work, also for type inhabitation:

```
?- type([], E, A -> A).
E = lam(_G1555, var(_G1555)) .
```

In the following sections, we discuss how to add polymorphic features to the specification. The specifications with the extended features also serve as machine executable reference implementations, which are able to perform both type checking and type inference.

2.2   HM + Type Constructor Polymorphism + Kind Polymorphism

Modern functional languages such as Haskell support rich flavors of polymorphism beyond type polymorphism. For example, consider a generic tree datatype

$$\textbf{data } \textit{Tree } c \textit{ a } = \textit{ Leaf } a \mid \textit{Node } (c \textit{ (Tree } c \textit{ a)})$$

where c determines the branching structure at the *Nodes* and a determines the type of the value hanging on the *Leafs*. For instance, it instantiates to a binary

---

[3] Here, in this subsection, we consider non-recursive bindings only but the specification of HM can be easily modified to support recursive bindings (see Sect. 3.1).

tree when c instantiates to a pair constructor and a rose tree when c instantiates to a list constructor. The type system of Haskell infers that c has kind $* \rightarrow *$ and a has kind $*$. That is, this generic tree datatype is polymorphic on the unary type constructor variable c as well as on the type variable a. Haskell's type system is also able to infer types for polymorphic functions defined over *Trees*, which may involve polymorphism over type constructors as well as over types. Furthermore, recent versions of the Glasgow Haskell Compiler support kind polymorphism [34].

The Prolog specification in Fig. 2 describes type constructor polymorphism and kind polymorphism, in only 32 lines (excluding empty lines). We get kind polymorphism for free because we can reuse the same `instantiate` predicate for kinds, which was used for types in the HM specification. However, the instantiation for types needs to be modified, as in `inst_type`, to ensure that the kinds of freshly generated type constructor variables match with the corresponding variables in the polymorphic type. For example, each use of *Node* :: $\forall c\ a.\ c\ (Tree\ c\ a) \rightarrow Tree\ c\ a$ generates two variables, say c' and a', and the type system should make sure that c' has the same kind ($* \rightarrow *$) as c and a' the same kind ($*$) as a. The `samekinds` predicate used in `inst_type` generates such kinding relations exactly for this reason. Other than ensuring same kinds for freshly generated variables, `inst_type` instantiates polymorphic types just as `instantiate` does. In the remainder of this section, we focus our discussion on the modifications to support type constructor variables.

Supporting type constructor variables of arbitrary kinds introduces the possibility of ill-kinded type (constructor) formation (e.g., $F\ G$ when $F : * \rightarrow *$ but $G : * \rightarrow *$ or $A \rightarrow B$ when $A : * \rightarrow *$). In our Prolog specification, we use the atomic symbol `o` to represent the kind usually denoted by $*$ (e.g., in Haskell) because $*$ is predefined as a built-in infix operator in Prolog. The `kind` predicate transcribes the kinding rules for well-formed kinds, which is self-explanatory (HM without `let`-binding duplicated on the type level instead of term level).

The typing rules (`type`) need some modifications from the rules of HM, in order to invoke checks for well-kindedness using the kinding rules (`kind`). We discuss the modification in three steps.

The first step is to have the typing rules take an additional argument for the kinding context (`KC`) along with the typing context (`C`). The typing rules should keep track of the kinding context in order to invoke `kind` from `type`. That is, we change the definition of the `type` predicate from `type(C,...)` to `type(KC,C,...)`.

The second step is to invoke well-kindedness checks from the necessary places among the typing rules. We follow the formulation of Pure Type Systems [7], a generic theory of typed lambda calculi, which indicates that well-kindedness checks are required at the formation of function types, that is, in the typing rule for lambda expressions. One would naturally attempt the following modification:

```
type(KC,C,lam(X,E),A->B)  :- type(KC,C,[X:mono(A)|C],E,B),
                             kind(KC,A->B,o).
```

```
kind(KC,var(Z),K1) :- first(Z:K,KC), instantiate(K,K1).
kind(KC,F $ G, K2) :- kind(KC,F,K1 -> K2), kind(KC,G,K1).
kind(KC,A -> B,o)  :- kind(KC,A,o), kind(KC,B,o).

type(KC,C,var(X),    T1) --> { first(X:T,C) }, inst_type(KC,T,T1).
type(KC,C,lam(X,E), A->B) --> type(KC, [X:mono(A)|C],E,B), [kind(KC,A->B,o)].
type(KC,C,X $ Y,       B) --> type(KC,C,X,A->B), type(KC,C,Y,A).
type(KC,C,let(X=E0,E1),T) --> type(KC,C,E0,A), type(KC, [X:poly(C,A)|C],E1,T).

first(X:T,[X1:T1|Zs]) :- X = X1, T = T1.
first(X:T,[X1:T1|Zs]) :- X\==X1, first(X:T, Zs).

instantiate(poly(C,T),T1) :- copy_term(t(C,T),t(C,T1)).
instantiate(mono(T),T).

inst_type(KC,poly(C,T),T2) --> { copy_term(t(C,T),t(C,T1)) },
  { free_variables(T,Xs), free_variables(T1,Xs1) }, % Xs, Xs1 same length
  samekinds(KC,Xs,Xs1), { T1=T2 }. % unify T1 T2 later (T2 may not be var)
inst_type(KC,mono(T),T) --> [].

samekinds(KC,[X|Xs],[Y|Ys]) --> { X\==Y }, [kind(KC,X,K),kind(KC,Y,K)],
                                    samekinds(KC,Xs,Ys).
samekinds(KC,[X|Xs],[X|Ys]) --> [], samekinds(KC,Xs,Ys).
samekinds(KC,[],     []    ) --> [].

variablize(var(X)) :- gensym(t,X).

infer_type(KC,C,E,T) :-
  phrase( type(KC,C,E,T), Gs0 ), % 1st stage of typing in this line
  copy_term(Gs0,Gs),             % 2nd stage of kinding from here
  bagof(Ty, member(kind(_,Ty,_),Gs), Tys),
  free_variables(Tys,Xs), % collect all free tyvars in Xs
  maplist(variablize,Xs), % concretize tyvar with var(t) where t fresh
  bagof(A:K, member(var(A),Xs), KC1), % kind bindngs for var(t)
  appendKC(Gs,KC1,Gs1), % extend each KC with KC1 for new vars
  maplist(call,Gs1).    % run all goals in Gs1

appendKC([],_,[]).
appendKC([kind(KC,X,K)|Gs],KC1,[kind(KC2,X,K)|Gs1]) :-
  append(KC1,KC,KC2), appendKC(Gs,KC1,Gs1).
```

Fig. 2. HM + type constructor polymorphism + kind polymorphism in Prolog (without pattern matching).

This second step modification is intuitive as a specification, but rather fragile as a reference implementation. For instance, a simple type inference query for the identity function fails (where the HM specification successfully infers T = A -> A):

```
?- type([],[],lam(x,var(x)),T).
ERROR: Out of local stack
```

There are mainly two reasons for the erratic behavior. Firstly, there is not enough information at the moment of well-kindedness checking. At the invocation of kind, the only available information is that it is a function type A -> B. Whether A and B are variables, type constructor applications, or function types may be determined later on, when there are other parts of the expression to be type checked (or inferred). Secondly, we have a conflicting view on type variables at the typing level and at the kinding level. At the typing level, we think of type variables as unification variables, implemented by Prolog variables in order to exploit the unification natively supported in Prolog. At the kinding level, on the contrary, we think of type variables as concrete names that can be looked up in the kinding context (just like term variables in the typing context).

The last step of the modification addresses the erratic behavior of the second step. A solution for these two problems mentioned above is to stage the control flow: first, get as much information as possible at the typing level, and then, concretize Prolog variables with atomic names for the rest of the work at the kinding level. Instead of directly invoking kind within type, we collect the list of all the necessary well-kindedness assertions into a list to be handled later. This programming technique is known as *delayed goals* in logic programming, which is like building up a to-do list or continuation. We use the Definite Clause Grammar (DCG) rules [25,31] to collect delayed goals using a neat syntax. The DCG rules were originally designed for describing production rules of formal grammar, where nonterminals are specified within the brackets and context-sensitive conditions are specified within curly braces using ordinary Prolog predicates. Here, we exploit DCG rules (as many others do) as a neat syntax for a *writer monad* that collects kind assertions as a side-output within the brackets (e.g., [kind(KC,A->B,o)]) and pure computations appear in curly braces (e.g., first(X:T,C)). The infer_type predicate implements the two-staged solution as follows:

1. The 1st line is the first stage at the typing level. For example,
   ```
   ?- phrase( type([],[],lam(x,var(x)),T), Gs0 ).
   T = (_G1643->_G1643),
   Gs0 = [kind([], (_G1643->_G1643), o)] .
   ```
   it infers the most generic type (_G1643->_G1643) of the identity function and generates one delayed goal, namely kind([], (_G1643− > _G1643), o).

2. In the 2nd line, we make a copied version of the delayed goals using copy_term in order to decouple the variables of the first stage from the variables of the second stage. After the 2nd line, Gs contains a copied version of Gs0 with freshly renamed variables, say Gs = [kind([], (_G2211->_G2211), o)].

3,4. The 3rd and 4th lines collects all the type variables in Gs into Xs, that is, Xs=[_G2211], continuing with the identity function example.

5. The 5th line maplist(variablize,Xs) instantiates the Prolog variables collected in Xs into concrete type variables with fresh names. In variablize, gensym(t,X) generates atoms with fresh names that start

with t. For instance, X=t1, X=t2, · · ·. After the 5th line, where it is con-
cretized as _G2211=var(t1), we have Xs = [var(t1)] and Gs = [kind([],
(var(t1)->var(t1)), o)].

6,7. Freshly generated type variables need to be registered to the kinding context
in order to be well-kinded. The 6th line monomorphically binds all the
variable names in Xs and collects them into KC1. Continuing with the identity
function example, KC1=[t1:mono(K1)] after the 6th line. The 7th line extends
each kinding context in Gs with KC1 for the freshly generated variables. The
goals with extended contexts are collected in Gs1. After 7th line, we have
Gs1 = [kind([t1:mono(K1)], (var(t1)->var(t1)), o)].

8. Finally, the delayed well-kindedness assertions in Gs1 are called on as goals,
which amounts to the following query for our identity function example:

```
?- kind([t1:mono(K1)], (var(t1)->var(t1)), o).
K1 = o
```

3   Supporting Other Language Features

The purpose of this section is to demonstrate that our Prolog specification for
polymorphic features is extensible for supporting other orthogonal features in
functional languages including general recursion (Sect. 3.1), pattern matching
over algebraic datatypes (Sect. 3.2), and recursion schemes over non-regular algebraic datatypes with user provided annotations (Sect. 3.3). The specification for
the pattern-matching and the recursion schemes in this section are extensions
that build upon the specification in Sect. 2.2.

Discussions on the details of the Prolog code is kept relatively brief, compared to the previous section, because our main purpose here is to demonstrate
that supporting these features does not significantly increase the size and the
complexity of our specification. Readers with further interest are encouraged to
experiment with our specifications available online (see Sect. 1, p. 2).

3.1   Recursive Let-Bindings

Adding recursive let-bindings is obvious. We simply add a monomorphic binding
for the let-bound variable (X) when inferring the type of the expression (E0)
defining the let-bound value as follows:

```
type(KC,C,letrec(X=E0,E1),T) --> type(KC,[X:mono(A)  |C],E0,A),
                                  type(KC,[X:poly(C,A)|C],E1,T).
```

We could also allow polymorphic recursion by type annotations on the let-
bound variable, like we will do for Mendler-style iteration over non-regular
datatypes in Sect. 3.3.

3.2   Pattern Matching for Algebraic Datatypes

In Fig. 3 (on p. 9), we specify pattern matching expressions without the scrutinee,
which is also known as pattern-matching lambdas. A pattern lambda is a function
that awaits an expression to be passed in as an argument to pattern match its

```
type(KC,C,Alts,A->T) --> type_alts(KC,C,Alts,A->T), [kind(KC,A->T,o)].

type_alts(KC,C,[Alt],            A->T) --> type_alt(KC,C,Alt,A->T).
type_alts(KC,C,[Alt,Alt2|Alts],A->T) --> type_alt(KC,C,Alt,A->T),
                                          type_alts(KC,C,[Alt2|Alts],A->T).

type_alt(KC,C,P->E,A->T) --> % assume single depth pattern (C x0 .. xn)
  { P =.. [Ctor|Xs], upper_atom(Ctor), % when P='Cons'(x,xs) then Xs=[x,xs]
    findall(var(X),member(X,Xs),Vs),   %     Vs = [var(x),var(xs)]
    foldl_ap(var(Ctor),Vs,PE),         %     PE=var('Cons')$var(x)$var(xs)
    findall(X:mono(Tx),member(X,Xs),C1,C) }, % extend C with bindings for Xs
  type(KC,C1,PE,A), type(KC,C1,E,T).

upper_atom(A) :- atom(A), atom_chars(A,[C|_]), char_type(C,upper).

% foldl_ap(E, [E1,...,En], E$E1$...$En).
foldl_ap(E, []      , E).
foldl_ap(E0,[E1|Es], E) :- foldl_ap(E0$E1, Es, E).
```

Fig. 3. A Prolog specification of non-nested pattern-matching lambdas (coverage checking not included).

```
kind(KC,mu(F), K)  :- kind(KC,F, K -> K).

type(KC,C,in(N,E), T) --> type(KC,C,E,T0),
                          { unfold_N_ap(1+N,T0,F,[mu(F)|Is]),
                            foldl_ap(mu(F),Is,T) }.

type(KC,C,mit(X,Alts),mu(F)->T) -->
  { is_list(Alts), gensym(r,R),
    KC1 = [R:mono(o)|KC], C1 = [X:poly(C,var(R)->T)|C] },
  type_alts(KC1,C1,Alts,F$var(R)->T).

type(KC,C,mit(X,Is-->T0,Alts),A->T) -->
  { is_list(Alts), gensym(r,R),
    foldl_ap(mu(F),Is,A), foldl_ap(var(R),Is,RIs),
    KC1 = [R:mono(K)|KC], C1 = [X:poly(C,RIs->T0)|C] },
  [kind(KC,F,K->K), kind(KC,A->T,o)], % delayed goals
  { foldl_ap(F,[var(R)|Is],FRIs) },
  type_alts(KC1,C1,Alts,FRIs->T).

% unfold_N_ap(N, E$E_1$...$E_N, E, [E_1,...,E_N]).
unfold_N_ap(0,E,     E,[]).
unfold_N_ap(N,E0$E1,E,Es) :- N>0, M is N-1,
                             unfold_N_ap(M,E0,E,Es0), append(Es0,[E1],Es).
```

Fig. 4. A Prolog specification for Mendler-style iteration on algebraic datatypes (including non-regular nested datatypes).

value. For example, let $\{p_1 \rightarrow e_1; \cdots ; p_n \rightarrow e_n\}$ be a pattern-matching lambda. Then, the application $\{p_1 \rightarrow e_1; \cdots ; p_n \rightarrow e_n\}\, e$ corresponds to a pattern matching expressions in Haskell of the form **case** e **of** $\{p_1 \rightarrow e_1; \cdots ; p_n \rightarrow e_n\}$.

We represent pattern-matching lambdas in Prolog as a list of clauses that match each pattern to a body, for instance, `['Nil'-->E1, 'Cons'(x,xs)-->E2]` where E1 and E2 are expressions of the bodies. For simplicity, we implement the most simple design of non-nested patterns. That is, a pattern is either an atom that represents a nullary data constructor, such as `'Nil'`, or a complex term with an n-ary function symbol that represents an n-ary data constructor and n variables as its arguments, such as `'Cons'(x,xs)`. Here, we are using the convention that names of type constructors and data constructors start with uppercase letters while names of term variables (including pattern variables) start with lowercase letters. We also add a delayed well-kindedness goal because pattern lambdas introduce function types (`A -> T`), just like ordinary lambda expressions.

3.3   Recursion Schemes for Non-Regular Algebraic Datatypes

Consider the following two recursive datatype declarations in Haskell:

$$\textbf{data } List\ a\ =\ N_L \mid C_L\ a\ (List\ a)$$
$$\textbf{data } Bush\ a\ =\ N_B \mid C_B\ a\ (Bush\ (Bush\ a))$$

List is a homogeneous list, which is either empty or an element tailed by a *List* that contains (zero or more) elements of *the same type as the prior element*. *Bush* is a list-like structure that is either empty or has an element tailed by a *Bush* that contains (zero or more) elements *but their type* (*Bush a*) *is different from the type of the prior element* (*a*).

Every recursive component of *List*, which is the tail of a list, has exactly the same type argument (*a*) as the *List* containing the tail. Because the types of recursive occurrences in *List* are always the same, or *regular*, and *List* is therefore categorized as a *regular datatype*. The recursive component of *Bush*, on the contrary, has a type argument (*Bush a*) different from the type argument (*a*) of its containing *Bush*. Due to this non-regularity of the types in its recursive occurrences, *Bush* is categorized as a *non-regular datatype*, which is also known as a *nested datatype* [8] because the types of recursive components typically become nested as the recursion goes deeper.

In order to define interesting and useful recursive functions over non-regular datatypes, one needs polymorphic recursion, whose type inference is known to be undecidable without the aid of user supplied type annotations. In Fig. 4 (on p9), we specify a subset of a functional language that supports a recursion scheme, which naturally generalizes from regular datatypes to non-regular datatypes. In particular, we specify the Mendler-style iteration [1,21] supported in the Nax language [2]. In Nax, all recursive constructs, both at the type level and at the term level, are defined using the primitives provided by the language, avoiding uncontrolled general recursion.

```
getKC0([ 'N':mono(o->o)             % Nat    = mu(var('N'))
       , 'L':mono(o->o->o)          % List A = mu(var('L')$A)
       , 'B':mono((o->o)->(o->o))   % Bush A = mu(var('B'))$A
       ]).


getC0(% Ctors of N
      [ 'Z':poly([] , N$R1)
      , 'S':poly([] , R1 -> N$R1)
      % Ctors of L
      , 'N':poly([] , L$A2$R2)
      , 'C':poly([] , A2-> R2-> L$A2$R2)
      % Ctors of B
      , 'BN':poly([] , B$R3$A3)
      , 'BC':poly([] , A3 -> R3$(R3$A3) -> B$R3$A3)
      % used in bsum example
      , 'plus':poly([], mu(N) -> mu(N) -> mu(N))
      ])
   :- N = var('N'), L = var('L'), B = var('B').

infer_len :- % length of List
  TM_len = mit(len,['N'        ->Zero,
                    'C'(x,xs)->Succ$(var(len)$var(xs))]),
  Zero = in(0,var('Z')),
  Succ = lam(x,in(0,var('S')$var(x))),
  getKC0(KCtx), getC0(Ctx),
  infer_type(KCtx,Ctx,TM_len,T), writeln(T).

%%%% ?- infer_len. % corresponds to "List a -> Nat"
%%%% mu(var(L)$_G1854)->mu(var(N))
%%%% true .

infer_bsum :- % sum of all elements in Bush of natural numbers
  TM_bsum = mit(bsum, [I]-->((I->mu(var('N')))->mu(var('N'))),
               [ 'BN'        -> lam(f,Zero)
               , 'BC'(x,xs) -> lam(f, % f : I -> Nat
                    var(plus) % f x + bsum xs (\ys -> bsum ys f)
                       $ (var(f)$var(x)) % calculate Nat value from x
                       $ (var(bsum) $ var(xs)   % recursive call on xs
                               $ lam(ys,var(bsum)$var(ys)$var(f)))) 
               ]),
  Zero = in(0,var('Z')),
  getKC0(KCtx), getC0(Ctx),
  infer_type(KCtx,Ctx,TM_bsum,T), writeln(T).

%%%% ?- infer_bsum. % corresponds to "Bush i -> (i -> Nat) -> Nat"
%%%% mu(var(B))$_G1452-> (_G1452->mu(var(N)))->mu(var(N))
%%%% true .
```

Fig. 5. Example queries of type inference: list length and bush sum.

The `mu(F)` appearing in the Prolog specification corresponds to a recursive type μF constructed by the fixpoint type operator μ applied to a base structure F, which is not recursive by itself. Here, we require that F is either a type constructor introduced by a (non-recursive) datatype declaration or a partial application of such a type constructor. We add a kinding rule for the fixpoint type operator by adding another rule of the `kind` predicate for `mu(F)`. We also add two accompanying rules for recursive values. The expression `in(N,E)` constructs a recursive value of type `mu(F)$I_0$...$I_N`. In case of regular datatypes, where `mu(F)` does not require additional type arguments (i.e., `mu(F):o`), N is 0. The Mendler-style iteration expressions define (terminating) recursive computation over recursive values. There are two rules for Mendler-style iteration – one for regular datatypes and the other for non-regular datatypes.

The Mendler-style iteration over regular datatypes (`mit(X,Alts)`) does not need any type annotation. The Mendler-style iteration over non-regular datatypes (`mit(X,Is-->T0,Alts)`) needs an annotation (`Is-->T0`) to guide the type inference because it is likely to rely on polymorphic recursion. We require that `Is` must be list of variables. For instance, `mit(X,[I1,I2,I3]-->T0,Alts)` has type `(mu(F)$I1$I2$I3)->T0` for some F. The specification for Mendler-style iteration relies on pattern-matching lambdas discussed in the previous subsection. Once we have properly set up the kinding context and typing context for the name of the recursive call (`X`), the rest amounts to inferring types for pattern-matching lambdas. Pointers to further details on Mendler-style recursion [1,3,33] and Nax [2] are available in the references section at the end of this article. Here, in Fig. 5, we provide type inference queries on some example programs using Mendler-style iteration.

A missing part from a typical functional language's type system, which we have not discussed in this paper, is the initial phase of populating the kinding context and typing context from the list of algebraic datatype declarations prior to type checking the expressions using them. With fully functioning basic building blocks for kind inference (`kind`) and type inference (`type`), inferring kinds of type constructor names and inferring types for their associated data constructors should be straightforward.

4   Future Work

We plan to continue our work on several additional features, including generalized algebraic datatypes (GADTs) and real term-indices in GADTs (as in Nax).

GADTs add the complexity of introducing local constraints within a pattern-matching clause, which should not escape the scope of the clause, unlike global unification constraints in HM. It would be interesting to see whether Prolog's built-in support for handling unification variables and symbols could help us express the concept of local constraints as elegantly as we expressed polymorphic instantiation in Sect. 2.

The kind structure needed for type constructor polymorphism is exactly the kinds supported in the higher-order polymorphic lambda calculus, known as System F_ω [17]. Type constructors in F_ω can have types as arguments. For example, the type constructor *List* for lists has kind $* \to *$, which means that it needs one type argument to be fully applied as a type (e.g. *List* Nat : $*$).

kind in System F_ω	$\kappa :: = * \mid \kappa \to \kappa$
kind in System F_i	$\kappa :: = * \mid \kappa \to \kappa \mid \{A\} \to \kappa$

To support terms, as well as types, to be supplied to type constructors as arguments, the kind structure needs to be extended. System F_i [4], which Nax is based on, extends the kind structure with $\{A\} \to \kappa$ to support term indices in types. This extension allows type constructors such as *Vec* : $* \to \{Nat\} \to *$ for vectors (a.k.a. length indexed lists). For instance, *Vec Bool* $\{8\}$ is a type of boolean vectors of length 8. There are two ramifications regarding type inference:

- the unification is modulo equivalence of terms: For instance, the type system should consider *Vec Bool* $\{n\}$ and *Vec Bool* $\{(\lambda x.x)\ n\}$ as equivalent types.
- Type inference/checking and kind inference/checking invoke each other: A typing rule has to invoke a kinding rule to support type constructor polymorphism (Sect. 2.2). In the extended kind structure, types can appear in kinds (A in $\{A\} \to \kappa$) and therefore kinding rules need to invoke typing rules.

Extending our specification with term indices would be an interesting future work that might involve resolving possible challenges from these two ramifications.

In addition, we are planning to develop specifications for more practical language constructs such as records with named fields and modules for organizing definitions in different namespaces. To support high degree of polymorphism with records and modules, we will also need to support *row polymorphism* [16] and *first-class polymorphism* (e.g., [27]).

5   Related Work

5.1   HM($\mathcal{X}$), CHR, and Typol

The idea of using logic programming (LP) to specify type systems is not new, for instance, Typol [12] and HM($\mathcal{X}$) [24].

Typol is a specification language for both static semantics (i.e. type systems) and dynamic semantics of programming languages, where type checkers and interpreters could be generated directly from Typol specifications by compiling the specification into Prolog code. Although Despeyroux [12] demonstrated that Typol can be used for type system based on HM (more specifically, the core of ML), it was mainly used for language specifications without parametric polymorphism — in the 80's, there were not as much practical programming languages supporting parametric polymorphism as in the 21st century.

In the late 90's, Odersky, Sulzmann, and Wehr [24] defined a general framework called HM($\mathcal{X}$) for specifying extensions of HM (e.g., records, type classes, intersection types) and Alves and Florido [5] implemented HM($\mathcal{X}$) using Constraint Handling Rules (CHR) in Prolog. Testing a type system extension in the HM($\mathcal{X}$) framework provides a certain level of confidence that the extension would work well with type polymorphism in HM. Testing an extension by extending our specification provides additional confidence that the extension would work well with type constructor polymorphism and kind polymorphism, as well as with type polymorphism.

CHR have been used for type inference in many other occasions. For instance, Csorba et al. [11] discuss *"Pros and Cons of using CHR for Type Inference"* of the Q programming language, which is a functional language well suited for complex calculations on large volume of data. Although Q was designed to be strongly typed, prior implementations dynamically checked those types during runtime execution. They implemented a static type inference for Q using CHR in Prolog. Interestingly, our work using Prolog for type inference shares a common *Con* (difficulties they had to overcome by workaround) in their work using CHR in Prolog for type inference. One of their difficulties was to "influence the firing order of rules with different heads", which corresponds to our need to process `kind` predicates after processing `type` predicates. Such *Cons* seem to be common in LP regardless of the use of CHR.

5.2   Delayed Goals and Control Flow in Logic Programming

The concept of delayed goals has been used in many different contexts in LP. An AILog textbook [26] introduces delaying goals as one of the useful abilities of a meta-interpreter. Several Prolog systems including SWI and SICStus provide built-in support for delaying a goal until certain conditions are met using the predicates such as `freeze` or `when`. In our specification, we could not simply use `freeze` or `when` because we pre-process the collected delayed goals (see `variablize` in Sect. 2.2). Recently, Schrijvers et al. [29] implemented delimited continuations for Prolog, which might be a useful abstraction for the delayed goals used in our work.

5.3   Other Logic Programming Systems

Some experimental Prolog implementations support interesting features such as nominal abstraction in αProlog [10] and a (restricted version of) higher-order unification in λProlog [23]. However, we have not found a relational specification of a polymorphic type systems using them. The αProlog developer attempted to implement the HM type inference for mini-ML in αProlog, but failed to produce a working version.[4] The Teyjus λProlog compiler version 2 includes a PCF [30] example, which is similar to HM but without polymorphic `let`-bindings. In both example implementations, they define the type inference predicate tailored for type inference only (unlike our relational specification that works for both type checking and inference) and the unification used in their type inference are manually crafted rather than relying on the native unification of the LP systems.

---

[4] See `miniml.apl` in the examples directory of the αProlog version 0.4 or 0.3.

Kanren[5] [14] is a declarative LP system embedded in a pure functional subset of Scheme. A relational implementation of HM is provided in the Kanren repository, which works for both type checking, type inference, and also for type inhabitance searching, as in our HM specification in Prolog. A simplified version called miniKanren [9] has been implemented in several dialects of Scheme [6] and an even further simplified kernel μKanren [18] is being implemented in growing number of host languages as an embedded Domain Specific Language (eDSL) for LP. By design, Kanren does not provide concrete syntax, therefore, it is not best suited for a specification language. However, Kanren has its benefits of being flexible, simple, and portable. If one is to build a tool based on LP concepts and wishes to support interfaces to one or more programming languages, μKanren may be a good choice to target as the backend.

Executable type system specifications in Prolog have been studied for supporting static types in Prolog itself (e.g., [28]). Recently, there has been research on type inference using LP with non-standard semantics (e.g., corecursive, coinductive) for object-oriented languages (e.g., featherweight Java) but functional languages were left for future work [6]. Johann et al. [19] have developed S-resolution, which is proven [15] to produce the same results when the depth-first-search style SLD-resolution used in Prolog is proven to be inductive. S-resolution can also answer some queries for which SLD-resolution fails to terminate. S-resolution might be useful for us to eliminate the need for delayed goals in our specification.

5.4   Descriptions of Type Inference Algorithms in ITPs

There are several formal descriptions of type inference algorithms using Interactive Theorem Provers (ITPs) such as Coq [13] and Isabelle/HOL [32]. The primary motivation in such work is to formally prove theoretical properties (e.g., soundness, principal typing) of type inference algorithms, which is different from our motivation of providing a human readable and machine executable specification for the type system to reduce the gap between theoretical specification and practical implementation. Some of those descriptions are not even executable because the unification is merely specified as a set of logical axioms. Formally describing certifiable type inference in ITPs is challenging (and therefore also challenging to extend or modify) for two reasons. First, fresh names should be monitored more explicitly and rigorously for the sake of formal proof. Second, algorithms may need to be massaged differently from their usual representations, in order to convince the termination checker of the ITP (e.g. [22]).

6   Conclusions

During this work, we searched for relational specifications of type systems that are executable in logic programming systems, only to find out that there are sur-

---

prisingly few (Sect. 5.3); we found a few for HM but were not able to find specifications for more sophisticated polymorphisms. Our work is a pioneering case study on this subject matter, demonstrating the possibility of relational specification for advanced polymorphic features, highlighting the benefits of relational specifications, and identifying limitations of the LP systems presently available.

There are novel features and designs scattered around in different theories/systems that could be useful for relational specifications of type systems, as discussed in Sect. 5 (e.g., nominal logic in LP, embedded DSLs for LP, abstractions for control flow in LP, alternative resolution semantics). We believe that there should be a tool that makes it easy to develop relational specifications of type systems. Such a tool can open a new era in language construction, analogous to the impact when parser generators such as Yacc were first introduced. But to realize such a tool for applications pedagogical examples, we need a combined effort of both functional and logic programing communities to seamlessly put together such novel ideas accomplished individually in different settings into the context of *"relational specifications of polymorphic type systems"*.

Acknowledgements. Thanks to Patricia Johann for helping us clarify the specification for Mendler-style iteration, Ekaterina Komendantskaya and Frantisek Farka for the discussions on S-Resolution, Peng Fu for pointers to Kanren, Chris Warburton for careful proofreading, and FLOPS'16 reviewers for their feedback.

References

1. Abel, A., Matthes, R., Uustalu, T.: Generalized iteration and coiteration for higher-order nested datatypes. In: FoSSaCS 2003 (2003)
2. Ahn, K.Y.: The Nax language. Ph.D. thesis, Department of Computer Science, Portland State University, November 2014
3. Ahn, K.Y., Sheard, T.: A hierarchy of Mendler-style recursion combinators. In: ICFP 2011. ACM (2011)
4. Ahn, K.Y., Sheard, T., Fiore, M., Pitts, A.M.: System Fi: a higher-order polymorphic lambda calculus with erasable term indices. In: TLCA 2013 (2013)
5. Alves, S., Florido, M.: Type inference using Constraint Handling Rules. In: WFLP 2001, vol. 64 of Electronic Notes in TCS, pp. 56–72. Elsevier (2002)
6. Ancona, D., Lagorio, G.: Coinductive type systems for object-oriented languages. In: Drossopoulou, S. (ed.) ECOOP 2009. LNCS, vol. 5653, pp. 2–26. Springer, Heidelberg (2009)
7. Barendregt, H.: Introduction to generalized type systems. J. Funct. Program. **1**(2), 125–154 (1991)
8. Bird, R., Meertens, L.: Nested datatypes. In: MPC: 4th International Conference on Mathematics of Program Construction (1998)
9. Byrd, W.E.: Relational programming in miniKanren: techniques, applications,and implementations. Ph.D. thesis, Indiana University (2009)
10. Cheney, J., Urban, C.: αProlog: A logic programming language with names, binding, and α-equivalence. In: Demoen, B., Lifschitz, V. (eds.) ICLP 2004. LNCS, vol. 3132, pp. 269–283. Springer, Heidelberg (2004)
11. Csorba, J., Zombori, Z., Szeredi, P.: Pros and cons of using CHR for type inference. In: CHR 2012, KU Leuven, Deptarment of CS, Tech-report CW 624 (2012)

12. Despeyroux, T.: Executable specification of static semantics. In: MacQueen, D.B., Plotkin, G., Kahn, G. (eds.) Semantics of Data Types 1984. LNCS, vol. 173, pp. 215–233. Springer, Heidelberg (1984)
13. Dubois, C.: Proving ML type soundness within Coq. In: Aagaard, M.D., Harrison, J. (eds.) TPHOLs 2000. LNCS, vol. 1869, pp. 126–144. Springer, Heidelberg (2000)
14. Friedman, D.P., Byrd, W.E., Kiselyov, O.: The Reasoned Schemer. MIT Press, Cambridge (2005). ISBN 978-0-262-56214-0
15. Fu, P., Komendantskaya, E.: A type theoretic approach to structural resolution. In: Pre-Proceedings of LOPSTR 2015 (2015)
16. Gaster, B.R., Jones, M.P.: A polymorphic type system for extensible records and variants. Technical report (1996)
17. J.-Y. Girard. Interprétation fonctionelle et élimination des coupures de l'arithmétique d'ordre supérieur. Ph.D. thesis, Université Paris VII (1972)
18. Hemann, J., Friedman, D.P.: μKanren: A minimal functional core for relational programming. In: Scheme 2013 (2013)
19. Johann, P., Komendantskaya, E., Komendantskiy, V.: Structural resolution for logic programming. In: Techincal Communications of ICLP (2015)
20. Jones, M.P.: Typing Haskell in Haskell. In: Haskell 1999, October 1999
21. Matthes, R.: Extensions of System F by Iteration and Primitive Recursion on Monotone Inductive Types. Ph.D. thesis, Ludwig-Maximilians University (1998)
22. McBride, C.: First-order unification by structural recursion. J. Func. Program. **13**, 1061–1075 (2003). ISSN 1469-7653
23. Mitchell, D.J., Nadathur, G.: System description: teyjus - a compiler and abstract machine based implementation of λprolog. In: Ganzinger, H. (ed.) CADE 1999. LNCS (LNAI), vol. 1632, pp. 287–291. Springer, Heidelberg (1999)
24. Odersky, M., Sulzmann, M., Wehr, M.: Type inference with constrained types. Theor. Pract. Object Syst. **5**(1), 35–55 (1999). ISSN 1074-3227
25. Pereira, F.C.N., Warren, D.H.D.: Definite clause grammars for language analysis. Artif. Intell. **13**, 231–278 (1980)
26. Poole, D., Mackworth, A.K.: Artificial Intelligence - Foundations of Computational Agents. Cambridge University Press, Cambridge (2010)
27. Russo, C.V., Vytiniotis, D.: Qml: explicit first-class polymorphism for ml. In: ML 2009, pp. 3–14. ACM, New York (2009)
28. Schrijvers, T., Costa, V.S., Wielemaker, J., Demoen, B.: Towards typed prolog. In: Garcia de la Banda, M., Pontelli, E. (eds.) ICLP 2008. LNCS, vol. 5366, pp. 693–697. Springer, Heidelberg (2008)
29. Schrijvers, T., Demoen, B., Desouter, B., Wielemaker, J.: Delimited continuations for prolog. In: Proceedings of ICLP 2013 TPLP (2013)
30. Scott, D.S.: A type-theoretic alternative to CUCH ISWIM OWHY. Manuscript (1969)
31. SWI-Prolog team. SWI-Prolog reference manual (section 4.2) (2005)
32. Urban, C., Nipkow, T.: Nominal verification of algorithm W. In: From Semantics to Computer Science, pp. 363–382. Cambridge University Press (2009)
33. Vene, V.: Categorical Programming with Inductive and Coinductive Types. Ph.D. thesis, Department of Computer Science, University of Tartu, August 2000
34. Yorgey, B.A., Weirich, S., Cretin, J., Peyton Jones, S., Vytiniotis, D., Magalhães, J.P.: Giving Haskell a promotion. In: TLDI 2012. ACM (2012)

Proof Relevant Corecursive Resolution

Peng Fu[1]([✉]), Ekaterina Komendantskaya[1], Tom Schrijvers[2],
and Andrew Pond[1]

[1] Computer Science, University of Dundee, Dundee, UK
pfu@dundee.ac.uk
[2] Department of Computer Science, KU Leuven, Leuven, Belgium

Abstract. Resolution lies at the foundation of both logic programming
and type class context reduction in functional languages. Terminating
derivations by resolution have well-defined inductive meaning, whereas
some non-terminating derivations can be understood coinductively. Cycle
detection is a popular method to capture a small subset of such derivations. We show that in fact cycle detection is a restricted form of coinductive proof, in which the atomic formula forming the cycle plays the
rôle of coinductive hypothesis.

This paper introduces a heuristic method for obtaining richer coinductive hypotheses in the form of Horn formulas. Our approach subsumes cycle detection and gives coinductive meaning to a larger class
of derivations. For this purpose we extend resolution with Horn formula
resolvents and corecursive evidence generation. We illustrate our method
on non-terminating type class resolution problems.

Keywords: Horn clause logic · Resolution · Corecursion · Haskell type
class inference · Coinductive proofs

1 Introduction

Horn clause logic is a fragment of first-order logic known for its simple syntax,
well-defined models, and efficient algorithms for automated proof search. It is
used in a variety of applications, from program verification [3] to type inference
in object-oriented programming languages [1]. Similar syntax and proof methods
underlie type class inference in functional programming languages [17,24]. For
example, the following declaration specifies equality class instances for pairs and
integers in Haskell:

> **instance** *Eq Int* **where** ...
> **instance** (*Eq x, Eq y*) $\Rightarrow$ *Eq (x, y)* **where** ...

P. Fu—This author is supported by EPSRC grant EP/K031864/1.

A. Pond—This author is supported by Carnegie Trust Scotland.

O. Kiselyov and A. King (Eds.): FLOPS 2016, LNCS 9613, pp. 126–143, 2016.
DOI: 10.1007/978-3-319-29604-3_9

It corresponds to a Horn clause program Φ_{Pair} with two clauses κ_{Int} and κ_{Pair}:

$\kappa_{Int} : Eq\ Int$
$\kappa_{Pair} : (Eq\ x, Eq\ y) \Rightarrow Eq\ (x, y)$

Horn clause logic uses SLD-resolution as an inference engine. If a derivation for a given formula A and a Horn clause program Φ terminates successfully with substitution θ, then θA is logically entailed by Φ, or $\Phi \vdash \theta A$. The search for a suitable θ reflects the problem-solving nature of SLD-resolution. When the unification algorithm underlying SLD-resolution is restricted to matching, resolution can be viewed as theorem proving: the successful terminating derivations for A using Φ will guarantee $\Phi \vdash A$. For example, $Eq\ (Int, Int) \rightsquigarrow Eq\ Int, Eq\ Int \rightsquigarrow Eq\ Int \rightsquigarrow \emptyset$. Therefore, we have: $\Phi_{Pair} \vdash Eq\ (Int, Int)$. For the purposes of this paper, we always assume resolution by term-matching.

To emphasize the proof-theoretic meaning of resolution, we will record proof evidence alongside the derivation steps. For instance, $Eq\ (Int, Int)$ is proven by applying the clauses κ_{Pair} and κ_{Int}. We denote this by $\Phi_{Pair} \vdash Eq\ (Int, Int) \Downarrow \kappa_{Pair}\ \kappa_{Int}\ \kappa_{Int}$.

Horn clause logic can have inductive and coinductive interpretation, via the least and greatest fixed points of the *consequence operator* F_Φ. Given a Horn clause program Φ, and a set S containing (ground) formulas formed from the signature of Φ, $F_\Phi(S) = \{\sigma A \mid \sigma B_1, \ldots, \sigma B_n \in S \text{ and } B_1, \ldots B_n \Rightarrow A \in \Phi\}$ [18]. Through the Knaster-Tarski construction, the least fixed point of this operator gives the set of all finite ground formulas *inductively entailed* by Φ. Extending S to include infinite terms, the greatest fixed point of F_Φ defines the set of all finite and infinite ground formulas *coinductively entailed* by Φ.

Inductively, SLD-resolution is sound: if $\Phi \vdash A$, then A is inductively entailed by Φ. It is more difficult to characterise coinductive entailment computationally; several approaches exist [16,18,22]. So far the most popular solution is to use cycle detection [22]: given a Horn clause program Φ, if a cycle is found in a derivation for a formula A, then A is coinductively entailed by Φ.

Consider, as an example, the following Horn clause program Φ_{AB}:

$\kappa_A : B\ x \Rightarrow A\ x$
$\kappa_B : A\ x \Rightarrow B\ x$

It gives rise to an infinite derivation $A\ x \rightsquigarrow B\ x \rightsquigarrow A\ x \rightsquigarrow \ldots$. By noticing the cycle, we can conclude that (an instance) of $A\ x$ is coinductively entailed by Φ_{AB}. We can *construct* a proof evidence that reflects the circular nature of this derivation: $\alpha = \kappa_A\ (\kappa_B\ \alpha)$. This being a recursive equation expecting the greatest fixed point solution, we can represent it with the greatest fix point ν operator, $\nu\alpha.\kappa_A\ (\kappa_B\ \alpha)$. Now we have $\Phi_{AB} \vdash A\ x \Downarrow \nu\alpha.\kappa_A\ (\kappa_B\ \alpha)$. From now on, we call the evidence containing ν-term a *corecursive evidence*.

According to Gibbons and Hutton [7] and inspired by Moss and Danner [20], a corecursive program is defined to be a function whose range is a type defined recursively as the greatest solution of some equation (i.e. whose range is a coinductive type). We can informally understand the Horn clause Φ_{AB} as the following Haskell data type declarations:

data $B\ x = K_B\ (A\ x)$
data $A\ x = K_A\ (B\ x)$

So the corecursive evidence $\nu\alpha.\kappa_A\ (\kappa_B\ \alpha)$ for $A\ x$ corresponds to the corecursive program $(d :: A\ x) = K_A\ (K_B\ d)$. In our case, the corecursive evidence d is that function, and its range type $A\ x$ can be seen as a coinductive type.

Corecursion also arises in type class inference. Consider the following mutually recursive definitions of lists of even and odd length in Haskell:

data $OddList\ a\ = OCons\ a\ (EvenList\ a)$
data $EvenList\ a = Nil\ |\ ECons\ a\ (OddList\ a)$

They give rise to Eq type class instance declarations that can be expressed using the following Horn clause program $\Phi_{EvenOdd}$:

$\kappa_{Odd} : (Eq\ a, Eq\ (EvenList\ a)) \Rightarrow Eq\ (OddList\ a)$
$\kappa_{Even} : (Eq\ a, Eq\ (OddList\ a)) \Rightarrow Eq\ (EvenList\ a)$

When resolving the type class constraint $Eq\ (OddList\ Int)$, Haskell's standard type class resolution diverges. The state-of-the-art is to use cycle detection [17] to terminate otherwise infinite derivations. Resolution for $Eq\ (OddList\ Int)$ exhibits a cycle on the atomic formula $Eq\ (OddList\ Int)$, thus the derivation can be terminated, with corecursive evidence $\nu\alpha.\kappa_{Odd}\ \kappa_{Int}\ (\kappa_{Even}\ \kappa_{Int}\ \alpha)$.

The method of cycle detection is rather limited: there are many Horn clause programs that have coinductive meaning, but do not give rise to detectable cycles. For example, consider the program Φ_Q:

$\kappa_S : (Q\ (S\ (G\ x)), Q\ x) \Rightarrow Q\ (S\ x)$
$\kappa_G : Q\ x \Rightarrow Q\ (G\ x)$
$\kappa_Z : Q\ Z$

It gives rise to the following derivation without cycling:
$Q\ (S\ Z) \rightsquigarrow Q\ Z, Q\ (S\ (G\ Z)) \rightsquigarrow Q\ Z, Q\ (G\ Z), Q\ (S\ (G\ (G\ Z))) \rightsquigarrow \dots$ When such derivations arise, we cannot terminate the derivation by cycle detection.

Let us look at a similar situation for type classes. Consider a datatype-generic representation of perfect trees: a nested datatype [2], with fixpoint Mu of the higher-order functor $HPTree$ [12].

data $Mu\ h\ a = In\ \{\ out :: h\ (Mu\ h)\ a\}$
data $HPTree\ f\ a = HPLeaf\ a\ |\ HPNode\ (f\ (a, a))$

These two datatypes give rise to the following Eq type class instances.

instance $Eq\ (h\ (Mu\ h)\ a) \Rightarrow Eq\ (Mu\ h\ a)$ **where**
$\quad In\ x \equiv In\ y = x \equiv y$
instance $(Eq\ a, Eq\ (f\ (a, a))) \Rightarrow Eq\ (HPTree\ f\ a)$ **where**
$\quad HPLeaf\ x\ \equiv HPLeaf\ y\ = x \equiv y$

$$HPNode \; xs \equiv HPNode \; ys = xs \equiv ys$$
$$\_ \qquad\qquad \equiv \_ \qquad\quad = False$$

The corresponding Horn clause program Φ_{HPTree} consists of Φ_{Pair} and the following two clauses :

$$\kappa_{Mu} : Eq \; (h \; (Mu \; h) \; a) \Rightarrow Eq \; (Mu \; h \; a)$$
$$\kappa_{HPTree} : (Eq \; a, Eq \; (f \; (a, a))) \Rightarrow Eq \; (HPTree \; f \; a)$$

The type class resolution for $Eq \; (Mu \; HPTree \; Int)$ cannot be terminated by cycle detection. Instead we get a context reduction overflow error in the Glasgow Haskell Compiler, even if we just compare two finite data structures of the type $Mu \; HPTree \; Int$.

To find a solution to the above problems, let us view infinite resolution from the perspective of coinductive proof in the Calculus of Coinductive Constructions [4,8]. There, in order to prove a proposition F from the assumptions $F_1, .., F_n$, the proof may involve not only natural deduction and lemmas, but also F, provided the use of F is *guarded*. We could say that the existing cycle detection methods treat the atomic formula forming a cycle as a *coinductive hypothesis*. We can equivalently describe the above-explained derivation for Φ_{AB} in the following terms: when a cycle with a formula $A \; x$ is found in the derivation, Φ_{AB} gets extended with a coinductive hypothesis $\alpha : A \; x$. So to prove $A \; x$ coinductively, we would need to apply the clause κ_A first, and then clause κ_B, finally apply the coinductive hypothesis. The resulting proof witness is $\nu\alpha. \; \kappa_A \; (\kappa_B \; \alpha)$.

The next logical step we can make is to use the above formalism to extend the syntax of the coinductive hypotheses. While cycle detection only uses atomic formulas as coinductive hypotheses, we can try to generalise the syntax of coinductive hypotheses to full Horn formulas.

For example, for program Φ_Q, we could prove a lemma $e : Q \; x \Rightarrow Q \; (S \; x)$ coinductively, which would allow us to form finite derivation for $Q \; (S \; Z)$, which is described by $(e \; \kappa_Z)$. The proof of $e : Q \; x \Rightarrow Q \; (S \; x)$ is of a coinductive nature: if we first assume $\alpha : Q \; x \Rightarrow Q \; (S \; x)$ and $\alpha_1 : Q \; C$, then all we need to show is $Q \; (S \; C)$.[1] To show $Q \; (S \; C)$, we apply κ_S, which gives us $Q \; C$, $Q \; (S \; (G \; C))$. We first discharge $Q \; C$ with α_1 and then apply the coinductive hypothesis α which yields $Q \; (G \; C)$, and can be proved with κ_G and α_1. So we have obtained a coinductive proof for e, which is $\nu\alpha.\lambda\alpha_1.\kappa_S \; (\alpha \; (\kappa_G \; \alpha_1)) \; \alpha_1$. We can apply similar reasoning to show that $\Phi_{HPTree} \vdash Eq \; (Mu \; HPTree \; Int) \; \Downarrow$ $(\nu\alpha.\lambda\alpha_1.\kappa_{Mu} \; (\kappa_{HPTree} \; \alpha_1 \; (\alpha \; (\kappa_{Pair} \; \alpha_1 \; \alpha_1)))) \; \kappa_{Int}$ using the coinductively proved lemma $Eq \; x \Rightarrow Eq \; (Mu \; HPTree \; x)$.[2]

To formalise the above intuitions, we need to solve several technical problems.

1. How to generate suitable lemmas? We propose to observe a more general notion of a loop invariant than a cycle in the non-terminating resolution.

---

[1] Note that here C is an eigenvariable.

[2] The proof term can be type-checked with polymorphic recursion.

In Sect. 3 we devise a heuristic method to identify potential loops in the resolution tree and extract *candidate lemmas* in Horn clause form.

In general, it is very challenging to develop a practical method for generating candidate lemmas based on loop analysis, since the admissibility of a loop in reduction is a semi-decidable problem [25].

2. How to enrich resolution to allow coinductive proofs for Horn formulas? and how to formalise the corecursive proof evidence construction? Coinductive proofs involve not only applying the axioms, but also modus ponens and generalization. Therefore, the resolution mechanism will have to be extended in order to support such automation.

In Sect. 4, we introduce proof relevant *corecursive resolution* – a calculus that extends the standard resolution rule with two further rules: one allows us to resolve Horn formula queries, and the other to construct corecursive proof evidence for non-terminating resolution.

3. How to give an operational semantics to the evidence produced by corecursive resolution of Sect. 4? In particular, we need to show the correspondence between corecursive evidence and resolution seen as infinite reduction. In Sect. 5, we prove that for every non-terminating resolution resulting from a *simple loop*, a coinductively provable candidate lemma can be obtained and its evidence is *observationally equivalent* to the non-terminating resolution process.

In type class inference, the proof evidence has computational meaning, i.e. the evidence will be run as a program. So the corecursive evidence should be able to recover the original infinite resolution trace.

In Sects. 6 and 7 we survey the related work, explain the limitations of our method and conclude the paper. We have implemented our method of candidate lemma generation based on loop analysis and corecursive resolution, and incorporated it in the type class inference process of a simple functional language. Additional examples and implementation information are provided in the extended version.

2   Preliminaries: Resolution with Evidence

This section provides a standard formalisation of resolution with evidence together with two derived forms: a *small-step* variant of resolution and a reification of resolution in a resolution tree.

We consider the following syntax.

Definition 1 (Basic Syntax).

Term	t	$::=$	$x \mid K \mid t\,t'$
Atomic Formula	A, B, C, D	$::=$	$P\,t_1 \ldots t_n$
Horn Formula	H	$::=$	$B_1, ..., B_n \Rightarrow A$
Proof/Evidence	e	$::=$	$\kappa \mid e\,e'$
Axiom Environment	Φ	$::=$	$\cdot \mid \Phi, (\kappa : H)$

We consider first-order applicative terms, where K stands for some constant symbol. Atomic formulas are predicates on terms, and Horn formulas are defined as usual. We assume that all variables x in Horn formulas are implicitly universally quantified. There are no *existential variables* in the Horn formulas, i.e., $\bigcup_i \mathrm{FV}(B_i) \subseteq \mathrm{FV}(A)$ for $B_1, \ldots, B_n \Rightarrow A$. The axiom environment Φ is a set of Horn formulas labelled with distinct evidence constants κ. Evidence terms e are made of evidence constants κ and their applications. Finally, we often use $\underline{A}$ to abbreviate $A_1, \ldots, A_n$ when the number n is unimportant.

The above syntax can be used to model the Haskell type class setting as follows. Terms denote Haskell types like Int or (x, y), and atomic formulas denote Haskell type class constraints on types like $Eq\,(Int, Int)$. Horn formulas correspond to the type-level information of type class instances.

Our evidence e models type class dictionaries, following Wadler and Blott's dictionary-passing elaboration of type classes [24]. In particular the constants κ refer to dictionaries that capture the term-level information of type class instances, i.e., the implementations of the type class methods. Evidence application $(e\,e')$ accounts for dictionaries that are parametrised by other dictionaries. Horn formulas in turn represent type class instance declarations. The axiom environment Φ corresponds to Haskell's global environment of type class instances. Note that the treatment of type class instance declaration and their corresponding evidence construction here are based on our own understanding of many related works ([14,15,23]), which are also discussed in Sect. 6.

In order to define resolution together with evidence generation, we use resolution judgement $\Phi \vdash A \Downarrow e$ to state that the atomic formula A is entailed by the axioms Φ, and that the proof term e witnesses this entailment. It is defined by means of the following inference rule.

Definition 2 (Resolution). $\boxed{\Phi \vdash A \Downarrow e}$

$$\frac{\Phi \vdash \sigma B_1 \Downarrow e_1 \quad \cdots \quad \Phi \vdash \sigma B_n \Downarrow e_n}{\Phi \vdash \sigma A \Downarrow \kappa\, e_1 \cdots e_n} \quad \text{if } (\kappa : B_1, \ldots, B_n \Rightarrow A) \in \Phi$$

Using this definition we can show $\Phi_{Pair} \vdash Eq\,(Int, Int) \Downarrow \kappa_{Pair}\, \kappa_{Int}\, \kappa_{Int}$.

In case resolution is diverging, it is often more convenient to consider a *small-step* resolution judgement (in analogy to the small step operational semantics) that performs one resolution step at a time and allows us to observe the intermediate states.

The basic idea is to rewrite the initial query A step by step into its evidence e. This involves *mixed terms* on the way that consist partly of evidence, and partly of formulas that are not yet resolved.

Definition 3 (Mixed Terms).

Mixed term	q	$::=$	$A \mid \kappa \mid q\,q'$
Mixed term context	$\mathcal{C}$	$::=$	$\bullet \mid \mathcal{C}\,q \mid q\,\mathcal{C}$

At the same time we have defined mixed term contexts $\mathcal{C}$ as mixed terms with a hole $\bullet$, where $\mathcal{C}[q]$ substitutes the hole with q in the usual way.

Definition 4 (Small-Step Resolution). $\boxed{\Phi \vdash q \to q'}$

$$\frac{}{\Phi \vdash \mathcal{C}[\sigma A] \to \mathcal{C}[\kappa\ \sigma \underline{B}]} \quad if\ (\kappa : \underline{B} \Rightarrow A) \in \Phi$$

For instance, we resolve $Eq\ (Int, Int)$ in three small steps: $\Phi_{Pair} \vdash Eq\ (Int, Int) \to \kappa_{Pair}\ (Eq\ Int)\ (Eq\ Int)$, $\Phi_{Pair} \vdash \kappa_{Pair}\ (Eq\ Int)\ (Eq\ Int) \to \kappa_{Pair}\ \kappa_{Int}\ (Eq\ Int)$ and $\Phi_{Pair} \vdash \kappa_{Pair}\ \kappa_{Int}\ (Eq\ Int) \to \kappa_{Pair}\ \kappa_{Int}\ \kappa_{Int}$. We write $\Phi \vdash q \to^* q'$ to denote the transitive closure of small-step resolution.

The following theorem formalizes the intuition that resolution and small-step resolution coincide.

Theorem 1. $\Phi \vdash A \Downarrow e$ iff $\Phi \vdash A \to^* e$.

The proof tree for a judgement $\Phi \vdash A \Downarrow e$ is called a *resolution tree*. It conveniently records the history of resolution and, for instance, it is easy to observe the ancestors of a node. This last feature is useful for our heuristic loop invariant analysis in Sect. 3.

Our formalisation of trees in general is as follows: We use w, v to denote positions $\langle k_1, k_2, ..., k_n \rangle$ in a tree, where $k_i \geqslant 1$ for $1 \leqslant i \leqslant n$. Let ϵ denote the empty position or *root*. We also define $\langle k_1, k_2, ..., k_n \rangle \cdot i = \langle k_1, k_2, ..., k_n, i \rangle$ and $\langle k_1, k_2, ..., k_n \rangle + \langle l_1, ..., l_m \rangle = \langle k_1, k_2, ..., k_n, l_1, ..., l_m \rangle$. We write $w > v$ if there exists a non-empty v' such that $w = v + v'$. For a tree T, $T(w)$ refers to the node at position w, and $T(w, i)$ refers to the edge between $T(w)$ and $T(w \cdot i)$. We use $\square$ as a special proposition to denote success.

Resolution trees are defined as follows, note that they are a special case of *rewriting trees* [13,16]:

Definition 5 (Resolution Tree). *The resolution tree for atomic formula A is a tree T satisfying:*

- $T(\epsilon) = A$.
- $T(w \cdot i) = \sigma B_i$ and $T(w, i) = \kappa^i$ with $i \in \{1, ..., n\}$ if $T(w) = \sigma D$ and $(\kappa : B_1, ..., B_n \Rightarrow D) \in \Phi$. When $n = 0$, we write $T(w \cdot i) = \square$ and $T(w, i) = \kappa$ for any $i > 0$.

In general, the resolution tree can be infinite, this means that resolution is non-terminating, which we denote as $\Phi \vdash A \Uparrow$. Figure 1 shows a finite fragment of the infinite resolution tree for $\Phi_{HPTree} \vdash Eq\ (Mu\ HPTree\ Int) \cdot \Uparrow$.

We note that Definitions 2 and 4 describe a special case of SLD-resolution in which unification taking place in derivations is restricted to term-matching. This restriction is motivated by two considerations. The first one comes directly from the application area of our results: type class resolution uses exactly this restricted version of SLD-resolution. The second reason is of more general nature.

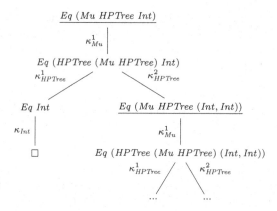

Fig. 1. The infinite resolution tree for $\Phi_{HPTree} \vdash Eq \ (Mu \ HPTree \ Int) \Uparrow$

As discussed in detail in [6,16], SLD-derivations restricted to term-matching reflect the *theorem proving* content of a proof by SLD-resolution. That is, if A can be derived from Φ by SLD-resolution with term-matching only, then A is inductvely entailed by Φ. If, on the other hand, A is derived from Φ by SLD-resolution with unification and computes a substitution σ, then σA is inductively entailed by Φ. In this sense, SLD-resolution with unification additionally has a *problem-solving* aspect. In developing proof-theoretic approach to resolution here, we thus focus on resolution by term-matching.

The resolution rule of Definition 2 resembles the definition of the consequence operator [18] used to define declarative semantics of Horn clause Logic. In fact, the forward and backward closure of the rule of Definition 2 can be directly used to construct the usual least and greatest Herbrand models for Horn clause logic, as shown in [16]. There, it was also shown that SLD-resolution by term-matching is sound but incomplete relative to the least Herbrand models.

3   Candidate Lemma Generation

This section explains how we generate candidate lemma from a potentially infinite resolution tree. Based on Paterson's condition we obtain a finite pruned approximation (Definition 8) of this resolution tree. Anti-unification on this approximation yields an abstract atomic formula and the corresponding abstract approximated resolution tree. It is from this abstract tree that we read off the candidate lemma (Definition 11).

We use $\Sigma(A)$ and $\mathrm{FVar}(A)$ to denote the multi-sets of respectively function symbols and variables in A.

Definition 6 (Paterson's Condition). *For* $(\kappa : \underline{B} \Rightarrow A) \in \Phi$, *we say* κ *satisfies Paterson's condition if* $(\Sigma(B_i) \cup \mathrm{FVar}(B_i)) \subset (\Sigma(A) \cup \mathrm{FVar}(A))$ *for each* B_i.

Paterson's condition is used in Glasgow Haskell Compiler to enforce termination of context reduction [23]. In this paper, we use it as a practical criterion to detect problematic instance declarations. Any declarations that do not satisfy the condition could potentially introduce diverging behavior in the resolution tree.

If $\kappa : A_1, ..., A_n \Rightarrow B$, then we have $\kappa^i : A_i \Rightarrow B$ for projection on index i.

Definition 7 (Critical Triple). *Let $v = (w \cdot i) + v'$ for some v'. A critical triple in T is a triple $\langle \kappa^i, T(w), T(v) \rangle$ such that $T(v, i) = T(w, i) = \kappa^i$, and κ^i does not satisfy Paterson's condition.*

We will omit κ^i from the triple and write $\langle T(w), T(v) \rangle$ when it is not important. Intuitively, it means the nodes $T(w)$ and $T(v)$ are using the same problematic projection κ^i, which could give rise to infinite resolution.

The absence of a critical triple in a resolution tree means that it has to be finite [23], while the presence of a critical triple only means that the tree is *possibly* infinite. In general the infiniteness of a resolution tree is undecidable and the critical triples provide a convenient over-approximation.

Definition 8 (Closed Subtree). *A closed subtree T is a subtree of a resolution tree such that for all leaves $T(v) \neq \square$, the root $T(\epsilon)$ and $T(v)$ form a critical triple.*

The critical triple in Fig. 1 is formed by the underlined nodes. The closed subtree in that figure is the subtree without the infinite branch below node *Eq (Mu HPTree (Int, Int))*. A closed subtree can intuitively be understood as a finite approximation of an infinite resolution tree. We use it as the basis for generating candidate lemma by means of anti-unification [21].

Definition 9 (Anti-Unifier). *We define the least general anti-unifier of atomic formulas A and B (denoted by $A \sqcup B$) and the least general anti-unifier of the terms t and t' (denoted by $t \sqcup t'$) as:*

- $P\ t_1\ ..., t_n\ \sqcup P\ t'_1\ ..., t'_n = P\ (t_1 \sqcup t'_1)\ ...\ (t_n \sqcup t'_n)$
- $K\ t_1\ ...\ t_n \sqcup K\ t'_1\ ...\ t'_n = K\ (t_1 \sqcup t'_1)\ ...\ (t_n \sqcup t'_n)$
- *Otherwise, $A \sqcup B = \phi(A, B), t \sqcup t' = \phi(t, t')$, where ϕ is an injective function from a pair of terms (atomic formulas) to a set of fresh variables.*

Anti-unification allows us to extract the common pattern from different ground atomic formulas.

Definition 10 (Abstract Representation). *Let $\langle T(\epsilon), T(v_1) \rangle, ..., \langle T(\epsilon), T(v_n) \rangle$ be all the critical triples in a closed subtree T. Let $C = T(\epsilon) \sqcup T(v_1) \sqcup ... \sqcup T(v_n)$, then the abstract representation T' of the closed subtree T is a tree such that:*

- $T'(\epsilon) = C$

- $T'(w \cdot i) = \sigma B_i$ and $T'(w, i) = \kappa^i$ with $i \in \{1, ..., n\}$ if $T'(w) = \sigma D$ and $(\kappa : B_1, ..., B_n \Rightarrow D) \in \Phi$. When $n = 0$, we write $T'(w \cdot i) = \square$ and $T'(w, i) = \kappa$ for any $i > 0$.
- $T'(w)$ is undefined if $w > v_i$ for some $1 \leqslant i \leqslant n$.

The abstract representation unfolds the anti-unifier of all the critical triples. Thus the abstract representation can always be embedded into the original closed subtree. It is an abstract form of the closed subtree, and we can extract the candidate lemma from the abstract representation.

Definition 11 (Candidate Lemma). *Let T be an abstract representation of a closed subtree, then the candidate lemma induced by this abstract representation is $T(v_1), ..., T(v_n) \Rightarrow T(\epsilon)$, where the $T(v_i)$ are all the leaves for which $T(v_i) \Rightarrow T(\epsilon)$ satisfies Paterson's condition.*

Figure 2 shows the abstract representation of the closed subtree of Fig. 1. We read off the candidate lemma as $Eq\ x \Rightarrow Eq\ (Mu\ HPTree\ x)$.

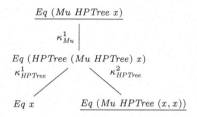

Fig. 2. The abstract representation of the closed subtree of Fig. 1

The candidate lemma plays a double role. Firstly, it allows us to construct a finite resolution tree. For example, we know that $Eq\ (Mu\ HPTree\ Int)$ gives rise to infinite tree with the axiom environment Φ_{HPTree}. However, a finite tree can be constructed with $Eq\ x \Rightarrow Eq\ (Mu\ HPTree\ x)$, since it reduces $Eq\ (Mu\ HPTree\ Int)$ to $Eq\ Int$, which succeeds trivially with κ_{Int}. Next we show how to prove the candidate lemma coinductively, and such proofs will encapsulate the infinite aspect of the resolution tree. Since an infinite resolution tree gives rise to infinite evidence, the finite proof of the lemma has to be coinductive. We discuss such evidence construction in detail in Sects. 4 and 5.

4   Corecursive Resolution

In this section, we extend the definition of resolution from Sect. 2 by introducing two additional rules: one to handle coinductive proofs, and another – to allow Horn formula goals, rather than atomic goals, in the derivations. We call the resulting calculus *corecursive resolution*.

Definition 12 (Extended Syntax).

$$
\begin{array}{llll}
Proof/Evidence & e & ::= & \kappa \mid e\ e' \mid \alpha \mid \lambda\alpha.e \mid \nu\alpha.e \\
Axiom\ Environment & \varPhi & ::= & \cdot \mid \varPhi, (e : H)
\end{array}
$$

To support coinductive proofs, we extend the syntax of evidence with functions $\lambda\alpha.e$, variables α and fixed point $\nu\alpha.e$ (which models the recursive equation $\alpha = e$ expecting the greatest solution). Also we allow the Horn clauses H in the axiom environment $\varPhi$ to be supported by any form of evidence e (and not necessarily by constants κ).

Definition 13 (Corecursive Resolution). *The following judgement for corecursive resolution extends the resolution in Definition 2.*

$$
\frac{\varPhi \vdash \sigma B_1 \Downarrow e_1 \quad \cdots \quad \varPhi \vdash \sigma B_n \Downarrow e_n}{\varPhi \vdash \sigma A \Downarrow e\ e_1 \cdots e_n} \quad if\ (e : B_1, ..., B_m \Rightarrow A) \in \varPhi
$$

$$
\frac{\varPhi, (\alpha : \underline{A} \Rightarrow B) \vdash \underline{A} \Rightarrow B \Downarrow e \quad \mathrm{HNF}(e)}{\varPhi \vdash \underline{A} \Rightarrow B \Downarrow \nu\alpha.e} \ (\mathrm{Mu}) \qquad \frac{\varPhi, (\underline{\alpha} : \underline{A}) \vdash B \Downarrow e}{\varPhi \vdash \underline{A} \Rightarrow B \Downarrow \lambda\underline{\alpha}.e} \ (\mathrm{Lam})
$$

Note that $\mathrm{HNF}(e)$ means e has to be in *head normal form* $\lambda\underline{\alpha}.\kappa\ \underline{e}$. This requirement is essential to ensure the corecursive evidence satisfies the *guardedness* condition.[3] The Lam rule implicitly assumes the treatment of *eigenvariables*, i.e. we instantiate all the free variables in $\underline{A} \Rightarrow B$ with fresh term constants.

We implicitly assume that axiom environments are well-formed.

Definition 14 (Well-Formedness of Environment).

$$
\frac{}{\cdot \vdash \mathsf{wf}} \qquad \frac{\varPhi \vdash \mathsf{wf}}{\varPhi, \alpha : H \vdash \mathsf{wf}} \qquad \frac{\varPhi \vdash \mathsf{wf}}{\varPhi, \kappa : H \vdash \mathsf{wf}} \qquad \frac{\varPhi \vdash H \Downarrow e}{\varPhi, e : H \vdash \mathsf{wf}}
$$

As an example, let us consider resolving the candidate lemma $Eq\ x \Rightarrow Eq\ (My\ HPTree\ x)$ against the axiom environment $\varPhi_{HPTree}$. This yields the following derivation, where $\varPhi_1 = \varPhi_{HPTree}, (\alpha : Eq\ x \Rightarrow Eq\ (Mu\ HPTree\ x))$ and $\varPhi_2 = \varPhi_1, (\alpha_1 : Eq\ C)$:

$$
\cfrac{
\cfrac{
\cfrac{
\cfrac{\varPhi_2 \vdash Eq\ C \Downarrow \alpha_1 \quad \varPhi_2 \vdash Eq\ C \Downarrow \alpha_1}{\varPhi_2 \vdash Eq\ (C, C) \Downarrow (\kappa_{Pair}\ \alpha_1\ \alpha_1)}
}{\varPhi_2 \vdash Eq\ C \Downarrow \alpha_1 \quad \varPhi_2 \vdash Eq\ (HPTree\ (C, C)) \Downarrow \alpha\ (\kappa_{Pair}\ \alpha_1\ \alpha_1)}
}{
\cfrac{\varPhi_2 \vdash Eq\ (HPTree\ (Mu\ HPTree\ C)) \Downarrow \kappa_{HPTree}\ \alpha_1\ (\alpha\ (\kappa_{Pair}\ \alpha_1\ \alpha_1))}{
\cfrac{(\varPhi_2 = \varPhi_1, \alpha_1 : Eq\ C) \vdash Eq\ (Mu\ HPTree\ C) \Downarrow \kappa_{Mu}\ (\kappa_{HPTree}\ \alpha_1\ (\alpha\ (\kappa_{Pair}\ \alpha_1\ \alpha_1)))}{\varPhi_1 \vdash Eq\ x \Rightarrow Eq\ (Mu\ HPTree\ x) \Downarrow \lambda\alpha_1.\kappa_{Mu}\ (\kappa_{HPTree}\ \alpha_1\ (\alpha\ (\kappa_{Pair}\ \alpha_1\ \alpha_1)))}
}
}
}{\varPhi_{HPTree} \vdash Eq\ x \Rightarrow Eq\ (Mu\ HPTree\ x) \Downarrow \nu\alpha.\lambda\alpha_1.\kappa_{Mu}\ (\kappa_{HPTree}\ \alpha_1\ (\alpha\ (\kappa_{Pair}\ \alpha_1\ \alpha_1)))}
$$

---

[3] See the extended version for a detailed discussion.

Once we prove $Eq\ x \Rightarrow Eq\ (Mu\ HPTree\ x)$ from Φ_{HPTree} by corecursive resolution, we can add it to the axiom environment and use it to prove the ground query $Eq\ (Mu\ HPTree\ Int)$. Let $\Phi' = \Phi_{HPTree}, (\nu\alpha.\lambda\alpha_1.\kappa_1\ (\kappa_2\ \alpha_1\ (\alpha\ (\kappa_3\ \alpha_1\ \alpha_1)))) :$ $Eq\ x \Rightarrow Eq\ (Mu\ HPTree\ x))$. We have the following derivation.

$$\frac{\Phi' \vdash Eq\ Int \Downarrow \kappa_{Int}}{\Phi' \vdash Eq\ (Mu\ HPTree\ Int) \Downarrow (\nu\alpha.\lambda\alpha_1.\kappa_{Mu}\ (\kappa_{HPTree}\ \alpha_1\ (\alpha\ (\kappa_{Pair}\ \alpha_1\ \alpha_1))))\ \kappa_{Int}}$$

5   Operational Semantics of Corecursive Evidence

The purpose of this section is to give operational semantics to corecursive resolution, and in particular, we are interested in giving operational interpretation to the corecursive evidence constructed as a result of applying corecursive resolution. In type class applications, for example, the evidence constructed for a query will be run as a program. It is therefore important to establish the exact relationship between the non-terminating resolution as a process and the proof-term that we obtain via corecursive resolution. We prove that corecursive evidence indeed faithfully captures the otherwise infinite resolution process of Sect. 2.

In general, we know that if $\Phi \vdash A \rightarrow^* \mathcal{C}[\sigma A]$, then we can observe the following looping infinite reduction trace:

$$\Phi \vdash A \rightarrow^* \mathcal{C}[\sigma A] \rightarrow^* \mathcal{C}[\sigma\mathcal{C}[\sigma^2 A]] \rightarrow^* \mathcal{C}[\sigma\mathcal{C}[\sigma^2\mathcal{C}[\sigma^3 A]]] \rightarrow \dots$$

Each iteration of the loop gives rise to repeatedly applying substitution σ to the reduction context $\mathcal{C}$.

In principle, this mixed term context $\mathcal{C}$ may contain an atomic formula B that itself is normalizing, but σB spawns another loop. Clearly this is a complicating factor. For instance, a loop can spawn off additional loops in each iteration. Alternatively, a loop can have multiple iteration points such as $\Phi \vdash A \rightarrow^*$ $\mathcal{C}[\sigma_1 A, \sigma_2 A, ..., \sigma_n A]$.[4] These complicating factors are beyond the scope of this section. We focus only on *simple loops*. These are loops with a single iteration point that does not spawn additional loops.

We use $|\mathcal{C}|$ to denote the set of atomic formulas in the context $\mathcal{C}$. If all atomic formulas $D \in |\mathcal{C}|$ are irreducible with respect to Φ, then we call $\mathcal{C}$ a *normal context*.

Definition 15 (Simple Loop). *Let* $\Phi \vdash B \rightarrow^* \mathcal{C}[\sigma B]$, *where* $\mathcal{C}$ *is normal. If for all* $D \in |\mathcal{C}|$, *we have that* $\Phi \vdash \sigma D \rightarrow^* \mathcal{C}'[D]$ *with* $|\mathcal{C}'| = \emptyset$, *then we call* $\Phi \vdash B \rightarrow^* \mathcal{C}[\sigma B]$ *a simple loop.*

---

[4] Note that we abuse notation here to denote contexts with multiple holes. Also we abbreviate identical instantiation of $\mathcal{C}[D, \dots, D]$ those multiple holes to $\mathcal{C}[D]$.

In the above definition, the normality of $\mathcal{C}$ ensures that the loop has a single iteration point. Likewise the condition $\Phi \vdash \sigma D \rightarrow^* \mathcal{C}'[D]$, which implies that $\Phi \vdash \sigma^n D \rightarrow^* \mathcal{C}'^n[D]$, guarantees that each iteration of the loop spawns no further loops.

Definition 16 (Observational Point). *Let $\Phi \vdash B \rightarrow^* \mathcal{C}'[\sigma B]$ be a simple loop and $\Phi \vdash B \rightarrow^* q$. We call q an observational point if it is of the form $\mathcal{C}[\delta B]$. We use $\mathcal{O}(B)_\Phi$ to denote the set of observational points in the simple loop.*

For example, we have the following infinite resolution trace generated by the simple loop (with the subterms of observational points underlined).

$$\Phi_{HPTree} \vdash \underline{Eq\ (Mu\ HPTree\ x)} \rightarrow \kappa_{Mu}\ \underline{(Eq\ (HPTree\ (Mu\ HPTree)\ x))} \rightarrow$$
$$\kappa_{Mu}\ (\kappa_{HPTree}\ (Eq\ x)\ \underline{(Eq\ (Mu\ HPTree\ (x,x))))} \rightarrow$$
$$\kappa_{Mu}\ (\kappa_{HPTree}\ (Eq\ x)\ (\kappa_{Mu}\ \underline{(Eq\ (HPTree\ (Mu\ HPTree)\ (x,x)))))) \rightarrow$$
$$\kappa_{Mu}(\kappa_{HPTree}(Eq\ x)(\kappa_{Mu}(\kappa_{HPTree}(Eq(x,x))\underline{(Eq(Mu\ HPTree\ ((x,x),(x,x)))))))) \rightarrow$$
$$\kappa_{Mu}(\kappa_{HPTree}(Eq\ x)(\kappa_{Mu}(\kappa_{HPTree}(\kappa_{Pair}(Eq\ x)(Eq\ x)))\underline{(Eq\ (Mu\ HPTree\ ((x,x),(x,x))))))) \rightarrow \cdots$$

In this case, we have $\sigma = [(x,x)/x]$ and $\Phi \vdash \sigma(Eq\ x) \rightarrow \kappa_{Pair}\ (Eq\ x)\ (Eq\ x)$.

The corecursive evidence encapsulates an infinite derivation in a finite fix-point expression. We can recover the infinite resolution by reducing the corecursive expression. To define small-step *evidence reduction*, we first extend mixed terms to cope with richer corecursive evidence.

Definition 17. *Mixed term* $q ::= A \mid \kappa \mid q\ q' \mid \alpha \mid \lambda\alpha.q \mid \nu\alpha.q$

Now we define the small-step evidence reduction relation $q \rightsquigarrow q'$.

Definition 18 (Small Step Evidence Reduction). $\boxed{q \rightsquigarrow q'}$

$$\overline{\mathcal{C}[\nu\alpha.q] \rightsquigarrow_\nu \mathcal{C}[[\nu\alpha.q/\alpha]q]} \qquad \overline{\mathcal{C}[(\lambda\alpha.q)\ q'] \rightsquigarrow_\beta \mathcal{C}[[q'/\alpha]q]}$$

Note that for simplicity we still use the mixed term context $\mathcal{C}$ as defined in Sect. 2, but we only allow the reduction of an outermost redex, i.e., a redex that is not a subterm of some other redex. In other words, reduction unfolds the evidence term strictly downwards from the root, this follows closely the way evidence is constructed during resolution.

We call the states where we perform a ν-transition *corecursive points*. Note that ν-transitions unfold a corecursive definition. These correspond closely to the observational points in resolution.

Definition 19 (Corecursive Point). *Let $q' \rightsquigarrow^* q$. We call q a corecursive point if it is of the form $\mathcal{C}[(\nu\alpha.e)\ q_1\ldots q_n]$. We use $\mathcal{S}(q')$ to denote the set of corecursive points in $q' \rightsquigarrow^* q$.*

Let $e \equiv \nu\alpha.\lambda\alpha_1.\kappa_{Mu}\ (\kappa_{HPTree}\ \alpha_1\ (\alpha\ (\kappa_{Pair}\ \alpha_1\ \alpha_1)))$. We have the following evidence reduction trace (with the subterms of corecursive points underlined):

$$e \ (Eq \ x) \leadsto_\nu (\lambda\alpha_1.\kappa_{Mu} \ (\kappa_{HPTree} \ \alpha_1 \ (e \ (\kappa_{Pair} \ \alpha_1 \ \alpha_1)))) \ (Eq \ x) \leadsto_\beta$$
$$\kappa_{Mu} \ (\kappa_{HPTree} \ (Eq \ x) \ \underline{(e \ (\kappa_{Pair} \ (Eq \ x) \ (Eq \ x)))}) \leadsto_\nu$$
$$\kappa_{Mu} \ (\kappa_{HPTree} \ (Eq \ x) \ ((\lambda\alpha_1.\kappa_{Mu} \ (\kappa_{HPTree} \ \alpha_1 \ (e \ (\kappa_{Pair} \ \alpha_1 \ \alpha_1)))) \ (\kappa_{Pair} \ (Eq \ x) \ (Eq \ x)))) \leadsto_\beta$$
$$\kappa_{Mu}(\kappa_{HPTree}(Eq \ x)(\kappa_{Mu}(\kappa_{HPTree}(\kappa_{Pair}(Eq \ x)(Eq \ x))\underline{(e(\kappa_{Pair}(\kappa_{Pair}(Eq \ x)(Eq \ x))(\kappa_{Pair}(Eq \ x)(Eq \ x))))})))$$
$$\leadsto_\nu \ ...$$

Observe that the mixed term contexts of the observational points and the corecursive points in the above traces coincide. This allows us to show observational equivalence of resolution and evidence reduction without explicitly introducing actual infinite evidence.

The following theorem shows that if resolution gives rise to a simple loop, then we can obtain a corecursive evidence e (Theorem 2 (1)) such that the infinite resolution trace is observational equivalent to e's evidence reduction trace (Theorem 2 (2)).

Theorem 2 (Observational Equivalence). *Let $\Phi \vdash B \to^* C[\sigma B]$ be a simple loop and $|\mathcal{C}| = \{D_1, ..., D_n\}$. Then:*
1. *We have $\Phi \vdash D_1, ..., D_n \Rightarrow B \Downarrow \nu\alpha.\lambda\alpha_1....\lambda\alpha_n.e$ for some e.*
2. *$C[\delta B] \in \mathcal{O}(B)_\Phi$ iff $C[(\nu\alpha.\lambda\underline{\alpha}.e) \ \underline{q}] \in \mathcal{S}((\nu\alpha.\lambda\underline{\alpha}.e) \ \underline{D})$.*

The proof can be found in the extended version.

6   Related Work

Calculus of Coinductive Constructions. Interactive theorem prover Coq pioneered implementation of the *guarded coinduction principle* ([4,8]). The Coq termination checker may prevent some nested uses of coinduction, e.g. a proof term such as $(\nu\alpha.\lambda x.\kappa_0 \ (\kappa_1 \ x \ (\alpha \ (\alpha \ x)))) \ \kappa_2$ is not accepted by Coq, while from the outermost reduction point of view, this proof term is productive.

Loop detection in term rewriting. Distinctions between cycle, loop and non-looping has long been established in term rewriting research ([5,25]). For us, detecting loop is the first step of invariant analysis, but we also want to extract corecursive evidence such that it captures the infinite reduction trace.

Non-terminating type-class resolution. Hughes (Sect. 4 [11]) observed the cyclic nature of the instance declarations **instance** $Sat \ (EqD \ a) \Rightarrow Eq \ a$ and **instance** $Eq \ a \Rightarrow Sat \ (EqD \ a)$. He proposed to treat the looping context reduction as failure, in which case the compiler would need to search for an alternative reduction.

The cycle detection method [17] was proposed to generate corecursive evidence for a restricted class of non-terminating resolution. It is supported by the current Glasgow Haskell Compiler.

Hinze and Peyton Jones [10] came across an example of an instance of the form **instance** $(Binary \ a, Binary \ (f \ (GRose \ f \ a))) \Rightarrow Binary \ (GRose \ f \ a)$, but discovered that it causes resolution to diverge. They suggested the following as a replacement: **instance** $(Binary \ a, \forall b \ . \ Binary \ b \Rightarrow Binary \ f \ b) \Rightarrow$

Binary (GRose f a). Unfortunately, Haskell does not support instances with *polymorphic higher-order instance contexts*. Nevertheless, allowing such implication constraints would greatly increase the expressitivity of corecursive resolution. In the terminology of our paper, it amounts to extending Horn formulas to intuitionistic formulas. Working with intuitionistic formulas would require a certain amount of searching, as the non-overlapping condition for Horn formulas is not enough to ensure uniqueness of the evidence. For example, consider the following axioms:

$$\kappa_1 : (A \Rightarrow B\ x) \Rightarrow D\ (S\ x)$$
$$\kappa_2 : A, D\ x \Rightarrow B\ (S\ x)$$
$$\kappa_3 : \Rightarrow D\ Z$$

We have two distinct proof terms for $D\ (S\ (S\ (S\ (S\ Z)))))$:

$$\kappa_1\ (\lambda\alpha_1.\kappa_2\ \alpha_1\ (\kappa_1\ (\lambda\alpha_2.\kappa_2\ \underline{\alpha_1}\ \kappa_3)))$$
$$\kappa_1\ (\lambda\alpha_1.\kappa_2\ \alpha_1\ (\kappa_1\ (\lambda\alpha_2.\kappa_2\ \underline{\alpha_2}\ \kappa_3)))$$

This is undesirable from the perspective of generating evidence for type class.

Instance declarations and (Horn Clause) logic programs. The process of simplifying type class constraints is formally described as the notion of *context reduction* by Peyton Jones et. al. [15], Sect. 3.2 of the same paper also describes the form of type class instance declarations. Type class evidence in its connection with type system is studied in Mark Jones's thesis [14, Chapter 4.2]. Instance declarations can also be interpreted as single head *simplification* rules in Constraints Handling Rules (CHR) [23], which implies that instance declarations can be modeled as Horn formulas naturally. To our knowledge, the tradition of studying logic programming proof-theoretically dates back to Girard's suggestion that the cut rule can model resolution for Horn formulas [9, Chapter 13.4]. Alternatively, Miller et. al. [19] model Horn formulas using cut-free sequent calculus. Context reduction, instance declaration and their connection to proof relevant resolution are also discussed under the name of *LP-TM* (logic programming with term-matching) in Fu and Komendantskaya [6, Sect. 4.1].

7   Conclusion and Future Work

We have introduced a novel approach to non-terminating resolution. Firstly, we have shown that the popular cycle detection methods employed for logic programming or type class resolution can be understood via more general coinductive proof principles ([4,8]). Secondly, we have shown that resolution can be enriched with rules that capture the intuition of richer coinductive hypothesis formation. This extension allows to provide corecursive evidence to some derivations that could not be handled by previous methods. Moreover, corecursive resolution is formulated in a proof-relevant way, i.e. proof-evidence construction is an essential part of corecursive resolution. This makes it easier to integrate it directly into type class inference.

We have implemented the techniques of Sects. 3 and 4, and have incorporated them as part of the evidence construction process for a simple language that admits previously non-terminating examples.[5]

Future Work. In general, the interactions between different loops can be complicated. Consider Φ_{Pair} with the following declarations (denoted by Φ_M):

$$\kappa_M : Eq\ (h_1\ (M\ h_1\ h_2)\ (M\ h_2\ h_1)\ a) \Rightarrow Eq\ (M\ h_1\ h_2\ a)$$
$$\kappa_H : (Eq\ a, Eq\ ((f_1\ a),(f_2\ a))) \Rightarrow Eq\ (H\ f_1\ f_2\ a)$$
$$\kappa_G : Eq\ ((g\ a),(f\ (g\ a))) \Rightarrow Eq\ (G\ f\ g\ a)$$

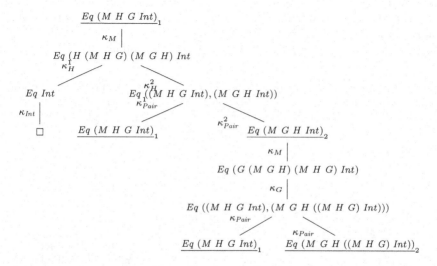

Fig. 3. A Partial Resolution tree for $\Phi_M \vdash Eq\ (M\ H\ G\ Int) \Uparrow$

A partial resolution tree generated by the query $Eq\ (M\ H\ G\ Int)$ is described in Fig. 3. In this case the cycle (underlined with the index 1) is mutually nested with a loop (underlined with index 2). Our method in Sect. 3 is not able to generate any candidate lemmas. Yet there are two candidate lemmas for this case (with the proof of e_2 refer to e_1):

$$e_1 : (Eq\ x, Eq\ (M\ G\ H\ x)) \Rightarrow Eq\ (M\ H\ G\ x)$$
$$e_2 : Eq\ x \Rightarrow Eq\ (M\ H\ G\ x)$$

We would like to improve our heuristics to allow generating multiple candidate lemmas, where their corecursive evidences mutually refer to each other.

---

[5] See the extended version for more examples and information about the implementation. Extended version is available from authors' homepages.

There are situations where resolution is non-terminating but does not form any loop such as $\Phi \vdash A \rightarrow^* \mathcal{C}[\sigma A]$. Consider the following program Φ_D:

$$\kappa_1 : D\ n\ (S\ m) \Rightarrow D\ (S\ n)\ m$$
$$\kappa_2 : D\ (S\ m)\ Z \Rightarrow D\ Z\ m$$

For query $D\ Z\ Z$, the resolution diverges without forming any loop. We would have to introduce extra equality axioms in order to obtain finite corecursive evidence.[6] We would like to investigate the ramifications of incorporating equality axioms in the corecursive resolution in the future.

We plan to extend the observational equivalence result of Sect. 5 to cope with more general notions of loop and extend our approach to allow intuitionistic formulas as candidate lemmas. Another avenue for future work is a formal proof that the calculus of Definition 13 is sound relative to the the greatest Herbrand models [18], and therefore reflects the broader notion of the coinductive entailment for Horn clause logic as discussed in the introduction.

Acknowledgements. We thank Patricia Johann and the FLOPS'16 reviewers for their helpful comments, and František Farka for many discussions. Part of this work was funded by the Flemish Fund for Scientific Research.

References

1. Ancona, D., Lagorio, G.: Idealized coinductive type systems for imperative object-oriented programs. RAIRO - Theor. Inf. Appl. **45**(1), 3–33 (2011)
2. Bird, R.S., Meertens, L.: Nested datatypes. In: Jeuring, J. (ed.) MPC 1998. LNCS, vol. 1422, pp. 52–67. Springer, Heidelberg (1998)
3. Bjørner, N., Gurfinkel, A., McMillan, K., Rybalchenko, A.: Horn clause solvers for program verification. In: Beklemishev, L.D., Blass, A., Dershowitz, N., Finkbeiner, B., Schulte, W. (eds.) Gurevich Festschrift II 2015. LNCS, vol. 9300, pp. 24–51. Springer, Heidelberg (2015)
4. Coquand, T.: Infinite objects in type theory. In: Barendregt, H., Nipkow, T. (eds.) TYPES 1993. LNCS, vol. 806. Springer, Heidelberg (1994)
5. Dershowitz, N.: Termination of rewriting. J. Symb. Comput. **3**, 69–115 (1987)
6. Fu, P., Komendantskaya, E.: A type-theoretic approach to resolution. In: 25th International Symposium, LOPSTR 2015. Revised Selected Papers (2015)
7. Gibbons, J., Hutton, G.: Proof methods for corecursive programs. Fundam. Inf. Spec. Issue Program Transform. **66**(4), 353–366 (2005)
8. Gimenez, C.E.: Un calcul de constructions infinies et son application a la vérification de systèmes communicants (1996)
9. Girard, J.-Y., Taylor, P., Lafont, Y.: Proofs and Types, vol. 7. Cambridge University Press, Cambridge (1989)
10. Hinze, R., Peyton-Jones, S.: Derivable type classes. Electron. Notes Theor. Comput. Sci. **41**(1), 5–35 (2001)

---

[6] See the extended version for a solution in Haskell using type family and more discussion.

11. Hughes, J.: Restricted data types in Haskell. In: Haskell Workshop, vol. 99 (1999)
12. Johann, P., Ghani, N.: Haskell programming with nested types: a principled approach (2009)
13. Johann, P., Komendantskaya, E., Komendantskiy, V.: Structural resolution for logic programming. In: Technical Communications of ICLP 2015, July 2015
14. Jones, M.P.: Qualified Types: Theory and Practice, vol. 9. Cambridge University Press, Cambridge (2003)
15. Jones, S.P., Jones, M., Meijer, E.: Type classes: an exploration of the design space. In: Haskell Workshopp (1997)
16. Komendantskaya, E., Johann, P. Structural resolution: a framework for coinductive proof search and proof construction in Horn clause logic. Submitted
17. Lämmel, R., Peyton-Jones, S.: Scrap your boilerplate with class: extensible generic functions. In: Proceedings of 10th ACM SIGPLAN International Conference on Functional Programming, ICFP 2005, pp. 204–215, New York, NY, USA. ACM (2005)
18. Lloyd, J.W.: Foundations of Logic Programming. Springer Science & Business Media, Heidelberg (1987)
19. Miller, D., Nadathur, G., Pfenning, F., Scedrov, A.: Uniform proofs as a foundation for logic programming. Ann. Pure Appl. Log. **51**(1), 125–157 (1991)
20. Moss, L.S., Danner, N.: On the foundations of corecursion. Log. J. IGPL **5**(2), 231–257 (1997)
21. Plotkin, G.D.: A note on inductive generalization. Mach. Intell. **5**, 153–163 (1970)
22. Simon, L., Gupta, G., Mallya, A., Bansal, A.: Co-logic programming: extending logic programming with coinduction. In: Arge, L., Cachin, C., Jurdziński, T., Tarlecki, A. (eds.) ICALP 2007. LNCS, vol. 4596, pp. 472–483. Springer, Heidelberg (2007)
23. Sulzmann, M., Duck, G.J., Peyton Jones, S.L., Stuckey, P.J.: Understanding functional dependencies via constraint handling rules. J. Funct. Program. **17**(1), 83–129 (2007)
24. Wadler, P., Blott, S.: How to make ad-hoc polymorphism less ad hoc. In: Proceedings of 16th ACM SIGPLAN-SIGACT Symposium on Principles of Programming Languages, pp. 60–76. ACM (1989)
25. Zantema, H., Geser, A.: Non-looping rewriting. Universiteit Utrecht, Faculty of Mathematics & Computer Science (1996)

A Coq Library for Internal Verification of Running-Times

Jay McCarthy[1]([⊠]), Burke Fetscher[2], Max New[2], Daniel Feltey[2],
and Robert Bruce Findler[2]

[1] University of Massachusetts at Lowell, Lowell, USA
jay.mccarthy@gmail.com
[2] Northwestern University, Evanston, USA
{burke.fetscher,max.new,daniel.feltey,robby}@eecs.northwestern.edu

Abstract. This paper presents a Coq library that lifts an abstract yet precise notion of running-time into the type of a function. Our library is based on a monad that counts abstract steps, controlled by one of the monadic operations. The monad's computational content, however, is simply that of the identity monad so programs written in our monad (that recur on the natural structure of their arguments) extract into idiomatic OCaml code. We evaluated the expressiveness of the library by proving that red-black tree insertion and search, merge sort, insertion sort, Fibonacci, iterated list insertion, BigNum addition, and Okasaki's Braun Tree algorithms all have their expected running times.

1 Introduction

For some programs, proving that they have correct input-output behavior is only part of the story. As Crosby and Wallach (2003) observed, incorrect performance characteristics can also lead to security vulnerabilities. Indeed, some programs and algorithms are valuable precisely because of their performance characteristics. For example, mergesort is preferable to insertion sort only because of its improved running time. Unfortunately, defining functions in Coq or other theorem proving systems does not provide enough information in the types to be able to state these intensional properties.

Our work provides a monad (implemented as a library in Coq) that enables us to include abstract running times in types. We use this library to prove several important algorithms have their expected running times. Our library has two benefits over Danielsson (2008)'s. First, it allows programmers to write idiomatic code without embedding invariants in data types, so we can reason about a wider variety of programs. Second, and more significantly, our monad adds no complexity computations to the extracted OCaml code, so it has no verification overhead on running time. We elaborate these details and differences throughout the paper and, in particular, in Sect. 8.

The rest of the paper is structured as follows. In Sect. 2, we give an overview of how the library works and the style of proofs we support. In Sect. 3, we discuss the cost model our proofs deal with. In Sect. 4, we explain the extraction of

© Springer International Publishing Switzerland 2016
O. Kiselyov and A. King (Eds.): FLOPS 2016, LNCS 9613, pp. 144–162, 2016.
DOI: 10.1007/978-3-319-29604-3_10

our programs to OCaml. In these first three sections, we use a consistent example that is introduced in Sect. 2. Following this preamble, Sect. 5 walks through the definition and design of the monad itself. Section 6 describes the results of our case study, wherein we proved properties of a variety of different functions. Section 7 discusses accounting for the runtimes of various language primitives. Finally, Sect. 8 provides a detailed account of our relation to similar projects. Our source code and other supplementary material is available at http://github. com/rfindler/395-2013.

2   Overview of Our Library

The core of our library is a monad that, as part of its types, tracks the running time of functions. To use the library, programs must be explicitly written using the usual return and bind monadic operations. In return, the result type of a function can use not only the argument values to give it a very precise specification, but also an abstract step count describing how many primitive operations (function calls, matches, variable references etc.) that the function executes.

To give a sense of how code using our library looks, we start with a definition of Braun trees (Braun and Rem 1983) and the insertion function where the contributions to the running time are explicitly declared as part of the body of the function. In the next section, we make the running times implicit (and thus not trusted or spoofable).

Braun trees, which provide for efficient growable vectors, are a form of balanced binary trees where the balance condition allows only a single shape of trees for a given size. Specifically, for each interior node, either the two children are exactly the same size or the left child's size is one larger than the right child's size.

Because this invariant is so strong, explicit balance information is not needed in the data structure that represents Braun trees; we can use a simple binary tree definition.

```
Inductive bin_tree {A:Set} : Set :=
| bt_mt   : bin_tree
| bt_node : A -> bin_tree -> bin_tree -> bin_tree.
```

To be able to state facts about Braun trees, however, we need the inductive Braun to specify which binary trees are Braun trees (at a given size n).

```
Inductive Braun {A:Set} : (@bin_tree A) -> nat -> Prop :=
| B_mt   : Braun bt_mt 0
| B_node : forall (x:A) s s_size t t_size,
    t_size <= s_size <= t_size+1 ->
    Braun s s_size -> Braun t t_size ->
    Braun (bt_node x s t) (s_size+t_size+1).
```

This says that the empty binary tree is a Braun tree of size 0, and that if two numbers s_size, t_size are the sizes of two Braun trees s t, and

```
Program Fixpoint insert {A:Set} (i:A) (b:@bin_tree A)
: {! res !:! @bin_tree A !<! c !>!
     (forall n, Braun b n -> (Braun res (n+1) /\ c = fl_log n + 1)) !} :=
  match b with
  | bt_mt        => += 1; <== (bt_node i bt_mt bt_mt)
  | bt_node j s t => t' <- insert j t;
                     += 1; <== (bt_node i t' s)
  end.
```

Fig. 1. Braun tree insertion

if s_size < = t_size < = s_size + 1, then combining the s and t into a single tree produces a Braun tree of size s_size+t_size+1.

Figure 1 shows the insertion function. Let us dig into this function, one line at a time. It accepts an object i (of type A) to insert into the Braun tree b. Its result type uses a special notation: {! «result id» !:! «simple type» !<! «running time id !>! «property»!} where the braces, exclamation marks, colons, less than, and greater than are all fixed parts of the syntax and the portions enclosed in «» are filled in based on the particulars of the insert function. In this case, it is saying that insert returns a binary tree and, if the input is a Braun tree of size n, then the result is a Braun tree of size n+1 and the function takes fl_log n + 1 steps of computation (where fl_log computes the floor of the base 2 logarithm).

These new {! ... !} types are the types of computations in the monad. The monad tracks the running time as well as tracking the correctness property of the function.

The body of the insert function begins with the match expression that determines if the input Braun tree is empty or not. If it is empty, then the function returns a singleton tree that is obtained by calling bt_node with two empty children. This case uses <==, the return operation that injects simple values into the monad and += that declares that this operation takes a single unit of computation. That is, the type of += insists that += accepts a natural number k and a computation in the monad taking some number of steps, say n. The result of += is also a computation in the monad just like the second argument, except that the running time is n+k.

In the non-empty case, the insertion function recurs with the right subtree and then builds a new tree with the subtrees swapped. This swapping is what preserves the Braun invariant. Since we know that the left subtree's size is either equal to or one larger than the right's, when we add an element to the right and swap the subtrees, we end up with a new tree whose left subtree's size is either equal to or one greater than the right.

The «var» <- «expr»; «expr» notation is the monadic bind operator; using a let-style notation. The first, right-hand side expression must be a computation in the monad; the result value is pulled out of the monad and bound to var for use in the body expression. Then, as before, we return the new tree in the monad after treating this branch as a single abstract step of computation.

We exploit Sozeau (2006)'s `Program` to simplify proving that these functions have their types. In this case, we are left with two proof obligations, one from each of the cases of the function. The first one is:

```
forall n, Braun bt_mt n ->
  Braun (bt_node i bt_mt bt_mt) (n + 1) /\1 = fl_log n + 1
```

The assumption is saying that n is the size of the empty Braun tree, which tells us that n must be zero. So simplifying, we are asked to prove that:

```
Braun (bt_node i bt_mt bt_mt) 1 /\1 = fl_log 0 + 1
```

both of which follow immediately from the definitions. This proof request corresponds exactly to what we need to know in order for the base case to be correct: the singleton tree is a Braun tree of size 1 and the running time is correct on empty input.

For the second case, we are asked to prove:

```
forall i j s t bt an n,
  (forall m : nat, Braun t m -> Braun bt (m + 1) /\an = fl_log m + 1) ->
  Braun (bt_node j s t) n ->
  Braun (bt_node i bt s) (n + 1) /\an + 1 = fl_log n + 1
```

Thus, we may assume a slightly more general inductive hypothesis (the inner `forall`) than we need (it is specialized to the recursive call that `insert` makes, but not the size of the tree) and that the tree `bt_node j s t` is a Braun tree of size n. So, we must show that `bt_node i bt s` is a Braun tree of size n + 1 and that the running time is correct.

Because the size information is not present in the actual insertion function, Coq does not know to specialize the inductive hypothesis to the size of t. To clarify that, we can replace m with `t_size` and, since we know that the tree is not empty, we can replace n with `s_size + t_size + 1` and simplify to arrive at this goal:

```
forall i j s t bt an s_size t_size,
  Braun bt (t_size + 1) ->
  an = fl_log t_size + 1 ->
  Braun (bt_node j s t) (s_size + t_size + 1) ->
  Braun (bt_node i bt s) (s_size + t_size + 1 + 1) /\
  an + 1 = fl_log (s_size + t_size + 1) + 1
```

which we can prove by using facts about logarithms and the definition of Braun trees.

This theorem corresponds precisely to what we need to know in order to prove that the recursive case of `insert` works. The assumptions correspond to the facts we gain from the input to the function and from the result of the recursive call. The conclusion corresponds to the facts we need to establish for this case. This precision of the obligation is thanks to `Program` and the structure of our monad.

3   Implicit Running Times

One disadvantage to the code in the previous section is that the running times
are tangled with the body of the insertion function. Even worse, making mistakes
when writing += expressions can produce un-provable claims or cause our proofs
about the running times to be useless, as they will prove facts that are irrelevant
to the functions we are using.

To handle this situation, we've written a simple Coq-to-Coq translation function that accepts functions written in our monad without any += expressions and
turns them into ones with += expressions in just the right places.

Our translation function accepts a function written in the monad, but without the monadic type on its result, and produces one with it. For example, the
insert function shown on the left in Fig. 2 is translated into the one on the
right. As well as adding += expressions, the translation process also generates
a call to insert_result in the monadic result type. The user must define this
function separately and the translation's output must be used in that context:

```
Definition insert_time n := 9 * fl_log n + 6.
Definition insert_result (A : Set) (i : A) (b:bin_tree) (res:bin_tree) c :=
  (forall n, Braun b n ->
             (Braun res (S n) /\
             (forall xs, SequenceR b xs -> SequenceR res (i::xs)) /\
             c = insert_time n)).
```

Unlike the previous version, this one accounts for the larger constant factors
and it also includes a stricter correctness condition. Specifically, the new con-
junct uses SequenceR (a proposition we wrote) to insist that if you linearize the
resulting Braun tree into a list, then it is the same as linearizing the input and
consing the new element onto the list.

Rather than develop a novel, and potentially controversial cost semantics,
we show the utility of our monad by adopting the Rosendahl (1989) cost model.

```
Program Fixpoint

  insert {A:Set} (i:A) (b:@bin_tree A)
: @bin_tree A :=
match b with
  | bt_mt =>
    <== bt_node i bt_mt bt_mt
  | bt_node j s t =>
    t' <- insert j t;
    <== bt_node i t' s
end.
```

```
Program Fixpoint insert {A:Set} (i:A)
(b:@bin_tree A)
: {! res !:! @bin_tree A !<! c !>!
    insert_result A i b res c !} :=
match b with
  | bt_mt =>
    += 6;
    <== (bt_node i bt_mt bt_mt)
  | bt_node j s t =>
    t' <- insert j t;
    += 9;
    <== (bt_node i t' s)
end.
```

Fig. 2. Inserting += into insert

This model treats each function call, variable lookup, and case-dispatch as a single unit of abstract time. In Fig. 2, the first return is annotated with a cost of 6 because it references 4 variables, calls 1 function, and does 1 case-dispatch. The second return is annotated with a cost of 9 because it references 6 variables (the self-reference is not counted), calls 2 functions, and does 1 case-dispatch.

Our translation function is straightforward and is included in the supplementary materials (add-plusses/check-stx-errs in rkt/tmonad/main.rkt). Our monad could support different cost semantics, without modification, provided a function could map them to the program's syntax in a straightforward way.

An alternative approach would be to follow Danner et al. (2013) and build a Coq model of a machine and programming language. We would then define a cost judgement for this machine and prove its soundness with respect to the machine's reduction lengths. Finally, we would show that our monadic types allow incremental proofs of their cost results. In some sense, this "deep embedding" would be a more direct study of cost and cost proofs, but it would be no more directly connected with the running time of the programs, unless we could establish a connection to the OCaml VM.

4 Extracting the insert Function

One of the important benefits of our library is that none of the correctness conditions and running time infrastructure affect Coq's extraction process. In particular, our monad extracts as the identity monad, which means that the OCaml code produced by Coq does not require any modifications. For example, here is how insert extracts:

```
type 'a bin_tree = | Bt_mt
                   | Bt_node of 'a * 'a bin_tree * 'a bin_tree

let rec insert i = function
| Bt_mt            -> Bt_node (i, Bt_mt, Bt_mt)
| Bt_node (j, s, t) -> Bt_node (i, (insert j t), s)
```

The only declarations we added to aid Coq's extraction was the suggestion that it should inline the monad operations. And since the extracted version of our monad is the identity monad, the monad operations simply evaporate when they are inlined.

More importantly, however, note that this code does not have any proof residue; there are no extra data-structures or function arguments or other artifacts of the information used to prove the running time correct.

5 The Monad

One way to account for cost is to use the monad to pair an actual value (of type B) with a natural number representing the computation's current cost, and then ensure that this number is incremented appropriately at each stage of the computation. Unfortunately, this cost would be part of the dynamic behavior of the algorithm. In other words, `insert x bt` would return a new tree and a number, violating our goal of having no complexity residue in extracted programs.

In Coq parlance, the problem is that we have a pair of two `Set` values—the B and the `nat`—and `Set`s are, by definition, part of the computational content. Instead, we need to have a `Set` paired with something from the universe of truth propositions, `Prop`. The trouble is finding the right proposition.

We use a new function `C` that consumes a type and a proposition that is parameterized over values of the type and numbers. Specifically, we define `C`:

```
Definition C (A:Set) (P:A -> nat -> Prop) : Set :=
  {a : A | exists (an:nat), (P a an)}.
```

For a given A and P, `C A P` is a dependent pair of `a`, a value of type A, and a proof that there exists some natural number `an` related to `a` by P. The intention is to think of the natural number as the running time and P as some specification of running time (and possibly also correctness) specific to the particular function. Importantly, the right-hand side of this pair is a proposition, so it contributes no computational content when extracted into OCaml. To see this in practice, consider `insert`'s result type:

```
: {! res !:! @bin_tree A !<! c !>!
    (forall n, Braun b n -> (Braun res (n+1) /\ c = fl_log n + 1)) !}
```

This is a shorthand (using Coq's `notation` construct) for the following call to `C`, in order to avoid duplicating the type between `!:!` and `!<!`:

```
(C (@bin_tree A) (fun (res:@bin_tree A) (c:nat) =>
    (forall n, Braun b n -> (Braun res (n+1) /\ c = fl_log n + 1))))
```

One important aspect of the `C` type is that the `nat` is bound only by an existential, and thus is not necessarily connected to the value or the runtime. Therefore, when we know an expression has the type `C A P`, we do not know that its running time is correct, because the property might be about anything and the proof might supply any `nat` to satisfy the existential. Thus, in order to guarantee the correct running times, we treat types of the form `C A P` as private to the monad's defining module. We build a set of operations that can be combined in arbitrary ways but subject to the restriction that the `nat` must actually be the running time.

The first of these operations is the monadic unit, `ret`. Suppose a program returns an empty list, `<== nil`. Such a program takes no steps to compute, because the value is readily available. This logic applies to all places where a computation ends. To do this, we define `<== x` to be `ret__ x_`, a use of the monad operator `ret`. The underscores ask Coq to fill in well-typed arguments (asking the user to provide proofs, if necessary, as we saw in Sect. 2). This is the type[1] of `ret`:

---

[1] The definition of `ret`, and all other monadic operations, are in the supplementary material and our public Github repo. The types are the most interesting part, however, so we focus on them.

```
Definition ret (A:Set) (P:A -> nat -> Prop) (a:A) (Pa0:P a 0) : C A P.
```

This specifies that `ret` will construct a C A P only when given a proof, Pa0, that the correctness/runtime property holds between the actual value returned a and the natural number 0. In other words, `ret` requires P to predict the running time as 0.

There are two other operations in our monad: `inc` that adds to the count of the running time, and `bind` that combines two computations in the monad, summing their running times. We tackle `inc` next.

Suppose a program returns a value a, with property P, that takes exactly one step to compute. We represent such a program with the expression:

```
+= 1; <== a
```

We would like our proof obligation for this expression to be P a 1. We know, however that the obligation on `<==`, namely P a 0, is irrelevant or worse, wrong. There is a simple way out of this bind: what if the P for the `ret` were different than the P for of the entire expression? In code, what if the obligation were P' a 0? At worst, such a change would be irrelevant because there may not be a connection between P' and P. But, we can choose a P' such that P' a 0 is the same as P a 1.

We previously described P as a relation between As and nats, but in Coq this is just a function that accepts an A and a nat and returns a proposition. So, we can make P' be the function `fun a an => P a (an+1)`. This has the effect of transforming the runtime obligation on `ret` from what was described above. The proof P' a 0 becomes P a 1. In general, if the cost along a control-flow path to a `ret` has k units of cost, the proof will be P a k. Thus, we accrue the cost inside of the property itself.

The monadic operator `inc` encapsulates this logic and introduces k units of cost:

```
Definition inc (A:Set) k (PA : A -> nat -> Prop)
          (x:C A (fun x xn => forall xm, xn + k = xm -> PA x xm))
 : C A PA.
```

In programs using our monad, we write `+= k; e`, a shorthand for `inc_ k_ e`. The key point in the definition is that the property in x's type is *not* PA, but a modified function that ensures the argument is at least k.

In principle, the logic for `bind` is very similar. A `bind` represents a composition of two computations: an A-producing one and an A-consuming, B-producing one. If we assume that the property for A is PA and PB for B, then an attempt at a type for `bind` is:

```
Definition bind1 (A:Set) (PA:A -> nat -> Prop)
               (B:Set) (PB:B -> nat -> Prop)
               (am:C A PA) (bf:A -> C B PB)
 : C B PB.
```

This definition is incorrect from the cost perspective, because it does not ensure that the cost for producing the A is accounted for along with the cost of producing the B.

Suppose that the cost of generating the A was 7, then we should transform the property of the B computation to be `fun b bn => PB b (bn+7)`. Unfortunately, we cannot "look inside" the A computation to know that it costs 7 units. Instead, we have to show that *whatever* the cost for A was, the cost of B is still as expected. This suggests a second attempt at a definition of `bind`:

```
Definition bind2 (A:Set) (PA:A -> nat -> Prop)
                 (B:Set) (PB:B -> nat -> Prop)
                 (am:C A PA)
                 (bf:A -> C B (fun b bn => forall an, PB b (bn+an)))
  : C B PB.
```

Unfortunately, this is far too strong of a statement because there are some costs an that are too much. The only an costs that our `bind` proof must be concerned with are those that respect the PA property given the *actual* value of a that the A computation produced. We can use a dependent type on `bf` to capture the connection between the costs in a third attempt at the type for `bind`.

```
Definition bind3 (A:Set) (PA:A -> nat -> Prop)
                 (B:Set) (PB:B -> nat -> Prop)
                 (am:C A PA),
                 (bf:forall (a:A),
                     C B (fun b bn => forall an, PA a an -> PB b (bn+an)))
  : C B PB.
```

This version of `bind` is complete, from a cost perspective, but has one problem for practical theorem proving. The body of the function `bf` has access to the value a, but it does not have access to the correctness part of the property PA. At first blush, the missing PA appears not to matter because the proof of correctness for the result of `bf` *does* have access through the hypothesis PA a an, but that proof context is not available when producing the b result. Instead, `bind` assumes that b has already been computed. That assumption means if the proof of PA is needed to compute b, then we will be stuck. The most common case where PA is neccessary occurs when `bf` performs non-structural recursion and must construct a well-foundness proof to perform the recursive call. These well-foundness proofs typically rely on the correctness of the a value. Some of the functions we discuss in our case study in Sect. 6 could not be written with this version of `bind`, although some could.

It is simple to incorporate the PA proof into the type of `bf`, once you realize the need for it, by adding an additional proposition argument that corresponds to the right-hand side of the C A PA value am:

```
Definition bind (A:Set) (PA:A -> nat -> Prop)
                (B:Set) (PB:B -> nat -> Prop)
                (am:C A PA)
```

```
                 (bf:forall (a:A) (pa:exists an, PA a an),
                    C B (fun b bn => forall an, PA a an -> PB b (an+bn)))
  : C B PB.
```

When writing programs we use the notation «x»<-«expr1»; «expr2» as a shorthand for bind_ _ _ _ expr1 (fun (x : _) (am : _) => expr2)

Because all of the interesting aspects of these operations happen in their types, the extractions of these operations have no interesting dynamic content. Specifically ret is simply the identity function, inc is a function that just returns its second argument and bind applies its second argument to its first.

Furthermore, we have proven that they obey variants of the monad laws that incorporate the proof obligations (see the file monad/laws.v in the supplementary material). Our versions of the monad law proofs use an auxiliary relation, written sig_eqv, rather than equality. This relation ensures that the values returned by monadic commands are equal and that their proofs are equivalent. In practice, this means that although the theorems proved by expressions such as (m >>= (\x -> f x >>= g)) and ((m >>= f) >>= g) are written differently, they imply each other. In particular, for that pair of expressions, one proves that (n_m + (n_f + n_g)) is an accurate prediction of running time and the other proves that ((n_m + n_f) + n_g) is an accurate prediction of running time, which are equivalant statements.

In summary, the monad works by requiring the verifier to predict the running-time in the PA property and then prove that the actual cost (starting at 0 and incrementing as the property passes down) matches the prediction.

6   Case Study

To better understand how applicable our monad is, we implemented a variety of functions: search and insert for red-black trees, insertion sort, merge sort, both the naive recursive version of the nth Fibonacci number function and the iterative version, a function that inserts m times into a list at position n using both lists and zippers, BigNum add1 and plus, and all of the algorithms mentioned in Okasaki (1997)'s paper, *Three Algorithms on Braun Trees*. We chose these algorithms by first selecting Okasaki's papers, because the project originated in a class and we knew Okasaki's paper to be well-written and understandable to undergraduates. From that initial selection, we moved to an in-order traversal of Cormen et al. (2009) looking for functional algorithms that would challenge the framework.

To elaborate on the Braun tree algorithms, Okasaki's paper contains several versions of each of the three functions, each with different running times, in each case culminating with efficient versions. The three functions are:

- size: computes the size of a Braun tree (a linear and a log squared version)
- copy: builds a Braun tree of a given size filled entirely with a given element (a linear, a fib ∘ log, a log squared, and a log time version), and
- make_array: converts a list into a Braun tree (two n log n and a linear version).

```
Program Fixpoint copy_log_sq {A:Set} (x:A) (n:nat) {measure n}
 : {! res !:! bin_tree !<! c !>! copy_log_sq_result A x n res c !} :=
    match n with
      | 0    => += 3; <== bt_mt
      | S n' => t <- copy_log_sq x (div2 n');
                if (even_odd_dec n')
                then (+= 13; <== (bt_node x t t))
                else (s <- insert x t; += 16; <== (bt_node x s t))
    end.
```

Fig. 3. copy_log_sq

In total, we implemented 19 different functions using the monad. For all of them, we proved the expected O running times. For merge sort, we proved it is $\Theta(n \log(n))$. For the naive fib, we proved that it is Θ of itself, $O(2^n)$, and $\Omega(2^{n/2})$, all assuming that the addition operation is constant time. For the iterative fib, we prove that it is $O(n^2)$. For the list insertion functions, we prove that when m is positive, the zipper version is O of the list version (because the zipper version runs in $O(m + n)$ while the list version runs in $O(n * m)$.) For BigNum arithmetic, we prove that add1 is $O(\log(n))$ and that plus is $\Theta(\log(n))$. In all cases, except for make_array_linear and red-black tree insertion, the proofs of running time include proof of correctness of the algorithm. Finally, in the proofs for BigNum arithmetic and about the Fibonacci functions, we use a simplified cost model that reduces all inc constants to 1. The supplementary material contains all of the Coq code for all of the functions in our case study.

6.1   Line Counts

Our supplementary material contains a detailed account of the lines of Coq code produced for our study. We separate the line counts into proofs that are inside obligations (and thus correspond to establishing that the monadic types are correct) and other lines of proofs. In total there are 12,870 lines of code. There are 5,321 lines that are not proofs. There are 1,895 lines of code in obligations and 5,654 lines of other proofs.

We have built a library of general proofs about the monad (such as the monad laws), an asymptotic complexity library, a Log library, and some common facts and definitions about Braun trees. This library accounts for over 25 % of the code of each category.

With the exception of the make_array_linear and the red-black tree insertion function, the proofs inside the obligations establish the correctness of the functions and establish a basic running time result, but not an asymptotic one in terms of O.

For example, Fig. 3 is the definition of the copy_log_sq function, basically mirroring Okasaki's definition, but in Coq's notation. The monadic result type is

```
Definition copy_log_sq_result (A:Set) (x:A) (n:nat) (b:@bin_tree A) (c:nat) :=
  Braun b n /\ SequenceR b (mk_list x n) /\ c = copy_log_sq_time n.
```

which says that the result is a Braun tree whose size matches the input natural number, that linearizing the resulting tree produces the input list, and that the running time is given by the function `copy_log_sq_time`.

The running time function, however, is defined in parallel to `copy_log_sq` itself, not as the product of the logs:

```
Program Fixpoint copy_log_sq_time (n:nat) {measure n} :=
  match n with
    | 0    => 3
    | S n' => if (even_odd_dec n')
                then 13 + copy_log_sq_time (div2 n')
                else 16 + copy_log_sq_time (div2 n') + insert_time (div2 n')
  end.
```

This parallel definition allows a straightforward proof that `copy_log_sq`'s running time is `copy_log_sq_time`, but leaves as a separate issue the proof that `copy_log_sq_time` is $O(\log^2 n)$. There are 56 lines of proof to guarantee the result type of the function is correct and an additional 179 lines to prove that `copy_log_sq_time` is $O(\log^2 n)$.

For simple functions (those with linear running time except `make_array_linear`), the running time can be expressed directly in the monadic result (with precise constants). However, for most of the functions the running time is first expressed precisely in a manner that matches the structure of the function and then that running time is proven to correspond to some asymptotic complexity, as with `copy_log_sq`.

6.2 Extraction

The extracted functions naturally fall into three categories.

In the first category are functions that recur on the natural structure of their inputs, e.g., functions that process lists from the front, functions that process trees by processing the children and combining the result, and so on. In the second category are functions that recursively process numbers by counting down by one from a given number. In the third category are functions that "skip" over some of their inputs. For example, some functions recur on natural numbers by dividing the number by 2 instead of subtracting one, and merge sort recurs by dividing the list in half at each step.

Functions in the first category extract into precisely the OCaml code that you would expect, just like `insert`, as discussed in Sect. 2.

Functions in the second category could extract like the first, except because we extract Coq's `nat` type, which is based on Peano numerals, into OCaml's `big_int` type, which has a different structure, a natural `match` expression in Coq becomes a more complex pattern in OCaml. A representative example of this pattern is `zip_rightn`. Here is the extracted version:

```
let rec zip_rightn n z =
  (fun f0 fS n -> if (eq_big_int n zero_big_int) then f0 () else fS (pred_big_int n))
    (fun_ ->
    z)
    (fun np ->
    zip_rightn np (zip_right z))
    n
```

The body of this function is equivalent to a single conditional that returns z
when n is 0 and recursively calls `zip_rightn` on n-1 otherwise. This artifact in
the extraction is simply a by-product of the mismatch between **nat** and **big_int**.
We expect that this artifact can be automatically removed by the OCaml compiler. This transformation into the single conditional corresponds to modest
inlining, since f0 and fS occur exactly once and are constants.

Functions in the third category, however, are more complex. They extract
into code that is cluttered by Coq's support for non-simple recursion schemes.
Because each function in Coq must be proven to be well-defined and to terminate
on all inputs, functions that don't simply follow the natural recursive structure of
their input must have supplemental arguments that record the decreasing nature
of their input. After extraction, these additional arguments clutter the OCaml
code with useless data structures equivalent to the original set of arguments.

The function `cinterleave` is one such function. Here is the extracted version:

```
let rec cinterleave_func x =
  let e = let a,p = let x0,h = x in h in a in
  let o = let x0,h = let x0,h = x in h in h in
  let cinterleave0 = fun e0 o0 -> let y = _,(e0,o0) in cinterleave_func y in
  (match e with
   | Nil -> o
   | Cons (x0, xs) -> Cons (x0, (cinterleave0 o xs)))


let cinterleave e o =
  Obj.magic (cinterleave_func (_,((Obj.magic e),(Obj.magic o))))
```

All of the extra pieces beyond what was written in the original function
are useless. In particular, the argument to `cinterleave_func` is a three-deep
nested pair containing _ and two lists. The _ is a constant that is defined at
the top of the extraction file that is never used for anything and behaves like
unit. That piece of the tuple corresponds to a proof that the combined length
of the two lists is decreasing. The function starts by destructuring this complex
argument to extract the two lists, e and o. Next it constructs a version of the
function, `cinterleave0`, that recovers the natural two argument function for use
recursively in the body of the `match` expression. Finally, this same two argument
interface is reconstructed a second time, `cinterleave`, for external applications.
The external interface has an additional layer of strangeness in the form of
applications of `Obj.magic` which can be used to coerce types, but here is simply
the identity function on values and in the types. These calls correspond to use

of `proj1_sig` in Coq to extract the value from a Sigma type and are useless and always successful in OCaml.

All together, the OCaml program is equivalent to:

```
let rec cinterleave e o =
    match e with | Nil         -> o
                 | Cons (x, xs) -> Cons (x, (cinterleave o xs))
```

This is exactly the Coq program and idiomatic OCaml code. Unlike the second category, it is less plausible that the OCaml compiler already performs this optimization and removes the superfluity from the Coq extraction output. However, it is plausible that such an optimization pass could be implemented, since it corresponds to inlining, de-tupling, and removing an unused unit-like argument. In summary, the presence of these useless terms is unrelated to our running time monad, but is an example of the sort of verification residue we wish to avoid and do successfully avoid in the case of the running time obligations.

The functions in the first category are: `insert`, `size_linear`, `size`, `make_array_naive`, `foldr`, `make_array_naive_foldr`, `unravel`, `to_list_naive`, `isort`'s `insert`, `isort`, `clength`, `minsert_at`, `to_zip,from_zip`, `zip_right`, `zip_left`, `zip_insert`, `zip_minsert`, `minsertz_at`, `bst_search`, `rbt_blacken`, `rbt_balance`, `rbt_insert`. The functions in the second category are: `fib_rec`, `fib_iter`, `sub1`, `mergesort`'s `split`, `insert_at`, `zip_rightn`, `zip_leftn`, `add1`, `tplus`. The functions in the third category are: `copy_linear`, `copy_fib`, `copy_log_sq`, `copy2`, `diff`, `make_array_td`, `cinterleave`, `merge`, `mergesort`. Some of the functions in the second category are also in the third category.

7   Accounting for Language Primitives

Rosendahl (1989)'s cost function counts all primitive functions as constant (simply because it counts a call as unit time and then doesn't process the body). For most primitives, this is the right behavior. For example, field selection functions (e.g., `car` and `cdr`) are certainly constant time. Structure allocation functions (e.g., `cons`) are usually constant time when using a two-space copying collector, as most garbage-collected languages do. Occasionally, allocation triggers garbage collection, which we can assume amortized constant time (but not something our framework handles).

More interestingly, and more often overlooked, however, are numeric primitives. In a language implementation with BigNums, integers are generally represented as a list of digits in some large base and grade-school arithmetic algorithms implement the various operations. Most of these operations do not take constant time.

If we assume that the base is a power of 2^2, then division by 2, evenness testing, and checking to see if a number is equal to 0 are all constant-time operations. The algorithms in our study use two other numeric operations: `+` and `sub1` (not counting the abstract comparison in the sorting functions).

---

[2] This is the case if BigNums are represented as lists of bits.

In general, addition of BigNums is not constant time. However, certain uses of addition can be replaced by constant-time bit operations. For instance, doubling and adding 1 can be replaced by a specialized operation that conses a 1 on the front of the bitstring. Fortunately, every time we use addition in one of the functions in our Braun library, the operation can be replaced by one of these efficient operations.

One of the more interesting uses is in the linear version of `size`, which has the sum `lsize+rsize+1` where `lsize` and `rsize` are the sizes of two subtrees of a Braun tree. This operation, at first glance, doesn't seem to take constant-time. But the Braun invariant tells us that `lsize` and `rsize` are either equal, or that `lsize` is `rsize+1`. Accordingly, this operation can be replaced with either `lsize*2+1` or `lsize*2`, both of which are constant-time operations. Checking to see which case applies is also constant time: if the numbers are the same, the digits at the front of the respective lists will be the same and if they differ by 1, those digits will be different.

The uses of addition in `fib`, however, are not constant time. We did not account for the time of additions in the recursive implementation of `fib`. We have proved, however, that the iterative `fib` function, which requires linear time when additions are not counted, requires quadratic time when we properly account for primitive operations.

Our implementation of addition has a run time that is linear in the number of bits of its input. Using this fact, we can prove that iterative `fib` has a run time that is asymptotic to the square of its input. To prove that `fib`'s run time is bounded below by n^2, we first observe that for all $n \geq 6$ we have that $2^{n/2} \leq fib(n)$. In the nth iteration of the loop, `fib` adds numbers with $\frac{n}{2}$ bits in their binary representation, which takes time on the order of $\frac{n}{2}$. For large enough n, this implies that the run time of the additions in the iterative `fib` function are bounded below by $\frac{1}{2}(6 + 7 + \cdots + n)$. This sum has a quadratic lower bound. Since the other primitives used in calculating `fib` run in constant time, the run time is dominated by the addition operations, thus the run time of `fib` is bounded below by a factor of n^2.

A similar argument shows that the run time of `fib` has a quadratic upper bound. Combining these two results proves that the run time of the iterative version of `fib` is asymptotically n^2 when we account for primitive operations. The supplementary material contains proofs of these facts in Coq (`fib/fib_iter.v`).

Although our analysis of `fib` properly accounts for addition, it does not consider all language primitives. Specifically, the above analysis of the `fib` function ignores the subtraction that occurs in each iteration of the loop. For example, in the extracted OCaml code for `fib`, pattern matching against `S n` becomes a call to the `pred_big_int` function. Subtracting 1 from a number represented in binary requires more than constant time; `sub1` may need to traverse the entire number to compute its predecessor.

To be certain that the non-constant run time of `sub1` does not affect our calculation of `fib`'s run time, we argue that the implicit subtractions in the implementation of `fib` take amortized constant time. Although subtraction by 1 is not always a constant time operation, it does require constant time on half of its possible inputs. On any odd number represented in binary, subtracting by 1 is a constant time operation. It follows that any number equivalent to 2 modulo 4 will require 2 units of time to perform the sub1 operation because sub1 will terminate after two iterations. In general, there is a $\frac{1}{2^n}$ chance that sub1 terminates after n iterations. To account for all uses of sub1 in the implementation of fib, we note that we will perform the sub1 operation on each number from 1 to n. This gives a cost in terms of the iterations required by sub1 that is bounded above by $n * (\frac{1}{2} + \frac{2}{4} + \frac{3}{8} + \cdots + \frac{n}{2^n} + \cdots)$. One can show that this infinite sum converges to $2 * n$, thus for a sequence of n sub1 operations this shows that subtraction implicit in the definition of fib requires amortized constant time. Overall, the run time of the additions performed by fib will dwarf the time required by subtraction. This justifies the fact that we do not explicitly consider the time taken by sub1 operations.

Although we can account for the recursion pattern using sub1 described above that counts down from n to 0, there are several other recursive uses of sub1 found in our library. For example, our implementations of copy2 and copy_insert loop by subtracting 1 then dividing by 2. As for fib, we have not explicitly accounted for these other uses of sub1. We do, however, believe that the overhead of using sub1 in these functions does not change their asymptotic complexity, but we have verified this only by testing and informal arguments.

8   Related Work

The most closely related work to ours is Danielsson (2008), which presents a monad that carries a notion of abstract time. Unlike our monad, his does not carry an invariant – in our terms his construction does not have the P argument. In our opinion, figuring out the design of monad operations that support the P argument is our major technical advance. Accordingly, his system cannot specify the running time of many of the Braun functions, since the size information is not available without the additional assumption of Braunness. Of course, one can bake the Braun invariants into the Braun data-structure itself, which would provide them to his monad via the function arguments, but this restricts the way the code is written, leaves residue in the extracted code, and moves the implementation away from an idiomatic style. Also, his monad leaves natural numbers in the extracted code; avoiding that is a major goal of this work.

While Crary and Weirich (2000)'s work does not leverage the full expressiveness of a theorem proving system like Coq's, it does share a similar resemblance to our approach. Also like Danielsson (2008)'s and unlike ours, it does not provide a place to carry an invariant of the data structures that can be used to establish running times.

Weegen and McKinna (2009) give a proof of the average case complexity of Quicksort in Coq. They too use monads, but design a monad that is specially tailored to counting only comparison operations. They side-step the extraction problem by abstracting the implementation over a monad transformer and use one monad for proving the correct running times and another for extraction.

Xi and Pfenning first seriously studied the idea of using dependent types to describe invariants of data structures in practical programming languages (Xi 1999a,b; Xi and Pfenning 1999) and, indeed, even used Braun trees as an example in the DML language, which could automatically prove that, for example, `size_log_sq` is correct.

Filliâtre and Letouzey (2004) implemented a number of balanced binary tree implementations in Coq with proofs of correctness (but not running time), with the goal of high-quality extraction. They use an "external" approach, where the types do not carry the running time information, which makes the proofs more complex.

Swierstra (2009)'s Hoare state monad is like our monad in that it exploits monadic structure to make proof obligations visible at the right moments. However, the state used in their monad has computational content and thus is not erased during extraction.

Charguéraud (2010) and Charguéraud and Pottier (2015)'s characteristic formula generator seems to produce Coq code with obligations similar to what our monad produces, but it does not consider running time.

Others have explored automatic techniques for proving that programs have particular resource bounds using a variety of techniques (Gulwani et al. 2009; Hoffmann and Shao 2015; Hofmann and Jost 2003; Hughes and Pareto 1999) These approaches are all weaker than our approach, but provide more automation.

Similarly, others have explored different approaches for accounting for various resource bounds and costs, but we do not provide any contribution in this area. Instead, we take an off-the-shelf cost semantics (Rosendahl (1989))'s) and use it. We believe our approach applies to other cost models.

We have consistently used the word "monad" to describe what our library provides and believe that is a usefully evocative word to capture the essence of our library. However, they are not technically monads for two reasons. First, the monad laws are written using an equality, but we use an equivalence relation appropriate to our type. Second, our types have more parameters than the single parameter used in monads, due to the proof information residing in the types, so our "monad" is actually a generalized form of a monad, a specialization of Atkey (2009)'s or Altenkirch et al. (2010)'s. Swierstra (2009) and Swamy et al. (2013) follow this same evocative naming convention.

Our code uses Sozeau (2006)'s `Program` facility in Coq for writing dependently-typed programs by separating idiomatic code and detail-oriented proofs in the program source. Without `Program`, our programs would have to mix the running time proofs in with the program, which would greatly obscure the code's connection to the original algorithm, as one does in Danielsson (2008).

We have experimented with supporting proofs about imperative programs by combining our monad's types with a variation of the Swierstra (2009) and Swamy et al. (2013) monads. The types and proofs work out, but are considerably more complicated, due in part to the complexity of proofs about imperative programs.

We consider it future work to study whether there is a more elegant approach and develop a detailed case study.

Acknowledgments. Thanks to reviewers of previous versions of this paper. Thanks to Neil Toronto for help with the properties of integer logarithms (including efficient implementations of them). This work grew out of a PL seminar at Northwestern; thanks to Benjamin English, Michael Hueschen, Daniel Lieberman, Yuchen Liu, Kevin Schwarz, Zach Smith, and Lei Wang for their feedback on early versions of the work.

References

Altenkirch, T., Chapman, J., Uustalu, T.: Monads need not be endofunctors. In: Proceedings of the Foundations of Software Science and Computation Structure (2010)

Atkey, R.: Parameterised notions of computation. JFP **19**(3–4), 335–376 (2009)

Braun, W., Rem, M.: A logarithmic Implementation of Flexible Arrays. Eindhoven University of Technology, MR83/4 (1983)

Charguéraud, A.: Characteristic Formulae for Mechanized Program Verification. Ph.D. dissertation, Université Paris Diderot (Paris 7) (2010)

Charguéraud, A., Pottier, F.: Machine-checked verification of the correctness and amortized complexity of an efficient union-find implementation. In: Proceedings of the ITP (2015)

Cormen, T.H., Leiserson, C.E., Rivest, R.L., Stein, C.: Introduction to Algorithms, 3rd edn. MIT Press, Cambridge (2009)

Crary, K., Weirich, S.: Resource bound certification. In: Proceedings of the POPL (2000)

Crosby, S.A., Wallach, D.S.: Denial of service via algorithmic complexity attacks. In: Proceedings of the USENIX Security Symposium (2003)

Danielsson, N.A.: Lightweight semiformal time complexity analysis for purely functional data structures. In: Proceedings of the POPL (2008)

Danner, N., Paykin, J., Royer, J.S.: A static cost analysis for a higher-order language. In: Proceedings of the Workshop on Programming Languages meets Program Verification (2013)

Filliâtre, J.-C., Letouzey, P.: Functors for proofs and programs. In: Schmidt, D. (ed.) ESOP 2004. LNCS, vol. 2986, pp. 370–384. Springer, Heidelberg (2004)

Gulwani, S., Mehra, K.K., Chilimbi, T.: SPEED: precise and efficient static estimation of program computational complexity. In: Proceedings of the POPL (2009)

Hoffmann, J., Shao, Z.: Automatic static cost analysis for parallel programs. In: Vitek, J. (ed.) ESOP 2015. LNCS, vol. 9032, pp. 132–157. Springer, Heidelberg (2015)

Hofmann, M., Jost, S.: Static prediction of heap space usage for first-order functional programs. In: Proceedings of the POPL (2003)

Hughes, J., Pareto, L.: Recursion and Dynamic Data-structures in bounded space: towards embedded ML programming. In: Proceedings of the ICFP (1999)

Okasaki, C.: Three algorithms on braun trees. JFP **7**(6), 661–666 (1997)

Rosendahl, M.: Automatic complexity analysis. In: Proceedings of the International Conference on Functional Programming Languages And Computer Architecture (1989)

Sozeau, M.: Subset coercions in Coq. In: Proceedings of the TYPES (2006)

Swamy, N., Weinberger, J., Schlesinger, C., Chen, J., Livshits, B.: Verifying higher-order programs with the dijkstra monad. In: Proceedings of the PLDI (2013)

Swierstra, W.: A hoare logic for the state monad. In: Proceedings of the TPHOLS (2009)

van der Weegen, E., McKinna, J.: A machine-checked proof of the average-case complexity of quicksort in Coq. In: Berardi, S., Damiani, F., de'Liguoro, U. (eds.) TYPES 2008. LNCS, vol. 5497, pp. 256–271. Springer, Heidelberg (2009)

Xi, H.: Dependently typed data structures. In: Proceedings of the Workshop on Algorithmic Aspects of Advanced Programming Languages (1999a)

Xi, H.: Dependently Types in Practical Programming. Ph.D. dissertation, Carnegie Mellon University (1999b)

Xi, H., Pfenning, F.: Dependently types in practical programming. In: Proceedings of the POPL (1999)

A Transformational Approach to Parametric Accumulated-Cost Static Profiling

R. Haemmerlé[1], P. López-García[1,2]([✉]), U. Liqat[1], M. Klemen[1],
J.P. Gallagher[1,3], and M.V. Hermenegildo[1,4]

[1] IMDEA Software Institute, Madrid, Spain
[2] Spanish Council for Scientific Research (CSIC), Madrid, Spain
pedro.lopez@imdea.org
[3] Roskilde University, Roskilde, Denmark
[4] Technical University of Madrid (UPM), Madrid, Spain

Abstract. Traditional static resource analyses estimate the total resource usage of a program, without executing it. In this paper we present a novel resource analysis whose aim is instead the *static profiling of accumulated cost*, i.e., to discover, for selected parts of the program, an estimate or bound of the resource usage accumulated in each of those parts. Traditional resource analyses are parametric in the sense that the results can be functions on input data sizes. Our static profiling is also parametric, i.e., our accumulated cost estimates are also parameterized by input data sizes. Our proposal is based on the concept of cost centers and a program transformation that allows the static inference of functions that return bounds on these accumulated costs depending on input data sizes, for each cost center of interest. Such information is much more useful to the software developer than the traditional resource usage functions, as it allows identifying the parts of a program that should be optimized, because of their greater impact on the total cost of program executions. We also report on our implementation of the proposed technique using the CiaoPP program analysis framework, and provide some experimental results.

1 Introduction and Motivation

The execution of software consumes resources such as time, energy, and memory. The goal of automatic program resource analysis is to infer the resources that a program uses as a function of the size of the input data or other environmental parameters of the program, without actually executing the program. Previous work on this topic, mainly for inferring asymptotic time complexity bounds, goes back to the 1970s. Recent research has adapted and extended these techniques for inferring other resources, including for example energy [14,15].

In this paper we investigate an extension of this problem which, although based on the same essential techniques, has a different range of applications. Rather than estimating the total resource usage of a program, we wish to perform *static profiling* of its resource usage. This means that we intend to discover,

© Springer International Publishing Switzerland 2016
O. Kiselyov and A. King (Eds.): FLOPS 2016, LNCS 9613, pp. 163–180, 2016.
DOI: 10.1007/978-3-319-29604-3_11

for selected parts of the program, an estimate of the resources used by those parts. As before, the estimates will be parameterised by input sizes. However, these input sizes will be of the entry predicate/function, unlike the input sizes of the selected parts, as in the standard resource analysis.

There are several motivations for this research. Firstly, a profile of the resource usage of the program can show the developer which parts of the program are the most resource critical. For example, it can expose the cost of functions that are perhaps not particularly resource hungry by themselves but which are called many times. Such parts are natural targets for optimization, since there a small improvement can yield important savings. Secondly, there are cases where the overall resource functions of a program might not be obtainable. This can be for instance because some program parts are too complex for analysis or because the code for some parts is not available and the cost cannot even be reasonably estimated. In this case useful information may still be obtained by excluding such parts from the analysis, obtaining information about the resource usage for the rest of the program. Thirdly, resource usage models (for example Tiwari's energy consumption model [29]) are sometimes based on summing the individual resource usage of basic components of the program. The analysis presented here fits naturally with such models. Finally, in cases where a program has mutually recursive functions/predicates, the standard cost analysis infers similar resource functions for each recursive function. In such cases, a static profile finds precisely the resource functions for each mutually recursive part of the program, and helps identify the parts that are responsible for most of the cost.

The traditional profiling techniques are dynamic (i.e., require executing the program on some particular input) and are based either on code instrumentation, i.e., introducing additional pieces of code in the sections to be measured, or on running a process that performs the profiling together with the measured program. In both cases, the dynamic profiler introduces an overhead in the resource measured that needs to be properly discriminated, which is non trivial. For example, it may be the case that an instruction in the original program has a very different energy consumption in the presence of code added by the profiler just before it. In contrast, the static profiling approach we propose in this paper obtains safe upper and lower bounds on resource consumption, because it is based on the semantics of the program rather than particular executions of it. I.e., the results are valid for all possible program inputs.

Our starting point is the well-developed technique of extracting recurrence relations that express resource usage functions [1,5–7,25,32]. These are then solved to get a closed-form function expressing the (bounds on) parameterised resource usage. In our work we will make use the CiaoPP program analysis framework, which includes a set of generic resource analyses based on these techniques. In particular, we will use the analysis described in [28]. CiaoPP operates on an intermediate semantic program representation based on Horn Clauses [16], that we will refer to as the "HC IR." By transforming the input language into this intermediate representation, the CiaoPP framework has been shown capable of analyzing imperative programs at the source, bytecode, or binary level with competitive precision and efficiency (see [14–16,20,21] for details).

Our approach to static profiling is based on a transformation that is performed at the level of the CiaoPP Horn Clause-based intermediate representation. The proposed transformation allows a standard cost analyzer (CiaoPP in our experiments) to statically infer functions that return bounds on *accumulated costs* depending on input data sizes, for a number of predefined program points of interest (predicates in our case), referred to as cost centers. Intuitively, given a program $\mathcal{P}$, the cost accumulated in a given predicate $p \in \mathcal{P}$ is defined in the context of the execution of a single call to another predicate $q \in \mathcal{P}$. It expresses the addition of (part of) the resource usages corresponding to the execution of all calls to predicate p generated by a single call to predicate $q \in \mathcal{P}$.

In the rest of the paper, Sect. 2 presents informally a general model of (dynamic) profiling and how we turn it into a static version. Section 3 reviews established techniques for cost analysis based on extracting and solving cost relations. Section 4 formalizes our notion of *accumulated cost*. Section 5 describes the implementation of the technique, based on a source-to-source transformation. Section 6 reports some experimental results. In Sect. 7 we comment on some related work and finally Sect. 8 concludes, discussing future directions.

2   From Dynamic Profiling to Static Profiling

We start by presenting informally a general model of (dynamic) profiling and how we turn it into a static version. Our model is based on the notion of *cost centers*, inspired from the work of Sansom and Peyton Jones [26] and Morgan and Jarvis [18]. This approach was also applied to Logic Programs and extended to perform run-time checking of non-functional properties in [17]. Intuitively a cost center provides a dynamic scoping mechanism to uniquely attribute the execution costs of a part of the code to an identifier. The scope of the cost center is dynamic in the sense that execution costs of code that are not explicitly associated to a cost center are dynamically attributed to the same cost center as the caller. For a number of languages it is convenient to identify the cost centers with (a subset of) functions, procedures, or predicates. In this paper we follow this path. Alternatively, cost centers can be defined by special scoping constructs [26].

As an example,[1] assume that a programmer wishes to profile a program which uses the following `variance()` function (`variance()` naively computes the variance of an array of integers):

---

[1] As mentioned in the introduction, CiaoPP's analyses deal with programs written in such C-like languages (among others) by analyzing corresponding Horn Clause representations.

```
1  int   variance(int * arr, int size){
2    int tmp[size], i = size;
3    while(i > 0) {
4      i--;
5      tmp[i] = (arr[i] - mean(arr, size));
6      tmp[i] = tmp[i] * tmp[i]; }
7    return mean(tmp, size);
8  }
```

Assume that mean() is a given function that computes the mean of an integer array. First consider that both mean() and variance() are cost centers. In this case the actual execution costs of the code that appears textually within the variance() function will be aggregated at each call to such function and will be attributed to the variance() cost center. However the cost of calls to mean() –including those made from variance()– will not be attributed to variance(). Now consider the case where variance() is declared a cost center, but mean() is not. In this case the execution costs of calls to mean() made from the variance() function will be also aggregated to those of variance() (but not those made from other points in the program).

Returning to the case where both variance() and mean() are declared as cost centers, assume that the programmer profiles the energy consumption (measured as nano joules, nJ) of a call to the variance() function over the array $\{1, 2, 3, 4\}$, on some particular architecture. Assume that the result of the profiler is that 74.7 units of energy are accumulated in the variance() cost center and 464.4 units in the mean() cost center. Since mean() is called 4 times, the cost of a single call to it (with the array above) would be 116.1 nJ (464.4/4). If only variance() were declared a cost center, the profiler would have accumulated all the cost in it, i.e., $464.4 + 74.7$ nJ. In such a case, the cost measured by the profiler would be the same as what we call the standard cost of a (single) call to variance() with the given array (i.e., 539 nJ).

Since the accumulated value in the mean() cost center is much larger than that accumulated in the variance() cost center, this indicates that for this particular call most of the energy is consumed inside the mean() function, i.e., that this function is responsible for most of the standard cost of the call to variance(). This can be a strong indicator that it may be worthwhile to either optimize the body of mean() or try to reduce the number of times it is called. Note, however, that with just this data, which come from a run with a particular input, the programmer does not really have any guarantees that the results are representative of the general behavior of the program for all inputs. This problem is usually tackled by repeating the process on a large set of different inputs. This can lead to more indicative results, but still has several drawbacks. First, this process can be very long, because profiling usually introduces additional execution costs, which get multiplied by the number of inputs. Second, and more importantly, even if a large number of inputs is used, this still does not provide a strong guarantee, i.e., there may be some corner case inputs for which the call behaves in a very different way. Finally, the approach does not allow the comparison of the asymptotic cost accumulated in the different cost centers.

To overcome the problems outlined above, we propose to *statically* infer (lower and upper) bounds on the cost accumulated in the cost centers as functions of the sizes of the input data to the profiled call (the call variance() in our example). In the example above, the system we have implemented infers (for the resource "energy"[2]) that for a call to variance() with a list of size *size*, the costs accumulated in the variance and mean() functions are $24.32 + size \times 12.59$ and $23.03 + 17.46 \times size^2 + 40.49 \times size$ energy units (nano joules) respectively. In this case the system infers these expressions for both the upper and lower bounds, which means that they are exact costs. Hence, the programmer does have the guarantee that for all non-trivial calls (i.e., for all calls with non-empty lists) *and for any input data*, the code of mean() consumes most of the energy. In this case an obvious improvement can be made, since the call to mean(arr, size) can be safely moved outside the loop:

```
1   int  variance(int * arr, int size){
2     int tmp[size];
3     int i = size;
4     int m = mean(arr, size);
5     while(i > 0) {
6       i--;
7       tmp[i] = (arr[i] - m);
8       tmp[i] = tmp[i] * tmp[i];
9     }
10    return mean(tmp, size);
11  }
```

For this version of the program, the system infers that the costs accumulated in the variance() and mean() functions are $28.18 + size \times 8.73$ and $46.06 + 34.92 \times size$ energy units (nano joules) respectively. For brevity and simplicity we chose a program that is rather naive and where the optimization is obvious (and would in fact be done by some compilers automatically), but the same reasoning applies to more complex cases that are not easy to spot without profiling information. Furthermore, the static profiling functions can also be used for guiding automatic optimization by the compiler.

3   The Classical Cost Relations-Based Parametric Static Analysis

The approach to cost analysis based on setting up and solving recurrence equations was proposed in [32] and has been developed significantly in subsequent work. For example, in [25] an automatic upper-bound analysis was presented based on an abstract interpretation of a step-counting version of a functional

---

[2] Using as back-end analysis the energy analysis of [14, 15] on an XCore XS1 processor with the program compiled by the XMOS xcc compiler without optimization.

program, in order to infer both execution time and execution steps. However, size measures could not automatically be inferred and the experimental section showed few details about the practicality of the analysis. In the context of Logic Programming, a semi-automatic analysis was presented in [5,6] that inferred upper-bounds on the number of execution steps, given as functions on the input data sizes. This work also proposed techniques to address the additional challenges posed by the Logic Programming paradigm, as, for example, dealing with the generation of multiple solutions via backtracking. However, a shortcoming of the approach was its loss in precision in the presence of divide-and-conquer programs in which the sizes of the output arguments of the "divide" predicates are dependent. This approach was later fully automated (by integrating it into the CiaoPP system and automatically providing *modes and size measures*) and extended to inferring both upper- and lower-bounds on the number of *execution steps* (which is non-trivial because of the possibility of failure) in [7,10]. In addition, [7] introduced the setting up of non-deterministic recurrence relations for the class of divide-and-conquer programs mentioned above, and proposed a technique for computing approximated closed form bound functions for some of them. Such a technique was based on bounding the number of terminal and non-terminal nodes in the set of computation trees corresponding to the evaluation of the non-deterministic recurrence relations, and bounding the cost of such nodes. Non-deterministic recurrence relations were also used and further developed in [1] (named Cost Relations). The approach in [5–7] was generalized in [22] to infer *user-defined resources* (by using an extension of the Ciao assertion language [11]), and was further improved in [28] by defining the resource analysis itself as an *abstract domain* that is integrated into the PLAI abstract interpretation framework [19,24] of CiaoPP, obtaining features such as *multivariance*, efficient fixpoints, and assertion-based verification and user interaction. A significant additional improvement brought about by [28] is that it is combined with a *sized types* abstract domain, which allows the inference of non-trivial cost bounds when they depend on the sizes of input terms and their subterms at any position and depth. Recently, many other approaches have been proposed for resource analysis [1,2,8,9,12,13,23,30]. While based on different techniques, all these analyses infer, for all predicates p of a given program $\mathcal{P}$, an approximation of the notion of cost that we call the *standard cost* or *single call cost*. Most of them infer an upper bound, while others infer both upper and lower bounds. The following example shows this (for the case of CiaoPP) and also illustrates that this concept of cost may not be directly useful for locating performance bottlenecks.

Example 1. Consider the following implementation of an eval(E,M,R) predicate that evaluates modulo 2^M a given expression E built from additions and multiplications. This implementation assumes that two predicates are given: add(A,B,M,R) and mult(A,B,M,R), that respectively add and multiply two infinite precision numbers A and B modulo 2^M, and unify the result with R.

```
1  eval(const(A),M,R)   :- eval_const(A,M,R).
2  eval(A+B,      M,R)  :- eval_add(A,B,M,R).
3  eval(A*B,      M,R)  :- eval_mult(A,B,M,R).
4
5  eval_const(A,_,R)    :- R=A.
6  eval_add(A,B,M,R)    :- eval(A,M,RA), eval(B,M,RB), add(RA,RB,M,R).
7  eval_mult(A,B,M,R):- eval(A,M,RA),  eval(B,M,RB),mult(RA,RB,M,R).
```

For the sake of simplicity, assume that all the costs are null except those related to the evaluation of add/4 and mult/4. Assume that the cost of the evaluation of add(A,B,M,R) is M and the cost of the evaluation of mult(A,B,M,R) is M^2. Under these assumptions, the standard CiaoPP cost analysis infers that the cost of the evaluation of eval(E,M,R) is bounded by $(2^{\text{depth}(E)} - 1) \times (M + M^2)$ where depth(E) stands for the depth of the expression E – note that the exact bound is $(2^{\text{depth}(E)} - 1) \times M^2$. However, such an analysis does not help finding precisely which part of the code is responsible for most of the cost. Indeed since all the predicates (eval/3, eval_add/4, and eval_mult/4) are mutually recursive, the system will infer a similar cost for eval_add/4 and eval_mult/4. Furthermore, those costs will be expressed in terms of different input variables making the actual comparison difficult.

4 Parametric Accumulated-Cost Static Profiling

We now formalize the new notion of cost that we propose, the *accumulated cost*, which has been intuitively described in Sect. 1. As mentioned before, our approach is based on the notion of cost centers: user-defined program points (predicates, in our case) to which execution costs are assigned during the execution of a program. Data about computational events is accumulated by the cost center each time the corresponding program point is reached by the program execution control flow.

We start by presenting a formal *profiled semantics* for Logic Programming. For this purpose we assume given a program $\mathcal{P}$. We also assume that each predicate p is associated with a cost $\text{cost}_p \in \mathbb{R}$ and that the cost centers are defined as a set $\Diamond$ of predicate symbols. In the following we will use overlined symbols such as $\bar{t}$, $\bar{x}$, or $\bar{e}$ to denote a sequence of terms, variables, or arithmetic expressions.

We define a *predicate call with context* as a tuple of the form $r : p(\bar{t})$, where r, the *context*, is a cost center (i.e., a predicate from $\Diamond$) and $p(\bar{t})$ is a predicate call. Then, we define *profiled states* as tuples of the form $\langle \alpha ; \theta ; \kappa \rangle$ where α is a sequence of predicate calls with context, θ is a substitution that maps variables to calling data, and κ, the *cost assignment*, is a family of real numbers indexed by the cost centers $\Diamond$. The *profiled resource semantics* is defined as the smallest relation $\rightarrow_{\mathcal{P}}$ over profiled states satisfying:

$$\frac{q = \text{update}_\Diamond(p, r) \quad (p(\bar{s}) : - \beta) \in \mathcal{P}\rho \quad \sigma \text{ is an m.g.u. of } \bar{s} \text{ and } \bar{t}\theta}{\langle r : p(\bar{t}), \alpha \,;\, \theta \,;\, \kappa \rangle \to_\mathcal{P} \langle q : \beta, \alpha \,;\, \theta \circ \sigma \,;\, \kappa[q \mapsto \kappa_q + \text{cost}_p] \rangle}$$

$$\frac{\sigma \text{ is an m.g.u. of } t \text{ and } [s\theta]}{\langle r :(t \text{ is } s), \alpha \,;\, \theta \,;\, \kappa \rangle \to_\mathcal{P} \langle \alpha \,;\, \theta \circ \sigma \,;\, \kappa \rangle}$$

where:

- $q : \beta, \alpha$ is a notation for the sequence $q : p_1(\bar{s}_1), ..., q : p_n(\bar{s}_n), \alpha$, assuming β is the sequence $p_1(s_1), ..., p_n(s_n)$.
- $[s]$ stands for the arithmetic evaluation of s (if s is not a ground arithmetic expression, then $[s]$ is not defined, as well as the rule using it),
- ρ stands for a renaming with fresh variables,
- $\kappa[q \mapsto c]$ is the assignment that maps p to c if $p = q$ or to κ_p otherwise, and
- $\text{update}_\Diamond(p, r)$ equals either p if $p \in \Diamond$, or r otherwise.

The first rule can be understood as an extension of SLD resolution with cost. Concretely, the cost cost_p of the called predicate p is added to the value of the current cost center, the cost center being updated beforehand to the current predicate if the latter is in fact a cost center, and left unchanged otherwise. The latter rule characterizes the semantics of the built-in is/2, where we assume w.l.o.g. that the operation has no cost. Standard left-to-right evaluation is simply recovered by ignoring the cost assignment together with the calling contexts. In the following section, we will use the notation $(\alpha \,;\, \theta)$, where α is a sequence of predicate calls and θ a substitution, to denote a standard (non-profiled) LP state.

In the following, we use Π as the set of tuples of terms, and $\mathbb{R}$ to denote the set of real numbers. For any cost center $p \in \Diamond$, the *profiled resource usage function* is the function $\mathcal{C}_\Diamond^p : 2^\Pi \to 2^{\mathbb{R}^n}$ defined as:

$$\mathcal{C}_\Diamond^p(\bar{T}) = \begin{cases} \{\kappa \mid \bar{t} \in \bar{T} \ \& \ \langle p : p(\bar{t}) \,;\, \epsilon \,;\, \bar{0} \rangle \to_\mathcal{P}^* \langle \Box \,;\, \theta \,;\, \kappa \rangle \} & \text{if } p(\bar{t}) \text{ terminates} \\ & \text{universally } \forall \bar{t} \in \bar{T} \\ \mathbb{R}^n & \text{otherwise} \end{cases}$$

where $\bar{0}$ stands for the trivial cost assignment that maps any cost center to 0, $\to_\mathcal{P}^*$ is the reflexive and transitive closure of $\to_\mathcal{P}$, $\Box$ denotes the empty sequence of predicate calls, ϵ is the identity substitution, and n is the number of cost centers. We use the "top" element in $2^{\mathbb{R}^n}$ (i.e., $\mathbb{R}^n$) to denote a "don't know" cost for non-terminating programs, which, for simplicity, are currently not defined in our framework. Note that the cost κ_p in an infinite derivation can be (asymptotically) different from $+\infty$ as (1) p can be the context of only a finite number of the steps involved in an infinite derivation, and (2) because costs of predicates can be zero or negative. The profiled semantics is a natural generalization of the standard resource usage semantics which is able to handle several costs which are accumulated in the cost centers. Indeed the resource usage function inferred by the standard analysis can be understood as the function $\mathcal{C}^p = \mathcal{C}_{\{P\}}^p$ defined over a unique cost center.

$\mathcal{C}_q^p(\bar{T})$ denotes the cost accumulated in q from the calls $p(\bar{t})$ $(\bar{t} \in \bar{T})$, that is, the union of the ith component of all tuples in $\mathcal{C}_\Diamond^p(\bar{T})$ if q is the ith cost center in $\Diamond$ (formally $\mathcal{C}_q^p(\bar{T}) = \{\kappa_q \mid \kappa \in \mathcal{C}_\Diamond^p(\bar{T})\}$). In particular, if $p(\bar{t})$ deterministically succeeds (e.g., when it is obtained by translation of some imperative program) the cost accumulated in q from $p(\bar{t})$ is unique, i.e., $\mathcal{C}_q^p(\{\bar{t}\}) = \{c\}$ for some $c \in \mathbb{R}$. In such a case, by a slight abuse of notation, we denote the unique value by $\mathcal{C}_q^p(\bar{t})$.

Example 2. Consider the deterministic program given in Example 1. If we profile the program, defining all the predicates of the program as cost centers except add/4 and mult/4, the costs accumulated in eval_const/3, eval_add/4 and eval_mult/4 for a call of the form eval(E,M,R) are respectively bounded by 0, $(0.5 \times 2^{\text{depth}(E)} \times M)$, and $(0.5 \times 2^{\text{depth}(E)} \times M^2)$. This makes it easier to spot the source of most of the cost, i.e., eval_mult/4. Therefore, to improve the efficiency of the whole program, it can be useful to concentrate on this predicate, either by optimizing its implementation or by reducing the number of times it is called.

We write $p \rightsquigarrow q$ if q is reachable from q, that is, if $q(\bar{t}) \rightarrow_\mathcal{P}^* (p(\bar{s}), \alpha)$ for some calling data $\bar{t}$ and $\bar{s}$, and some sequence of calls α. Given a set $\Diamond$ of cost centers assigned to a program $\mathcal{P}$ and some predicate p, we define the set of *reachable cost centers* from p as the sequence $\Diamond_p = \{q \mid q \in \Diamond \wedge p \rightsquigarrow^* q\}$.

Theorem 1. *Let $\mathcal{P}$ be a program and $\Diamond \subseteq pred(\mathcal{P})$ a set of cost centers for it. Then, for all $p \in \Diamond$: for all $\bar{T} \subset \Pi$ it holds that: $\mathcal{C}_p(\bar{T}) = \left\{\sum_{q \in \Diamond_p} \mathcal{C}_q^p(\bar{T})\right\}$. In particular, if $p(\bar{t})$ deterministically succeeds $\mathcal{C}_p(\bar{t}) = \sum_{q \in \Diamond_p} \mathcal{C}_q^p(\bar{t})$.*

Note that Theorem 1 provides the basis for a compositional and modular definition of the standard (i.e., single call) cost analysis, from the results of the accumulated cost analysis. Note also that (by definition of reachable cost center) p is always reachable from itself, even though p does not call itself.

5   Inferring Accumulated Cost via Transformation

As mentioned before, our implementation of the static profiler is based on a source-to-source transformation. In this section we show such a transformation that allows obtaining accumulated cost information for cost centers by performing a sized type analysis in CiaoPP. Basically, the transformation consists of adding *shadow arguments* to each predicate of the Horn clauses that represent the accumulated cost for each cost center.

5.1   The Transformation

In this section we assume there is exactly n cost centers and $\Diamond$ is defined as the family $\{p_i\}_{i \in 0..n-1}$. The transformation proposed consists of adding $n+1$ shadow arguments to each predicate, such that on success those variables will be assigned to the costs accumulated in the program. There are n shadow arguments for the cost accumulated in the cost centers called by the predicate, and an additional one for the cost associated with the calling context, which is not known statically.

Formally, the transformation is defined by the functions $[\![\cdot]\!]_\Diamond$ and $[\![\cdot]\!]_n$ that respectively translate clauses and goals. The function $[\![\cdot]\!]_n : \mathcal{A}^* \to (\mathcal{A}^* \times E^{n+1})$ (E is the set of possibly non-ground arithmetic expressions) that translates sequences of atoms is defined recursively on the length of the goal as:

- $[\![q(\bar{t}), \alpha]\!]_n = ((q(\bar{t}, \bar{x}), \beta), \bar{x} + \bar{e})$ where $(\beta, \bar{e}) = [\![\alpha]\!]_n$
- $[\![\Box]\!]_n = (\Box, \bar{0})$

where $\bar{x}$ (resp. $\bar{0}$) stands for a sequence of $(n + 1)$ fresh variables (a sequence of $(n + 1)$ zeros). On the other hand the function $[\![\cdot]\!]_\Diamond : \mathcal{C} \to \mathcal{C}$ is defined by cases as follows:

$$
[\![q(\bar{t}) : - \alpha]\!]_\Diamond = \begin{cases} (q(\bar{t}, \bar{x}) : - \beta, & \\ \quad \bar{x} \text{ is } \bar{e}[\bar{e}_n \leftarrow 0][\bar{e}_i \leftarrow (cost_q + e_i + e_n)] & \text{if } q = p_i \in \Diamond \\ (q(\bar{t}, \bar{x}) : - \beta, & \\ \quad \bar{x} \text{ is } \bar{e}[\bar{e}_n \leftarrow (cost_q + e_n)] & \text{otherwise} \end{cases}
$$

where $(\beta, \bar{e}) = [\![\alpha]\!]_n$, $\bar{x}$ is a sequence of $n + 1$ fresh variables, and $\bar{x}$ is $\bar{e}$ is a notation for x_0 is e_0, ..., x_n is e_n (assuming $\bar{x} = (x_0, \dots, x_n)$ and $\bar{e} = (e_0, \dots, e_n)$).

The translation of a clause is defined by case on the predicate q it defines. Suppose q is some cost center $p_i \in \Diamond$. In this case the costs associated with q itself (i.e., $cost_q$) are assigned to the argument corresponding to q, namely e_i. Furthermore the costs in evaluating q that are not associated to any other cost center (i.e., e_n) are also assigned to e_i. Thus we have $\bar{e}[\bar{e}_n \leftarrow 0][\bar{e}_i \leftarrow (cost_q + e_i + e_n)]$. On the other hand, if q is not a cost center, then the costs associated with q are associated to its context, namely e_n, and thus we have $\bar{e}[\bar{e}_n \leftarrow (cost_q + e_n)]$.

Example 3. We show now the translation of the code corresponding to our running example, given in Example 1, assuming that the cost centers are eval/3, eval_const/4, eval_add/4, and eval_mult/4. In the translation the output arguments Ce, Cc, Ca, and Cm correspond to the cost accumulated in the respective cost centers. On the other hand, the output C is the cost that has not been accumulated in any of the cost centers. Within the translation we leave the actual implementations of add/4 and mult/4 unspecified and marked by (...).

```
1   eval(const(A),M,R,Ce,Cc,Ca,Cm,C)  :-
2     eval_const(A,M,R,De,Dc,Da,Dm,D),
3     Ce is De+D, Cc is Dc, Ca is Da, Cm is Dm, C is 0.
4   eval(A+B,M,R,Ce,Cc,Ca,Cm,C)  :-
5     eval_add(A,B,M,R,De,Dc,Da,Dm,D),
6     Ce is De+D,  Cc is Dc, Ca is Da, Cm is Dm, C is 0.
7   eval(A*B,M,R,Ce,Cc,Ca,Cm,C)  :-
8     eval_mult(A,B,M,R,De,Dc,Da,Dm,D),
9     Ce is De+D,  Cc is Dc, Ca is Da, Cm is Dm, C is 0.
10  eval_const(A,_M,R,Ce,Cc,Ca,Cm,C)  :- R=A,
11    Ce is 0, Cc is 0, Ca is 0, Cm is 0, C is 0.
12  eval_add(A,B,M,R,Ce,Cc,Ca,Cm,C)  :-
13    eval(A,M,RA,De,Dc,Da,Dm,D), eval(B,M,RB,Ee,Ec,Ea,Em,E),
14    add(RA,RB,M,R,Fe,Fc,Fa,Fm,F),
15    Ce is De+Ee+Fe, Cc is Dc+Ec+Fc, Ca is Da+Ea+Fa+D+E+F,
16    Cm is Dm+Em+Fm, C is 0.
17  eval_mult(A,B,M,R,Ce,Cc,Ca,Cm,C)  :-
18    eval(A,M,RA,De,Dc,Da,Dm,D), eval(B,M,RB,Ee,Ec,Ea,Em,E),
19    mult(RA,RB,M,R,Fe,Fc,Fa,Fm,F),
20    Ce is De+Ee+Fe, Cc is Dc+Ec+Fc, Ca is Da+Ea+Fa,
21    Cm is Dm+Em+Fm+D+E+F, C is 0.
22  add(RA,RB,M,R,Ce,Cc,Ca,Cm,C)  :-
23    (...)
24    Ce is 0, Cc is 0, Ca is M, Cm is 0, C is 0.
25  mult(RA,RB,M,R,Ce,Cc,Ca,Cm,C)  :-
26    (...)
27    Ce is 0, Cc is 0, Ca is 0, Cm is M*M, C is 0.
```

The following theorem states that the translation of a given program simulates the original one, while reifying the cost assignment as a first-order argument.

Theorem 2. *Assume a given program $\mathcal{P}$ profiled according n cost centers $\Diamond = \{p_0, \ldots, p_{n-1}\}$ and a predicate p different from* is.

(Soundness). *If $(p(\bar{t}, \bar{x}) ; \theta) \rightarrow^*_{[\![\mathcal{P}]\!]_\Diamond} (\square ; \sigma)$ (for some sequence of pairwise $\bar{x}$ distinct variables free in $\bar{t}$ and θ) then there exists a derivation of the form $\langle p_i : p(\bar{t}) ; \theta ; \bar{0}\rangle \rightarrow^*_{\mathcal{P}} \langle \square ; \sigma' ; \kappa\rangle$, with $\bar{t}\sigma' = \bar{t}\sigma$, $\kappa_{p_j} = x_j\sigma$ (for $j \in 1, \ldots, n-1$ and $j \neq i$), and $\kappa_i = x_i\sigma + x_n\sigma$.*

(Completeness). *If $\langle p_i : p(\bar{t}) ; \epsilon ; \bar{0}\rangle \rightarrow^*_{\mathcal{P}} \langle \square ; \theta ; \kappa\rangle$, then there exists a derivation of the form $(p(\bar{t}, \bar{x}) ; \epsilon) \rightarrow^*_{[\![\mathcal{P}]\!]_\Diamond} (\square ; \sigma)$, with $\bar{t}\theta = \bar{t}\sigma$, $\kappa_{p_k} = x_j\sigma$ (for $j \in 1, \ldots, n-1$ and $j \neq i$), and $\kappa_i = x_i\sigma + x_n\sigma$.*

5.2 Performing the Resource Usage Analysis

The Horn Clause program resulting from the transformation described above, whose predicates are augmented with shadow output arguments representing the accumulated cost for each cost center, is analyzed in order to infer lower and upper bounds on the sizes of such arguments, which actually represent bounds on the respective accumulated costs.

In order to obtain such bounds, we use the size analysis presented in [27, 28], integrated in the CiaoPP system. The goal of this analysis is to infer lower and upper bounds on the sizes of output arguments as a function on the sizes of input arguments. This analysis is based on the abstract interpretation framework present in CiaoPP, and basically infers *sized types* for output arguments. Sized types are representations that incorporate structural (shape) information and allow expressing both lower and upper bounds on the size of a set of terms and their subterms at any position and depth. For a more detailed explanation of this process, we refer the reader to [27].

Continuing with our running example, consider the output argument Ca, which represents the accumulated cost of the cost center eval_add/4 when it is called from eval/4. In a preprocessing step, the program is unfolded in order to avoid mutual recursion, which makes the analysis harder. After the unfolding step, the analysis infers types for the predicate arguments by using an existing analysis for regular types [31]. This analysis infers that for a call to a transformed version of eval/4 (with shadow variables) of the form:

$$eval(Exp, M, R, Ce, Cc, Ca, Cm, C)$$

with Exp and R bound and the rest of arguments as free variables, then Ca gets bound to a number upon success, i.e., a term of type num. From the inferred regular type, the analysis derives a *sized type schema*, which is just a sized type with variables in bound positions, along with a set of constraints over those variables.

In this case, the corresponding sized type for **num** is $\mathbf{num}^{(\alpha,\beta)}$, where α and β are variables representing lower and upper bounds on the size of the elements that belong to such type. The metric we use for the size of a number is its actual value, since **num** is a basic type. For compound types, e.g., lists, trees or arithmetic expressions, we can use several metrics for the size of any term belonging to them, such as the depth of such term (as in our example), or the number of type rule applications needed for the type definition to succeed for such term.

The next step involves setting up recurrence relations between size variables. Thus, for β, that represents the upper bound of the size of Ca, we obtain the following equation (where $Size_{arg}^{pred}$ is the size of the argument *arg* corresponding to predicate *pred*):

$$\beta = Size_{Ca}^{eval}(Size_{exp}, M) = \begin{cases} 2 * Size_{Ca}^{eval}(Size_{exp} - 1, M) + M & \text{if } Size_{exp} > 1 \\ 0 & \text{otherwise} \end{cases}$$

At this point, we have obtained a recurrence relation that represents the size of the output argument. However, such expression is not useful for some applications. One disadvantage of using recurrence relations is that the evaluation of them given concrete input values usually takes longer than the evaluation of an equivalent non-recursive expression. In addition, it is not easy to see the complexity order of a given procedure just by looking at its recurrence relation, and the comparison with other functions is also more difficult. For this reason, the analysis uses a solver for obtaining closed-form representations for recurrence relations. Such closed forms can be either exact solutions or safe overapproximations. In our example, the closed-form version for the recurrence is:

$$\beta = Size_{Ca}^{eval}(Size_{exp}, M) = (2^{Size_{exp}} - 1) * M$$

Assuming that the metric for the size of arithmetic expressions is the depth of the term representing them, we have that $Size_{exp} = depth(exp)$. Thus, we can finally conclude that the accumulated cost of eval_add/4 when called from eval/3 (i.e., the size of Ca in the transformed version of the program), is given by

$$(2^{depth(exp)} - 1) * M.$$

6   Experimental Results

We have performed an experimental evaluation of our techniques with the prototype implementation described in Sect. 5 over a number of selected benchmarks from [28]. The benchmarks are written directly as Horn Clause programs (in Ciao). In each benchmark, a number of predicates are marked as cost centers. The results are shown in Table 1. Static profiling was performed for each cost center, capturing the accumulated cost with respect to an entry predicate (marked with a *star*, e.g., *appendAll2**). While in the experiments both upper and lower bounds were inferred, for the sake of brevity we only show upper bound functions. Also, each clause body is assumed to have unitary cost.

Column 1 of Table 1 shows the list of benchmarks while column 2 provides the list of cost centers for each benchmark. Column 3 shows the parametric accumulated cost inferred for each cost center, as a resource usage upper bound function on input data sizes of the entry predicate.Column 4 compares the parametric accumulated cost function of each cost center from column 3 with the results from a dynamic profiling tool [17]. Although the analysis infers upper bounds on the accumulated cost, for some benchmarks these are exact upper bounds (in fact, exact costs) and for others these are correct but relatively imprecise. The imprecision introduced in the benchmarks *listfact* and *appendAll2* is due to the fact that the cost not only depends on the input data sizes but also on the sizes of the sub-terms in the input data, since the analysis statically assumes an upper bound on the sizes of the sub-terms. Note that CiaoPP is the only analysis tool that infers concrete upper bound functions over sized types (costs that depend on the sizes of subterms) [28].

Column 5 shows for comparison the cost inferred by the standard (i.e., non-accumulated) cost analysis [28] for each program and its auxiliary predicates (also marked as cost centers). The comparison of the accumulated and standard cost functions (columns 3 vs. 5) shows the usefulness of our approach: the upper bounds on cost centers display accumulated costs for program parts that were

Table 1. Experimental results.

Program	Cost-Center Predicate	Accumulated Cost UB	Static vs. Dyn	Standard Cost UB	#Calls
appendAll2	$appendAll2^*$	b_1	0 %	$2b_1 b_2 b_3 + b_1 b_2 + b_1$	1
	$appendAll$	$b_1 b_2$	33 %	$b_1 b_2$	b_1
	$append$	$2b_1 b_2 b_3$	61 %	β	$b_1 b_2 + b_1$
hanoi	$hanoi^*$	$2^v - 1$	0 %	$2^{v+1} - 2$	1
	$processMove$	$2^v - 1$	0 %	1	$2^v - 1$
coupled	$coupled^*$	1	0 %	$v + 1$	1
	f	$\frac{v}{2} + \frac{(-1)^v}{4} + \frac{3}{4}$	1.2 %	v	$\frac{v}{2} - \frac{(-1)^v}{4} + \frac{1}{4}$
	g	$\frac{v}{2} + \frac{(-1)^v}{4} - \frac{1}{4}$	0 %	v	$\frac{v}{2} + \frac{(-1)^v}{4} - \frac{1}{4}$
minsort	$minsort^*$	$\beta + 1$	0 %	$\frac{(\beta+1)^2}{2} + \frac{\beta+1}{2}$	1
	$findmin$	$\frac{(\beta+1)^2}{2} + \frac{\beta-1}{2}$	7 %	β	$\beta + 1$
dyade	$dyade^*$	β_1	0 %	$\beta_1(\beta_2 + 1)$	1
	$mult$	$\beta_1 \beta_2$	0 %	β	β_1
variance_naive	$variance^*$	1	0 %	$2\beta^2$	1
	sq_diff	$\beta - 1$	0 %	$2\beta_2 \beta_1 - 2\beta_2$	$\beta - 1$
	$mean$	$2\beta^2 - \beta$	0 %	$\beta - 1$	β
variance	$variance^*$	1	0 %	$5\beta + 3$	1
	sq_diff	β	0 %	β	β
	$mean$	$4\beta + 2$	0 %	$2\beta + 1$	2
listfact	$listfact^*$	β	0 %	$\beta(\delta + 2)$	1
	$fact$	$\beta\delta + \beta$	47 %	$\delta + 1$	β

- $ln^{(\alpha_i, \beta_i)}(n^{(\gamma_i, \delta_i)})$ represents the size of the list of numbers L_i, where β_i and δ_i (resp. α_i and γ_i) denote the upper (resp. lower) bounds on the length of the list and the size of its numbers respectively.
- $lln^{(a_1, b_1)}(lln^{(a_2, b_2)}(ln^{(a_3, b_3)}(n^{(a_4, b_4)})))$ represents the size of the list of lists of lists of numbers similarly.
- $n^{(\mu, v)}$ denotes the size of a number with lower- and upper-bounds μ and v respectively.

not visible with the standard analysis. For instance, similarly to Example 1, the *coupled* benchmark has two auxiliary mutually recursive predicates f and g that are processing elements of a list alternatively until the list becomes empty. The standard analysis infers almost the same upper bound for both functions due to the mutual recursion, whereas the accumulated cost precisely points out the source of cost in the mutually recursive parts. Similarly, in *hanoi*, although the cost of *processMove* (processing a single *hanoi* move) is unitary, we can see that it is called an exponential number of times. The analysis is providing hints to the programmer about the parts of the program that are most profitable candidates for optimization. Note that the upper bound cost functions inferred by static profiling for each cost center predicate are on the input data sizes of the program (entry predicate), in contrast to the standard analysis where the cost functions are on the input data sizes of the predicate that the cost function corresponds to.

Finally, in column 6 an additional *#Calls* cost is presented, indicating the number of times each predicate is called, as a function of input data sizes of the entry predicate. These cost functions are inferred using the standard analysis by defining explicitly a *#Calls resource* for each cost center predicate. A big complexity order in the number of calls to a predicate (in relation to that of a single call) might give hints to reduce the number of calls to such predicate in order to effectively reduce its impact on the overall cost of the program (i.e., the cost of a call to the entry point). More interestingly, since both the *Accumulated* and *#Calls* costs of a predicate q are expressed as functions of input data sizes of the entry predicate, their quotient (Column 3 / Column 6) is meaningful and will give an approximation of the cost of a single call to q as a function of the input data sizes *of the entry predicate*. Note that the standard analysis (Column 5) also provides an upper-bound approximation of this cost but as a function of the input data sizes of predicate q.

7   Related Work

Static profiling in the context of Worst Case Execution Time (WCET) Analysis of real-time programs is presented in [4]. It proposes an approach to computing worst-case timing information for all code parts of a program using a complementary metric, called *criticality*. Every statement of a real-time program is assigned with a criticality value, expressing how critical the respective code is for the global WCET. Our approach is not limited to WCET, since it is able to obtain results for a general class of *user-defined* resources. Furthermore, our inferred metrics are parametric on the input data sizes of the main program, in contrast to the *criticality* metric, which is a numeric value in the range [0, 1]. In addition, our approach is modular and compositional, able to compute accumulated costs w.r.t. calls originating from different procedures of the program, and not only the main program entry point. In [3] the authors present static profiling techniques to estimate the execution *likelihood* and *frequency* of program points in order to assess whether the cost of certain compile-time optimizations would pay off. To this end, they explore the use of some static analysis techniques for predicting the result of conditional branches, such as assuming uniform distribution over all branches, making heuristic based predictions, and performing value range propagation. In this context, our approach can be used to infer bounds on the number of times a certain program point will be called from a given entry point, as functions on input data sizes, in contrast with a single value representing the execution likelihood or frequency. Besides, since our techniques are supported mainly by the theory of abstract interpretation, the approximations inferred are *correct* by design.

8   Conclusions

In this paper we have presented a novel approach of *static profiling of accumulated cost* that infers upper- and lower-bounds of the resource usage accumulated in particular parts of a program as a functions on the input data sizes of the program. We have constructed a prototype implementation of the proposed approach using the CiaoPP program analysis framework. Preliminary experimental results with the tool support the usefulness of our approach where precise accumulated upper bound cost functions were inferred for parts of the program for which the standard analysis was not able to infer precise information. The upper bound functions inferred by the static profiling were also evaluated against a dynamic profiling tool [17], and showed promising accuracy for the static analysis. However in cases where the cost depended on the sizes of the sub-terms of the input, the upper bound accumulated cost loses precision.

Acknowledgements. This research has received funding from the European Union 7th Framework Program agreement no 318337, ENTRA, Spanish MINECO TIN'12-39391 *StrongSoft* project, and the Madrid M141047003 *N-GREENS* program.

References

1. Albert, E., Arenas, P., Genaim, S., Puebla, G.: Closed-form upper bounds in static cost analysis. J. Autom. Reasoning **46**(2), 161–203 (2011)
2. Albert, E., Genaim, S., Masud, A.N.: More precise yet widely applicable cost analysis. In: Jhala, R., Schmidt, D. (eds.) VMCAI 2011. LNCS, vol. 6538, pp. 38–53. Springer, Heidelberg (2011)
3. Boogerd, C., Moonen, L.: On the use of data flow analysis in static profiling. In: Eighth IEEE International Working Conference on Source Code Analysis and Manipulation, pp. 79–88, September 2008
4. Brandner, F., Hepp, S., Jordan, A.: Static profiling of the worst-case in real-time programs. In: Proceedings of the 20th International Conference on Real-Time and Network Systems, RTNS 2012, pp. 101–110. ACM, New York (2012)
5. Debray, S.K., Lin, N.W.: Cost analysis of logic programs. ACM Trans. Program. Lang. Syst. **15**(5), 826–875 (1993)
6. Debray, S.K., Lin, N.-W., Hermenegildo, M.: Task Granularity Analysis in Logic Programs. In: Proceeding of the 1990 ACM Conference on Programming Language Design and Implementation, pp. 174–188. ACM Press, June 1990
7. Debray, S.K., López-García, P., Hermenegildo, M., Lin, N.-W.: Lower bound cost estimation for logic programs. In: 1997 International Logic Programming Symposium, pp. 291–305. MIT Press, Cambridge, October 1997
8. Giesl, J., Ströder, T., Schneider-Kamp, P., Emmes, F., Fuhs, C.: Symbolic evaluation graphs and term rewriting: a general methodology for analyzing logic programs. In: PPDP, pp. 1–12. ACM (2012)
9. Grobauer, B.: Cost recurrences for DML programs. In: Proceedings of the Sixth ACM SIGPLAN International Conference on Functional Programming, ICFP 2001, pp. 253–264. ACM, New York (2001)
10. Hermenegildo, M., Puebla, G., Bueno, F., Lopez-Garcia, P.: Integrated program debugging, verification, and optimization using abstract interpretation (and the Ciao system preprocessor). Sci. Comput. Program. **58**(1–2), 115–140 (2005)
11. Hermenegildo, M.V., Bueno, F., Carro, M., López, P., Mera, E., Morales, J.F., Puebla, G.: An overview of Ciao and its design philosophy. Theor. Pract. Logic Program. **12**(1–2), 219–252 (2012). arxiv.org/abs/1102.5497

12. Hoffmann, J., Aehlig, K., Hofmann, M.: Multivariate amortized resource analysis. ACM Trans. Program. Lang. Syst. **34**(3), 14:1–14:62 (2012)
13. Igarashi, A., Kobayashi, N.: Resource usage analysis. In: Proceedings of the 29th ACM SIGPLAN-SIGACT Symposium on Principles of Programming Languages, POPL 2002, pp. 331–342. ACM, New York (2002)
14. Liqat, U., Georgiou, K., Kerrison, S., Lopez-Garcia, P., Hermenegildo, M.V., Gallagher, J.P., Eder, K.: Inferring energy consumption at different software levels: ISA vs. LLVM IR. In: Van Eekelen, M., DalLago, U. (eds.) FOPARA 2015, LNCS. Springer (2016, to appear)
15. Liqat, U., et al.: Energy consumption analysis of programs based on XMOS ISA-level models. In: Gupta, G., Peña, R. (eds.) LOPSTR 2013, LNCS 8901. LNCS, vol. 8901, pp. 72–90. Springer, Heidelberg (2014)
16. Méndez-Lojo, M., Navas, J., Hermenegildo, M.V.: A flexible, (C)LP-based approach to the analysis of object-oriented programs. In: King, A. (ed.) LOPSTR 2007. LNCS, vol. 4915, pp. 154–168. Springer, Heidelberg (2008)
17. Mera, E., Trigo, T., Lopez-García, P., Hermenegildo, M.: Profiling for run-time checking of computational properties and performance debugging in logic programs. In: Rocha, R., Launchbury, J. (eds.) PADL 2011. LNCS, vol. 6539, pp. 38–53. Springer, Heidelberg (2011)
18. Morgan, R.G., Jarvis, S.A.: Profiling large-scale lazy functional programs. J. Funct. programing **8**(3), 201–237 (1998)
19. Muthukumar, K., Hermenegildo, M.: Compile-time derivation of variable dependency using abstract interpretation. J. Logic Program. **13**(2/3), 315–347 (1992)
20. Navas, J., Méndez-Lojo, M., Hermenegildo, M.: Safe upper-bounds inference of energy consumption for java bytecode applications. In: The Sixth NASA Langley Formal Methods Workshop (LFM 2008), pp. 29–32, April 2008. (Extended Abstract)
21. Navas, J., Méndez-Lojo, M., Hermenegildo, M.: User-definable resource usage bounds analysis for java bytecode. In: Proceedings of the Workshop on Bytecode Semantics, Verification, Analysis and Transformation (BYTECODE 2009), vol. 253. Electronic Notes in Theoretical Computer Science, pp. 65–82. Elsevier, North Holland, March 2009
22. Navas, J., Mera, E., López-García, P., Hermenegildo, M.V.: User-definable resource bounds analysis for logic programs. In: Dahl, V., Niemelä, I. (eds.) ICLP 2007. LNCS, vol. 4670, pp. 348–363. Springer, Heidelberg (2007)
23. Nielson, F., Riis Nielson, H., Seidl, H.: Automatic complexity analysis. In: Le Métayer, D. (ed.) ESOP 2002. LNCS, vol. 2305, pp. 243–261. Springer, Heidelberg (2002)
24. Puebla, G., Hermenegildo, M.: Optimized algorithms for incremental analysis of logic programs. In: Cousot, Radhia, Schmidt, D.A. (eds.) SAS 1996. LNCS, vol. 1145. Springer, Heidelberg (1996)
25. Rosendahl, M.: Automatic complexity analysis. In: 4th ACM Conference on Functional Programming Languages and Computer Architecture (FPCA 1989), pp. 144–156. ACM Press (1989)
26. Sansom, P.M., Peyton Jones, S.L.: Time and space profiling for non-strict, higher-order functional languages. In: Proceedings of the 22nd ACM SIGPLAN-SIGACT Symposium on Principles of Programming Languages, POPL 1995, pp. 355–366. ACM, New York (1995)

27. Serrano, A., Lopez-Garcia, P., Bueno, F., Hermenegildo, M.: Sized type analysis for logic programs (technical communication). In: Swift, T., Lamma, E. (eds.) Theory and Practice of Logic Programming, 29th International Conference on Logic Programming (ICLP 2013) Special Issue, On-line Supplement, vol. 13, pp. 1–14. Cambridge University Press, August 2013
28. Serrano, A., Lopez-Garcia, P., Hermenegildo, M.: Resource usage analysis of logic programs via abstract interpretation using sized types. In: 30th International Conference on Logic Programming (ICLP 2014) Theory and Practice of Logic Programming, vol. 14(4–5), pp. 739–754 (2014). (special issue)
29. Tiwari, V., Malik, S., Wolfe, A.: Power analysis of embedded software: a first step towards software power minimization. IEEE Trans. VLSI Syst. **2**(4), 437–445 (1994)
30. Vasconcelos, P.B., Hammond, K.: Inferring cost equations for recursive, polymorphic and higher-order functional programs. In: Trinder, P., Michaelson, G.J., Peña, R. (eds.) IFL 2003. LNCS, vol. 3145, pp. 86–101. Springer, Heidelberg (2004)
31. Bueno, F., Vaucheret, C.: More precise yet efficient type inference for logic programs. In: Hermenegildo, M.V., Puebla, G. (eds.) SAS 2002. LNCS, vol. 2477, pp. 102–116. Springer, Heidelberg (2002)
32. Wegbreit, B.: Mechanical program analysis. Commun. ACM **18**(9), 528–539 (1975)

Polymorphic Types in Erlang
Function Specifications

Francisco J. López-Fraguas[(✉)], Manuel Montenegro,
and Juan Rodríguez-Hortalá

Departamento de Sistemas Informáticos Y Computación,
Universidad Complutense de Madrid, Madrid, Spain
fraguas@sip.ucm.es, {montenegro,juanrh}@fdi.ucm.es

Abstract. Erlang is a concurrent functional programming language
developed by Ericsson, well suited for implementing distributed systems.
Although Erlang is dynamically typed, the Dialyzer static analysis tool
can be used to extract implicit type information from the programs, both
for documentation purposes and for finding errors that will definitively
arise at program execution. Dialyzer is based on the notion of success
types, that correspond to safe over-approximations for the semantics of
expressions. Erlang also supports user given function specifications (or
just *specs*), that are contracts providing more information about the
semantics of functions. Function specs are useful not only as documentation, but also can be employed by Dialyzer to improve the precision of
the analysis. Even though specs can have a polymorphic shape, in practice Dialyzer is not able to exploit all their potential. One reason for that
is that extending the notion of success types to a polymorphic setting
is not trivial, and several interpretations are possible. In this work we
propose a precise formulation for a novel interpretation of function specs
as polymorphic success types, and a program transformation that allows
us to apply this new interpretation on the call sites of functions with a
declared spec. This results in a significant improvement in the number
of definite errors that Dialyzer is able to detect.

1 Introduction

Erlang [2] is an eager concurrent functional programming language developed
by Ericsson. It is a dynamically typed language, in contrast with languages like
Haskell or ML where programs must be recognized as well typed by a static
analysis, according typically with some variant of Hindley-Milner system [4],
ensuring statically type safety, i.e., that the evaluation of a well-typed expression
within a well-typed program will not incur a type clash at any step. This kind of
analysis is conservative in the sense that it rejects programs that could be free

Work partially supported by the Spanish MINECO project CAVI-ART (TIN2013-
44742-C4-3-R), Madrid regional project N-GREENS Software-CM (S2013/ICE-
2731) and UCM-Santander grants GR3/14-910502, GR3/14-910398.

© Springer International Publishing Switzerland 2016
O. Kiselyov and A. King (Eds.): FLOPS 2016, LNCS 9613, pp. 181–197, 2016.
DOI: 10.1007/978-3-319-29604-3_12

of runtime errors in purely operational terms, but that are not detected as such by the analysis.

Dynamic typing provides usually more liberality; however, runtime error detection means probably late error detection, a serious inconvenience in practice. To address this in Erlang, the Dialyzer static analysis tool was proposed in [7] with two essential design principles: it should be applicable to already existing Erlang programs and should not produce *false positives*: signalling a type error must imply that a runtime error will certainly happen. As it is said in [14], the lemma *'well-typed programs never go wrong'* of Hindley-Milner types is replaced in the Dialyzer approach by *'ill-typed programs always fail'*.

Dialyzer, Success Types and Type Specifications. Dialyzer considers primitive types *integer, atom,...*, tuple types $\{\tau_1, \ldots, \tau_n\}$, list types $[\tau]$, functional types $(\tau_1, \ldots, \tau_n) \to \tau, \ldots$. Each individual Erlang value v is itself a type and the union $\tau_1 | \tau_2$ of two types is also a type. Types represent sets of values that can be ordered by set inclusion. The empty and the total set of values are represented by the types *none* and *any*[1].

Dialyzer tries to infer *success types* [9] that are over-approximations for the semantics of expressions: τ is a success type for e if τ contains all the possible values to which e can be reduced. A type $(\tau_1, \ldots, \tau_n) \to \tau$ is a success type for a function f if whenever $f(e_1, \ldots, e_n)$ reduces to a value v then $v \in \tau$ and each e_i reduces to a value $v_i \in \tau_i$. Notice that *any* is a success type for any expression, that $(any, \ldots, any) \to any$ is a success type for any f, and that if *none* is a success type for e then e cannot be reduced to any value, thus indicating a definite error, not just a possible one. Singleton and union types allow Dialyzer to infer frequently quite precise success types, as this simple example shows:

```
f(0) -> 1 ; f(1) -> 0.    g(2) -> 0.           h(0) -> 0.
e1() -> f(0).             e2() -> g(e1()).      e3() -> h(e1()).
```

Dialyzer (more exactly, its associated tool Typer [8]) infers the following success types, reported in the form of specs (type specifications or signatures):

```
-spec f(0 | 1) -> 0 | 1.      -spec e1() -> 0 | 1.
-spec g(2) -> 0.              -spec e2() -> none.
-spec h(0) -> 0.             -spec e3() -> 0.
```

Dialyzer has detected that e_2 is not reducible to any value. The rest of specs are strict overapproximations of the corresponding semantics, but are nevertheless more precise than types like $Int \to Int$ (for f) or Int (for e_i) that would have been inferred in ML or Haskell. But, as we will see soon, Dialyzer has also important limitations which are the focus of this paper.

User given type specifications were considered in [6] and later on incorporated to Erlang, as contracts specifying the intended behavior of functions. They are useful as documentation and also used by Dialyzer to refine its analysis. For instance, the user could give the specification -spec f(0) -> 1 ; (1) -> 0 that allows Dialyzer to refine its analysis, obtaining

---

[1] Written in actual Erlang as none(), any(), but we omit those () for types.

```
-spec e₁() -> 1.      -spec e₂() -> none.      -spec e₃() -> none.
```

which corresponds better (perfectly, in this case) to reality. In this paper we assume that user specs correspond indeed to success types, i.e., that the contract corresponding to each spec is fulfilled by its function definition. In practice, Dialyzer only checks that user specs are compatible with the inferred success types. In presence of user specs, errors reported by Dialyzer anticipate definite runtime errors or violations of the contract given by the specs. It is in this sense that the absence of false positives must be understood.

Dialyzer, Polymorphism and this Work. The limitations of Dialyzer become quickly apparent with polymorphic functions. The simplest example is given by the function `id(X) -> X`, whose Hindley-Milner type would be $\forall \alpha.\alpha \to \alpha$. What Dialyzer infers is `-spec id(any) -> any`, with no connection between the two *any*'s. This causes a great loss of precision: for the function f above, Dialyzer infers *none* for $f(2)$, but $0|1$ for $f(id(2))$, since $id(2)$ is analyzed as *any*.

Could user specs come to our rescue? Yes ... in principle. User specs permit polymorphic specifications like `-spec id(X) -> X when X::any` where a condition `X::`τ expresses that `X` is a subtype of τ (so, in this case, any `X` fulfils `X::any`). Erlang's documentation [1] says that 'it is up to the tools that process the specifications to choose whether to take this extra information into account or not'. However, Dialyzer does not use it in a sensible way, but replaces each occurrence of X by its bound *any*, thus falling exactly into the same imprecisions as before. We do not know of any other Erlang tool that improves the situation. Moreover, it is not obvious how polymorphism of function specs must be interpreted, due to the union nature of success types.

Those are precisely the problems addressed in this paper: how to interpret polymorphic specifications in a setting of success types and how to improve Dialyzer's treatment of them. We do not investigate here inference of polymorphic success types, a subject of obvious interest but left to future work. We postpone until Sect. 3 the discussion of suitable interpretations of polymorphism, but we elaborate a bit more via examples our ideas for improving Dialyzer's behavior.

The kind of imprecisions pointed out with *id* occur with any other polymorphic function. Consider for instance *map* and two applications of it.

```
map(F,[]) when is_function(F) -> [] ;
map(F,[X|Xs]) -> [F(X)|map(F,Xs)] .
```

```
e₁() -> map(fun(X)->not(X) end,[1,2]). %this expression will fail
e₂() -> map(fun(X)->not(X) end,[true,false]).
```

Dialyzer infers the rather imprecises `-spec map(fun(),[any]) -> [any]` and `-spec eᵢ() -> [any]`. Adding the polymorphic `-spec map(fun((A) -> B),[A1])` `-> [B] when A1::A` does not help too much: we still obtain `-spec eᵢ() -> [any]`.

Forcing Dialyzer to be Polymorphic. To overcome the diagnosed problem we could have tried to identify which parts of Dialyzer should be changed or even to build a completely new inference system and tool. Instead, we have done something much more lightweight: we run Dialyzer (as it is, no change in the tool) not over the original program but over a program transformation so that the effect is as if Dialyzer had used properly the polymorphic specifications provided in the program. The key idea is replacing *inline* each application of a function with a polymorphic spec by an expression having the same type as the original application and where the dependencies between types –lost in the direct use of Dialyzer– are kept and properly managed by Dialyzer because of the inlining. A convenient way of doing such a transformation is by means of parameterized Erlang macros, that are expanded at compile time. Abstracting out the macros to auxiliary functions would not be useful, because those functions would suffer of the same problems of the original ones. To get an idea of how this works, consider the *map* example: we distil a macro MAP(F,L) from the polymorphic spec of *map* and replace each application of *map* by one of ?MAP.

```
-define(MAP(F,L),begin
                  F1 = F , L1 = L,
                  receive {A,A1,B} ->
                    F1 = ?FUN(A,B),
                    L1 = ?LIST(A1),
                    A = A1,
                    ?LIST(B)
                  end
              end).
% Other auxiliary macros FUN/2, LIST/2, ALT/2, ...
e1() -> ?MAP(fun(X)->not(X) end,[1,2]).
e2() -> ?MAP(fun(X)->not(X) end,[true,false]).
```

We leave detailed explanations for Sect. 4; but we remark that the transformation does not pretend to preserve evaluation, since MAP is not based on the code of *map* but only on its spec. The noticeable fact is that now Dialyzer infers for e_i the expected 'good' types: -spec e1() -> none and -spec e2() -> [boolean]. That is precisely the purpose of the transformation. Section 4 contains a complete transformation scheme that, being automatic and general, produces a slightly more complex code.

Organization of the Paper. The two main sections come after formalizing simple success types in Sect. 2. In Sect. 3 we discuss and propose a precise interpretation of function specifications as polymorphic success types. Section 4 contains the program transformation that forces Dialyzer to simulate polymorphic specs, as well as some results about its correctness. Some auxiliary technical contents, including proof sketches, have been left to a technical report [10].

2   Simple Success Types

In this section we formalize an interpretation of Dialyzer success types, which is hopefully equivalent to the original notion from [8,9]. The main idea is that a

$$\begin{array}{l|l}
\mathcal{CS}^0 = Atom \uplus Integer \uplus Float \uplus & DVal \simeq Atom \oplus Integer \oplus Float \oplus Pid \oplus \{[]\} \oplus \\
\quad\quad \{[]\} \uplus Pid & \quad\quad \bigoplus_{c \in \mathcal{CS}^n} \{c\} \otimes DVal \otimes \ldots^n \otimes DVal \ \oplus \\
\mathcal{CS}^2 = \{[\_|\_], \{\_,\_\}\} & \\
\mathcal{CS}^n = \{\{\_, \ldots^n, \_\}\} \ \forall n \in \mathbb{N}\backslash\{2\} & \quad\quad \bigoplus_{n \in \mathbb{N}} (DVal \otimes \ldots^n \otimes DVal) \hookrightarrow \mathcal{P}(DVal)
\end{array}$$

Fig. 1. Definition of the set of Erlang values

success type τ for an expression e represents a safe over-approximation for the semantics of e, formalized through a denotational semantics for expressions and types that gives e a smaller denotation than that for τ in a preorder over the semantic domain.

For this task we use a variation of Core Erlang [3], that is expressive enough to represent most Erlang programs, but that allows for a simpler presentation. A detailed description of the syntax and denotational semantics of the considered language is available in [10]. We use a reflexive semantic domain $DVal$ (see Fig. 1), whose definition is based on standard primitive domains and standard domain constructors, which ensure it is correctly defined [5]. The denotation of expressions is defined by the semantic function $\mathcal{E}[\![\_]\!] : Exp \to (\mathcal{UFS} \to Exp) \to \mathcal{P}(DVal)$ where Exp is the set of expressions, and definitional environments $\Lambda \in \mathcal{UFS} \to Exp$ are mappings from user function symbols to Exp that serve to model programs. We write $\mathcal{E}[\![e]\!]^\Lambda$ for the semantics of e within Λ and frequently omit Λ when implied by the context. In general $\mathcal{E}[\![e]\!]$ is a set of values, due to the non-determinism caused by concurrency primitives like `receive`. Note that values can be functions, hence $\mathcal{E}[\![e]\!]$ can be a set of functions. We will need some notations regarding (sets of) functions: we write $f|_C$ for the restriction of a function f to a subset C of its domain; the range restriction of f is denoted by $f|_C^{-1}$, and is defined by $f|_C^{-1}(x) = f(x)$ iff $f(x) \in C$; $f|_C^{-1}(x)$ is undefined otherwise. This is extended to set of functions as $fs|_C(x) = \{f|_C(x) \mid f \in fs\}$, and $fs|_C^{-1}(x) = \{f|_C^{-1}(x) \mid f \in fs\}$. We define the application of a set of functions fs with common domain to a set of values vs in that domain as $fs(vs) = \{f(v) \mid f \in fs, v \in vs\}$, and to a value as $fs(v) = fs(\{v\})$.

We consider a preorder $e \sqsubseteq e'$ on $DVal$ (see [10]) and extend it to $\mathcal{P}(DVal)$ to capture the notion that $\mathcal{E}[\![e']\!]$ is more powerful than $\mathcal{E}[\![e]\!]$, in the sense that for each value in $\mathcal{E}[\![e]\!]$ there is a greater one in $\mathcal{E}[\![e']\!]$ (i.e. a function with a greater graph, a tuple with greater elements, ...).

We refer to the original success types from [8,9] as *simple* success types, to stress their difference to the success *type schemes* we will consider for function specs in Sect. 3, reminding to what is usually done also in Hindley-Milner-like type systems. We assume a set of type variables $\mathcal{TV}$ and use $\alpha, \beta \in \mathcal{TV}$. The set of simple types $\mathcal{T}$ is defined in Fig. 2. To better reflect its meaning, we write here $\tau \cup \tau'$ instead of the concrete Erlang syntax $\tau \mid \tau'$. Notice that individual values $v \in Val$ are types, where Val is a subset of Exp that only contains (intensional) values. We assume the existence of a denotation $\mathcal{V}[\![\_]\!]$ of these intensional values— see [10] for details—. The type $nelist(\tau, \tau')$ stands for (possibly improper) not empty lists with elements of type τ and ending of type τ'; note all the variant

$$\mathcal{TC}^0 \ni C^0 ::= none \mid any \mid atom \mid integer \mid float \mid pid \mid v \quad (v \in Val)$$
$$\mathcal{TC}^2 \ni C^2 ::= \_ \cup \_ \mid nelist(\_,\_) \quad \mathcal{TC}^n \ni C^n ::= \{\_,\dots{}^n,\_\}$$
$$\mathcal{TC}^{n+1} \ni C^{n+1} ::= (\_,\dots{}^n,\_) \to \_$$
$$\mathcal{T} \ni \tau ::= \alpha \mid C^n(\tau_1,\dots,\tau_n)$$

$\mathcal{T}[\![none]\!] = \emptyset \quad \mathcal{T}[\![any]\!] = DVal \quad \mathcal{T}[\![atom]\!] = Atom \quad \mathcal{T}[\![integer]\!] = Integer$

$\mathcal{T}[\![float]\!] = Float \quad \mathcal{T}[\![pid]\!] = Pid \quad \mathcal{T}[\![v]\!] = \{\mathcal{V}[\![v]\!] \, [\,]\} \quad \mathcal{T}[\![\tau_1 \cup \tau_2]\!] = \mathcal{T}[\![\tau_1]\!] \cup \mathcal{T}[\![\tau_2]\!]$

$\mathcal{T}[\![nelist(\tau_v,\tau_c)]\!] =$

$\quad lfp \, (\lambda Z.\{([\,|\,],v,c) \mid v \in \mathcal{T}[\![\tau_v]\!], c \in \mathcal{T}[\![\tau_c]\!]\} \cup \{([\,|\,],v,z) \mid v \in \mathcal{T}[\![\tau_v]\!], z \in Z\})$

$\mathcal{T}[\![\{\tau_1,\dots,\tau_n\}]\!] = \{(\{,\dots{}^n,\},v_1,\dots,v_n) \mid \forall i \in \{1..n\}.v_i \in \mathcal{T}[\![\tau_i]\!]\}$

$\mathcal{T}[\![(\tau_1,\dots,\tau_n) \to \tau]\!] = \{\bigoplus\limits_{z \in Dom} \hat{\lambda}z.\mathcal{T}[\![\tau]\!]\}$ where $Dom \stackrel{def}{=} \prod_{i=1}^n \mathcal{T}[\![\tau_i]\!]$

Fig. 2. Syntax and semantics of simple types

types for lists from [1] can be expressed with *nelist* and $\cup$: for example `list(0 | 1)` can be expressed as $nelist(0 \cup 1,[\,])$, as $[\,] \in \mathcal{CS}^0$ implies $[\,] \in Val$, hence $[\,] \in \mathcal{TC}^0$ and so $[\,] \in \mathcal{T}$. Type substitutions $\pi \in TSubst$ are finite mappings $\pi : TV \to \mathcal{T}$. We say π is ground when $\pi(\alpha)$ is ground for any α.

The denotation $\mathcal{T}[\![\tau]\!]$ of a simple type τ is a set of semantic values in $DVal$ given by the mapping $\mathcal{T}[\![\_]\!] : \mathcal{T} \to \mathcal{P}(DVal)$ defined in Fig. 2. The notation $\hat{\lambda}v_1.v_2$ denotes a function with a single binding from v_1 to v_2 —i.e., with a single point as graph— whereas the $\oplus$ operator merges two functions provided their domains are disjoint. Note $\mathcal{T}[\![\,]\!]$ is for example able to distinguish the type *any* from the type $(any) \to any$, as $\mathcal{T}[\![any]\!] = \mathcal{P}(DVal)$ and $\mathcal{T}[\![(any) \to any]\!] = DVal \hookrightarrow DVal$, and therefore $\mathcal{T}[\![any]\!] \ni 0 \notin \mathcal{T}[\![(any) \to any]\!]$, showing that *any* contains more values than $(any) \to any$.

We formalize that hierarchy among types by overloading the preorder $\sqsubseteq$ on $DVal$ to $\mathcal{T}$ as $\tau_1 \sqsubseteq \tau_2$ iff $\mathcal{T}[\![\tau_1]\!] \sqsubseteq \mathcal{T}[\![\tau_2]\!]$. Note none of the overloadings of $\sqsubseteq$ is a partial order, as they are not antisymmetric: for example, with $\tau_1 = 0 \cup integer$, $\tau_2 = integer$ we have $\tau_1 \sqsubseteq \tau_2$ and $\tau_2 \sqsubseteq \tau_1$, but τ_1 and τ_2 are different types. Nevertheless, as is standard, this preorder defines a partial order on the quotient set for the equivalence relation $\tau' \sqsubseteq \tau \wedge \tau \sqsubseteq \tau'$, which is a lattice [8,9] with *any* as $\top$ and *none* as $\bot$. For the remainder of the paper, when using $\sqcup$ or $\sqcap$ on elements of $\mathcal{T}$, we implicitly work modulo that equivalence relation. We can now use the denotational semantics to formulate with precision the notion of success types.

Definition 1 (Success Type, for Simple Types). *We say that* $\tau \in \mathcal{T}$ *is a success type for* $e \in Exp$, *written* $e : \tau$, *iff* $\mathcal{E}[\![e]\!] \sqsubseteq \mathcal{T}[\![\tau]\!]$.

Example 1. $\tau_1 = (0 \cup 1) \to 0 \cup 1$ is a success type for the expression $e = fun(X) \to case \, X \, of \, 0 \to 0$, as $\mathcal{E}[\![e]\!] = \hat{\lambda}(0).\{0\} \sqsubseteq \hat{\lambda}(0).\{0,1\} \oplus \hat{\lambda}(1).\{0,1\} = \mathcal{T}[\![(0 \cup 1) \to 0 \cup 1]\!]$. The type τ_1 is not the only valid success type for e. For example, $(0) \to 0$ is a more precise one.

This formulation tries to generalize Definition 1 from [9], that is only defined for functions, to arbitrary expressions. In general, expressions may have more than one success type, because $e : \tau_1$ and $\tau_1 \sqsubseteq \tau_2$ imply $e : \tau_2$. In particular $e : any$ for all expressions e. On other other hand, $e : none$ is equivalent to $\mathcal{E}[\![e]\!] \sqsubseteq \mathcal{T}[\![none]\!] = \emptyset$, which implies that no value can be computed for e, i.e. that evaluating e will surely lead to a runtime error.

3   Success Type Schemes

Following the official Erlang documentation [1], we define the set of success type schemes $\mathcal{TS}$ as: $\mathcal{TS} \ni \sigma :: = \forall \alpha_1, \ldots, \alpha_m. \tau \mid \tau_1^1 \sqsubseteq \tau_2^1, \ldots, \tau_1^l \sqsubseteq \tau_2^l$ for $\alpha_i \in \mathcal{TV}$, $\tau, \tau_i^j \in \mathcal{T}$. This notion of type schemes expresses a form of bounded polymorphism, as type variables can be instantiated only with types that respect the corresponding type inclusion constraint. We use the semantics above to characterize these constraints, so $\tau_1 \sqsubseteq \tau_2$ is satisfied iff $\emptyset \neq \mathcal{T}[\![\tau_1]\!]$ and $\tau_1 \sqsubseteq \tau_2$. Note success type schemes are just another presentation of Erlang function specs, and that $\mathcal{TS}$ contains type schemes corresponding to overloaded specs, which have the general form $\forall \alpha_1, \ldots, \alpha_m. (\tau_{p_1}^1, \ldots, \tau_{p_n}^1) \rightarrow \tau_r^1 \cup \ldots \cup (\tau_{p_1}^o, \ldots, \tau_{p_n}^o) \rightarrow \tau_r^o \mid \tau_1^1 \sqsubseteq \tau_2^1, \ldots, \tau_1^l \sqsubseteq \tau_2^l$ for a given $f \in \mathcal{FS}^n$. For this reason we will use the terms 'function spec' and 'type scheme' interchangeably for the rest of the paper. Notice that, in this system, overloaded schemes can be understood as union types (represented with the $\cup$ operator), since success types overapproximate the behaviour of programs. This contrasts with the traditional approach in which overloading is achieved via intersection types [12].

Just like we have characterized whether a simple type is a success type for an expression or not, we are interested in defining when a type scheme is a success type scheme for a function. We discuss here the issue.

A first obvious approach would be trying to mimic Definition 1, for which we would need a suitable definition for the denotation of a success type scheme $\mathcal{TS}[\![\_]\!] : \mathcal{TS} \rightarrow \mathcal{P}(DVal)$, and then require $\mathcal{E}[\![f]\!] \sqsubseteq \mathcal{TS}[\![\sigma]\!]$ for σ to be a success type scheme of f. Let us consider for now a simplified setting where specs σ have the shape $\forall \overline{\alpha_j \sqsubseteq \tau_j}. \tau$. A first possible definition of $\mathcal{TS}[\![\sigma]\!]$ could be $\mathcal{TS}[\![\sigma]\!] = \mathcal{T}[\![C(\sigma)]\!]$ where $C(\sigma)$ is the *compaction* of σ, the simple type resulting of replacing type variables by their bounds, i.e., $C(\forall \overline{\alpha_j \sqsubseteq \tau_j}. \tau) = \tau[\overline{\alpha_j/\tau_j}]$. However, this corresponds to the observed behaviour of Dialyzer, as described through the examples of *id* and *map* in Sect. 1, for which we know that the polymorphism nature of type schemes is lost.

We could also consider the other extreme, with the following "singleton" interpretation of success type schemes in which a polymorphic type variable is instantiated with individual values taken from the denotation of its bound:

$$\mathcal{TS}[\![\forall \overline{\alpha_j \sqsubseteq \tau_j}. \tau]\!] = \bigcup_{v_j \in \mathcal{T}[\![\tau_j]\!] \cap DVal} \mathcal{T}[\![\tau[\overline{\alpha_j/v_j}]]\!]$$

Just like the previous interpretation was too loose, this interpretation is too strict; for instance, when applied to *take* $: \forall \alpha_e \sqsubseteq any, \alpha_t \sqsubseteq any. (integer, [\,] \cup nelist(\alpha_e, \alpha_t)) \rightarrow [\,] \cup nelist(\alpha_e, \alpha_t)$ it does not allow α_e to be instantiated with $0 \sqcup 1$, because that does not correspond to a value but to a set of values. Therefore $take(1, [0 \mid [1 \mid []]])$ would be considered a contract violation. So maybe we should try with something in the middle. The following interpretation allows to instantiate the type variables of a type scheme with any subtype of its bound.

$$\mathcal{TS}[\![\overline{\forall \alpha_j \subseteq \tau_j}. \tau]\!] = \bigcup_{\overline{\tau'_j \subseteq \tau_j}} \mathcal{T}[\![\tau \overline{[\alpha_j/\tau'_j]}]\!]$$

This seems to corresponds to the polymorphic treatment of the list constructor that can be observed in Dialyzer: for example the type $nelist(0 \cup 1, [])$ is inferred for the list $[1, 0]$. Sadly, the condition $\mathcal{E}[\![f]\!] \sqsubseteq \mathcal{TS}[\![\sigma]\!]$ for this $\mathcal{TS}$ is just as strong as $\mathcal{E}[\![f]\!] \sqsubseteq \mathcal{T}[\![C(\sigma)]\!]$, i.e., the first $\mathcal{TS}$ we considered. The problem is that the supremum of $\{\tau \overline{[\alpha_j/\tau'_j]} \mid \tau'_j \subseteq \tau_j\}$ is precisely $C(\sigma)$. So this interpretation is as loose as the first one.

Nevertheless, we are quite close to the final interpretation of type schemes we propose in this paper, which at the end does not define a semantics $\mathcal{TS}[\![\sigma]\!]$ for type schemes, but needs to be more complex. Let us define the decomposition of a type scheme, $D(\_) : \mathcal{TS} \to \mathcal{P}(\mathcal{T})$ as $D(\overline{\forall \alpha_j \subseteq \tau_j}. \tau) = \{\tau \overline{[\alpha_j/\tau'_j]} \mid \tau'_j \subseteq \tau_j\}$. It is easy to check that for any type scheme $\bigsqcup D(\sigma) = C(\sigma)$, and that $C(\sigma) \in D(\sigma)$. What it is interesting about $D(\sigma)$ is that it corresponds to a decomposition of the semantics $\mathcal{T}[\![C(\sigma)]\!]$ as $\{\mathcal{T}[\![\tau]\!] \mid \tau \in D(\sigma)\} \in \mathcal{P}(\mathcal{P}(DVal))$. The idea then is that σ is a success type scheme for f iff $f : C(\sigma)$ and $\mathcal{E}[\![f]\!]$ can be decomposed following $D(\sigma)$. We formalize this idea through several conditions that must be satisfied by the semantics of any function for which a type scheme is declared. These are understood as additional conditions that are part of the contract the programmer assumes when declaring a function spec. We continue focusing on simplified declarations $f : \sigma$ for $\sigma = \overline{\forall \alpha_j \subseteq \tau_j}. (\overline{\tau_p}) \to \tau_r$. Then $D(\sigma)$ defines the following decomposition of $\mathcal{T}[\![C(\sigma)]\!]$:

$$\{\mathcal{T}[\![((\overline{\tau_p}) \to \tau_r)\overline{[\alpha_j/\tau'_j]}]\!] \mid \overline{\tau'_j \subseteq \tau_j}\}$$

For $f : \sigma$ we require the following condition to hold for any $\overline{\tau'_j \subseteq \tau_j}$:

$$\mathcal{E}[\![f]\!]|_{\mathcal{T}[\![(\overline{\tau_p})\overline{[\alpha_j/\tau'_j]}]\!]} \sqsubseteq \mathcal{T}[\![((\overline{\tau_p}) \to \tau_r^l)\overline{[\alpha_j/\tau'_j]}]\!]$$

With this condition we are saying that f defines a relation between input arguments and function results that respects the shape of the semantics decomposition expressed by σ. Consider for example the identity function $id = fun(X) \to X$, and assume we declare $id : \forall \alpha \subseteq any. (\alpha) \to \alpha$. It is easy to see that for $\tau \subseteq any$ we have that $id|_{\mathcal{T}[\![\tau]\!]} \in \mathcal{T}[\![(\tau) \to \tau]\!]$, because id just returns its input argument. Now we can use the inequality above to conclude that $id(0) : 0$, reasoning only with the specification $id : \forall \alpha \subseteq any. (\alpha) \to \alpha$, regardless of the concrete definition of id, in the line of Wadler's 'free theorems' [15].

Proof. $\mathcal{E}[\![id(0)]\!] = \mathcal{E}[\![id]\!](\mathcal{E}[\![0]\!]) = \mathcal{E}[\![id]\!]|_{\mathcal{E}[\![0]\!]}(\mathcal{E}[\![0]\!]) = \mathcal{E}[\![id]\!]|_{\mathcal{T}[\![0]\!]}(\mathcal{E}[\![0]\!])$, as $\mathcal{E}[\![0]\!] \sqsubseteq \mathcal{T}[\![0]\!]$. But then by $id : \forall \alpha \subseteq any. (\alpha) \to \alpha$ and using the inequality above with $\tau'_j = 0$ we have $\mathcal{E}[\![id]\!]|_{\mathcal{T}[\![0]\!]}(\mathcal{E}[\![0]\!]) \sqsubseteq \mathcal{T}[\![(0) \to 0]\!](\mathcal{E}[\![0]\!])$, and we can use $0 : 0$ to get $T[\![(0) \to 0]\!](\mathcal{E}[\![0]\!]) \sqsubseteq T[\![(0) \to 0]\!](T[\![0]\!]) = (\hat{\lambda}0.\{0\})(\{0\}) = \{0\}$. So we have $\mathcal{E}[\![id(0)]\!] \sqsubseteq \{0\} \sqsubseteq T[\![0]\!]$, i.e. $id(0) : 0$.

On the other hand, for $g = fun(X) \to case\ X\ of\ \{Y_1\ when\ is\_integer(X) \to 0, Y_2\ when\ true \to X\}$ that inequality does not hold for the declaration $g : \forall \alpha \sqsubseteq any.\ (\alpha) \to \alpha$, because for $\tau = 1$ we have that $\mathcal{E}[\![g]\!]|_{T[\![1]\!]}(1) = \{0\} \not\subseteq T[\![(1) \to 1]\!](1)$. One way to see this, that might be familiar to functional programmers, is that the inequality condition above tries to capture the notion of parametricity first proposed in Reynolds' abstraction theorem [13], and later exploited in [15]. The function g breaks parametricity, because its rules inspect the variable X, which has a polymorphic type α. Conversely, id respects parametricity, because it does not inspect its polymorphic argument, and just returns it untouched.

That was a form of bottom-up information flow, where the type of a function argument affects the type of the whole function application. For $f : \sigma$ with $\sigma = \forall \alpha_j \sqsubseteq \tau_j.\ (\overline{\tau_p}) \to \tau_r$ we also require the following inequality condition, that corresponds to top down information flow, that should hold for any $\overline{\tau'_j \sqsubseteq \tau_j}$:

$$\mathcal{E}[\![f]\!]^{-1}_{T[\![\tau_r[\overline{\alpha_j/\tau'_j}]]\!]} \sqsubseteq T[\![((\overline{\tau_p}) \to \tau'_r)[\overline{\alpha_j/\tau'_j}]]\!]$$

We can use this inequality for equational reasoning with id, but now with top-down information flow, where the type of a function application affects the type of its arguments. In particular we will conclude (again by using *only* the type specification of id) that if $id(a)$ is evaluated to some value $v : 0$, then in that evaluation a must be reduced to a value $v_a : 0$, i.e. 0 is a value for a.

Proof. By hypothesis $\mathcal{E}[\![id(a)]\!] \sqsubseteq T[\![0]\!]$. Also $\mathcal{E}[\![id(a)]\!] = \mathcal{E}[\![id]\!](\mathcal{E}[\![a]\!])$, hence $\mathcal{E}[\![id(a)]\!] = \mathcal{E}[\![id]\!]^{-1}_{T[\![0]\!]}(\mathcal{E}[\![a]\!]) \sqsubseteq T[\![(0) \to 0)]\!](\mathcal{E}[\![a]\!])$ using the inequality above with $\overline{\tau'_j} = 0$. So, given $v \in \mathcal{E}[\![id(a)]\!]$ we have $v \in T[\![(0) \to 0]\!](\mathcal{E}[\![a]\!])$. This implies that to compute any $v \in \mathcal{E}[\![id(a)]\!]$ we need compute some $v_a \in \mathcal{E}[\![a]\!]$ such that $v_a \in dom(T[\![(0) \to 0]\!]) = T[\![0]\!]$, i.e. $v_a : 0$.

Additionally, for $f : \sigma$ we require $f : C(\sigma)$, in order to avoid accepting trivially small type schemes. For example, that condition rejects $id : (0) \to 0$, since $(0) \to 0$ is not a success type for id.

After giving the intuitions, we generalize the previous conditions to arbitrary types schemes for function symbols of the shape $\forall \overline{\alpha_j}.\ \bigcup_{l=1}^o (\overline{\tau^l_{p_i}}) \to \tau^l_r \mid \overline{\tau^k_1 \sqsubseteq \tau^k_2}$. We first need to generalize the notion of compaction. For any conjunction of constraints $\overline{\tau^k_1 \sqsubseteq \tau^k_2}$ the set of its solutions is the set $Sol(\overline{\tau^k_1 \sqsubseteq \tau^k_2})$ of ground $\pi \in TSubst$ such that $var(\overline{\tau^k_1 \sqsubseteq \tau^k_2}) \subseteq dom(\pi)$ and $(\overline{\tau^k_1 \sqsubseteq \tau^k_2})\pi$ is satisfied. For any $\sigma \in TS$, given $\sigma = \forall \overline{\alpha_j}.\ \bigcup_{l=1}^o (\overline{\tau^l_{p_i}}) \to \tau^l_r \mid \overline{\tau^k_1 \sqsubseteq \tau^k_2}$ we assume $var(\sigma) \subseteq var(\overline{\tau^k_1 \sqsubseteq \tau^k_2})$ without loss of generality, by adding additional trivial constraints $\alpha \sqsubseteq any$ for any $\alpha \in var(\sigma) \setminus var(\overline{\tau^k_1 \sqsubseteq \tau^k_2})$. Then the compaction of σ is defined as $C(\sigma) = (\bigcup_{l=1}^o (\overline{\tau^l_{p_i}}) \to \tau^l_r)\pi_s$ for $\pi_s = \bigsqcup Sol(\overline{\tau^k_1 \sqsubseteq \tau^k_2})$.

Definition 2 (Success Type, for Type Schemes). *For any $f \in \mathcal{FS}^n$ and $\sigma \in TS$ we say that σ is a success type scheme for f, denoted $f : \sigma$, iff given*

$\sigma = \forall \overline{\alpha_j}. \bigcup_{l=1}^o (\overline{\tau_{p_i}^l}) \to \tau_r^l \mid \overline{\tau_1^k \subseteq \tau_2^k}$ we have $f : C(\sigma)$ and the following conditions are met for $\pi_s = \bigsqcup Sol(\overline{\tau_1^k \subseteq \tau_2^k})$:

1. For any $\pi \in Sol(\overline{\tau_1^k \subseteq \tau_2^k})$, given $\pi_p^l = \pi|_{var(\overline{\tau_p^l})}$ then

$$\mathcal{E}[\![f]\!]|_{\bigcup_{l=1}^o \mathcal{T}[\![(\overline{\tau_{p_i}^l})\pi_p^l]\!]} \sqsubseteq \bigcup_{l=1}^o \mathcal{T}[\![(\overline{\tau_{p_i}^l})\pi_p^l \to \tau_r^l \pi_p^l \pi_s]\!]$$

2. For any $\pi \in Sol(\overline{\tau_1^k \subseteq \tau_2^k})$, given $\pi_r^l = \pi|_{var(\tau_r^l)}$ then

$$\mathcal{E}[\![f]\!]|_{\bigcup_{l=1}^o \mathcal{T}[\![\tau_r^l \pi_r^l]\!]}^{-1} \sqsubseteq \bigcup_{l=1}^o \mathcal{T}[\![(\overline{\tau_{p_i}^l})\pi_r^l \pi_s \to \tau_r^l \pi_r^l]\!]$$

3. For any ground π_p such that $dom(\tau_p) \subseteq \bigcup_{l=1}^o var(\overline{\tau_p^l})$ and $Sol((\overline{\tau_1^k \subseteq \tau_2^k})\pi_p) = \emptyset$ then $\mathcal{E}[\![f]\!]|_{\bigcup_{l=1}^o \mathcal{T}[\![(\overline{\tau_{p_i}^l})\pi_p]\!]} = \emptyset$

4. For any ground π_r such that $dom(\tau_p) \subseteq \bigcup_{l=1}^o var(\tau_r^l)$ and $Sol((\overline{\tau_1^k \subseteq \tau_2^k})\pi_r) = \emptyset$ then $\mathcal{E}[\![f]\!]|_{\bigcup_{l=1}^o \mathcal{T}[\![\tau_r^l \pi_r]\!]}^{-1} = \emptyset$

Items 1. and 2. of Definition 2 express the relation between function input and outputs. These are basically the same we discussed above, with minor modifications over the domain of solutions π, that for the sake of readability were omitted in the presentation above. To understand these changes, let's consider a function f with declared spec $f : \sigma$ with $\sigma = \forall \alpha. (\alpha) \to 0 \mid \alpha \subseteq any$. A function with this type can only return 0 regardless of its argument. So for any expression e used as an argument for f, we have $\mathcal{E}[\![f(e)]\!] = \mathcal{E}[\![f]\!]|_{\mathcal{T}[\![0]\!]}^{-1}(\mathcal{E}[\![e]\!])$, and we should not be able to say a thing about the type of e, because α does not appear in the right hand side of σ. If we could, then we would be able to perform wrong deductions, thus introducing false positives in Dialyzer. A less artificial example would be the case of map, assuming the same spec as in Sect. 1: $\forall \alpha, \alpha_1, \beta. ((\alpha) \to \beta, list(\alpha_1)) \to list(\beta) \mid \alpha_1 \subseteq \alpha, \alpha \subseteq any, \beta \subseteq any$. Assuming for instance a call $map(g, [e])$, in a context that forces $map(g, [e])$ to $[true \cup false]$, then β should be instantiated to $true \cup false$, but we should not be able to infer derive any constraint about the domain of g from that.

Regarding items 3. and 4. of Definition 2, they express relationships between polymorphic variables, which can be used to fail when an instantiation of the variables results in unsolvable constraints. Consider again the example of map together with the function not defined as $fun(X) \to case\ X\ of\ \{true \to false; false \to true\}$; then it is clear that the call $map(fun(X) \to not(X), [1, 2])$ will fail. We can use item 3. of Definition 2 to deduce $\mathcal{E}[\![map(fun(X) \to not(X), [1, 2])]\!] = \mathcal{E}[\![map]\!]|_{((\alpha) \to \beta, list(\alpha_1))\pi_p}(\mathcal{E}[\![(fun(X) \to not(X)]\!], \mathcal{E}[\![[1, 2]]\!])) = \emptyset(\mathcal{E}[\![(fun(X) \to not(X)]\!], \mathcal{E}[\![[1, 2]]\!])) = \emptyset = \mathcal{T}[\![none]\!]$ for $\pi_p = [\alpha/true \cup false, \alpha_1/1 \cup 2, \beta/true \cup false]$, as $1 \cup 2 \subseteq true \cup false$ has no solution.

Although certainly complex, the notion of success type scheme given by us corresponds to the intuitive idea of parametricity honouring function. That can be understood in simple terms considering that polymorphic functions should not inspect data variables with a polymorphic variable as type, i.e. data variables with a polymorphic variable as type are a kind of opaque data container. Note we can still perform matching against the constructed part of a polymorphic variable, as for example in $head$ defined by $fun(Xs) \rightarrow case\ Xs\ of\ [X|_] \rightarrow X$, declared as $head : \forall \alpha.\ nelist(\alpha) \rightarrow \alpha \mid \alpha \subseteq any$. In this case we inspect Xs, but only for the constructed fragment $nelist$ of its type $nelist(\alpha, [\,])$. The same applies to the typical operations in polymorphic lists like $map, take, filter, \ldots$ These notions should be familiar to the seasoned functional programmer, that would then have an intuitive understanding of the additional contract she is accepting by assuming Definition 2.

At the time of writing, Erlang only allows the programmer to place specs in top-level function definitions. However, we can also apply Definition 2 to expressions that are always evaluated to a function.

4   A Program Transformation for Simulating Success Types Schemes

In this section we introduce an algorithm that transforms a given program by substituting macro expansions for polymorphic function calls. For each ground type τ there is a macro which is replaced with an Erlang term with the same semantics as $\mathcal{T}[\![\tau]\!]$. We can build these terms in a compositional way. For each function definition f/n with a monomorphic type $\overline{\tau_i}^n \rightarrow \tau$, the algorithm generates a macro with n arguments, and is expanded to a term that overapproximates $\mathcal{T}[\![\tau]\!]$ provided the set of possible arguments of the macro overapproximate their corresponding $\mathcal{T}[\![\tau_i]\!]$. If f/n has a polymorphic type $\forall \overline{\alpha_i}.\tau_f$, the macro generates fresh variables corresponding to the $\overline{\alpha_i}$, which are subsequently bound to ground types during type inference.

The generation of the macro for a type scheme requires the latter to be left linear, that is, that no variable occurs twice in the types of the parameters. In the presence of union types, nonlinearity can be a source of misconceptions. For instance, assume a function $f/2$ with type scheme $\forall \alpha.(\alpha, \alpha) \rightarrow true$. Although it seems at first sight that the definition f(0,a) -> true does not fit into this scheme, it actually does under the instance $[\alpha/0 \cup a]$. In fact, we can prove by using Definition 2 that this scheme is equivalent to $\forall \alpha_1, \alpha_2.(\alpha_1, \alpha_2) \rightarrow true$. In a similar way we can establish the equivalence between $\forall \alpha.(\alpha, \alpha) \rightarrow \alpha$ and $\forall \alpha.(\alpha_1, \alpha_2) \rightarrow \alpha_1 \cup \alpha_2$. If the programmer intends to convey the constraint of both parameters being equal, she would have to add the conditions $\alpha_1 \subseteq \alpha_2$ and $\alpha_2 \subseteq \alpha_1$ to the previous scheme. The resulting scheme would exclude any function f such that $\mathcal{E}[\![f(v_1, v_2)]\!] \neq \emptyset$ for some values $v_1, v_2 \in DVal$ such that there exist two types τ_1 and τ_2 that "separate" these values, that is, $v_1 \in \mathcal{T}[\![\tau_1]\!] \backslash \mathcal{T}[\![\tau_2]\!]$ and $v_2 \in \mathcal{T}[\![\tau_2]\!] \backslash \mathcal{T}[\![\tau_1]\!]$. In this case, the third condition of Definition 2 would not be satisfied, since we would get $Sol(\{\tau_1 \subseteq \tau_2, \tau_2 \subseteq \tau_1\}) = \emptyset$ but $\mathcal{E}[\![f]\!]|_{\mathcal{T}[\![(\tau_1, \tau_2)]\!]} \sqsupseteq \mathcal{E}[\![f]\!]|_{\mathcal{E}[\![(v_1, v_2)]\!]} \sqsupseteq \emptyset$. With the current type system there are values that cannot be separated by types. For instance, let us consider $fun(X) \rightarrow X + 1$

and $fun(X) \to X - 1$. Each of these expressions has $(integer) \to integer$ as the smallest type containing its semantics, so the expressions cannot be separated.

In order to left-linearize a type scheme we rename each occurrence of the same variable with different type variables and substitute, in the right-hand side of the type scheme, the union of these variables for the original one.

Definition 3. *Given a type scheme* $\sigma = \forall \overline{\alpha_i}.(\overline{\tau_j}) \to \tau \mid C$, *we say that a type scheme* $\sigma' = \forall \overline{\alpha_i}'.(\overline{\tau_j}') \to \tau' \mid C'$ *is a left linearization of* σ *iff* σ' *does not contain free type variables, no type variable occurs twice in* $\overline{\tau_j}'$ *and there exists a substitution* $\pi : \{\overline{\alpha_i}'\} \to \{\overline{\alpha_i}\}$ *such that:*

1. $\tau_j' \pi = \tau_j$ *for every* j.
2. *If we define the substitution* $\pi_{img} = \overline{[\alpha_i / \cup_{\beta \in \pi^{-1}(\{\alpha_i\})} \beta]}$ *then* $\tau' = \tau \pi_{img}$.
3. $C' = \{\tau_1' \subseteq \tau_2' \mid var(\{\tau_1', \tau_2'\}) \subseteq \{\overline{\alpha_i}'\}, (\pi(\tau_1') \subseteq \pi(\tau_2')) \in C\}$.

The first condition of this definition requires the types of the parameters τ_j to be instantiations of their counterparts τ_j' in which type variables are replaced by type variables. The second condition states that whenever we replace a variable α by several variables $\alpha_1', \ldots, \alpha_n'$, the left linearization of σ replaces α by $\alpha_1' \cup \ldots \cup \alpha_n'$ in the result type of the function. The last condition specifies the set of constraints C' in the linearized type scheme. The constraints occurring in the original (non-linear) type scheme have to be replicated in the linear type scheme with their corresponding variables. For instance, the linearization of $\forall \alpha.(\alpha, \alpha) \to integer \mid \alpha \subseteq integer$ yields $\forall \alpha_1, \alpha_2.(\alpha_1, \alpha_2) \to integer \mid \alpha_1 \subseteq integer, \alpha_2 \subseteq integer$ as a result.

Now we show how to transform a type τ into an Erlang term or macro expansion with the same semantics. The function BT_{fun} (Fig. 3) does this transformation. It is given the simple type τ to be transformed. If τ is a type constructor applied to several arguments $\overline{\tau_i}^n$, the function receives a list of expressions $\overline{e_i}^n$ such that each e_i is an overapproximation of the semantics of τ_i. In the translation we assume function definitions such as 'ANY', 'NONE', etc. These functions are defined in [10], and their semantics are those of their corresponding type. For instance, $\mathcal{E}[\![\,'\mathtt{ANY}'()]\!] = \mathcal{T}[\![any]\!]$. We assume an environment Λ^0 containing these auxiliary definitions. The ALT macro represents a nondeterministic choice between its arguments. The macro NELIST expands to a list of arbitrary length with elements of a given type. Finally, we have a family of macros $\{\mathtt{FUN}_n\}_n i \in \mathbb{N}$ representing the functions of arity n. Each macro is parametric on the variables corresponding to the input arguments and the variable corresponding to the result. From these macro definitions we specify the translation of compound types in the right column of Fig. 3.

As we shall see later, the macro generated for a given function binds its parameters to the translation of their corresponding types. We could perform this translation directly via the BT_{fun} function, but the notion of parametricity implied by Definition 2 allows us to generate macros that reflect a given type scheme in a more accurate way. For instance, assume a function $f/1$ with type

$$BT_{fun} \; [\![none]\!] \, [\,] = \text{'NONE'}() \qquad\qquad BT_{fun} \; [\![v]\!] \, [\,] = v \text{ where } v \in Val$$
$$BT_{fun} \; [\![any]\!] \, [\,] = \text{'ANY'}() \qquad\qquad BT_{fun} \; [\![\_ \cup \_]\!] \, [e_1, e_2] = \text{?ALT}(e_1, \; e_2)$$
$$BT_{fun} \; [\![atom]\!] \, [\,] = \text{'ATOM'}() \qquad\quad BT_{fun} \; [\![\{\_, \overset{n}{\cdots}, \_\}]\!] \, [\overline{e_i}^{\,n}] = \{\overline{e_i}^{\,n}\}$$
$$BT_{fun} \; [\![integer]\!] \, [\,] = \text{'INTEGER'}() \;\; BT_{fun} \; [\![nelist(\_, \_)]\!] \, [e_1, e_2] = \text{?NELIST}(e_1, \; e_2)$$
$$BT_{fun} \; [\![float]\!] \, [\,] = \text{'FLOAT'}() \qquad BT_{fun} \; [\![(\_, \overset{n}{\cdots}, \_) \to \_]\!] \, [\overline{e_i}^{\,n}, e] = \text{?FUN}_n(\overline{e_i}^{\,n}, \; e)$$
$$BT_{fun} \; [\![pid]\!] \, [\,] = \text{'PID'}()$$

Fig. 3. Translation of type constructors into expressions.

$$TR_{par} \; [\![C()]\!] \, \eta \, \overline{\alpha_i}^{\,n} = \{\{\overline{fun() \to \text{'NONE'}()}^{\,n}\}, BT_{fun} \; [\![C]\!] \, [\,]\} \; (\text{if } C \in \mathcal{TC}^0)$$

$$TR_{par} \; [\![\alpha]\!] \, \eta \, \overline{\alpha_i}^{\,n} = \{\{\overline{e_i}^{\,n}\}, \eta(\alpha)\} \text{ where } \forall i. e_i = \begin{cases} fun() \to \eta(\alpha) & \text{if } \alpha_i = \alpha \\ fun() \to \text{'NONE'}() & \text{otherwise} \end{cases}$$

$$TR_{par} \; [\![\tau_1 \cup \tau_2]\!] \, \eta \, \overline{\alpha_i}^{\,n} = \text{?ALT}(TR_{par} \; [\![\tau_1]\!] \, \eta \, \overline{\alpha_i}^{\,n}, TR_{par} \; [\![\tau_2]\!] \, \eta \, \overline{\alpha_i}^{\,n})$$
$$TR_{par} \; [\![C(\overline{\tau_j}^{\,m})]\!] \, \eta \, \overline{\alpha_i}^{\,n} = \{\{\bigsqcup \overline{e_{j,1}}^{\,m}, \dots, \bigsqcup \overline{e_{j,n}}^{\,m}\}, BT_{fun} \; [\![C]\!] \, [\overline{e_j}^{\,m}]\}$$
$$\text{where } \forall j \in \{1..m\}. \{\{e_{j,1}, \dots, e_{j,n}\}, e_j\} = TR_{par} \; [\![\tau_j]\!] \, \eta \, \overline{\alpha_i}^{\,n}$$
$$\text{if } C \in \{nelist(\_, \_), \{\_, \overset{m}{\cdots} \_\}, (\_, \overset{m-1}{\cdots} \_) \to \_\}$$

$$e_1 \sqcup e_2 = \begin{cases} e_2 & \text{if } e_1 = fun() \to \text{'NONE'}() \\ e_1 & \text{otherwise} \end{cases} \qquad \bigsqcup \overline{e_i}^{\,n} = e_1 \sqcup (e_2 \sqcup \dots (e_{n-1} \sqcup e_n)\dots)$$

Fig. 4. Translation of the types of the parameters and type variable bindings

scheme $\forall \alpha. [\,] \cup nelist(\alpha) \to \alpha \cup false$. By using Definition 2 we can prove that $f([\,])$ can be evaluated only to $false$. In fact, for every simple type τ:

$$\mathcal{E}[\![f([\,])]\!] \subseteq \mathcal{E}[\![f]\!]|_{\mathcal{T}[\![[\,] \cup nelist(\tau)]\!]} (\mathcal{E}[\![[\,]]\!]) \subseteq \mathcal{T}[\![[\,] \cup nelist(\tau) \to \tau \cup false]\!] (\mathcal{E}[\![[\,]]\!]) \subseteq \mathcal{T}[\![\tau]\!] \cup \{false\}$$

In particular, for $\tau = 0$ and $\tau = 1$ we would obtain that $\mathcal{E}[\![f([\,])]\!]$ is a subset of both $\{0, false\}$ and $\{1, false\}$, so, if $f([\,])$ is evaluated to a value, then that value must be $false$. Thus, f has also the type scheme $\forall \alpha. ([\,] \to none \cup false) \cup (nelist(\alpha) \to \alpha \cup false)$, which is equivalent to the scheme shown previously. In general, when a function expects a parameter of type τ, but the type of the actual argument does not bind some of the variables in τ, these variables are bound to $none$ in f's result type. In Fig. 4 we define the TR_{par} function, which receives a simple type τ, a mapping η from type variables to program variables and a list of variables $\overline{\alpha_i}$. It returns a tuple whose second component is an Erlang term with the same semantics as τ, but replacing the type variables of the latter by program variables as specified by η. The first component of the result is another tuple with as many closures as type variables in the list $\overline{\alpha_i}$ given as third parameter. The i-th closure of the tuple will be evaluated to $\eta(\alpha_i)$ if α_i occurs free in τ, or to $\text{'NONE'}()$ otherwise. We return closures instead of plain values, since a $none$ value inside tuple component would make the whole tuple to have type $none$. As an example, let us assume $\eta = [\alpha/A]$. The result of $TR_{par} \; [\![0 \cup \alpha]\!] \, \eta \, [\alpha]$ is $\text{?ALT}(\{\{fun() \to \text{'NONE'}()\}, 0\}, \{\{fun() \to A\}, A\})$.

In Fig. 5 we show the *GenMacro* function which, given a type scheme σ for a function f/n it returns the definition of a macro $M_{f/n}$ overapproximating its

$$GenMacro(\forall\overline{\alpha_i}^m.\overline{\tau_j}^n \to \tau \mid \{\overline{\tau'_k \subseteq \tau''_k}^l\}) =$$

$$\texttt{-define}(M_{f/n}(\overline{X_j}^n),$$
$$\quad let \ \{\overline{Z_j = X_j}^n\} \ in$$
$$\quad receive \ \{\overline{A_i}^m\} \to let \ \overline{\{\{\eta'(\alpha_{j,k})\}, Z_j\} = TR_{par} \ [\![\tau_j]\!] \ \eta \ \overline{\alpha_{j,k}}}^n \ in$$
$$\quad\quad let \ \overline{\{\{\}, T_k\} = TR_{par} \ [\![\tau'_k]\!] \ \eta \ [\,]}^l \ in$$
$$\quad\quad let \ \overline{\{\{\}, T_k\} = TR_{par} \ [\![\tau''_k]\!] \ \eta \ [\,]}^l \ in$$
$$\quad\quad let \ \{\{\}, R\} = TR_{par} \ [\![\tau]\!] \ \eta'' \ [\,] \ in \ R$$
$$\quad end)$$
$$where \ \{\overline{Z_j}^n\}, \{\overline{T_k}^l\}, \{\overline{A_i}^m\}, \{\overline{A'_i}^m\} \ and \ R \ are \ fresh$$
$$\eta = [\alpha_i/A_i]^m, \eta' = [\alpha_i/A'_i]^m, \eta'' = [\alpha_i/A'_i()^m]$$
$$\forall j \in \{1..n\}.\{\overline{\alpha_{j,k}}\} = var(\tau_j)$$

Fig. 5. Translation of a function f of a type scheme σ into a macro

semantics. The macro receives as many parameters as the arity of f. Firstly, it assigns those parameters to fresh variables Z_j in order to avoid unnecesary code replication of the macro arguments at the macro expansion when the X_j occurs more than once in its definition. The *receive* statement brings the variables $\overline{A_i}^m$ into scope with type *any*. The types of these variables are subsequently bound to the types of the parameters Z_j by the assignments generated by TR_{par}, which also bind the $\overline{A'_i}$ variables to their corresponding closures containing either the A_i or 'NONE'(), as explained in the previous paragraph. Then, *GenMacro* translates the constraints of the type schemes into assignments to the same fresh variable T. Notice that, assuming that $e_1 : \tau_1$ and $e_2 : \tau_2$, the sequence $T = e_1, T = e_2$ is typable if τ_1 and τ_2 are *joinable* (i.e. non disjoint). This is a less accurate, but safe, overapproximation of the $\subseteq$ relation between types. Finally, the result of the macro expansion is the type of the result of the function, in which the closures assigned to the A'_i are invoked. As an example, we consider the macro generated for the type scheme $\forall\alpha.(int, [\,] \cup nelist(\alpha, [\,])) \to [\,] \cup nelist(\alpha, [\,])$:

```
-define(M(N, Xs), Z1 = N, Z2 = Xs,
    receive A ->
        {{}, Z1} = {{}, 'INT'()},
        {{AP}, Z2} = ?ALT({{fun 'NONE'/0}, []},
                          {{fun() -> A end}, ?NELIST(A,[]))),
        ?ALT([], ?NELIST(AP(),[]))
    end).
```

The definition of Fig. 5 only covers the case in which the input scheme is not overloaded. In the case of overloaded schemes we would have to generate an auxiliary macro for each of the specifications and another one defined as the disjunction (via ?ALT) of these auxiliary macros.

Once these macros have been generated, the transformation of the program is straightforward. Given an expression e, we denote by e^T the result of replacing each function call $f(e_1, \ldots, e_n)$ in e by the corresponding macro expansion

$?M_{f/n}(e_1, \ldots, e_n)$. Aditionally, the transformed environment Λ^T of Λ is the environment resulting from the transformation of the expressions occurring in the right-hand side of the bindings in Λ plus the bindings contained within Λ^0.

The following results prove the adequacy of the transformation. The first one shows three related things: that M_σ reflects the largest semantics compatible with σ, that the transformation overapproximates the semantics of expressions and, as a consequence, that the transformation is sound for computing success types, hence for detecting failures.

Proposition 1. *Let Λ be an environment and Λ^T its transformation. Then:*

(i) If $f/n : \sigma$, then $\mathcal{E}[\![f]\!]^\Lambda \sqsubseteq \mathcal{E}[\![fun(X_1, \ldots, X_n) \rightarrow ?M_\sigma(X_1, \ldots, X_n)]\!]^{\Lambda^0}$.
(ii) $\mathcal{E}[\![e]\!]^\Lambda \sqsubseteq \mathcal{E}[\![e^T]\!]^{\Lambda^T}$, for any e.
(iii) If $e^T : \tau$ for Λ^T then $e : \tau$ for Λ, for any e, τ.

All this would be useless if the loss of precision of the transformation with respect to the real semantics implied also a loss of precision in Dialyzer's analysis. We shall study now under which conditions the transformed program produces less accurate results than the original one. As it was stated in Sect. 3, Dialyzer uses the compaction of the polymorphic spec given by the user. Let us denote by Λ^C the environment that results from replacing in Λ every type scheme σ by $C(\sigma)$. If Dialyzer used the environment Λ^C for inferring success types, then we would ensure that it yields the same or more accurate results when applied to the transformed program.

Proposition 2. *If Dialyzer infers $e : \tau$ in an environment Λ^C, then it infers $e^T : \tau'$ in Λ^T for some $\tau' \sqsubseteq \tau$.*

The improvement is in fact strict in many cases, as proved by the examples of *id*, *map* and all usual polymorphic functions. This proposition applies when the user has specified a spec σ whose compaction $C(\sigma)$ is equal or more accurate than the type τ inferred by Dialyzer, as it happens in the great majority of cases. If it does not, then Dialyzer uses $\tau \sqcap C(\sigma)$ in the environment that is used for analysing the calls to f in the rest of the program. This may lead to a loss of precision when applying our transformation, as the following example shows:

```
-spec f(any()) -> any().          g() -> f(1).
f(0) -> 0.
```

Dialyzer would infer the call $g()$ to have type *none*, as it considers the type $((0) \rightarrow 0) \sqcap ((any) \rightarrow any) = 0 \rightarrow 0$ when analysing $f(1)$. However, our transformation replaces $f(1)$ by a term $?F(1)$ whose semantics is that of $(any) \rightarrow any$, so the expression $g()$ is inferred with type *any*. Nevertheless, we can adapt our transformation such that it uses $GenMacro(\tau)$ instead of $GenMacro(\sigma)$ whenever $\tau \subseteq C(\sigma)$. We just would have to apply Dialyzer twice, firstly to the original program without user-given specs, and then to the transformed program.

5   Conclusions and Future Work

Dialyzer is a great tool for preventing statically different kinds of failures in Erlang programs; in particular, runtime reduction errors are detected when Dialyzer infers the empty type *none* as the return success type for a function. The precision of the inference can be improved if the user provides more refined types by means of type *specs*, that can be even polymorphic and with subtyping constraints. However, polymorphism of specs is not fully exploited by Dialyzer, leading to a great loss of precision in many cases (for instance, most of the functions in the Erlang module `lists` have a polymorphic spec). Types inferred in previous proposals, like [11], were not better.

This weakness is probably not casual: as we have discussed in this paper, it is not obvious how polymorphic success types must be interpreted. Our first contribution has been a precise notion of what a polymorphic specification means, expressing the intuition, familiar to the seasoned functional programmer, that polymorphic functions are *parametric* and must not inspect argument positions corresponding to polymorphic data variables.

Our second contribution came from the observation that the content of polymorphic specs can expressed by pieces of Erlang code that, when inlined in a program replacing original function calls, force Dialyzer to really take into account the polymorphism of the function spec. This leads to a macro-based program transformation that, although losing precision from the point of view of the actual program semantics, permits Dialyzer to do a more refined analysis.

We think fair to say that our work improves significantly the present behavior of Dialyzer regarding polymorphism, and we see other positive aspects in the approach: it is lightweight, since no changes are needed in Dialyzer nor in user written programs, as far as the specifications are already in the program; it is scalable, because the macro expansions have a linear impact on the size of programs; and it is modular in the sense that only function specs are used for the transformation, so the actual definitions of function can be changed as far as specs are respected. We have implemented the transformation in an easy-to-use tool that can be found at http://dalila.sip.ucm.es/poly_erlang. Its source code is available at https://github.com/manuelmontenegro/erlang-poly-transformer. This tool runs under Dialyzer 2.7.3 with Erlang/OTP 17 (ERTS v6.13).

In this work we have assumed that the specs given by the user are correct, in the sense that they are success types schemes of the function to which they are attached, according to Definition 2. Checking that correctness of user-given specs is left to future work. We also aim to devise an inference algorithm for polymorphic specs, so that the programmer does not need to declare them.

Acknowledgements. The authors would like to thank Kostis Sagonas and Stavros Aronis, for many fruitful discussions about Dialyzer and success types, that have been fundamental for developing the intuitions about the meaning of polymorphic success types that is proposed in this paper.

References

1. Erlang reference manual user's guide v 6.4: 7. types and function specifications (2015). http://erlang.org/doc/reference_manual/typespec.html
2. Armstrong, J.: Programming Erlang: Software for a Concurrent World. The Pragmatic Programmers. Pragmatic Bookshelf (2013)
3. Carlsson, R.: An introduction to core erlang. In: Proceedings of the PLI 2001 Erlang Workshop. Citeseer (2001)
4. Damas, L., Milner, R.: Principal type-schemes for functional programs. In: Proceedings of the 9th ACM SIGPLAN-SIGACT Symposium on Principles of Programming Languages, pp. 207–212. ACM (1982)
5. Gunter, C.A., Mosses, P.D., Scott, D.S.: Semantic domains and denotational semantics. Technical report MS-CIS-89-16, Department of Computer and Information Science, University of Pennsylvania, February 1989
6. Jimenez, M., Lindahl, T., Sagonas, K.: A language for specifying type contracts in erlang and its interaction with success typings. In: Proceedings of the 2007 SIGPLAN Workshop on ERLANG Workshop, pp. 11–17. ACM (2007)
7. Lindahl, T., Sagonas, K.: Detecting software defects in telecom applications through lightweight static analysis: a war story. In: Chin, W.-N. (ed.) APLAS 2004. LNCS, vol. 3302, pp. 91–106. Springer, Heidelberg (2004)
8. Lindahl, T., Sagonas, K.: Typer: a type annotator of erlang code. In: Proceedings of the 2005 ACM SIGPLAN Workshop on Erlang, pp. 17–25. ACM (2005)
9. Lindahl, T., Sagonas, K.: Practical type inference based on success typings. In: Proceedings of the 8th ACM SIGPLAN International Conference on Principles and Practice of Declarative Programming, PPDP 2006, pp. 167–178, New York, NY, USA. ACM (2006)
10. López-Fraguas, F.J., Montenegro, M., Sánchez-Hernández, J.: Polymorphic types in Erlang function specifications (extended version). Technical report TR-3-15, Departamento de Sistemas Informáticos y Computación, Universidad Complutense de Madrid (2015)
11. Marlow, S., Wadler, P.: A practical subtyping system for erlang. In: Proceedings of the Second ACM SIGPLAN International Conference on Functional Programming, ICFP 1997, pp. 136–149, New York, NY, USA. ACM (1997)
12. Pierce, B.C.: Programming with intersection types and bounded polymorphism. Technical report (1991)
13. Reynolds, J.C.: Types, abstraction, and parametric polymorphism. In: Mason, R.E.A. (ed.) Information Processing 83. Elsevier Science Inc. (1983)
14. Sagonas, K.: Using static analysis to detect type errors and concurrency defects in erlang programs. In: Blume, M., Kobayashi, N., Vidal, G. (eds.) FLOPS 2010. LNCS, vol. 6009, pp. 13–18. Springer, Heidelberg (2010)
15. Wadler, P.: Theorems for free! In: Proceedings of the Fourth International Conference on Functional Programming Languages and Computer Architecture, pp. 347–359. ACM (1989)

Declarative Foreign Function Binding Through Generic Programming

Jeremy Yallop[✉], David Sheets, and Anil Madhavapeddy

University of Cambridge Computer Laboratory, Cambridge, UK
jeremy.yallop@cl.cam.ac.uk

Abstract. Foreign function interfaces are typically organised monolithically, tying together the *specification* of each foreign function with the *mechanism* used to make the function available in the host language. This leads to inflexible systems, where switching from one binding mechanism to another (say from dynamic binding to static code generation) often requires changing tools and rewriting large portions of code.

In contrast, approaching the design of a foreign function interface as a *generic programming* problem allows foreign function specifications to be written declaratively, with easy switching between a wide variety of binding mechanisms — static and dynamic, synchronous and asynchronous, etc. — with no changes to the specifications.

1 Introduction

The need to bind and call functions written in another language arises frequently in programming. For example, an OCaml programmer might call the C function `gettimeofday` to retrieve the current time:

```
int gettimeofday(struct timeval *, struct timezone *);
```

Before calling `gettimeofday`, the programmer must write a binding that exposes the C function as an OCaml function. Writing bindings presents many opportunities to introduce subtle errors [8, 12, 14], although it is a conceptually straightforward task: the programmer must convert the arguments of the bound function from OCaml values to C values, pass them to `gettimeofday`, and convert the result back to an OCaml value.

In fact, bindings for functions such as `gettimeofday` can be produced mechanically from their type definitions, and tools that can generate bindings (e.g. [2]) are widely available. However, using an external tool — i.e. operating *on* rather than *in* the language — can be damaging to program cohesiveness, since there is no connection between the types used within the tool and the types of the resulting code, and since tools introduce types and values into a program that are not apparent in its source code.

This paper advocates a different approach, based on generic programming (e.g. [9]), a collection of techniques for defining functions such as equality, serialisation, and traversal that can be applied at a wide variety of types. Generic programming involves introducing a representation of some collection of types,

© Springer International Publishing Switzerland 2016
O. Kiselyov and A. King (Eds.): FLOPS 2016, LNCS 9613, pp. 198–214, 2016.
DOI: 10.1007/978-3-319-29604-3_13

then writing generic functions, parameterised by that representation, that can operate across all of the corresponding types.

The starting point of generic programming is typically a representation of host language types. However, as this paper shows, generic programming techniques can also be applied to binding foreign functions, where the types of interest are the types of the foreign language, and the generic functions are binding strategies that turn the names and types of foreign-language functions into functions that can be called from the host language. In this way it is possible to eliminate the boilerplate needed to bind foreign functions — not by generating it with an external tool, but by using the abstraction mechanisms of the language to parameterise over the common type structure. The result is type-safe, flexible, and tightly integrated into the host language.

For concreteness, this paper focuses on *ocaml-ctypes*, a widely-used library for calling C functions from OCaml based on the generic programming approach, and assumes some knowledge of OCaml language features such as functors and generalized algebraic data types (GADTs) [13]. However, the techniques described in the following pages can be used to build a declarative foreign function library in any language that supports generic programming.

1.1   Outline

The generic programming approach presented here involves two key ingredients.

The first ingredient is an interpretation-independent representation of foreign language types as host language values (Sect. 2).

The second ingredient is an abstract binding interface that can be implemented in different ways to support different binding mechanisms. Section 3 develops various such mechanisms, including an evaluator for binding foreign functions dynamically (Sect. 3.1), a code generator for generating bindings statically (Sect. 3.2), an inverted approach for exposing host language functions to the foreign language, and some more exotic approaches, for asynchronous calls and out-of-process calls with improved memory safety (Sect. 3.3).

The techniques used for declarative binding of foreign-language functions can also be applied to determining the layout of foreign-language objects (Sect. 4).

The extended version of this paper offers more complete code listings of some of the generic functions and generated code from this edition and additional evidence for the practicality of the generic programming approach to foreign function interface design, including a description of a number of real-world uses of *ocaml-ctypes* in commercial and free software, and measurements that show that the performance of bindings generated by *ocaml-ctypes* is comparable to that of hand-written code.

2   Representing Foreign Types as Native Values

The first step in building a generic foreign function library is constructing a representation of foreign language types as host language values.

```
type _ ctype =
  Void    : unit ctype
| Char    : char ctype
| Int     : int ctype
| Pointer : α ctype → α ptr ctype
| View    : { read : β → α; write : α → β; ty: β ctype } → α ctype
| Struct  : struct_type → α structure ctype
| Funptr : α cfn → α funptr ctype
and _ cfn =
  Returns : α ctype → α cfn
| Fn : α ctype * β cfn → (α → β) cfn
and α structure = (* elided *) and struct_type = (* elided *)
and α ptr = (* elided *)
```

Fig. 1. C type representations, concretely

```
module type TYPE = sig
 type α cty
 val void: unit cty

 (* Scalar types *)
 val char: char cty
 val int: int cty
 val ptr: α cty → α ptr cty
 val view: (α → β) → (β → α) → α cty → β cty

 (* Aggregate types *)
 type τ structure and (α, τ) field
 module type STRUCTURE = sig
   type t
   val t : t structure cty
   val field: string → α cty → (α, t) field
   val seal: unit → unit
 end
 val structure: string → (module STRUCTURE)

 (* Functions and function pointers *)
 type α fn
 val returning: α cty → α fn
 val (@→): α cty → β fn → (α → β) fn

 type α funptr
 val funptr: α fn → α funptr cty
end
```

Fig. 2. C type representations, abstractly

Figure 1 defines generalized algebraic datatypes (GADTs) `ctype` and `cfn` for representing a variety of C object and function types. Each C type is mapped to a corresponding OCaml type, which is represented by the type parameter of `ctype`; for example, a value of type `int ctype` represents a C type that appears in OCaml as a value of type `int`.

The `TYPE` signature (Fig. 2) provides an abstract interface for building type representations, with an abstract type `cty` in place of the concrete type `ctype` and a function for each constructor. Using `cty` rather than using `ctype` directly introduces additional flexibility in mapping types as described by the user to concrete representations of types, as Sect. 4 will show.

Representing C Scalar Types. The constructors `Void`, `Char` and `Int` represent the C types with corresponding names, which are mapped to the OCaml types `unit`, `char` and `int`. (The full implementation supports the other scalar types — `float`, `short`, etc.) The `Pointer` constructor builds a C type representation from another C type representation, much as the C type constructor `*` builds a type from a type. (In the full implementation the parameterised type `ptr` comes with various operations for reading and writing values, but they are not needed in the exposition here.) The `View` constructor uses an isomorphism to vary the mapping between C types and OCaml types; for example, given functions for converting between `char ptr` and `string`

```
val string_of_ptr : char ptr → string
val ptr_of_string : string → char ptr
```

the following expression builds a value of type `string ctype` to represent values that appear in C as `char *` and in OCaml as `string`:

```
View {read = string_of_ptr; write = ptr_of_string; ty = Pointer Char}
```

Representing C Aggregate Types. Besides scalar types such as integers and pointers, C supports a number of aggregate types. The `TYPE` signature (Fig. 2) exports types `structure` and `field` for representing `structs` and `struct` fields, with a function `structure` for creating new `struct` types, and with a signature `STRUCTURE` that exposes a value `t` representing a `struct`, a function `field` that adds a field to an existing `struct` type, and a function `seal` that converts an incomplete type to a complete type that cannot be further extended. The two type parameters of `field` represent the type of the field and the type of the structure to which the field belongs. The type `t` in the `STRUCTURE` signature operates as a static tag: each call to `structure` generates an instance of `STRUCTURE` whose `t` is distinct from all other types in the program; this prevents `struct` representations from being used interchangeably, which would violate type safety.

Figure 3 shows the `STRUCTURE` machinery in action. Each line of OCaml code (on the right) corresponds to the corresponding line of the C code (on the left), which declares a `struct timeval` with two fields.

The first line creates a module `Tv` representing an initially empty struct type `timeval`. The actual representation of the struct type, based on the `Struct` constructor of Fig. 1, is internal to the `Tv` module; only the `field` and `seal` functions and the type representation `t` are exposed through the interface.

The second and third lines call the `Tv.field` function to add `unsigned long` fields with the names `tv_sec` and `tv_usec`. Calling `Tv.field` performs an effect and returns a value: that is, it extends the `struct` represented by `Tv` with an additional field, and it returns a value representing the new field, which may be used later in the program to access `struct tv` values.

The final line "seals" the struct type representation, turning it from an incomplete type into a fully-fledged object type with known properties such as size and alignment, just as the closing brace in the corresponding C declaration marks the point in the C program at which the struct type is completed. Adding fields to the struct representation is only possible before the call to `seal`, and creating values of the represented type is only possible afterwards; violation of either of these constraints results in an exception.

There are multiple possible implementations of the STRUCTURE interface and its operations `field` and `seal`, which are explored further in Sect. 4.

```
struct timeval {                 module Tv = (val structure "timeval")
    unsigned long tv_sec;        let sec  = Tv.field "tv_sec" ulong
    unsigned long tv_usec;       let usec = Tv.field "tv_usec" ulong
};                               let () = Tv.seal ()
```

Fig. 3. The `timeval` struct in C and OCaml

As with `ptr`, `structure` comes with various operations for reading and writing fields, allocating new structures, and so on, but they are again not needed in this exposition. Additionally, the full implementation supports `union` and array types.

Representing C Function Types. Finally, besides object (i.e. value) types, C supports function and function pointer types. The TYPE interface (Fig. 2) exports a type `fn` for representing C function types, along with constructors `returning` and `@→`, and a type `funptr` for representing C function pointer values, along with a value `funptr` for constructing function pointer type representations. The following expression constructs a representation of the type of `gettimeofday` from the introduction:

```
ptr Tv.t @→ ptr Tz.t @→ returning int
```

which has the following type, writing `tv` for `Tv.t structure`, and similarly for `tz`:

```
(tv ptr → tz ptr → int) fn
```

As the type parameter `tv ptr → tv ptr → int` indicates, the `@→` builds curried OCaml functions to represent C functions of multiple arguments. However, `returning` and `@→` carefully distinguish object types, which are represented with `cty`, from function types, which are represented with `fn`. A C function that takes

```
module type FOREIGN = sig
  type α res
  val foreign: string → α fn → α res
end
```

Fig. 4. The FOREIGN interface

```
module Bindings(F : FOREIGN) = struct
  let gettimeofday =
    F.foreign "gettimeofday" (ptr Tv.t @→ ptr Tz.t @→ returning int)
end
```

Fig. 5. Binding `gettimeofday`, abstractly

one argument and returns a function pointer that accepts another argument is quite different from a function of two arguments, and the coding represents them differently. More precisely, `returning` builds a representation of a function type from the object type that the function returns, and `@→` adds an object type as an additional argument to an existing function type. The `funptr` function supports the inverse conversion, turning object types into function types.

In the concrete representation of Fig. 1, the `ctype` datatype supports a additional constructor `Funptr` for representing function pointers. The `Returns` and `Fn` constructors of the datatype `fn` correspond to the `TYPE` functions `returning` and `@→` functions for building `fn` values.

3   Interpreting Type Representations

The type representations of Sect. 2 can support a number of generic operations including `sizeof`, allocation, and pretty-printing of types and values. This section focuses on various implementations of an abstract operation `foreign`, which builds a binding to a foreign function from its name and a representation of its type. Figure 4 shows the FOREIGN signature, which contains a single function, `foreign`. The return type, `res`, is left abstract so that each binding strategy can instantiate it appropriately.

Figure 5 shows a binding for `gettimeofday`, abstracted over the implementation of FOREIGN.

3.1   Dynamically Interpreting Foreign Function Bindings

Interpreting Calls. The first implementation of `foreign` evaluates the type representation to build bindings dynamically. The parameterised type `res` in the FOREIGN signature is instantiated with the alias $α$ `res =`$α$, so the type of `foreign` is as follows:

```
val foreign : string → α fn → α
```

```
typedef int ( *compar_t)(void*, void*);
int qsort(void*,size_t,size_t,compar_t)
```

Fig. 6. The C qsort function

That is, `foreign` turns a C function type description and a name into an OCaml function. Applying `foreign` to the name and type representation of `gettimeofday` in the top level returns a function that can be called immediately:

```
# let f = foreign "gettimeofday" (ptr Tv.t @→ ptr Tz.t @→ returning int)
val f : tv ptr → tz ptr → int = <fun>
```

The call to `foreign` resolves the name `"gettimeofday"` and dynamically synthesises a call description of the appropriate type. In the *ocaml-ctypes* implementation, dynamic name resolution is implemented by the POSIX function `dlsym` and call frame synthesis uses the `libffi` library to handle the low-level details.

Call synthesis involves two basic types. The first, `ffitype`, represents C types; there is a value of `ffi_type` for each scalar type:

```
type ffitype
val int_ffitype : ffitype
val char_ffitype : ffitype
val pointer_ffitype : ffitype
```

The second type, `callspec`, describes a call frame structure. There are primitive operations primitives for creating a new `callspec`, for adding arguments, and for marking the callspec as complete and specifying the return type:

```
type callspec
val alloc_callspec : unit → callspec
val add_argument : callspec → ffitype → int
val prepare_call : callspec → ffitype → unit
```

(The return type of `add_argument` represents an offset which is used for writing each argument into the appropriate place in a buffer when performing a call.)

Finally, the `call` function takes a function address, a completed `callspec`, and callback functions that write arguments and read return values from buffers.

```
val call : address → callspec → (address→unit) → (address→α) → α
```

The complete implementation of `foreign` may be found in the extended version of this paper.

Building a typed interface to these `libffi` primitives – that is, using them to implement `foreign` – is straightforward. Each call to `foreign` uses `alloc_callspec` to create a fresh `callspec`; each argument in the function representation results in a call to `add_argument` with the appropriate `ffitype` value. The `Returns` constructor results in a call to `prepare_call`; when the arguments of the function are supplied the `call` function is called to invoke the resolved C function. There is no compilation stage: the user can call `foreign` interactively, as shown above.

```
let compar_t = dfunptr (ptr void @→ ptr void @→ returning int)

module Bindings(F : FOREIGN) = struct
  let qsort = F.foreign "qsort"
    (ptr void @→ size_t @→ size_t @→ compar_t @→ returning void)
end
```

Fig. 7. Using `dfunptr` to bind to `qsort`

Interpreting Callbacks. The dynamic `foreign` implementation turns a function name and a function type description into a callable function in two stages: first, it resolves the name into a C function address; next, it builds a call frame from the address and the function type description. In fact, this second stage is sometimes useful independently, and it is supported as a separate operation:

val fn_of_ptr : α fn → unit ptr → α

Conversions in the other direction are also useful, since an OCaml function passed to C must be converted to an address:

val ptr_of_fn : α fn → α → unit ptr

The implementation of `ptr_of_fn` is based on the `callspec` interface used to build the call interpreter and uses an additional primitive operation, which accepts a `callspec` and an OCaml function, then uses `libffi` to dynamically construct and return a "trampoline" function which calls back into OCaml:

val make_function_pointer : callspec → (α →β) → address

These conversion functions are rather too low-level to expose directly to the user. Instead, the following view converts between addresses and pointers automatically:

```
let dfunptr fn = view (funptr fn) (fn_of_ptr fn) (ptr_of_fn fn)
val dfunptr : α fn → α cty
```

The `dfunptr` function builds object type representations from function type representations, just as C function pointers build object types from function types. Figure 7 shows `dfunptr` in action, describing the callback function for `qsort` (Fig. 6). The resulting `qsort` binding takes OCaml functions as arguments:

```
qsort arr nmemb sz
  (fun l r → compare (from_voidp int !@l) (from_voidp int !@r))
```

(The `from_voidp` function converts from a `void *` value to another pointer type.)

This scheme naturally supports even higher-order functions: function pointers which accept function pointer as arguments, and so on, allowing callbacks into OCaml to call back into C. However, such situations appear rare in practice.

3.2 Statically Compiling Foreign Function Bindings

Interpreting function type descriptions as calls is convenient for interactive development, but has a number of drawbacks. First, the implementation suffers from significant interpretative overhead (quantified in the extended version of this paper). Second, there is no check that the values passed between OCaml and C have appropriate types. The implementation resolves symbols to function addresses at runtime, so there is no checking of calls against the declared types of the functions that are invoked. Finally, it is impossible to make use of the many conveniences provided by the C language and typical toolchains. When compiling a function call a C compiler performs various promotions and conversions that are not available in the simple reimplementation of the call logic. Similarly, sidestepping the usual symbol resolution process makes it impossible to use tools like nm and objdump to interrogate object files and executables.

Fortunately, all of these problems share a common cure. Instead of basing the implementation of foreign on an *evaluation* of the type representation, the representation can be used to *generate* both C code that can be checked against the declared types of the bound functions and OCaml code that links the generated C code into the program.

Transforming the evaluator of Sect. 3.1 into a code generator can be seen as a form of *staging*, i.e. specializing the dynamic foreign function based on static information (i.e. the type description) in order to improve its performance when the time comes to supply the remaining arguments (i.e. the arguments to the bound function). As we shall see, the principles and techniques used in the staging and partial evaluation literature will be helpful in implementing the code-generating foreign.

Generating C. In all, three new implementations of the FOREIGN signature are needed. The first FOREIGN implementation, GenerateC, uses the name and the type representation passed to foreign to generate C code. The functor application Bindings(GenerateC) passes the name and type representation for gettimeofday to GenerateC.foreign, which generates a C wrapper for gettimeofday.

The generated C code, shown below, converts OCaml representations of values to C representations, calls gettimeofday and translates the return value representation back from C to OCaml[1]. If the user-specified type of gettimeofday is incompatible with the type declared in the C API then the C compiler will complain when building the generated source.

---

[1] There are no calls to protect local variables from the GC because the code generator can statically determine that the GC cannot run during the execution of this function. However, it is not generally possible to determine whether the bound C function can call back into OCaml, and so the user must inform the code generator if such callbacks may occur by passing a flag to foreign.

```
value ctypes_gettimeofday(value a, value b) {
    struct timeval  *c = ADDR_OF_PTR(a);
    struct timezone *d = ADDR_OF_PTR(b);
    int e = gettimeofday(c, d);
    return Val_int(e);
}
```

Generating OCaml. The second new FOREIGN implementation, GenerateML, generates an OCaml wrapper for ctypes_gettimeofday. The ctypes_gettimeofday function deals with low-level representations of OCaml values; the OCaml wrapper exposes the arguments and return types as typed values. The functor application Bindings(GenerateML) passes the name and type representation of gettimeofday to GenerateML.foreign, which generates an OCaml module GeneratedML that wraps ctypes_gettimeofday.

The OCaml module generated by GenerateML also matches the FOREIGN signature. The central feature of the generated code is the following foreign implementation that scrutinises the type representation passed as argument in order to build a function that extracts raw addresses from the pointer arguments to pass through to C:

```
external ctypes_gettimeofday : address → address → int
 = "ctypes_gettimeofday"

let foreign : type a. string → a cfn → a =
 fun name t → match name, t with
 | "gettimeofday",
    Fn (Pointer _, Fn (Pointer _, Returns Int)) →
     (fun x1 x2 → ctypes_gettimeofday (rawaddr x1) (rawaddr x2))
```

The type variable a is initially abstract but, since the type of t is a GADT, examining t using pattern matching reveals information about a. In particular, since the type parameter of cfn is instantiated to a function type in the definition of the Fn constructor (Fig. 1), the right-hand side of the first case of the definition of foreign above is also expected to have function type. Similar reasoning about the Pointer, Int and Returns constructors reveals that the right-hand side should be a function of type σ ptr $\to$ τ ptr $\to$ int for some types σ and τ, and this condition is met by the function expression in the generated code.

Linking the Generated Code. The generated OCaml module GeneratedML serves as the third FOREIGN implementation; it has the following type:

```
FOREIGN with type α fn = α
```

The application Bindings(GeneratedML) supplies GeneratedML as the argument F of the Bindings functor (Fig. 5). The generated foreign function above becomes F.foreign in the body of Bindings, and receives the name and type representation for gettimeofday as arguments. The inspection of the type representation in foreign serves as a form of type-safe linking, checking that the type specified by the user matches the known type of the bound function. In the general case, the type refinement in the pattern match within `foreign` allows the same generated implementation to serve for all the foreign function bindings in the `Bindings` functor, even if they have different types.

The Trick. The pattern match in the `GeneratedML.foreign` function can be seen as an instance of a binding-time improvement known in the partial evaluation community as The Trick [7]. The Trick transforms a program to introduce new opportunities for specialization by replacing a variable whose value is unknown with a branch over all its possible values. In the present case, the `GeneratedML.foreign` function will only ever be called with those function names and type representations used in the generation of the `GeneratedML` module. Enumerating all these possibilities as match cases results in simple non-recursive code that may easily be inlined when the `Bindings` functor is applied.

Cross-Stage Persistence. The scheme above, with its three implementations of `FOREIGN`, may appear unnecessarily complicated. It is perhaps not immediately obvious why we should not generate C code and a standalone OCaml module, eliminating the need to apply the `Bindings` functor to the generated code.

One advantage of the three-implementation scheme is that the generated code does not introduce new types or bindings into the program, since the generated module always has the same known type (i.e. `FOREIGN`). However, there is also a more compelling reason for the third implementation.

The `GeneratedML.foreign` function converts between typed arguments and return values and low-level untyped values which are passed to C. In the case where the type of an argument is a `view`, converting the argument involves applying the `write` function of the `view` representation. For example, the following binding to the standard C function `puts` uses the `string` view of Sect. 2 to support an argument that appears in OCaml as a `string` and in C as a `char *`:

```
let puts = foreign "puts" (string @→ returning int)
```

Calling `puts` with an argument s involves applying `ptr_of_string` to s to obtain a char*. However, there is no way of inserting `ptr_of_string` into the generated code. In the representation of a view the `write` function is simply a higher-order value, which cannot be converted into an external representation. This is analogous to the problem of *cross-stage persistence* in multi-stage languages: the generated code refers to a value in the heap of the generating program.

The three-implementation approach neatly sidesteps the difficulty. There is no need to externalise the `write` function; instead, the generated `foreign` implementation simply extracts `write` from the value representation at the point when `Bindings` is applied:

```
let foreign : type a. string → a cfn → a =
  fun name t → match name, t with
  | "puts", Fn (View {write}, Returns Int) →
    (fun x1 → ctypes_puts (write x1).addr)
  | (* ... *)
```

Thus, the third implementation of FOREIGN makes it possible to use views and other higher-order features in the type representation.

3.3 Further Interpretations

Inverted Bindings. Section 3.1 showed how to invert the call interpreter to support callbacks; Sect. 3.2 showed how to stage the call interpreter to improve safety and speed. The question naturally arises: Is there a use for an inverted, staged interpreter? It turns out that there is.

The primary use of *ocaml-ctypes* is making C libraries available to OCaml programs. However, as the discoveries of disastrous bugs in widely-used C libraries continue to accumulate, the need for safer implementations of those libraries written in high-level languages such as OCaml becomes increasingly pressing. As this section shows, it is possible to expose OCaml code to C via an interpretation of FOREIGN that interprets the parameter of the res type as a value to consume rather than a value to produce.

Specialising the res type of the FOREIGN signature (Fig. 5) with a type that consumes α values gives the following type for foreign:

```
val foreign : string → α fn → (α → unit)
```

that is, a function which takes a name and a function description and consumes a function. This consumer of functions is just what is needed to turn the tables: rather than resolving and binding foreign functions, this implementation of foreign exports host language functions under specified names.

Continuing the running example, this foreign implementation can export a function whose interface matches gettimeofday. Once again, it suffices to apply the Bindings functor from Fig. 5 to a suitable module. As with the staged call interpreter (Sect. 3.2), Bindings is applied multiple times – once to generate a C header and a corresponding implementation which forwards calls to OCaml callbacks, and again to produce an exporter which connects the C implementation with our OCaml functions.

As mentioned in Sect. 3, *ocaml-ctypes* includes a generic pretty-printing function that formats C type representations using the C declaration syntax. Applying the pretty-printer to the gettimeofday binding produces a declaration suitable for a header:

```
int gettimeofday(struct timeval *, struct timezone *);
```

The generation of the corresponding C implementation proceeds similarly to the staged call interpreter, except that the roles of OCaml and C are reversed: the generated code converts arguments from C to OCaml representations, calls back into OCaml and converts the result back into a C value before returning it. The addresses of the OCaml functions exposed to C are stored in an array in the generated C code. The size of the array is determined by the number of calls to foreign in the functor – one, in this case.

The generated OCaml module GeneratedInvML populates the array when the module is loaded by calling a function register_callback with a value of type t callback.

```
val register_callback : α callback → α → unit
```

The type parameter of the `callback` value passed to `register_callback` is the type of the registered function:

```
type _ callback = Gettimeofday : (address → address → int) callback
```

Finally, the generated `foreign` function is reminiscent of the staged implementation of Sect. 3.2; it scrutinises the type representation to produce a function consumer, which passes the consumed function to `register_callback`:

```
let foreign : type a. string → a cfn → (a → unit) =
  fun name t → match name, t with
 |"gettimeofday",
   Fn (Pointer tv, Fn (Pointer tz, Returns Int)) →
   (fun f → register_callback Gettimeofday
   (fun x1 x2 → f (makeptr tv x1) (makeptr tz x2)))
```

The applied module `Bindings(GeneratedInvML)` exports a single function, `gettimeofday`, which consumes an OCaml function to be exported to C:

```
val gettimeofday : (tv ptr → tz ptr → int) → unit
```

The complete code generated for the inverted binding may be found in the extended version of this paper.

Asynchronous Calls. Since the standard OCaml runtime has limited support for concurrency, many modern OCaml programs make use of cooperative concurrency libraries such as Lwt [16]. Cooperative concurrency requires taking care with potentially blocking calls, since a single blocking call can cause suspension of all threads. To help mitigate the problem, Lwt supports a primitive

```
val detach : (α → β) → α → β Lwt.t
```

which associates a potentially blocking computation with one of a pool of system threads. It is sometimes useful to wrap `detach` around calls to foreign functions.

As the signature of `detach` indicates, Lwt has a monadic interface: potentially blocking computations run in the `Lwt.t` monad. A simple generalization of the `TYPE` signature turns foreign calls into monadic computations:

```
module type TYPE' = sig
  type α comp
  val returning : α ctype → α comp fn
  (* otherwise the same as TYPE *)
end
```

(The original `TYPE` signature of Fig. 5 can be recovered from `TYPE'` by substituting type α comp = α.) The implementation of Sect. 3.2 requires corresponding changes: each foreign call in the generated OCaml code is enclosed in a call to `detach`, and each generated C call includes code to release OCaml's runtime lock.

Applying `Bindings` to this Lwt-specialised implementation of `FOREIGN` builds a binding to `gettimeofday` that runs in the Lwt monad:

```
val gettimeofday : tv structure ptr → tz structure ptr → int Lwt.t
```

Out-of-process Calls. High-level languages often make strong guarantees about type safety that are compromised by binding to foreign functions. Safe languages such as OCaml preclude memory corruption by isolating the programmer from the low-level details of memory access; however, a single call to a misbehaving C function can result in corruption of arbitrary parts of the program memory.

One way to protect the calling program from the corrupting influence of a C library is to allow the latter no access to the program's address space. This can be accomplished using a variant of the staged call interpreter (Sect. 3.2) in which, instead of invoking bound C functions directly, the generated stubs marshall the arguments into a shared memory buffer where they are retrieved by an entirely separate process which contains the C library.

Once again, this cross-process approach is straightforward to build from existing components. The data representation is based on C structs: for each foreign function the code generator outputs a struct with fields for function identifier, arguments and return value (Fig. 8). The struct is built using the type representation constructors (Sect. 2) and printed using the generic pretty printer. These structs are then read and written by the generated C code in the two processes. Besides the C and ML code generated for the staged interpreter, the cross-process interpretation also generates C code that runs in the remote process and a header file to ensure that the two communicants have a consistent view of the frame structs.

```
struct gettimeofday_frame {
    enum function_id id;
    struct timeval *tp;
    struct timezone *tz;
    int return_value;
};
```

Fig. 8. A `struct` for making cross-process calls to `gettimeofday`

The extended version of this paper describes experiments that quantify the overhead of these cross-process calls.

4   Interpreting Type Descriptions

As Sect. 2 showed, the `structure`, `field` and `seal` functions (Fig. 2, Sect. 2) can together be used to describe C `struct` types. The implementation of these operations must determine both the appropriate memory offsets of each field in the struct, and the size and alignment requirements of the whole `struct`; these numbers are determined by the order of the fields, the memory alignment requirements of each field type, and sometimes by additional compilation directives. As with FOREIGN, there are a variety of approaches to implementing the STRUCTURE interface.

Computing Layout Information. The simplest approach to implementing STRUCTURE is to give implementations of `field` and `seal` that simply compute the appropriate layout directly.

```
module Types(T: TYPE) = struct
 module Tv = (val T.structure "timeval")
 let sec  = Tv.field "tv_sec" ulong
 let usec = Tv.field "tv_usec" ulong
 let () = Tv.seal ()
end
```

Fig. 9. *timeval* layout, abstractly

The `structure` function builds an incomplete empty struct with no alignment requirements. The `field` function computes the next alignment boundary in the struct for its field argument, and updates the alignment requirements for the struct. The `seal` function inserts any padding necessary to align the struct and marks it as complete. The extended version of this paper gives the full code.

Computing structure layout in this way works for simple cases, but has a number of limitations that make it unsuitable to be the sole approach to laying out data. First, libraries may specify non-standard layout requirements (e.g. with the `__packed__` direction), and attempting to replicate these quickly becomes unmanageable. Second, some libraries, (e.g. `libuv`), define structs with interspersed internal fields which vary both across platforms and across versions. Replicating this variation in the bindings quickly leads to unmaintainable code.

Retrieving Layout Information. These drawbacks can be avoided with an alternative implementation of STRUCTURE that, instead of attempting to replicate the C compiler's structure layout algorithm, uses the C compiler itself as the source of layout information, much as the staged `foreign` (Sect. 3.2) generates C code to bind functions rather than using `libffi` to replicate the calling convention.

As with the staged `foreign` function, the idea is to use The Trick to transform `field` and `seal` from functions which compute the layout into functions which map particular concrete arguments into previously computed layout information. In order to bring the layout information directly into the OCaml program an additional stage is needed: first, the Types structure (Fig. 9) is applied to a module `Generate_C` to produce a C program which retrieves layout information with calls to `offsetof` and `sizeof`:

```
printf("{ftype;fname;foffset=%zu}\n", offsetof(struct timeval, tv_sec));
```

Compiling and running the C program produces an OCaml module `Types_impl` which satisfies the TYPE signature, and which contains implementations of `field` and `seal` specialized to the `struct`s and fields of the `Types` module:

```
let field s fname ftype = match s, fname with
 | Struct { tag = "timeval"}, "tv_sec" → {ftype; fname; foffset = 4}
 (* ... *)
```

The application `Types(Types_impl)` passes the layout information through to the calls to `Tv.field` and `Tv.seal`, making it available for use in the program.

This technique extends straightforwardly to retrieving other information that is available statically, such as the values of `enum` constants or preprocessor macros.

5   Related Work

The approach of representing foreign language types as native language values is inspired by several existing FFIs, including Python's ctypes, Common Lisp's Common FFI and Standard ML's NLFFI [4], each of which takes this approach.

This paper follows NLFFI's approach of indexing foreign type representations by host language types in order to ensure internal consistency (although OCaml's GADTs, unavailable to the author of NLFFI, make it possible to avoid most of the unsafe aspects of the implementation of that library). However, this paper departs from NLFFI in abstracting the declaration of C types from the mechanism used to retrieve information about those types, using OCaml's higher-order module system to perform the abstraction and subsequent selection.

The use of functors to abstract over interpretations of the `TYPE` and `FOREIGN` signatures is a central technique in this paper. Carette et al. [5] use functors in a similar way, first abstracting over the interpretation of an embedded object language (λ calculus), then developing a variety of increasingly exotic interpretations which perform partial evaluation, CPS translation and staging of terms.

The use of GADTs to represent foreign language types, and their indexes to represent the corresponding native language types (Sect. 2) can be viewed as an encoding of a *universe* of the kind used in dependently-typed programming [3, 15]. Altenkirch and McBride [1] use universes directly to represent the types of one programming language (Haskell) within another (OLEG) and then to implement generic functions over the corresponding values.

Mapping codes to types and their interpretations by abstracting over a parameterised type constructor is a well-known technique in the generic programming community [6,17]. Hinze [10] describes a library for generic programming in Haskell with a type class that corresponds quite closely to the `TYPE` signature of Sect. 2, except that the types described are Haskell's, not the types of a foreign language. There is a close connection between Haskell's type classes and ML's modules, and so Karvonen's implementation of Hinze's approach in ML [11] corresponds even more directly to this aspect of the design presented here.

References

1. Altenkirch, T., McBride, C.: Generic programming within dependently typed programming. In: Proceedings of the IFIP TC2/WG2.1 Working Conference on Generic Programming, pp. 1–20 (2003)
2. Beazley, D.M.: SWIG: An easy to use tool for integrating scripting languages with C and C++. In: USENIX Tcl/Tk Workshop (1996)
3. Benke, M., Dybjer, P., Jansson, P.: Universes for generic programs and proofs in dependent type theory. Nord. J. Comput. **10**(4), 265–289 (2003)

4. Blume, M.: No-longer-foreign: Teaching an ML compiler to speak C "natively". Electron. Notes Theoret. Comput. Sci. **59**(1), 36–52 (2001)
5. Carette, J., Kiselyov, O., Shan, C.: Finally tagless, partially evaluated: Tagless staged interpreters for simpler typed languages. J. Funct. Program. **19**(5), 509–543 (2009)
6. Cheney, J., Hinze, R.: A lightweight implementation of generics and dynamics. In: Haskell 2002, pp. 90–104. ACM, New York (2002)
7. Danvy, O., Malmkjær, K., Palsberg, J.: Eta-expansion does the trick. ACM Trans. Program. Lang. Syst. **18**(6), 730–751 (1996)
8. Furr, M., Foster, J.S.: Checking type safety of foreign function calls. In: PLDI 2005, pp. 62–72. ACM, New York (2005)
9. Gibbons, J.: Datatype-generic programming. In: Backhouse, R., Gibbons, J., Hinze, R., Jeuring, J. (eds.) SSDGP 2006. LNCS, vol. 4719, pp. 1–71. Springer, Heidelberg (2007)
10. Hinze, R.: Generics for the masses. J. Funct. Program. **16**(4–5), 451–483 (2006)
11. Karvonen, V.A.J.: Generics for the working ML'er. In: ML 2007. ACM (2007)
12. Kondoh, G., Onodera, T.: Finding bugs in java native interface programs. In: ISSTA 2008, pp. 109–118. ACM (2008)
13. Leroy, X., Doligez, D., Frisch, A., Garrigue, J., Rémy, D., Vouillon, J.: The OCaml system (release 3.12): Documentation and user's manual. In: INRIA, July 2011
14. Li, S., Tan, G.: Finding reference-counting errors in python/C programs with affine analysis. In: Jones, R. (ed.) ECOOP 2014. LNCS, vol. 8586, pp. 80–104. Springer, Heidelberg (2014)
15. Nordström, B., Petersson, K., Smith, J.M.: Programming in Martin-Löf Type Theory: An Introduction. Clarendon, New York (1990)
16. Vouillon, J.: Lwt: A cooperative thread library. In: ML 2008. ACM (2008)
17. Yang, Z.: Encoding types in ML-like languages. In: ICFP 1998. ACM (1998)

Incremental Computing with Abstract Data Structures

Akimasa Morihata$^{(\boxtimes)}$

University of Tokyo, Tokyo, Japan
morihata@graco.c.u-tokyo.ac.jp

Abstract. Incremental computing is a method of keeping consistency between an input and an output. If only a small portion of the input is modified, it is natural to expect that the corresponding output can be obtained more efficiently than full re-computation. However, for abstract data structures such as self-balancing binary search trees, even the most primitive modifications may lead to drastic change of the underlying structure. In this paper, we develop an incremental computing method, which can deal with complex modifications and therefore is suitable for abstract data structures. The key idea is to use shortcut fusion in order to decompose a complex modification to a series of simple ones. Based on this idea, we extend Jeuring's incremental computing method, which can deal with algebraic data structures, so as to deal with abstract data structures. Our method is purely functional and does not rely on any run-time support. Its correctness is straightforward from parametricity. Moreover, its cost is often proportional to that of the corresponding modification.

1 Introduction

It is common to process data that is gradually modified. *Incremental computing* (aka self-adjusting computing [1]) enables us to deal with such situations without full re-processing. Formally, given input x, objective function f, and modification *modify*, instead of calculating $f\ (modify\ x)$, incremental computing uses f_+ such that $f\ (modify\ x) = f_+\ (f\ x)$. It has many practical applications.

Interactive Editor: Incremental computing is useful for visualizing the effect of modifications to source data. For example, it may enable us to modify a HTML file while checking the rendering result.

Big Data Analysis: Incremental computing naturally leads to on-line processing and thus may make it possible to analyze data that are too large to store.

Error Recovery: When analyzing data sent from a server, we may detect, for example from the checksum, that the data is broken. By using incremental computing, we can start the calculation with the erroneous data and later fix the result.

Because of its importance, there are many studies for systematically developing programs that support incremental computing [1–11].

© Springer International Publishing Switzerland 2016
O. Kiselyov and A. King (Eds.): FLOPS 2016, LNCS 9613, pp. 215–231, 2016.
DOI: 10.1007/978-3-319-29604-3_14

For incremental computing, we usually assume modifications to be small. However, for abstract data structures, this assumption does not generally hold. As an example, consider a set implemented by a sorted list. To keep knowing its size while adding elements, we would like to have function s_+ such that $s_+\ e\ (size\ s) = size\ (insert\ e\ s)$, where *insert* adds an element to a set.

$$insert\ e\ s = \textbf{case}\ s\ \textbf{of}\ [] \to [e]$$
$$a : s' \to \textbf{if}\ e \equiv a\ \textbf{then}\ s$$
$$\textbf{else if}\ e < a\ \textbf{then}\ e : s\ \textbf{else}\ a : insert\ e\ s'$$

Note that $1 + size\ s$ is not always equal to $size\ (insert\ e\ s)$ because $insert\ e\ s = s$ if e is in s. In fact, the implementation of *insert* is not very simple and possibly reconstructs whole of the list. It is therefore unclear whether existing incremental computing methods are applicable to this case. Other abstract data structures have similar problems. In a queue implemented by a pair of lists, a dequeue operation may cause a list reversal. In self-balancing binary search trees, every modification, such as an insertion or a deletion, may lead to a series of rotations.

In this paper, we propose an incremental computing method, which is suitable for programs involving abstract data structures. Our development is based on the following observations:

- Most abstract data structures are implemented on simple structures such as lists and trees.
- Even though modifications for abstract data structures may be complex, each of them can be decomposed into a series of primitive ones for the underlying structure, such as constructor applications and pattern matching.

These observation indicate that incremental computing for programs with abstract data structures can be reduced to one for those with simpler underlying structures. For example, the sets discussed above is based on lists, and *insert* can be regarded as a series of list construction (cons) and pattern-matching; therefore, it is natural to expect that incremental computing methods for list operations can be extended to those for the set.

To make our idea concrete, we consult shortcut fusion [12,13], which uses polymorphic functions for capturing how intermediate data structures are constructed and/or destructed. For example, consider the following polymorphic function INSERT that implements *insert*.

$$insert = \text{INSERT}\ ([], (:))\ (\lambda l \to \textbf{case}\ l\ \textbf{of}\ [] \to \mathsf{Nothing};\ a : x \to \mathsf{Just}\ (a, x))$$
$$\text{INSERT}\ ::\ \forall \alpha.\ (\alpha, A \to \alpha \to \alpha) \to (\alpha \to \mathsf{Maybe}\ (A, \alpha)) \to A \to \alpha \to \alpha$$
$$\text{INSERT}\ (n, c)\ d\ e\ s$$
$$= \textbf{case}\ d\ s\ \textbf{of}\ \mathsf{Nothing} \to c\ e\ n$$
$$\mathsf{Just}\ (a, s') \to \textbf{if}\ e \equiv a\ \textbf{then}\ s$$
$$\textbf{else if}\ e < a\ \textbf{then}\ c\ e\ s$$
$$\textbf{else}\ c\ a\ (\text{INSERT}\ (n, c)\ d\ e\ s')$$

INSERT uses the parameters, n, c, and d, instead of the empty list, list extension, and pattern-matching, respectively. The polymorphic type of INSERT states that the output (of type α) is obtained by either using the parameters or returning the given list, s. Hence, incremental computing of *insert* seems possible if the both cases are managed. The latter is easy since it is sufficient to just reuse the previous value. For the former, we can utilize existing incremental computing methods for list operations. In fact, passing appropriate parameters to INSERT suffices. For instance, to compute *size*, consider the following s_+.

$$s_+ = \text{INSERT } (0, \lambda\_ \ x \rightarrow x+1) \ (\lambda x \rightarrow \text{if } x \equiv 0 \text{ then Nothing else Just } (\underline{a}, x-1))$$

Here, the arguments, 0, $(+1)$, and (-1), respectively correspond to $[]$, $(:)$, and pattern-matching. $\underline{a}$ is any value of the appropriate type. Regardless of $\underline{a}$, the polymorphic type of INSERT guarantees $s_+ \ e \ (size \ s) = size \ (insert \ e \ s)$, which is exactly what we hope to have.

Our approach has several benefits. First, it enables us to extend incremental computing methods for simple modifications to complex modifications. In this paper, we extend Jeuring's approach [8]. Second, not the program but the type is sufficient to see the correctness. In fact, correctness is straightforward from parametricity [14,15]. Third, since the incremental version just uses supplied functions instead of constructors and destructors, the cost of incremental computing is often proportional to that of the corresponding modification. Lastly, it is purely-functional source-to-source transformation and does not require any run-time support such as memoization. Therefore, it is easier to combine other functionalities, such as lazy evaluation and compiler optimizations.

Our major contributions are the following.

- We show two examples to demonstrate our approach: splay trees [16] (Sect. 2) and regular-expression matching (Sect. 3).
- We provide a datatype-generic formalism to our approach (Sect. 4), which subsumes both examples.

2   Incremental Computing on Splay Trees

We use Haskell for describing programs. We may abbreviate $(A \rightarrow B, B \rightarrow A)$ to $A \leftrightarrow B$. We deal with only purely functional, total, and terminating programs so as to simplify discussions concerning parametricity [14,15].

2.1   Splay Trees

In this section, we consider splay trees [16] that store integers. We implement them by the following node-labeled binary trees.

$$\textbf{data BTree} = \text{Nd BTree Int BTree} \ \mid \ \text{Lf}$$

Splay trees are binary search trees. To accelerate subsequent operations, they use a characteristic heuristic called *splaying*, which moves the accessed node to the root. Figure 1 shows a simplified implementation of the $lookup_k$ operation in the TreeStructures package[1] for Haskell, in which k denotes the integer located.

---

[1] https://hackage.haskell.org/package/TreeStructures-0.0.1.

$$lookup_k\ t\ =\ \textbf{case}\ t\ \textbf{of}$$

$$
\begin{aligned}
&\mathsf{Lf} \to t \\
&\mathsf{Nd}\ l\ v\ r \to \textbf{if}\ k \equiv v\ \textbf{then}\ t \\
&\qquad\qquad\quad \textbf{else if}\ k < v \\
&\qquad\qquad\qquad \textbf{then case}\ lookup_k\ l\ \textbf{of} \\
&\qquad\qquad\qquad\qquad \mathsf{Lf} \to t \\
&\qquad\qquad\qquad\qquad \mathsf{Nd}\ l'\ v'\ r' \to \mathsf{Nd}\ l'\ v'\ (\mathsf{Nd}\ r'\ v\ r) \\
&\qquad\qquad\qquad \textbf{else case}\ lookup_k\ r\ \textbf{of} \\
&\qquad\qquad\qquad\qquad \mathsf{Lf} \to t \\
&\qquad\qquad\qquad\qquad \mathsf{Nd}\ l'\ v'\ r' \to \mathsf{Nd}\ (\mathsf{Nd}\ l\ v\ l')\ v'\ r'
\end{aligned}
$$

Fig. 1. The *lookup* operation for splay trees.

We may want to associate structural information with splay trees. For example, if we consider avoiding splaying for short trees, we would like to incrementally calculate the size and the height.

2.2 Incremental Computing on Binary Trees

Our starting point is an incremental computing method by Jeuring [8]. His method is based on structural recursion, aka. *folds*.

$$
\begin{aligned}
&fold_{\mathsf{BTree}} :: \forall \alpha.\ (\mathsf{Maybe}\ (\alpha, \mathsf{Int}, \alpha) \to \alpha) \to \mathsf{BTree} \to \alpha \\
&fold_{\mathsf{BTree}}\ \phi\ \mathsf{Lf} \qquad\quad = \phi\ \mathsf{Nothing} \\
&fold_{\mathsf{BTree}}\ \phi\ (\mathsf{Nd}\ l\ v\ r) = \phi\ (\mathsf{Just}\ (fold_{\mathsf{BTree}}\ \phi\ l, v, fold_{\mathsf{BTree}}\ \phi\ r))
\end{aligned}
$$

Folds can implement several computations. For example, they subsume size and height.

$$
\begin{aligned}
size &= fold_{\mathsf{BTree}}\ \phi_{size} & height &= fold_{\mathsf{BTree}}\ \phi_{height} \\
\phi_{size}\ \mathsf{Nothing} &= 1 & \phi_{height}\ \mathsf{Nothing} &= 1 \\
\phi_{size}\ (\mathsf{Just}\ (l, a, r)) &= 1 + l + r & \phi_{height}\ (\mathsf{Just}\ (l, a, r)) &= 1 + max\ l\ r
\end{aligned}
$$

Unfortunately, folds are not generally suitable for incremental computing: when we destruct a tree, it is impossible to know the size and/or the height of a subtree from that of the parent. To remember values for each subtree and thereby avoid full re-computation, Jeuring's method employs a labeled version of binary trees, $\overline{\mathsf{BTree}}$, and *upward accumulation* [17,18], $ua_{\mathsf{BTree}}\ \phi$.

$$
\textbf{data}\ \overline{\mathsf{BTree}}\ a = \overline{\mathsf{Nd}}\ (\overline{\mathsf{BTree}}\ a)\ \mathsf{Int}\ (\overline{\mathsf{BTree}}\ a)\ a\ |\ \overline{\mathsf{Lf}}\ a
$$

$$
\begin{aligned}
&ua_{\mathsf{BTree}}\ \phi :: \forall \alpha.\ (\mathsf{Maybe}\ (\alpha, \mathsf{Int}, \alpha) \to \alpha) \to \mathsf{BTree} \to \overline{\mathsf{BTree}}\ \alpha \\
&ua_{\mathsf{BTree}}\ \phi = fold_{\mathsf{BTree}}\ \overline{\phi} \\
&\overline{\phi}\ \mathsf{Nothing} \qquad\quad = \overline{\mathsf{Lf}}\ (\phi\ \mathsf{Nothing}) \\
&\overline{\phi}\ (\mathsf{Just}\ (l', v, r')) = \overline{\mathsf{Nd}}\ l'\ v\ r'\ (\phi\ (\mathsf{Just}\ (val_{\mathsf{BTree}}\ l', v, val_{\mathsf{BTree}}\ r')))
\end{aligned}
$$

We in addition use an auxiliary function, val_{BTree}, which extracts the associated label: $val_{\mathsf{BTree}}\ (\overline{\mathsf{Lf}}\ a) = a$ and $val_{\mathsf{BTree}}\ (\overline{\mathsf{Nd}}\ \_\ \_\ \_\ a) = a$. It is easy to see

$val_{\mathsf{BTree}} \circ \mathsf{ua}_{\mathsf{BTree}}\ \phi = fold_{\mathsf{BTree}}\ \phi$, i.e., the value associated with the root is exactly the value of the corresponding fold; thus, we can reduce incremental computation of folds to that of upward accumulations.

Jeuring showed that, by using upward accumulations, we can incrementally calculate any folds when the structure is modified by either by a constructor application or pattern matching. Let $expose_{\mathsf{BTree}}\ (\overline{\mathsf{Lf}}\ \_) = \mathsf{Nothing}$ and $expose_{\mathsf{BTree}}\ (\overline{\mathsf{Nd}}\ l\ v\ r\ \_) = \mathsf{Just}\ (l, v, r)$. The keys are the the following equations.

$$\mathsf{ua}_{\mathsf{BTree}}\ \phi\ (\mathsf{Nd}\ l\ v\ r) = \overline{\phi}\ (\mathsf{Just}\ (\mathsf{ua}_{\mathsf{BTree}}\ \phi\ l, v, \mathsf{ua}_{\mathsf{BTree}}\ \phi\ r))$$

$$expose_{\mathsf{BTree}}\ (\mathsf{ua}_{\mathsf{BTree}}\ \phi\ (\mathsf{Nd}\ l\ v\ r)) = \mathsf{Just}\ (\mathsf{ua}_{\mathsf{BTree}}\ \phi\ l, v, \mathsf{ua}_{\mathsf{BTree}}\ \phi\ r)$$

The first shows that $\overline{\phi}$ calculates, from the results of the subtrees, that of larger tree. As the second shows, $expose_{\mathsf{BTree}}$ does the converse: it yields those of subtrees from that of the original tree.

Jeuring's method can be summarized as the following incremental computing algorithm.

- Given the objective function $fold_{\mathsf{BTree}}\ \phi$ and the initial structure t, calculate the labeled tree $\mathsf{ua}_{\mathsf{BTree}}\ \phi\ t$.
- For each construction by Nd, we update the labeled tree by $\overline{\phi} \circ \mathsf{Just}$.
- For each destruction by pattern-matching, we update the calculated value by $expose_{\mathsf{Tree}}$.
- If $(fold_{\mathsf{BTree}}\ \phi)$-value is required, apply val_{BTree} to the labeled tree.

2.3   Incremental Computing on Splay Trees

It seems difficult to extend Jeuring's method to splay trees. Splaying is a fairly complex operation and drastically change the structure. Therefore, it is nontrivial to know the height after splaying, for example, without full re-computation.

As mentioned in the introduction, we solve the difficulty by borrowing an idea from shortcut fusion [12,13]. Let $in_{\mathsf{BTree}} :: \mathsf{Maybe}\ (\mathsf{BTree}, \mathsf{Int}, \mathsf{BTree}) \to \mathsf{BTree}$ and $out_{\mathsf{BTree}} :: \mathsf{BTree} \to \mathsf{Maybe}\ (\mathsf{BTree}, \mathsf{Int}, \mathsf{BTree})$ be the functions that capture construction and destruction of BTree.

$$in_{\mathsf{BTree}}\ \mathsf{Nothing} \qquad = \mathsf{Lf} \qquad\qquad out_{\mathsf{BTree}}\ \mathsf{Lf} \qquad\quad = \mathsf{Nothing}$$
$$in_{\mathsf{BTree}}\ (\mathsf{Just}\ (l, v, r)) = \mathsf{Nd}\ l\ v\ r \qquad out_{\mathsf{BTree}}\ (\mathsf{Nd}\ l\ v\ r) = \mathsf{Just}\ (l, v, r)$$

Assume that a possibly complex modification, $modify :: \mathsf{BTree} \to \mathsf{BTree}$, can be implemented by supplying them to a polymorphic function, MOD, as follows.

$$modify\ t = \mathrm{MOD}\ (in_{\mathsf{BTree}}, out_{\mathsf{BTree}})\ t$$
$$\mathrm{MOD} :: \forall \alpha.\ (\mathsf{Maybe}\ (\alpha, \mathsf{Int}, \alpha) \leftrightarrow \alpha) \to \alpha \to \alpha$$

Figure 2 shows the case of $lookup_k$. The polymorphic function, LOOKUP_k, is obtained by substituting the parameters for every construction and destruction of BTree. As the polymorphic type explains, LOOKUP_k generates the output only by using the parameters. In other words, LOOKUP_k forms a skeleton that

$lookup_k$ = LOOKUP$_k$ $(in_{\mathsf{BTree}}, out_{\mathsf{BTree}})$
LOOKUP$_k$ :: $\forall \alpha.$ (Maybe $(\alpha, \mathsf{Int}, \alpha) \leftrightarrow \alpha) \to \alpha \to \alpha$
LOOKUP$_k$ (in, out) t
   = **case** out t **of**
       Nothing $\to t$
       Just $(l, v, r) \to$ **if** $k \equiv v$ **then** t
               else if $k < v$
                   then case out (LOOKUP$_k$ (in, out) l) **of**
                     Nothing $\to t$
                     Just $(l', v', r') \to in$ (Just $(l', v', in$ (Just $(r', v, r))))$
                 else case out (LOOKUP$_k$ (in, out) r) **of**
                     Nothing $\to t$
                     Just $(l, v', l') \to in$ (Just $(in$ (Just $(l, v, l')), v', r'))$

Fig. 2. Confirming incrementalizability of *lookup*.

expresses how primitive modifications, in_{BTree} and out_{BTree}, are composed to form a complex modification, $lookup_k$. We can similarly derive such skeletons for other modifications.

By using the polymorphic function, MOD, we can incrementally compute $fold_{\mathsf{BTree}}$ ϕ on splay trees as follows.

– Given the initial splay tree, $t :: \mathsf{BTree}$, calculate a labeled tree by ua_{BTree} ϕ t.
– Instead of modification $modify = \mathrm{MOD}$ $(in_{\mathsf{BTree}}, out_{\mathsf{BTree}})$, update the labeled tree by MOD $(\overline{\phi}, expose_{\mathsf{BTree}})$.
– If $(fold_{\mathsf{BTree}}$ $\phi)$-value is required, apply val_{BTree} to the labeled tree.

For example, to keep knowing the height, we first obtain the initial labeled tree by ua_{BTree} ϕ_{height} t where t is the initial splay tree, and for each $lookup_k$, we instead update the labeled tree by LOOKUP$_k$ $(\overline{\phi_{height}}, expose_{\mathsf{BTree}})$. The type of LOOKUP$_k$ guarantees the correctness of our approach.

$$\forall \phi.\ ua_{\mathsf{BTree}}\ \phi\ (lookup_k\ t) = \mathrm{LOOKUP}_k\ (\overline{\phi}, expose_{\mathsf{BTree}})\ (ua_{\mathsf{BTree}}\ \phi\ t)$$

Namely, calculating ua_{BTree} ϕ_{height} after the modification is equivalent to applying LOOKUP$_k$ $(\overline{\phi_{height}}, expose_{\mathsf{BTree}})$ after ua_{BTree} ϕ_{height}.

Efficiency. The cost of the incremental computing depends on the polymorphic function, MOD. For this case, the cost of LOOKUP$_k$ is proportional to that of $lookup_k$; thus, the overhead of the incremental computing is a constant factor. In general, it is natural to expect that the cost of MOD is proportional to that of $modify$ because the former is very often obtained by abstracting construction and destruction in the latter.

3 Incremental Regular Expression Matching on Zippers

3.1 Zippers and Associated Structural Recursions

Next we consider another example: incrementally checking whether a string matches a given regular expression.

In Haskell, strings are lists of characters. However, the usual lists, aka. *cons* lists, are not suitable for modification because direct access to their middle is not allowed. A better implementation is Huet's zipper [19], which consists of a pair of structures. For example, $([a_0, a_1, \ldots, a_{i-1}], [a_i, a_{i+1}, \ldots, a_n])$ represents sequence $a_0 a_1 \cdots a_n$ with a cursor at a_{i-1}. We can quickly access a_i, a_{i+1}, and so forth; to access $a_{i-1}, a_{i-2}, \ldots$ as well, we implement the first list by a *snoc* list, which is constructed from the empty list $[]$ and the snoc operator, $x \mathbin{\vec{:}} a$, which adds element a to the last of list x. In order to distinguish snoc lists from cons lists, we write the former SList A and the latter CList A.

We list four major modifications for zippers. For simplicity, we omit the case where the operation is not applicable.

Go Right. Move the cursor to right: *right* $(x, a : y) = (x \mathbin{\vec{:}} a, y)$.
Go Left. Move the cursor to left: *left* $(x \mathbin{\vec{:}} a, y) = (x, a : y)$.
Remove. Remove the element: *remove* $(x \mathbin{\vec{:}} a, y) = (x, y)$.
Insert. Insert an element: *insert* a $(x, y) = (x \mathbin{\vec{:}} a, y)$.

For calculating values for zippers, as the previous example, we introduce folds and upwards accumulations on zippers. Folds on zippers consumes the snoc list by *foldl* and the cons list by *foldr*, and then, combines the two results.

$$fold_{\mathsf{Zipper}} :: \forall \beta, \gamma, \delta.\ ((\gamma, \delta) \to \beta, \mathsf{Maybe}\ (\gamma, A) \to \gamma, \mathsf{Maybe}\ (A, \delta) \to \delta) \to$$
$$\qquad\qquad (\mathsf{SList}\ A, \mathsf{CList}\ A) \to \beta$$
$$fold_{\mathsf{Zipper}}\ (\phi_p, \phi_s, \phi_c)\ (s, c) = \phi_p\ (foldl\ \phi_s\ s, foldr\ \phi_c\ c)$$
$$foldl :: \forall \alpha.\ (\mathsf{Maybe}\ (\gamma, A) \to \gamma) \to \mathsf{SList}\ A \to \gamma$$
$$foldl\ \phi_s\ [] \quad = \phi_s\ \mathsf{Nothing}$$
$$foldl\ \phi_s\ (x \mathbin{\vec{:}} a) = \phi_s\ (\mathsf{Just}\ (foldl\ \phi_s\ x, a))$$
$$foldr :: \forall \delta.\ (\mathsf{Maybe}\ (A, \delta) \to \delta) \to \mathsf{CList}\ A \to \delta$$
$$foldr\ \phi_c\ [] \quad = \phi_c\ \mathsf{Nothing}$$
$$foldr\ \phi_c\ (a : x) = \phi_c\ (\mathsf{Just}\ (a, foldr\ \phi_c\ x))$$

$val_{\mathsf{pair}}\ (\_, \_, b) = b$		$expose_{\mathsf{pair}}\ (s, c, \_) = (s, c)$	
$val_{\mathsf{snoc}}\ (\mathsf{SNil}\ c)$	$= c$	$expose_{\mathsf{snoc}}\ (\mathsf{SNil}\ \_)$	$= \mathsf{Nothing}$
$val_{\mathsf{snoc}}\ (\mathsf{Snoc}\ \_\ \_\ c) = c$		$expose_{\mathsf{snoc}}\ (\mathsf{Snoc}\ x\ a\ \_)$	$= \mathsf{Just}\ (x, a)$
$val_{\mathsf{cons}}\ (\mathsf{CNil}\ d)$	$= d$	$expose_{\mathsf{cons}}\ (\mathsf{CNil}\ \_)$	$= \mathsf{Nothing}$
$val_{\mathsf{cons}}\ (\mathsf{Cons}\ \_\ \_\ d) = d$		$expose_{\mathsf{cons}}\ (\mathsf{Cons}\ a\ x\ \_)$	$= \mathsf{Just}\ (a, x)$

Fig. 3. Definitions of auxiliary functions

Upward accumulations remember the intermediate results of folds. The following defines labeled zippers and upward accumulations. Auxiliary functions are shown in Fig. 3. It is not difficult to see $val_{Pair} \circ ua_{Zipper} (\phi_p, \phi_s, \phi_c) = fold_{Zipper} (\phi_p, \phi_s, \phi_c)$.

$$
\begin{aligned}
&\textbf{type } \overline{\text{Zipper}} \ a \ b \ c \ d = (\overline{\text{SList}} \ a \ c, \overline{\text{CList}} \ a \ d, b) \\
&\textbf{data } \overline{\text{SList}} \ a \ c = \text{SNil} \ c \mid \text{Snoc} \ (\overline{\text{SList}} \ a \ c) \ a \ c \\
&\textbf{data } \overline{\text{CList}} \ a \ d = \text{CNil} \ d \mid \text{Cons} \ a \ (\overline{\text{CList}} \ a \ d) \ d \\[4pt]
&ua_{Zipper} (\phi_p, \phi_s, \phi_c) = fold_{Zipper} (\overline{\phi_p}, \overline{\phi_s}, \overline{\phi_c}) \\
&\overline{\phi_p} (s', c') = (s', c', \phi_p (val_{snoc} \ s', val_{cons} \ c')) \\
&\overline{\phi_s} \ \text{Nothing} \quad\ = \text{SNil} (\phi_s \ \text{Nothing}) \\
&\overline{\phi_s} (\text{Just} (x', a)) = \text{Snoc} \ x' \ a \ (\phi_s (\text{Just} (val_{snoc} \ x', a))) \\
&\overline{\phi_c} \ \text{Nothing} \quad\ = \text{CNil} (\phi_c \ \text{Nothing}) \\
&\overline{\phi_c} (\text{Just} (a, x')) = \text{Cons} \ a \ x' \ (\phi_c (\text{Just} (a, val_{cons} \ x')))
\end{aligned}
$$

3.2 Regular Expression Matching by Folds

Next, we implement regular expression matching by folds. For simplicity, we deal with a particular expression that checks whether a string denotes a binary decimal number. The integer part should be either 0 or a number starting from 1; the fractional part, if it exists, can be any 0/1-sequence following the decimal point.

$$(1[01]*|0)([.][01]+)?$$

We use a deterministic finite-state automaton (DFA) shown in Fig. 4. The following program implements the DFA-based matching, where τ_L is the transition function of the DFA.

$$match_L = (\lambda p \to p \in \{p_1, p_3, p_4\}) \circ foldl \ \tau_L \ p_0$$

Because the zipper generalizes a cons list, it is natural to consider a *foldr*-based implementation as well. Since *foldr* traverses a string from the tail, we use

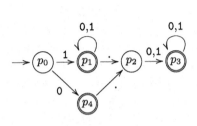

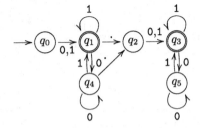

Fig. 4. DFA that accepts binary decimal numbers: p_0 is the initial state; p_1, p_3, and p_4 are the final states; the dead state is omitted.

Fig. 5. DFA that accepts the reverses of the binary decimal numbers: q_0 is the initial state; q_1 and q_3 are the final states; the dead state is omitted.

another DFA shown in Fig. 5, which corresponds to the reverse of the regular expression, $([01]+[.])?([01]*1|0)$; then, we have the following implementation, where $\tau'_R\ a\ q = \tau_R\ q\ a$ and τ_R is the transition function.

$$match_R = (\lambda q \to q \in \{q_1, q_3\}) \circ foldr\ \tau'_R\ q_0$$

The regular expression matching function on zippers, say $match$, can be specified by them. Let $(+\!\!+_S) :: \mathsf{SList}\ A \to \mathsf{CList}\ A \to \mathsf{SList}\ A$ and $(+\!\!+_C) :: \mathsf{SList}\ A \to \mathsf{CList}\ A \to \mathsf{CList}\ A$ be the append functions; then, $match$ should satisfy $match\ (x, y) = match_L\ (x +\!\!+_S y) = match_R\ (x +\!\!+_C y)$. However, these characterizations are not satisfactory. In order to incrementally compute $match$, we would like to implement it by $fold_{\mathsf{Zipper}}$. Fortunately, the third list-homomorphism theorem [20, 21] can be used for this purpose.

Theorem 1 ([21]). *For $h :: (\mathsf{SList}\ A, \mathsf{CList}\ A) \to C$, $g_1 :: B_1 \to C$, $f_1 :: B_1 \to A \to B_1$, $e_1 :: B_1$, $g_2 :: B_2 \to C$, $f_2 :: A \to B_2 \to B_2$, and $e_2 :: B_2$, assume the following.*

$$h\ (x, y) = g_1\ (foldl\ f_1\ e_1\ (x +\!\!+_S y)) = g_2\ (foldr\ f_2\ e_2\ (x +\!\!+_C y))$$

Then, there exists $(\oplus) :: B_1 \to B_2 \to C$ that satisfies the following equation.

$$h\ (x, y) = foldl\ f_1\ e_1\ x \oplus foldr\ f_2\ e_2\ y \qquad \square$$

Theorem 1 states that h is a fold on zippers if it can be expressed by both $foldl$ and $foldr$, exactly as our case. Moreover, it is possible to derive the merging operator, $\oplus$. Let ψ_L and ψ_R be functions that yield a string leading to the given state, i.e., $p = foldl\ \tau_L\ p_0\ (\psi_L\ p)$ and $q = foldr\ \tau'_R\ q_0\ (\psi_R\ q)$. Such a string is specified by a path from the initial state to that state. For example, path $q_0 \overset{0,1}{\to} q_1 \overset{0}{\to} q_4$ indicates that $\psi_R\ q_4$ may result in $[0, 0]$. In this way, we can obtain ψ_L and ψ_R as follows, where $\bot$ denotes the dead state.

$$
\begin{array}{ll}
\psi_L\ p_0 = [] & \psi_R\ q_0 = [] \\
\psi_L\ p_1 = [1] & \psi_R\ q_1 = [0] \\
\psi_L\ p_2 = [1, .] & \psi_R\ q_2 = [., 0] \\
\psi_L\ p_3 = [1, ., 0] & \psi_R\ q_3 = [0, ., 0] \\
\psi_L\ p_4 = [0] & \psi_R\ q_4 = [0, 0] \\
\psi_L\ \bot = [.] & \psi_R\ q_5 = [0, 0, ., 0] \\
& \psi_R\ \bot = [.]
\end{array}
$$

As the following calculation shows, the merging operator, $\oplus$, is given by $p \oplus q = match\ (\psi_L\ p, \psi_R\ q)$.

$$
\begin{aligned}
p \oplus q &= \{\text{definition of } \psi_L \text{ and } \psi_R\} \\
&\quad foldl\ \tau_L\ p_0\ (\psi_L\ p) \oplus foldr\ \tau'_R\ q_0\ (\psi_R\ q) \\
&= \{\text{Theorem 1}\} \\
&\quad match\ (\psi_L\ p, \psi_R\ q)
\end{aligned}
$$

Simplifying the equation yields the following.

$$p_i \oplus q_j \iff$$
$$i = 1 \vee (i, j) \in \{(0, 1), (0, 3), (2, 1), (2, 4), (3, 0), (3, 1), (3, 4), (4, 0), (4, 2)\}$$

In summary, $fold_{\text{Zipper}}\ ((\oplus), \tau_L, \tau_R')$ does the regular expression matching on zippers.

3.3   Incremental Computing on Zippers

As in the previous example, we prepare a skeleton that abstracts construction and destruction in each modification. The following in_{cons}, out_{cons}, in_{snoc}, out_{snoc}, in_{pair}, and out_{pair} are constructors and destructors of cons lists, snoc lists, and pairs.

$$
\begin{aligned}
in_{\text{cons}}\ \mathsf{Nothing} &= [] & out_{\text{cons}}\ [] &= \mathsf{Nothing} \\
in_{\text{cons}}\ (\mathsf{Just}\ (a, x)) &= a : x & out_{\text{cons}}\ (a : x) &= \mathsf{Just}\ (a, x) \\[4pt]
in_{\text{snoc}}\ \mathsf{Nothing} &= [] & out_{\text{snoc}}\ [] &= \mathsf{Nothing} \\
in_{\text{snoc}}\ (\mathsf{Just}\ (x, a)) &= x \mathbin{\vdots} a & out_{\text{snoc}}\ (x \mathbin{\vdots} a) &= \mathsf{Just}\ (x, a) \\[4pt]
in_{\text{pair}}\ (a, b) &= (a, b) & out_{\text{pair}}\ (a, b) &= (a, b)
\end{aligned}
$$

By abstracting all construction and destruction in four major modifications of zippers, we obtain polymorphic functions shown in Fig. 6. Their types verifies the following equation, where $(modify, \text{MOD})$ are either $(right, \text{RIGHT})$, $(left, \text{LEFT})$, $(remove, \text{REMOVE})$, or $(insert, \text{INSERT})$.

$$
\overline{\mathsf{ua}_{\text{Zipper}}\ (\phi_p, \phi_s, \phi_c) \circ modify}
$$
$$
= \text{MOD}\ (\overline{\phi_p}, expose_{\text{pair}})\ (\overline{\phi_s}, expose_{\text{snoc}})\ (\overline{\phi_c}, expose_{\text{cons}}) \circ \mathsf{ua}_{\text{Zipper}}\ (\phi_p, \phi_s, \phi_c)
$$

$\text{RIGHT}, \text{LEFT}, \text{REMOVE}, \text{INSERT} ::$
$$\quad \forall \beta, \gamma, \delta.\ ((\gamma, \delta) \leftrightarrow \beta) \to (\mathsf{Maybe}\ (\gamma, A) \leftrightarrow \gamma) \to (\mathsf{Maybe}\ (A, \delta) \leftrightarrow \delta) \to \beta \to \beta$$

$right = \text{RIGHT}\ (in_{\text{pair}}, out_{\text{pair}})\ (in_{\text{snoc}}, out_{\text{snoc}})\ (in_{\text{cons}}, out_{\text{cons}})$
$\text{RIGHT}\ (in_p, out_p)\ (in_s, out_s)\ (in_c, out_c)\ z = \mathbf{let}\ (x, y') = out_p\ z$
$$\qquad\qquad\qquad\qquad\qquad\qquad\quad \mathsf{Just}\ (a, y) = out_c\ y'$$
$$\qquad\qquad\qquad\qquad\qquad\qquad \mathbf{in}\ in_p\ (in_s\ (\mathsf{Just}\ (x, a)), y)$$

$left = \text{LEFT}\ (in_{\text{pair}}, out_{\text{pair}})\ (in_{\text{snoc}}, out_{\text{snoc}})\ (in_{\text{cons}}, out_{\text{cons}})$
$\text{LEFT}\ (in_p, out_p)\ (in_s, out_s)\ (in_c, out_c)\ z = \mathbf{let}\ (x', y) = out_p\ z$
$$\qquad\qquad\qquad\qquad\qquad\qquad\quad \mathsf{Just}\ (x, a) = out_s\ x'$$
$$\qquad\qquad\qquad\qquad\qquad\qquad \mathbf{in}\ in_p\ (x, in_c\ (\mathsf{Just}\ (a, y)))$$

$remove = \text{REMOVE}\ (in_{\text{pair}}, out_{\text{pair}})\ (in_{\text{snoc}}, out_{\text{snoc}})\ (in_{\text{cons}}, out_{\text{cons}})$
$\text{REMOVE}\ (in_p, out_p)\ (in_s, out_s)\ (in_c, out_c)\ z = \mathbf{let}\ (x', y) = out_p\ z$
$$\qquad\qquad\qquad\qquad\qquad\qquad\qquad \mathsf{Just}\ (x, a) = out_s\ x'$$
$$\qquad\qquad\qquad\qquad\qquad\qquad\quad \mathbf{in}\ in_p\ (x, y)$$

$insert = \text{INSERT}\ (in_{\text{pair}}, out_{\text{pair}})\ (in_{\text{snoc}}, out_{\text{snoc}})\ (in_{\text{cons}}, out_{\text{cons}})$
$\text{INSERT}\ (in_p, out_p)\ (in_s, out_s)\ (in_c, out_c)\ z = \mathbf{let}\ (x, y) = out_p\ z$
$$\qquad\qquad\qquad\qquad\qquad\qquad\quad \mathbf{in}\ in_p\ (in_s\ (\mathsf{Just}\ (x, a)), y)$$

Fig. 6. Polymorphic functions that implement major modifications on zippers.

Therefore, by using INSERT $(\overline{(\oplus)}, expose_{\mathsf{pair}})$ $(\overline{\tau_L}, expose_{\mathsf{snoc}})$ $(\overline{\tau_R'}, expose_{\mathsf{cons}})$ instead of *insert*, for example, we can incrementally calculate the regular expression matching. Moreover, the cost of INSERT is proportional to that of *insert*.

3.4 Comparison to Jeuring's Incremental Algorithm for Lists [8]

It is worth noting that our development is not specific to regular expression matching. We can incrementalize any fold on zippers. In fact, a similar result[2] is shown by Jeuring [8]. He observed that we can incrementally calculate divide-and-conquer operations on lists according to cursor moves, insertions, and deletions.

The most important point is that, as we will show in the next section, our result is an instance of a datatype-generic theory of incremental computing; hence, our approach subsumes Jeuring's. By virtue of the underlying theory, we can easily generalize the zipper-based incremental computation. In particular, because zippers and the third list-homomorphism theorem can deal with trees [21,22], essentially the same approach is applicable to zippers for trees, which may be useful for developing interactive structural editors, for example.

4 Datatype-Generic Incremental Computing

We have developed two incremental algorithms. We show that both are instances of a datatype-generic theory for incremental computing.

4.1 Datatype-Generic Folds

We, like Jeuring's [7], employ a datatype-generic formalism based on category theory. We explain a part necessary for our development. See literature such as a textbook [23] for further information.

A category consists of objects and arrows. In this paper, each object and each arrow correspond to a set and a total function between sets. $f :: A \to B$ denotes an arrow from object A to object B. A category must contain (i) the identity arrow, $id_A :: A \to A$, for each object A, and (ii) the composition, $g \circ f :: A \to C$, for each pair of arrows, $f :: A \to B$ and $g :: B \to C$.

A functor is a mapping between categories. Functor F maps object A and arrow $f :: A \to B$ to $\mathsf{F}A$ and $\mathsf{F}f :: \mathsf{F}A \to \mathsf{F}B$ so that $\mathsf{F}id_A = id_{\mathsf{F}A}$ and $\mathsf{F}(g \circ f) = \mathsf{F}g \circ \mathsf{F}f$. A bifunctor composes two categories and behaves as a functor if an operand is fixed. Formally, $\dagger$ is a bifunctor if $id_A \dagger id_B = id_{A\dagger B}$ and $(g_1 \dagger g_2) \circ (f_1 \dagger f_2) = (g_1 \circ f_1) \dagger (g_2 \circ f_2)$.

Functors can encode data structures and structural recursions. An F-algebra is a pair, (A, ϕ), where $\phi :: \mathsf{F}A \to A$. F-algebra $(\mu\mathsf{F}, in_\mathsf{F})$ is *initial* if for every F-algebra (A, ϕ), there exists a unique arrow h such that $\phi \circ \mathsf{F}h = h \circ in_\mathsf{F}$. The

---

[2] There is a minor difference: while Jeuring required the merging operator, $\oplus$, to be associative, we are not.

unique arrow to (A, ϕ) is called a *catamorphism* (aka. fold) and denoted by $(\!(\phi)\!)_F$. The initial F-algebra establishes an isomorphism between μF and $F\mu F$; thus, μF is the least fixed point of datatype equation $X \cong FX$. Catamorphisms correspond to structural recursions on the datatype. out_F denotes the inverse of in_F.

Example 1: BTree. BTree can be encoded by using polynomial functors. A polynomial functor is composed of the constant functor $!_A$, the identity functor I, product bifunctor $\times$, and coproduct bifunctor $+$. They are defined as follows, where A and B denote objects and f and g denote arrows:

$$
\begin{aligned}
!_A B &= A & A \times B &= \{(a, b) \mid a \in A, b \in B\} \\
!_A f &= id_A & (f \times g)\,(a, b) &= (f\,a, g\,b) \\
& & A + B &= \{\mathsf{Inl}\ a \mid a \in A\} \cup \{\mathsf{Inr}\ b \mid b \in B\} \\
\mathsf{I}A &= A & (f + g)\,(\mathsf{Inl}\ a) &= \mathsf{Inl}\ (f\ a) \\
\mathsf{I}f &= f & (f + g)\,(\mathsf{Inr}\ b) &= \mathsf{Inr}\ (g\ b)
\end{aligned}
$$

Let $T = I \times !_{\mathsf{Int}} \times I + !_{\{()\}}$; then, we have the initial T-algebra, $(\mu T, in_T)$, where μT is isomorphic to BTree. in_T, out_T, and $(\!(\phi)\!)_T$ are exactly in_{BTree}, out_{BTree}, and $fold_{\mathsf{BTree}}$ if we equate $\mathsf{Maybe}\ (A, B, A)$ with $A \times B \times A + \{()\}$.

Example 2: Zipper. It is well known (see [32], for example) that a composite data structure like zippers corresponds to the least fixed point in a category of tuples, in which every object and every arrow are tuples. Since zipper consists of three structures, two lists and a pair, we consider a category of triples.

Let $C = !_A \times I + !_{\{()\}}$; then, the initial C-algebra, $(\mu C, in_C)$ and catamorphism $(\!(\phi)\!)_C$ correspond to the cons lists and the *foldr* function. Similarly, the least fixed point of $S = I \times !_A + !_{\{()\}}$ and catamorphism $(\!(\phi)\!)_S$ correspond to *snoc* lists and *foldl*. Now, $Z(P, S, C) = (S \times C, SS, CC)$ is a functor on the category of triples; then, μZ formalizes the zipper structure. The first, the second, and the third components respectively correspond to the pair, the snoc list, and the cons lists. Initial algebra $(\mu Z, in_Z)$ is defined by $in_Z(p, s, c) = ((s, c), in_S\ s, in_C\ c)$. Catamorphisms consume the snoc list and the cons list by *foldl* and *foldr*, respectively, and then, merge these results. This is indeed $fold_{\mathsf{Zipper}}$.

4.2   Incremental Computing for Primitive Modifications

Jeuring [8] considered the following problem: Given objective function $h :: \mu F \rightarrow A$ and structure $t :: \mu F$, we would like to maintain the value of $h\ t$ even if t is modified by in_F or out_F. Incremental computation for this problem is possible if we have operators ϕ and ψ that correspond to these modifications.

Definition 1 ([8]). *An incremental catamorphism[3] on μF is triple $(h :: \mu F \rightarrow A, \phi :: FA \rightarrow A, \psi :: A \rightarrow FA)$ such that $h \circ in_F = \phi \circ Fh$ and $Fh \circ out_F = \psi \circ h$.* □

Any incremental catamorphism (h, ϕ, ψ) is associated with the following incremental computing algorithm.

---

[3] In the original paper, it is called an *incremental algorithm*.

- Given the initial structure $t :: \mu F$, calculate $h\ t$.
- For each modification by in_F, we update the calculated value by ϕ.
- For each modification by out_F, we update the calculated value by ψ.

The requirement ensures correctness of the algorithm. It is worth noting that the first equation, $h \circ in_F = \phi \circ Fh$, is equivalent to $h = (\!|\phi|\!)_F$; therefore, Definition 1 is applicable only when h is a catamorphism.

   Generic upward accumulation [17,18] is useful for developing incremental catamorphisms. Given a functor F, let $F_A = F \times !_A$. F_A adds a value of A to a structure by F. We assume that the least fixed point of F_A exists[4]. Two functions are associated: $val_F :: \mu F_A \rightarrow A$ extracts the associated value from the root; $expose_F :: \mu F_A \rightarrow F\mu F_A$ expands the root node so that its children can be accessed. They are defined as follows.

$$val_F\ v = \textbf{let}\ (\_, a) = out_{F_A}\ v\ \textbf{in}\ a$$
$$expose_F\ v = \textbf{let}\ (s, \_) = out_{F_A}\ v\ \textbf{in}\ s$$

   Given an F-algebra (A, ϕ), the upward accumulation by ϕ, denoted by $ua_F\ \phi$, is defined as follows.

$$ua_F\ \phi :: \mu F \rightarrow \mu F_A$$
$$ua_F\ \phi = (\!|\overline{\phi}|\!)_F \qquad \textbf{where } \overline{\phi}\ v = in_{F_A}\ (v, \phi\ (Fval_F\ v))$$

The upward accumulation can be used instead of the catamorphism.

Lemma 1 ([17]). *The following equation holds.*

$$val_F \circ ua_F\ \phi = (\!|\phi|\!)_F \qquad\qquad \square$$

Moreover, incremental computing of upward accumulations is possible if the modification is either in_F or out_F.

Theorem 2 ([8]). $(ua_F\ \phi, \overline{\phi}, expose_F)$ *is an incremental catamorphism on μF.*
$\qquad\qquad\qquad\qquad\qquad\qquad\qquad\qquad\qquad\qquad\qquad\qquad\qquad\qquad\qquad\qquad\qquad\square$

Example (Contd.). The above-mentioned definitions exactly match what we have seen in Sects. 2 and 3. For instance, μT_A, val_T, $expose_T$, and $ua_T\ \phi$ are identical to $\overline{BTree}\ A$, val_{BTree}, $expose_{BTree}$, and $ua_{BTree}\ \phi$.

4.3   Incremental Computing on Abstract Data Structures

Next we consider abstract data structures. An abstract data structure is characterized by the underlying structure and a set of modifications. For simplicity, we only deal with unary modifications, each of which takes only one structure. The discussion can be easily extended to non-unary cases such as the set union operator.

---

[4] This assumption holds for most of the practical cases. For instance, any algebraic datatype can be captured as the least fixed point of a container-type functor, and for any container-type functor F, F_A is container-type and therefore has the least fixed point [24].

Definition 2. *An abstract data structure (abbreviated to ADS) on T is a pair (T, M), where T is the underlying data structure and $M \subseteq T \to T$ is the set of modifications.*   □

The key to dealing with a complex modification, say $modify :: \mu\mathsf{F} \to \mu\mathsf{F}$, is to consider a skeleton function, MOD, that implements $modify$ and has the following polymorphic type.

$$modify \ t = \text{MOD} \ (in_\mathsf{F}, out_\mathsf{F}) \ t$$
$$\text{MOD} :: \forall\alpha. \ (\mathsf{F}\alpha \leftrightarrow \alpha) \to \alpha \to \alpha$$

The polymorphic type guarantees that MOD generates the output only by using the arguments: in_F, out_F, and t. We call such $modify$ incrementalizable.

Definition 3. *Modification $modify :: \mu\mathsf{F} \to \mu\mathsf{F}$ is incrementalizable if it is associated with a polymorphic function $\text{MOD} :: \forall\alpha. \ (\mathsf{F}\alpha \leftrightarrow \alpha) \to \alpha \to \alpha$ such that $modify = \text{MOD} \ (in_\mathsf{F}, out_\mathsf{F})$. ADS $(\mu\mathsf{F}, M)$ is incrementalizable if every modification in M is so.*   □

The following is the main theorem.

Theorem 3. *Let $(\mu\mathsf{F}, M)$ be an incrementalizable ADS and (h, ϕ, ψ) be an incremental catamorphism on $\mu\mathsf{F}$. Then, for any modification $M \ni modify = \text{MOD} \ (in_\mathsf{F}, out_\mathsf{F})$, the following equation holds.*

$$h \circ modify = \text{MOD} \ (\phi, \psi) \circ h$$

Proof. From parametricity [14,15] for the polymorphic type of MOD, it is sufficient to show $h \circ in_\mathsf{F} = \phi \circ \mathsf{F}h$ and $\mathsf{F}h \circ out_\mathsf{F} = \psi \circ h$, which are guaranteed from the fact that (h, ϕ, ψ) is an incremental catamorphism.   □

Consider keep knowing h on an incrementalizable ADS, $(\mu\mathsf{F}, M)$. If (h, ϕ, ψ) forms an incremental catamorphism, we have the following incremental computing algorithm.

- Given the initial structure $t :: \mu\mathsf{F}$, calculate $h \ t$.
- For each modification $M \ni modify = \text{MOD} \ (in_\mathsf{F}, out_\mathsf{F})$, we update the calculated value by $\text{MOD} \ (\phi, \psi)$.

Theorem 3 guarantees $h \ (modify \ t) = \text{MOD} \ (\phi, \psi) \ (h \ t)$ and thereby the correctness. In particular, by using upward accumulations, we can incrementally calculate any catamorphism if the underlying ADS is incrementalizable.

5   Related Work and Future Work

We have developed a method of incremental computing. There has been plenty of work already, including [1–11]. More studies can be found from these papers and an extensive survey by Ramalingam and Reps [25].

Our approach is purely functional and based on parametric polymorphism. While this enables us to develop a simple and clean theory, it makes our approach difficult to deal with the case where not modifications but the objective function is rather complex. Attribute-grammar-based methods [2,4–6] use value dependencies extracted from the syntactic definition. Self-adjusting computation [1,9,10] uses more precise value dependencies gathered at run-time. Because of absence of this, our approach fails to deal with accumulative objective functions, which the above-mentioned methods can.

Our method combines Jeuring's datatype-generic incrementalization [8] with two program transformations. Shortcut fusion [12] is a technique to eliminate intermediate data structures. The third list-homomorphism theorem [20] has been used for developing divide-and-conquer parallel programs. To the author's knowledge, neither has been used for incremental computing. Our method can also utilize methods related to them. Those for automating shortcut fusion [26–28] are useful for certifying incrementalizability. Those for automatic parallelization based on the third list-homomorphism theorem [29,30] can be used for deriving folds for composite data structures.

Our method is based on datatype-generic recursion schemes, folds and upward accumulations. More recursion schemes are studied in the literature, including anamorphisms, hylomorphisms [31], adjoint folds/unfolds [32], and conjugate hylomorphisms [33]. It would be interesting if our theory can be extended to these recursion schemes.

Acknowledgements. The author is grateful to anonymous reviewers whose comments were useful to improve the presentation. Especially, it is one of them who pointed out similarity between between a preliminary result and Jeuring's incremental algorithms on lists. The author is supported by the JSPS Grant-in-Aid for Young Scientists (B) 15K15965.

References

1. Acar, U.A., Blelloch, G.E., Harper, R.: Adaptive functional programming. ACM Trans. Program. Lang. Syst. **28**(6), 990–1034 (2006)
2. Demers, A.J., Reps, T.W., Teitelbaum, T.: Incremental evaluation for attribute grammars with application to syntax-directed editors. In: Conference Record of the Eighth Annual ACM Symposium on Principles of Programming Languages, pp. 105–116. ACM Press (1981)
3. Pugh, W., Teitelbaum, T.: Incremental computation via function caching. In: Conference Record of the Sixteenth Annual ACM Symposium on Principles of Programming Languages, pp. 315–328. ACM Press (1989)
4. Alblas, H.: Incremental attribute evaluation. In: Alblas, H., Melichar, B. (eds.) Attribute Grammars, Applications and Systems, International Summer School SAGA 1991. Lecture Notes in Computer Science, vol. 545, pp. 215–233. Springer, Heidelberg (1991)
5. Hudson, S.E.: Incremental attribute evaluation: a flexible algorithm for lazy update. ACM Trans. Program. Lang. Syst. **13**(3), 315–341 (1991)

6. Yellin, D.M., Strom, R.E.: INC: a language for incremental computations. ACM Trans. Program. Lang. Syst. **13**(2), 211–236 (1991)
7. Jeuring, J.: Incremental algorithms on lists. In: Proceedings of SION Computing Science in the Netherlands, pp. 315–335 (1991)
8. Jeuring, J.: Theories for algorithm calculation. Ph.D. thesis, Universiteit Utrecht (1993)
9. Acar, U.A., Blelloch, G.E., Harper, R., Vittes, J.L., Woo, S.L.M.: Dynamizing static algorithms, with applications to dynamic trees and history independence. In: Proceedings of the Fifteenth Annual ACM-SIAM Symposium on Discrete Algorithms, SODA 2004, pp. 531–540. SIAM (2004)
10. Chen, Y., Dunfield, J., Acar, U.A.: Type-directed automatic incrementalization. In: ACM SIGPLAN Conference on Programming Language Design and Implementation, PLDI 2012, pp. 299–310. ACM Press (2012)
11. Cai, Y., Giarrusso, P.G., Rendel, T., Ostermann, K.: A theory of changes for higher-order languages: incrementalizing λ-calculi by static differentiation. In: ACM SIGPLAN Conference on Programming Language Design and Implementation, PLDI 2014, pp. 145–155. ACM Press (2014)
12. Gill, A., Launchbury, J., Peyton Jones, S.: A short cut to deforestation. In: FPCA 1993 Conference on Functional Programming Languages and Computer Architecture, pp. 223–232. ACM Press (1993)
13. Takano, A., Meijer, E.: Shortcut deforestation in calculational form. In: Conference Record of FPCA 1995 SIGPLAN-SIGARCH-WG2.8 Conference on Functional Programming Languages and Computer Architecture, pp. 306–313. ACM Press (1995)
14. Reynolds, J.C.: Types, abstraction and parametric polymorphism. Inf. Process. **83**, 513–523 (1983)
15. Wadler, P.: Theorems for free! In: FPCA 1989 Conference on Functional Programming Languages and Computer Architecture, pp. 347–359. ACM Press (1989)
16. Sleator, D.D., Tarjan, R.E.: Self-adjusting binary search trees. J. ACM **32**(3), 652–686 (1985)
17. Bird, R.S., de Moor, O., Hoogendijk, P.F.: Generic functional programming with types and relations. J. Funct. Program. **6**(1), 1–28 (1996)
18. Gibbons, J.: Generic downwards accumulations. Sci. Comput. Program. **37**(1–3), 37–65 (2000)
19. Huet, G.P.: The zipper. J. Funct. Program. **7**(5), 549–554 (1997)
20. Gibbons, J.: The third homomorphism theorem. J. Funct. Program. **6**(4), 657–665 (1996)
21. Morihata, A.: A short cut to parallelization theorems. In: ACM SIGPLAN International Conference on Functional Programming, ICFP 2013, pp. 245–256. ACM Press (2013)
22. Morihata, A., Matsuzaki, K., Hu, Z., Takeichi, M.: The third homomorphism theorem on trees: downward & upward lead to divide-and-conquer. In: Proceedings of the 36th ACM SIGPLAN-SIGACT Symposium on Principles of Programming Languages, POPL 2009, pp. 177–185. ACM Press (2009)
23. Bird, R.S., de Moor, O.: Algebra of Programming. Prentice Hall, Upper Saddle River (1997)
24. Abbott, M., Altenkirch, T., Ghani, N.: Containers: constructing strictly positive types. Theor. Comput. Sci. **342**(1), 3–27 (2005)

25. Ramalingam, G., Reps, T.W.: A categorized bibliography on incremental computation. In: Conference Record of the Twentieth Annual ACM SIGPLAN-SIGACT Symposium on Principles of Programming Languages, pp. 502–510. ACM Press (1993)
26. Launchbury, J., Sheard, T.: Warm fusion: deriving build-catas from recursive definitions. In: Conference Record of FPCA 1995 SIGPLAN-SIGARCH-WG2.8 Conference on Functional Programming Languages and Computer Architecture, pp. 314–323. ACM Press (1995)
27. Chitil, O.: Type inference builds a short cut to deforestation. In: Proceedings of the 4th ACM SIGPLAN International Conference on Functional Programming, ICFP 1999, pp. 249–260. ACM Press (1999)
28. Yokoyama, T., Hu, Z., Takeichi, M.: Calculation rules for warming-up in fusion transformation. In: The 2005 Symposium on Trends in Functional Programming, TFP 2005, pp. 399–412 (2005)
29. Geser, A., Gorlatch, S.: Parallelizing functional programs by generalization. J. Funct. Program. **9**(6), 649–673 (1999)
30. Morita, K., Morihata, A., Matsuzaki, K., Hu, Z., Takeichi, M.: Automatic inversion generates divide-and-conquer parallel programs. In: Proceedings of the ACM SIGPLAN 2007 Conference on Programming Language Design and Implementation, pp. 146–155. ACM Press (2007)
31. Meijer, E., Fokkinga, M.M., Paterson, R.: Functional programming with bananas, lenses, envelopes and barbed wire. In: Hughes, J. (ed.) FPCA 1991. Lecture Notes in Computer Science, vol. 523, pp. 124–144. Springer, Heidelberg (1991)
32. Hinze, R.: Adjoint folds and unfolds - an extended study. Sci. Comput. Program. **78**(11), 2108–2159 (2013)
33. Hinze, R., Wu, N., Gibbons, J.: Conjugate hylomorphisms - or: the mother of all structured recursion schemes. In: Proceedings of the 42nd Annual ACM SIGPLAN-SIGACT Symposium on Principles of Programming Languages, POPL 2015, pp. 527–538. ACM Press (2015)

Declarative Programming with Algebra

Andre van Delft[1]($^{(\boxtimes)}$) and Anatoliy Kmetyuk[2]

[1] Rijswijk, The Netherlands
andre.vandelft@gmail.com
[2] Odessa, Ukraine
anatoliykmetyuk@gmail.com

Abstract. The Algebra of Communicating Processes (ACP) is a theory that views sequences and choices as mathematical operations: multiplication and addition. Based on these base constructs others are defined, such as parallel merge, interruption and disruption.

Conventional programming languages may be enriched with ACP features, to gain declarative expressiveness. We have done this in SubScript, an extension to the Scala language. SubScript has high level support for sequences, choices and iterations in a style similar to parser generator languages. It also offers parallel composition operations, such as and- and or- parallelism, and dataflow.

The declarative style is also present in the way various execution modes are supported. Conventional programming languages often require some boilerplate code to run things in the background, in the GUI thread, or as event handlers. SubScript supports the same execution modes, but with minimal boilerplate. It is also easy to compose programs from blocks having different execution modes.

This paper introduces ACP and SubScript; it briefly describes the current implementation, and gives several examples.

1 Introduction

The Algebra of Communicating Processes (ACP) [2] is a concurrency theory that allows for concise specifications of event-driven and concurrent processes. ACP and the related theories CSP [9] and CCS [11] appear to be largely ignored in R&D on declarative programming. This is unfortunate because ACP offers a solid mathematical foundation for reasoning about program behavior, and a uniform approach to high level process compositions such as sequence, choice, parallelism, interruption (a process being suspended while another one executes) and disruption (a process being canceled when another one starts).

It is well possible to program applications using ACP. We are developing an ACP based extension to Scala by the name of SubScript, with process refinements called *scripts*. SubScript contains several constructs and ideas such as or-parallelism, that are not yet covered by ACP; these are listed in [6].

The sequence and choice operators of ACP and Subscript are much like constructs in parser generator languages. SubScript code is therefore much like

© Springer International Publishing Switzerland 2016
O. Kiselyov and A. King (Eds.): FLOPS 2016, LNCS 9613, pp. 232–251, 2016.
DOI: 10.1007/978-3-319-29604-3_15

grammar descriptions. But the style extends to other composition operations such as parallelism, disruption and interruption.

SubScript also supports declarative specification of different code execution modes. In conventional programming languages such as Java, handling events is quite cumbersome: it requires creating, registering and later unregistering event listeners. Other boilerplate code is needed to let things happen in a background thread or in a GUI thread. In SubScript it is possible to largely abstract from this boiler plate. Like in ACP process specifications events to which a process reacts, appear just as actions; similar to internal actions.

It is also straightforward in SubScript to make compositions of code with different execution modes. This is useful for instance in interactive programs. E.g., a recurring pattern for handling user commands is to have a series of the following kinds of actions, that have 3 different execution modes:

- handle an event (e.g. a button being pressed)
- perform an action in the GUI thread (e.g. updating a status label)
- perform an action in the background thread (e.g. requesting data from a web server)
- perform an action in the GUI thread (e.g. showing the results)

SubScript also has anonymous scripts, also known as process lambdas. This comes almost for free from Scala's support for anonymous functions. Using these there is relatively simple syntactic sugar to define a sequential dataflow construct, which happens to be useful for exception handling as well. Another useful feature inspired by Scala is implicit conversion from data to processes.

All of Scala is available in SubScript. This includes concurrency features such as threads, actors and futures; SubScript allows wrapping those on a higher declarative level.

A SubScript implementation is available. It comes with a preprocessor that translates SubScript code into regular Scala code; some specific transformations are deferred to Scala macros. Script translate into methods; their bodies contain calls to the API of a SubScript Virtual Machine. There are also compatibility layer, for the Swing and Akka frameworks.

The rest of this paper is structured as follows: Sect. 2 introduces ACP; Sect. 3 gives two SubScript example applications; Sect. 4 lists language features; Sect. 5 describes a SubScript Virtual Machine; Sect. 6 highlights dataflow programming with SubScript; Sect. 7 discusses some related work.

The current paper is a follow up to a paper presented at the Scala Workshop 2013 [5] about dataflow programming support in SubScript, with application to actor systems.[1]

2   ACP

The Algebra of Communicating Processes is an algebraic approach to reasoning about concurrent systems. It is a member of the family of mathematical

---

[1] This paper contains some text fragments literally copied or adapted from the predecessor paper.

theories of concurrency known as process algebras or process calculi[2]. More so
than the other seminal process calculi (CCS and CSP), the development of ACP
focused on the algebra of processes, and sought to create an abstract, generalized
axiomatic system for processes.

ACP uses instantaneous, atomic actions $(a,b,c,...)$ as its main primitives. Two
special primitives are the deadlock process 0, also known as δ, and the empty
process 1, also known as ϵ. Expressions of primitives and operators represent
processes. The main operators can be roughly categorized as providing a basic
process algebra, concurrency, and communication:

- *Choice and sequencing* - the most fundamental of algebraic operators are the
  alternative operator $(+)$, which provides a choice between actions, and the
  sequencing operator $(\cdot)$, which specifies an ordering on actions. So, for example,
  the process $(a+b) \cdot c$ first chooses to perform either a or b, and then performs
  action c. How the choice between a and b is made does not matter and is left
  unspecified. Note that alternative composition is commutative but sequential
  composition is not (because time flows forward).
- *Concurrency* - to allow the description of concurrency, ACP provides the
  merge operator $\parallel$. This represents the parallel composition of two processes,
  the individual actions of which are interleaved. As an example, the process
  $(a \cdot b) \parallel (c \cdot d)$ may perform the atomic actions a, b, c, d in any of the sequences
  abcd, acbd, acdb, cabd, cadb, cdab.
- *Communication* - pairs of atomic actions may be defined as communicating
  actions, implying they cannot be performed on their own, but only together,
  when active in two parallel processes. This way, the two processes synchronize,
  and they may exchange data.

ACP fundamentally adopts an axiomatic, algebraic approach to the formal
definition of its various operators. Using the alternative and sequential composition operators, ACP defines a basic process algebra which satisfies the following
axioms:

$$x + y = y + x \qquad\qquad 0 + x = x$$
$$(x + y) + z = x + (y + z) \qquad\qquad 0 \cdot x = 0$$
$$x + x = x \qquad\qquad 1 \cdot x = x$$
$$(x + y) \cdot z = x \cdot z + y \cdot z \qquad\qquad x \cdot 1 = x$$
$$(x \cdot y) \cdot z = x \cdot (y \cdot z)$$

The primitives 0 and 1 behave much like the 0 and 1 that are usually neutral
elements for addition and multiplication in algebra. $x + 1$ means: *optionally* x.
This is shown by rewriting $(x + 1) \cdot y$ using the axioms:

$$(x + 1) \cdot y = x \cdot y + 1 \cdot y$$
$$= x \cdot y + y$$

---

[2] This description of ACP has largely been taken from Wikipedia.

The parallel merge operator $\parallel$ is defined in terms of the alternative and sequential composition operators. This definition also requires two auxiliary operators:

$$x \parallel y = x \mathbin{\lfloor\!\lfloor} y + y \mathbin{\lfloor\!\lfloor} x + x \mid y$$

- $x \mathbin{\lfloor\!\lfloor} y$ - "left-merge": first x is to execute an atomic action, and then the rest of x is done in parallel with y.
- $x \mid y$ - "communication merge": x and y start with a communication (as a pair of atomic actions), and then the rest of x is done in parallel with the rest of y.

The definitions of many new operators such as the left merge operator use a special property of closed process expressions with $\cdot$ and $+$: with the axioms as term rewrite rules from left to right (except for the commutativity axiom for $+$), each such expression reduces into one of the following normal forms: (x + y), $a \cdot x$, 1, 0. E.g. the axioms for the left merge operator are:

$$(x + y) \mathbin{\lfloor\!\lfloor} z = x \mathbin{\lfloor\!\lfloor} z + y \mathbin{\lfloor\!\lfloor} z \qquad\qquad 1 \mathbin{\lfloor\!\lfloor} x = 0$$
$$(a \cdot x) \mathbin{\lfloor\!\lfloor} y = a \cdot (x \parallel y) \qquad\qquad 0 \mathbin{\lfloor\!\lfloor} x = 0$$

Again these axioms may be applied as term rewrite rules so that each closed expression with the parallel merge operator $\parallel$ reduces to one of the four normal forms. This way it has been possible to extend ACP with many new operators that are defined precisely in terms of sequence and choice, e.g. interrupt and disrupt operators, process launching, and notions of time and priorities.

Since its inception in 1982, ACP has successfully been applied to the specification and verification of among others, communication protocols, traffic systems and manufacturing plants.

ACP's strict algebraic approach has an advantage over CSP and CCS: this way theorists can study multiple models that satisfy a given set of axioms. This fact was not relevant though choosing ACP as a base for SubScript rather than CSP or CCS. The main reasons were:

- CSP has Two Choice Operators: a deterministic one and a nondeterministic one. This distinction appears unnecessary as CCS and ACP can do without.
- CSP and CCS have *Action Prefixing*: a kind of sequential composition where the left hand side must be an atomic action (an *event*, in CSP terms); the right hand side cannot be an atomic action. In CCS this is an inconvenient limitation. CSP has a separate sequential composition operator, but also this is an unnecessary complication. ACP treats sequences much like mainstream programming languages do: operands may be atomic, like assignments, or composed, like method calls.

SubScript supports *anonymous processes*, also known as *process lambdas*. These constructs have never been formalized for ACP, but they have been for CCS. In 1989, Henk Goeman unified Lambda Calculus with process expressions [8]. Shortly thereafter, Robin Milner et al. developed Pi-calculus [12], which also combines the two theories.

3   Two Simple GUI Applications

Suppose we need a simple program to look up
items in a database, based on a search string.
The user can enter a search string in the text
field and then press the Go button. This will
at first put a "Searching" message in the text
area at the lower part. Then the actual search
will be done at a database, which may take a

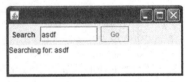

few seconds (simulated by a call to `Thread.sleep`). Finally the results from the
database are shown in the text area.

In plain Scala, the required code would be like:

```
val searchButton = new Button("Go")      {
  reactions += { case ButtonClicked(b) =>
    enabled = false
    outputTA.text = "Starting..."
    new Thread(new Runnable {
     def run() {
       Thread.sleep(3000)
       SwingUtilities.invokeLater(new Runnable{
         def run() {outputTA.text="Ready"; enabled = true
       }})
    }}).start
} }
```

Here `outputTA` denotes the output text area. This code looks very technical:
lots of indentations and braces. The control flow is hidden in nested functions.
Parallelism is done by calling the **start** method on a Thread object. This looks
like a usual method call, but something magic happens inside. Parallelism does
not get a similar basic treatment as statement sequences do.

The order in which the lines are executed is spaghetti-like:

- The first two lines are done during initialization, in the main thread.
- Then a call back block follows, which, executed when the button is pressed.
  Disabling the button and setting the "Starting..." text must be done in the
  Swing thread; this happens to be the case with the call back, so no special
  provision are needed.
- The call to **start** makes a background thread start that will execute a sleep
- After this sleep, the background thread schedules code for execution in the
  Swing thread, to set a "Ready" text and to enable the button.

Between the static program text and the dynamic process is a rather large
conceptual gap. The programming task is hard and boring. The result: many
applications fail to appropriately enable and disable their GUI widgets, or they
are not responsive, or they even hang every now and then. This not only holds
for Scala, but also for almost all imperative languages.

This situation is unnecessary. The SubScript notation is more concise and intuitive:

```
live = searchButton
       @gui: {:outputTA.text="Starting...":}
       {* Thread.sleep(3000) *}
       @gui: {:outputTA.text="Ready":}
       ...
```

The line breaks here denote sequential composition.[3]

- Line 1: `live` is a method like refinement called "script" for the controller behavior. `searchButton` is an object that is silently converted into a script call `clicked(searchButton)`. This is done by an extension of Scala's support for implicit conversions. This call "happens" when the user presses the search button.
- As a bonus, the call to `clicked` makes sure the button is exactly enabled when applicable, i.e. when the program is ready to handle a button click.
- Lines 2 and 4 each write a message in the text area. An annotation, `@gui:`, makes sure this happens in the Swing thread, as needed.
- Line 3 simulates the lasting database search using a sleep call. The asterisks next to the braces specify that this is done in a background thread, so that neither the GUI nor the main thread will be blocked meanwhile.
- Line 5 turns the foregoing into an "eternal" sequential loop (..., "etcetera") of search sequences.

SubScript programmers can easily specify the GUI controller life cycle, event handling, widget enabling, and switching to the GUI thread. This is not due to specific language features geared towards Swing, but through a custom Swing compatibility layer, with scripts such as `clicked` and methods such as `gui`.

3.1   Extending the Program

Now we add some realistic requirements to the program.

- Pressing the Enter key in the search text field triggers the search action as well.
- The search action requires that the input text field is not empty; only then should the search button be enabled
- Clicking button Cancel, or pressing the Escape key cancels an ongoing search.
- As long as the database search is ongoing, the progress should be indicated: 4 times per second a number is appended to the output text area.
- Clicking an Exit button or in the close box at the window's upper right corner exits the program, provided that the user confirms this in a dialog box.

---

[3] There is also a semicolon to denote sequences. SubScript has a similar semicolon inference for line breaks as Scala.

We can start by raising the abstraction level of the code above, giving names to each of its individual actions, so that we can implement these extensions by modifying the definitions of these named actions:

```
live                = searchSequence...

searchSequence      = searchCommand       showSearchingText
                      searchInDatabase  showSearchResults

searchCommand       = searchButton
searchInDatabase    = {* Thread.sleep(3000) *}
showSearchingText   = @gui: {:outputTA.text="Starting...":}
showSearchResults   = @gui: {:outputTA.text="Ready":}
```

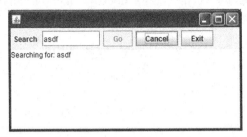

In a Java or Scala version the application state would need to be kept in variables; updating these would be nontrivial. The progress indicator would be cumbersome and error-prone to program (and that is why it is rarely present). It is easier to grow the SubScript version.

The three user commands will be:

```
searchCommand = searchButton + Key.Enter
cancelCommand = cancelButton + Key.Escape
exitCommand   = exitButton   + windowClosing
```

The first and second plus operators create exclusive choices between buttons and key codes. These operands are not processes, but data items for which implicit conversions to processes have been defined (such as `clicked` and `keyPressed`)[4].

The library script `windowClosing` acts on window closing events.

Exiting is implemented using a process named `exit` that runs in or-parallel composition to the rest. The or-parallel operator is | |. It means that both operands execute in parallel; as soon as one finishes successfully then the other is terminated and the whole composition terminates successfully. In this case, the left hand operand is an eternal loop of search sequences; the right hand operand is a (probably) finite loop.

The `exit` process starts with the exit command being given; then a confirmation dialog is run; all to be repeated while the result of the confirmation dialog

---

[4] We can combine this way any kind of item for which implicit conversions to scripts are in scope; this yields an algebra of general items rather than just of processes.

is false. The result of the confirmation dialog is transferred using a dataflow operator (explained later) to a while construct; this operator is a curly arrow that names and types the flowing data item.

```
live = searchSequence... || exit
exit = exitCommand
       @gui: {! confirmExit !} ~~(b:Boolean)~~> while !b
```

The @gui annotation in combination with special brace pairs around confirmExit ensure that the dialog is run asynchronously in the GUI thread; this way other parts of this program may remain active. The exclamation marks in the brace pairs denote that confirmExit is an atomic action in the ACP sense, which is relevant in choice contexts.

The while construct at the end does not require the conditional expression to be inside parentheses, as long as it is a simple expression that cannot be confused with the other parts of the script.

For the search sequence we now add items at the start and the end. searchGuard is an "active guard" containing a sequential loop. It first checks whether the text field (searchTF) contains some text. If it does, there is an "optional break". This means that the sequence and thus also the guard may end successfully, so that searchCommand becomes active.

However maybe an event happens at the text field before the user issues this search command; then the check needs to be redone, etc. (...).

Between searchGuard and searchCommand is a space. Like in Scala, this construct has a high priority, but unlike in Scala, it denotes sequential composition, in addition to semicolons and new lines.

After searchCommand a new line follows; this separates the first line from the remaining five lines. Therefore the rest, including cancelSearch, can only become active after the searchCommand has happened. cancelSearch is preceded by a slash symbol (/), which stands for disruption: the left hand side happens, possibly disrupted when the right hand side starts happening. The parentheses group the items on the preceding lines, so that the whole becomes the left hand side of the slash operator.

```
searchSequence      = searchGuard searchCommand
                      [ showSearchingText
                        searchInDatabase
                        showSearchResults ] / cancelSearch

searchGuard         = if !searchTF.text.isEmpty then break?
                      anyEvent(searchTF)
                      ...

cancelSearch        = cancelCommand showCanceledText
showSearchingText   = @gui: {:outputTA.text =...:}
showSearchResults   = @gui: {:outputTA.text =...:}
showCanceledText    = @gui: {:outputTA.text =...:}
```

The database search was mimicked by a few seconds of sleeping; we add a progress monitor process in an or-parallel composition. This `progressMonitor` is an eternal loop: wait a short time and then append a loop counter to the output text field, etc.

The pseudo-value **here** denotes "the current operand"; it is comparable to **this**, the "current object". Its field **pass** yields 0, 1, 2, ... in subsequent passes of the loop.

```
searchInDatabase   = {*Thread.sleep(3000)*}
                   || progressMonitor

progressMonitor    = {*Thread.sleep(250)*}
                     @gui: {:searchTF.text +=" " + here.pass:}
                     ...
```

4   SubScript Features

SubScript extends Scala with a construct named "script". This is a counterpart of ACP process refinements, that coexists with variables and methods in classes. The body of a script is an expression like the ACP process expressions.

4.1   Notation

ACP processes are notated with the mathematical expression syntax. The ACP symbol · for sequential composition is hard to type; therefore SubScript applies a semicolon (;) as known from Scala. As with multiplication in math, the semicolon symbol for sequence may also be omitted, but then some white space should separate the operands.[5]

The Scala symbols for and- and or-compositions of booleans, &, &&, | and | |, were reused for analogous flavors of parallelism in SubScript. Therefore the ACP symbol ‖ corresponds with an ampersand (&) in SubScript.

The special ACP processes 0 and 1 would clash with the usual notation for numbers. These are replaced by symbols: [-] and [+].[6]

Parentheses in ACP processes are replaced as rectangular brackets in SubScript scripts. This is because parentheses are already heavy in use in the base language Scala: for value expressions, tuple notation and parameter lists.

---

[5] In general Scala's operator precedence rules are followed, except for the dataflow operators; in Scala white space denotes function application; in SubScript it is sequential composition.

[6] Library scripts that refine into such special processes, may be more readable. For the time being we want a minimal set of new keywords.

Scripts are usually defined together in a section, e.g.,

```
script..
  hello =            {! print("Hello,") !}
  test  = hello & {! print("world!") !}
```

From here on the section header `script..` is mostly omitted for brevity.

4.2 Scala Code Fragments

`{! print(''Hello,'') !}` is a normal fragment of Scala code; by default it is executed in the main thread. Conceptually this corresponds with an atomic action happening in the sense of ACP. This atomic action is relevant for instance in a choice context such as `{! print(''Hello,'') !} + {! print(''world!'') !}`

Here as soon as the atomic action happens in the left hand side operand of the plus, the right hand side is excluded: its code fragment cannot be executed any more, and it is marked for deactivation.

There are different flavors of code fragments (`s` means some Scala code):

- `{! s !}` - normal code fragment; corresponds by default with one atomic action.
- `{* s *}` - code executed in a new thread; corresponds with two atomic actions.
- `{. s .}` - a code fragment executed by an event handler, e.g. a GUI listener; corresponds with an atomic action.
- `{... s ...}` - a code fragment that may be executed multiple times by a permanent event listener; each execution corresponds with an atomic action.
- `{: s :}` - a "tiny" code fragment. It does not correspond with an atomic action; therefore it is efficiently executed. Apart from the code being executed, this behaves neutrally in the ACP sense: it corresponds with 0 or 1; which one of these depends on nearest ancestor n-ary operator.

Normal code fragments may be manipulated to run in a distinct thread such as the GUI thread. In such cases there is a correspondence to two atomic actions instead of one: one atomic action happens just before the start of the code fragment execution, and one happens just after the end. The latter action will not happen when the executing code fragment had been disrupted, e.g. from the disruption operator `/`.

Threaded code fragments run in new threads; they also correspond with two such atomic actions. When disrupted while running, the thread will get an interrupt signal.

Scala expressions within code fragments may use a special value named **here**. It refers to the current node in the call graph (i.e. a generalization of a call stack, see Sect. 5), like **this** refers to the current object. **here** is in particular useful for implementing event handling scripts.[7]

---

[7] For convenience **here** is an implicit value so that it may be left out of parameter lists that have an implicit formal parameter of the node's type.

4.3   Annotations

An annotation is a piece of Scala code that is executed when the annotated part of a program is activated. The code may refer to its operand using the value named `there`. The code may in turn register callback code for other events that happen on the operand, e.g. when it is deactivated. This was applied for automatic GUI widget enabling and disabling, as seen in the previous examples.

Annotations can also change the execution behavior for code fragments. E.g. in

```
clearText = @gui: {: aTextField.text = " " :}
```

the tiny code fragment will be executed synchronously in the Swing GUI thread, using the Swing method `SwingUtilities.invokeAndWait()`.

When combined with a normal code fragment the annotation will execute the code asynchronously in the Swing GUI thread using `SwingUtilities.invokeLater()`; meanwhile other code fragments may be executed.[8]

4.4   Parallelism

For each of the boolean operators `&`, `&&`, `|` and `||` there is a counterpart parallel operator in SubScript: `&` and `&&` are and-like; they succeed when all operands succeed. `|` and `||` are or-like; they succeed when any operand succeeds.

`&` and `|` terminate when all operands terminate. `&&` denotes *strong and-parallelism*: it terminates when any operand terminates without success. `||` denotes *strong or-parallelism*: it terminates when any operand terminates successfully.

Between `{!print(''hello!'')!}` & `{!print(''world!'')!}`, each operand essentially contains a simple code fragment rather than code to be run in a separate thread. Therefore one operand will be executed before the other; the result is either "hello!world!" or "world!hello!". In general the atomic actions in parallel branches are shuffle merged, like one can shuffle card decks.

The most straightforward execution strategy will deterministically apply a left-to-right precedence for the code fragments that are operands to the operator `&`. However, alternative strategies are possible, e.g. for random simulations.

4.5   Disruption and Interruption

The slash operator denotes disruption: in `x/y`, both operands are activated; `x` is terminated as soon as an atomic action in `y` happens. For interruption there are two operators: in `x%/y` execution of `x` is suspended as soon as an atomic action

---

[8] In annotations `there` is implicit instead of `here`. Thus `@gui:` is equivalent to `@gui(there)`.

in y happens; it may resume when y has success. The operator %/%/ is for zero or more interruptions.[9]

4.6   Control and Iteration

SubScript has if-then-else, match, while, for and break constructs much like counterparts in Scala. The latter three are not limited to sequential contexts, so they enable alternative and parallel iteration control. Some special processes are:

- break? denotes an optional break. The nearest n-ary operator determines the exact behavior. E.g. x may or may not be executed in [break? x] y; this is much like [[+] + x] y.
- ... marks a loop; it is equivalent to while(true).
- ..? marks a loop and at the same time an optional break.

4.7   Scripts and Calls

A SubScript implementation will translate each script into a method that has return type Script[T] where T is the type of the script's result value (see below). This way most Scala language features for methods also apply to scripts: scripts may have both type parameters and data parameters; each parameter may be named or implicit. Variable length parameters and even script currying are possible.

The body of the example script test in Sect. 4.1 contains a call to script hello. This is much like a method call.

A script expression may also contain value terms such as variables, literals and Scala code between () or {}. If such a term is of type Unit then it is assumed to be in a tiny code fragment; if it is of type Script[T] then it is a script call; else there should be an implicit conversion to a Script[T].

ACP processes supports process communications as atomic actions that are shared by two or more parties. In SubScript this has been generalized to shared scripts that are called by multiple parties. E.g.

```
send, receive = {! println("Communication") !}
```

Synchronous calls to send and receive that do not exclude one another, may result in the execution of the shared script body. This is also a generalization of normal script calls; the latter may be considered to be special cases of communication with only one party involved.

---

[9] These operators start with a percent sign; they are members of a larger family of operators that can suspend and resume operands. These operators are not meant to be memorized; rather they may be encapsulated in higher level scripts with descriptive names.

4.8   Script Lambdas

For Scala value expressions there is a new kind of term: parameterless script lambdas (AKA closures). These appear as script expressions placed between rectangular brackets, such as [[a b+c] d]. These values of type Script[T] for some type T.

The Scala way of defining parameterized lambda expressions applies as well, essentially giving parameterized script lambdas, e.g., (i:Int) => [{:print(i):}].

4.9   Result Values

Code fragments and scripts have result values, which are comparable to method return values. A difference is that a method returns only once, whereas the script result value is available to the caller each time that the script has a success; this may be more than once, due to the 1-element of ACP. The following scripts each have result type Int:

```
s1:Int = {!5!}^
s2 = s1
s3 = s2 ^5
```

The first script has its result type explicitly stated; for the others the type is inferred. The caret as a postfix operator indicates that the script's result value is set from its operand. The second script has only one operand that is a script call or code fragment; in such cases the caret may be omitted.

The notation ^5 is shorthand for {:5:}^.[10]

A double caret is useful for operands that appear in loops, as in ..? x^^. The result of these zero or more x's is a list; on each success of an x, its result value is copied to the list at the position corresponding to the position of that x in the loop.

Double carets that immediately followed by integers creates a result tuple. E.g.

```
s = {:1:}^^1 {!"str"!}^^2
```

will produce a tuple (1,"str"), of type (Int,String).

[x]^ is shorthand for ([x])^, and likewise for double carets etc. This meaning is as follows: the parentheses enclose a Scala value, which is a script lambda having x as body. That has a Script type, which implies that the whole is a script call. But it is not entirely the same as x. Such a construct is useful for more complex result structures such as lists of tuples. E.g.,

```
s = ..? [x^^1 y^^2]^^
```

---

[10] 5^ is also valid syntax; this requires an implicit conversion to be in scope that turns the number into a script call.

results in a List[(X,Y)], where X and Y are the result types of x and y.

Apart from having success, a script may terminate in failure; that will often be due to an exception thrown from within a code fragment. The exception should be available as an alternative kind of result, similar to what can happen in *future* constructs used in functional reactive programming. Like in futures, a normal result is packed in a Success container, and an exception is packed in a Failure container.

5   The SubScript Virtual Machine

SubScript implementations have a Virtual Machine that executes scripts by internally doing graph manipulation.

5.1   Script Execution from Scala

From Scala code a so called *script executor* may execute a script lambda, as in executor.run([test]). The executor may be tailored for the type of application, e.g. discrete event simulations. After the execution ends, the executor may provide information on the execution, e.g. on whether the script ended successfully. The SubScript VM method _execute creates a fresh CommonExecutor (the default executor type) and then calls its run method with the script closure, e.g., _execute([test]).

Other types of executors could be more suited for specific application domains, such as discrete event simulations and multicore parallelism.

The code generated for the script closure calls library methods that build so-called "template trees", representing the static structure of the invoked scripts. Based on these template trees the script executor maintains a so called call graph. This is a generalization of a regular call stack. It is an acyclic graph; under its root node other nodes will be added and removed according to the template tree as the program is executed. These nodes represent process expression constructs, such as script calls, n-ary operators and code fragments. Recursive script calls lead to repeated occurrences, like in a call stack.

Each type of node has its own typical kind of life cycle. The executor maintains a prioritized queue of messages that direct the state transitions along these life cycles.

For instance, consider the following process which prints optionally "Hello", and then "world!":

```
Main = [{!print("H")!} + [+]] {!print("W")!}
```

[+] corresponds with 1 in ACP. Given the equivalence $(x + 1) \cdot y = x \cdot y + y$, this process should behave much like

```
Main = {!print("H")!} {!print("W")!} + {!print("W")!}
```

The following figure gives the template tree (in yellow) and 4 typical stages of the call graph (in green and red):

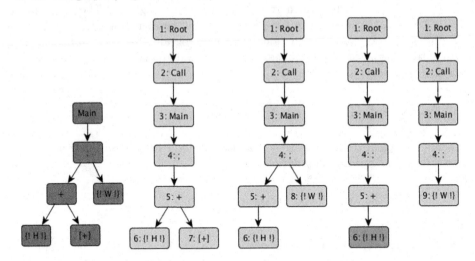

In the first depicted call graph, the left hand side of the semicolon has been activated. Node 7 now succeeds. Its success is propagated upwards, through node 5 until node 4.

This node does not react immediately; that has to wait until there is no more graph management to be done at its descendant nodes. Indeed, node 7 deactivates. Then node 4 takes action. Because of the received success, this sequential operator looks up in the template whether there would be a next operand to activate; indeed there is one, which will become node 8.

At that point there is no more call graph management to do. Then the code fragment of node 6 is executed (depicted in red). At the same time a conceptual atomic action happens; a message about this is propagated upwards in the call graph. The sequential node 4 reacts to this by excluding all its other operands; in this respect it acts the same as a `plus` node. Thus the branch with node 8 is deactivated as soon as node 6 starts executing.

After the execution, node 6 will succeed, and then again node 4 activates the next operand from the template, this time as node 9. Node 6 is deactivated, as is its parent node 5. The code fragment of node 9 executes. Then a success follows which propagates upwards to the root. Finally node 9 and its ancestors are deactivated.

Call graph management has a higher priority than executing code for atomic actions. Graph operations below a unary or n-ary operator has a higher priority than such operations at such an operator. This is achieved by collecting messages arriving at such operators in so called `Continuation` messages. This way the response at the n-ary operator can take into account all messages that have arrived.

The message types, in descending priority order, are:

- `Activation` - a node is to be added to the call graph, according to the template tree. This may also involve executing native code for annotations, process parameter evaluation, if- and while conditions, etc.
- `CFActivated` - a code fragment has been activated
- `AAHappened` - an atomic action has happened
- `Break` - a break has been encountered; a flag indicates whether it is optional
- `Success` - a success has been encountered
- `Exclude, Suspend, Resume` - atomic actions in descendants must be excluded, suspended or resumed
- `Deactivation` - a node is to be removed from the graph
- `Continuation` - collected messages for an operator node
- `CFExecutionFinished` - the execution of a code fragment has finished
- `CFToBeExecuted` - a code fragment is to be executed in the main thread

Messages `Exclude`, `Resume` and `Suspend` are propagated downwards in the call graph. Messages `AAHappened`, `CAActivated`, `CFActivated` are propagated upwards in the graph; they may have effects at the nodes that they pass by.

E.g., when a `AAHappened` message arrives from a child node at a + or ; node, `Exclude` messages for the sibling nodes are inserted in the message queue.

`Break` and `Success` are also propagated upwards, up to n-ary nodes. Such nodes have different ways to handle `Success` messages that arrived from their child nodes; often these result in sending new `Success` themselves.

Process communication involves multiple callers that call a single shared script. This binds branches of the call graph together; without communication the call graph would be a tree.

5.2   Implementation

The first SubScript implementation consisted only of a SubScript Virtual Machine: a library written in Scala, called from code with plain Scala syntax. The VM had been programmed using 2500 lines of Scala code. This is not a complete implementation; most notably support for ACP style communication is still to be done. When complete the VM may contain about 4000 lines.

In principle this approach suffices for writing the essence of SubScript programs. However, with the special syntax, e.g. for parameter lists, n-ary infix operators, various flavors of code fragments, specifications become considerably smaller, and these require much less parentheses and braces, which is important for clarity.

Therefore we made a special branch of the Scala compiler that translated the genuine SubScript syntax to the library calls. This took about 2000 lines of Scala code, mainly in the scanner, the parser and the typer. As of 2015 by a Parboiled [14] based preprocessor parses SubScript sources and generates Scala with some dedicated macro calls therein; the standard Scala compiler is thereafter invoked. This approach is leaner and more maintainable; however it leads to inconvenient compile error messages, and it is not suited for IDE integration.

6 Dataflow Programming

A relatively new SubScript language feature is dataflow, expressed by curly arrows as seen in the GUI controller example:

```
exit = exitCommand
       @gui: {! confirmExit !} ~~(b:Boolean)~~> while !b
```

We could also use a ternary version of the dataflow operator:

```
exit = exitCommand
       @gui: {! confirmExit !} ~~(b:Boolean  )~~> while !b
                               +~/~(e:Exception)~~> {:println(e
       );}
           ...
```

In case `confirmExit` would throw an exception, the code fragment would end in failure and its result would be a `Failure` wrapper containing the exception. Next, because of the failure, the arrow part with the slash would be followed, so that the exception is printed. The periods on the last line enforce that the script is a loop, even in case `while` has not been reached.

In general the dataflow operator can become analogous to a combination of match statements and exception handers. E.g., the dataflow on the left is syntactic sugar for a lower level dataflow on the right:

```
x ~~(b:Boolean       )~~> y1 |  x   ~~> case b:Boolean      => [y1]
+~~(i:Int if i<10 )~~> y2 |        case i:Int if i<10 => [y2]
+~~(  _              )~~> y3 |        case  _           => [y3]
+~/~(e:IOException)~~> z1 |  +~/~> case e:IOException => [z1]
+~/~(e:  Exception)~~> z2 |        case e:  Exception => [z2]
```

So it comes down to the meaning of x~~>y+~/~>z. In such a dataflow, y and z must be partial scripts, i.e. partial functions that return a `Script[T]` for some type T. The dataflow starts with x. When x has success, y is activated with x's normal result value passed as actual parameter. When x terminates as a failure, z is activated with x's resulting exception passed as actual parameter.

x~~>y is similar, except for that it ends in failure when x ends in failure.

x~/~>z is also similar, except for that it succeeds when x succeeds.

6.1 Example: Twitter Search

A simple Twitter search application contains an input text field and a result text area; when the user has changed the content of the input text field the application starts a request to the Twitter web service to get 10 tweets matching the input text.

But Twitter imposes request rate limit on its API, and the client should not exceed this. Therefore after each change in the text field the application waits 200 ms before sending the request to Twitter. If meanwhile the text field changes again, we will restart the wait. When the input text changes while a request had already been sent and the result was awaited, then that process is disrupted as well.

The searches may go wrong; we can (intentionally) send an empty search string, which will result in an error reply by the Twitter server.

A pure Scala version for the controller would contain something like:

```
def bindInputCallback = {
  listenTo(view.searchField.keys)
  val fWait   = InterruptableFuture {...}
  val fSearch = InterruptableFuture {...}

  reactions +=      {case _ ⇒ fWait.execute()}
        .flatMap    {case _ ⇒ fSearch.execute()}
        .onComplete{case Success(tweets)        ⇒ Swing.onEDT{...}
                    case Failure(e:Throwable) ⇒ Swing.onEDT{...}
} } }
```

InterruptableFutures are a flavor of futures that can be cancelled on demand. This functionality requires a bunch of ad-hoc utility code in pure Scala, whereas it is supported out-of-the-box in SubScript, backed by theory.

The SubScript version has a `live` script for the controller, containing a loop of complete search sequences.

```
live     = initialize; [mainSeq/..?]...

mainSeq = anyEvent(view.searchField)
             {* Thread.sleep(keyTypeDelay) *}
             {* searchTweets *} ~~(ts:Seq[Tweet])~~>updateView(ts)
                            +~/~(t: Throwable )~~>setErrorMsg(t)

updateView(ts: Seq[Tweet]) = @gui: {:...:}
setErrorMsg(t: Throwable ) = @gui: {:...:}
```

The slash and the iterator in `mainseq/..?` denote a disruptive loop that starts by activating 1 instance of `mainSeq`. As soon as the first atomic action therein happens (`anyEvent` in the search field) a next iteration of the disruptive loop is activated. Thus if a next event arrives soon enough, before the rest of the ongoing earlier `mainSeq` instance has terminated successfully, that ongoing instance is disrupted and a new delay starts, and a new instance of `mainSeq` is activated, etc. The disruptive loop ends when such a `mainseq` has terminated successfully.

A ternary dataflow operator directs the search result (of `searchTweets`) to the either `updateView` or `setErrorMsg`..

It is possible to create an implicit script that converts a future into an appropriate script. If such an implicit script were in scope, we may replace the threaded code fragment {*searchTweets*} by the future fSearch.

7   Related Work

Since the predecessor paper [5] we have improved the features for result values and dataflow.[11] The dataflow support now also covers pattern matching and exception handling. This improves the cooperation with futures and actors.

The predecessor paper contains an overview of other languages that show some resemblance to this work. Grammar notation formalisms are most related, as these have similar support for sequences and choices. SubScript result values were inspired by YACC [10] and by the parser combinator library FastParse[12].

SubScript has a delayed task execution. This also occurs in futures and the async idiom, known from functional reactive programming. Futures may terminate successfully or in a failure, which comparable to SubScript scripts; however they lack alternative compositions and a 1 element. In a way SubScript adds the expressiveness of grammar formalisms to the concurrency domain.

Other related approaches are Reactive-C [3] and its follow up SugarCubes [4]. These two have a similar execution mechanism with call graphs; yet they are not process algebra implementations since also they lack alternative compositions and a 1 element.

There are some papers that apply process algebra as a theoretical underpinning to actors: [1,7] use Pi-calculus, and [13] applies ACP.

8   Conclusion

SubScript offers constructs from the Algebra of Communicating Processes that supports a declarative programming style. This is useful for GUI controllers, text parsers and probably other areas.

Futures may conveniently placed in SubScript process expressions. Likewise SubScript processes may be converted into futures, but there is an "impedance mismatch". A variant of Futures that supports a kind of 1-element from ACP, could be interesting.

The performance is typically in the order of 10,000 actions per second on current mainstream personal computers. For most GUI controllers this speed is acceptable; for text processing that would depend on the input size.

---

[11] A useful definition for [x]^ (see Sect. 4.9) triggered several syntax changes. E.g. rectangular brackets replaced parentheses to delimit process expressions. Script lambda's are now also written between rectangular brackets. Script terms may now have the form (s) or {s}, with s a Scala value; such terms are method calls or script calls, possibly after implicit conversion. Normal code fragments had the form {s}; this became {!s!}.

[12] http://lihaoyi.github.io/fastparse/.

SubScript is an open source project[13]. It is currently implemented as a branch of the regular Scala compiler, bundled with a virtual machine and libraries for interfacing with Akka actors and Swing GUIs.

Acknowledgement. We thank the referees and especially the shepherd for their useful suggestions and other comments.

References

1. Thati, P., Agha, G.: An algebraic theory of actors and its application to a simple object-based language. In: Owe, O., Krogdahl, S., Lyche, T. (eds.) From Object-Orientation to Formal Methods. LNCS, vol. 2635, pp. 26–57. Springer, Heidelberg (2004)
2. Baeten, J.C.M.: A brief history of process algebra. Theor. Comput. Sci. **335**, 131–146 (2005)
3. Boussinot, F.: Reactive c: an extension of c to program reactive systems. Softw. Pract. Experiance **21**(4), 401–428 (1991)
4. Boussinot, F., Susini, J.F.: The sugarcubes tool box. In: Nets of Reactive Processes Implementation
5. van Delft, A.: Dataflow constructs for a language extension based on the algebra of communicating processes. In: Proceedings of 4th Workshop on Scala, SCALA 2013. ACM (2013)
6. van Delft, A.: Some new directions for ACP research. CoRR abs/1504.03719 (2015). http://arxiv.org/abs/1504.03719
7. Gaspari, M., Zavattaro, G.: An algebra of actors. In: Ciancarini, P., Fantechi, A., Gorrieri, R. (eds.) FMOODS, IFIP Conference Proceedings, vol. 139. Kluwer (1999)
8. Goeman, H.: Towards a theory of (self) applicative communicating processes: a short note. Inf. Process. Lett. **34**(3), 139–142 (1990)
9. Hoare, C.: Communicating sequential processes. ACM Comput. Surv. **7**(1), 80–112 (1985)
10. Johnson, S.: Yacc: Yet another compiler- compiler. Technical report, Bell Laboratories (1979)
11. Milner, R.: A Calculus of Communicating Systems. Springer-Verlag New York Inc., Secaucus (1982)
12. Milner, R., Parrow, J., Walker, D.: A calculus of mobile processes, part i. Inf. Comput. **100**, 1–40 (1989)
13. Wang, Y.: Fully abstract game semantics for actors. CoRR abs/1403.6563 (2014)
14. Wills, P.: No more regular expressions. Scala Exchange, Skills Matter, London (2014)

---

[13] Subscript web site: http://subscript-lang.org.

Author Index

Ahn, Ki Yung   109
Alpuim, Joao   29

Blot, Arthur   12
Brock-Nannestad, Taus   94

Carette, Jacques   62

Dagand, Pierre-Évariste   12

Feltey, Daniel   144
Fetscher, Burke   144
Findler, Robert Bruce   144
Fu, Peng   126

Gallagher, J.P.   163

Haemmerlé, R.   163
Hermenegildo, M.V.   163

Klemen, M.   163
Kmetyuk, Anatoliy   232
Komendantskaya, Ekaterina   126

Lawall, Julia   12
Liqat, U.   163
López-Fraguas, Francisco J.   181
López-García, P.   163

Mackie, Ian   80
Madhavapeddy, Anil   198

McCarthy, Jay   144
Montenegro, Manuel   181
Morihata, Akimasa   215

Narayanan, Praveen   62
New, Max   144

Pond, Andrew   126

Rodríguez-Hortalá, Juan   181
Romano, Wren   62

Sato, Shinya   80
Schrijvers, Tom   126
Shan, Chung-chieh   62
Sheets, David   198
Swierstra, Wouter   29

Triska, Markus   45

Ueda, Kazunori   1

van Delft, Andre   232
Vezzosi, Andrea   109

Yallop, Jeremy   198

Zinkov, Robert   62

Printed in the United States
By Bookmasters